**The Invisible Librarian**

To Anne

Keep up the
good work at keeping
us visible,

Aoife Lawton

CHANDOS

INFORMATION PROFESSIONAL SERIES

Series Editor: Ruth Rikowski
(email: Rikowskigr@aol.com)

Chandos' new series of books is aimed at the busy information professional. They have been specially commissioned to provide the reader with an authoritative view of current thinking. They are designed to provide easy-to-read and (most importantly) practical coverage of topics that are of interest to librarians and other information professionals. If you would like a full listing of current and forthcoming titles, please visit www.chandospublishing.com.

**New authors:** we are always pleased to receive ideas for new titles; if you would like to write a book for Chandos, please contact Dr Glyn Jones on g.jones.2@elsevier.com or telephone +44 (0) 1865 843000.

# The Invisible Librarian

## A Librarian's Guide to Increasing Visibility and Impact

*Aoife Lawton*

AMSTERDAM • BOSTON • HEIDELBERG • LONDON
NEW YORK • OXFORD • PARIS • SAN DIEGO
SAN FRANCISCO • SINGAPORE • SYDNEY • TOKYO
Chandos Publishing is an imprint of Elsevier

Chandos Publishing is an imprint of Elsevier
225 Wyman Street, Waltham, MA 02451, USA
Langford Lane, Kidlington, OX5 1GB, UK

**Notices**
Knowledge and best practice in this field are constantly changing. As new research and experience broaden our understanding, changes in research methods, professional practices, or medical treatment may become necessary.

Practitioners and researchers must always rely on their own experience and knowledge in evaluating and using any information, methods, compounds, or experiments described herein. In using such information or methods they should be mindful of their own safety and the safety of others, including parties for whom they have a professional responsibility.

To the fullest extent of the law, neither the Publisher nor the authors, contributors, or editors, assume any liability for any injury and/or damage to persons or property as a matter of products liability, negligence or otherwise, or from any use or operation of any methods, products, instructions, or ideas contained in the material herein.

ISBN: 978-0-08-100171-4 (print)
ISBN: 978-0-08-100174-5 (online)

**British Library Cataloguing-in-Publication Data**
A catalogue record for this book is available from the British Library

**Library of Congress Control Number:** 2015944253

  Working together
to grow libraries in
developing countries

www.elsevier.com • www.bookaid.org

# List of figures

## Introduction

## Chapter 1

## Chapter 2

## Chapter 3

## Chapter 4

## Chapter 5

# Chapter 6

# Chapter 7

# Chapter 8

# Chapter 9

# Chapter 10

# List of tables

# Chapter 5

# Chapter 6

# Chapter 7

# Chapter 8

# Biography

Aoife Lawton BA, MLIS works as a systems librarian at the Health Service Executive Library in Dr Steevens' Hospital in Dublin, Ireland. She coordinates electronic resources providing access to over 13,000 health service employees. Responsible for setting up and the management of the highly successful Irish health repository Lenus, she is actively involved in a range of specialist projects in the health service. She is former chair and an active member of the Irish Health Science Libraries Group, a section of the Library Association of Ireland.

# Preface

We are all living in uncertain times, and librarianship is a profession that is facing significant challenges. An opportunity to investigate the theme of visibility of the profession arose, which prompted this book. The visibility of librarians in society is something that presents as a paradox. Although a long-established and recognised profession, it is predominately misunderstood and persistently associated with books. The problem of the paradox is the potential for the profession to drift and its value and recognition in the world to slowly dissipate.

This book is written by a librarian for librarians, students interested in studying librarianship and anyone who wonders what it is exactly that librarians do. Readers are invited to navigate the world of a special, health, public, school or academic librarian in the first chapter. This is to give the reader an opportunity to adopt the character of a librarian and get an insider's view of the profession. Many librarians who were interviewed for the book gave up their free time in the evenings, early mornings or during lunch breaks to meet in person or online and share their experiences. A true insight into the real working life of librarians from many different countries and continents is captured through these interviews by way of case studies. Their stories will open up a world of intrigue and reveal the good, honest work that librarians do every day. The difference that they make to society generally and the dedication to the profession, which at its core, puts people first, is admirable.

I trust this book will empower librarians everywhere to increase their visibility, impact and value to the world around them. If you are reading this in print, then I wish you an enjoyable digital detox. If you are reading this online, then enjoy a different digital experience.

# Acknowledgement

I am indebted to the librarians who participated *in the interviews* and answered some thought-provoking questions with courage and honesty. I am grateful to the individuals and organisations who gave me permission to reproduce diagrams, quotations and photos in this book. As librarians, we are often at the beginning or end of a reader's journey, but rarely are we in the writer's shoes. This has been a personal challenge, and I owe tribute to my husband Dave, who provided some light relief by way of the illustrations in the book. I would like to thank my family and work colleagues and especially my parents, Angela and Herb, for their encouragement and to my Jack Russell, Sam, for pet therapy (see Chapter 9).

# Introduction

*You must be the change you wish to see in the world.*

**Mahatma Gandhi**

Librarians are not trendy anymore. It is unclear if they ever were or ever will be. The new problem facing librarians is that they are losing visibility. Google Trends paints a stark picture of declining visibility of the term 'library' and 'librarian' over the past 10 years (see Figures 1 and 2). This should act as a wake-up call to all librarians.

Is this a profession in decline? Google Trends data would suggest that it is. Are libraries and librarians losing their foothold in the world of disruptive technology? Do librarians want to reverse the trend and begin an upward slope with increased visibility? If the answer is yes, then this book offers a starting point. Librarians can take on this challenge and turn it into with what John Kotter, an authority on leadership and change, describes as 'A Big Opportunity (ABO)' (Kotter, 2014). Kotter describes ABO as 'A window into a winning future that is realistic, emotionally compelling and memorable' (p. 137). All that is needed is a willingness to change – together with inspiration, dedication and knowledge – characteristics that librarians have in abundance.

In the United States and Canada, Public Library Data Service (PLDS) statistical reports for 2013 and 2014 paint a picture of general decline. The decline is in the area of activities, which does not necessarily translate into a decline in impact or value. Paid full-time equivalent (FTE) staff numbers have been steadily reduced from a mean of 196.7 in 2009 to 181.5 in 2013. In four of the nine population groups, the mean public service hours (total hours open and convenient hours open) per week were reduced with a negative effect on activity statistics. Activity statistics extend to website visits, which was reduced by 18.4% per year since 2012. On the positive side, libraries are slowly embracing change, and in the past 3 years, more libraries declared that they offer a growing variety of technology equipment. Technology equipment included tablets, MP3 players, laptops and e-book readers. There was a significant increase (98%) in libraries' lending of tablets in the last 2 years. Libraries are embracing social media, with 97% of continuous responding libraries ($N = 288$) offering social networking. It is interesting to note that it was not until 2014 that outcome measures and a nod to evidence-based practice was being described in the statistical report. Operational statistics assist library managers in planning and managing, but evidence-based outcomes paint a picture of impact of public libraries that is essential for public accountability. The inclusion of outcomes in the report is a step in the right direction, with the 2014 report measuring libraries' plans for evidence-based demonstration of value in 12 areas.

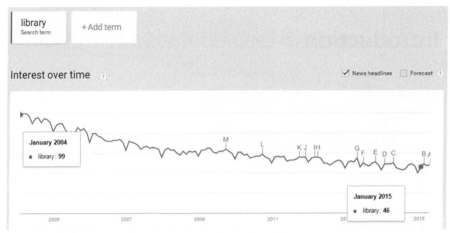

**Figure 1**   Google Trends library (www.google.com/trends).

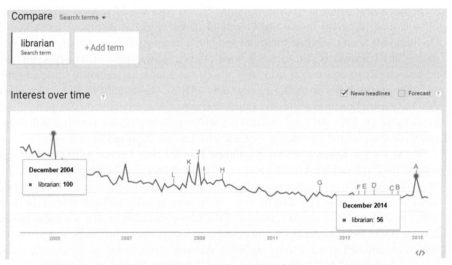

**Figure 2**   Google Trends librarian (www.google.com/trends).

Public libraries in the United Kingdom are under threat, and in some ways irreparable damage has been done to this cornerstone of democracy. Approximately 477 libraries in the United Kingdom have closed since 2004, and several others are under threat of closure (publiclibrarynews.com). According to the Chartered Institute of Public Finance and Accountancy, the number of library staff has fallen by 22% since 2009–2010. The problem? The value of public libraries and librarians is invisible to key decision-makers. The value of public libraries is wrongly perceived to be based on how 'busy' a library is, how many people visit it and how many people borrow books. The message about the value of public libraries having an economic, social and cultural dimension is being lost in translation. Value is not being properly communicated

LIBRARIES = BOOKS, INFORMATION, BUILDING, READING

| | TOTAL RESPONDENTS | AGE 18–24 | AGE 25–35 | AGE 36–50 | AGE 51–59 | AGE 60+ |
|---|---|---|---|---|---|---|
| BOOKS | 75% | 70% | 80% | 79% | 74% | 75% |
| INFORMATION | 12% | 18% | 9% | 8% | 11% | 8% |
| BUILDING (ENVIRONMENT) | 6% | 8% | 5% | 5% | 4% | 6% |
| READING | 3% | 2% | 2% | 3% | 4% | 4% |

What is the first thing you think of when you think of a library?

**Figure 3** OCLC graphic 1. Reused with permission from OCLC. *OCLC, At a Tipping Point: Education, Learning and Libraries*, 2014.

to government, to ordinary citizens and to librarians themselves. One of two key findings of the Sieghart report was that 'not enough decision-makers at national or local level appear sufficiently aware of the remarkable and vital value that a good library service can offer modern communities of every size and character' (Independent Library Report for England, 2014, p. 4).

The city of Birmingham library in the United Kingdom illustrates this point all too well. With a budget of £189 million, the library opened to much applause in 2013. It was opened by Malala Yousafzai, a teenager from Pakistan who was shot by the Taliban for speaking up for girls' rights to education, sending a powerful message about the role of libraries in learning, education and democracy (Culturehive.co.uk). However, less than 18 months later, the council announced reduced opening hours and a potential loss of 90 staff members. Thus, Birmingham is left with one big library and very few librarians. Coverage in the media captures a glimpse of public reaction: 'I do not know how many read books these days', and one person felt it would have a limited impact on tourism 'because people would take photos outside anyway and may not go inside' (Library of Birmingham, 2015). Therein lies a fundamental problem. Firstly, people equate public libraries with books, but librarians seem to be the only ones who know that there is much more to a public library than books, and it is their best kept secret. This perception is backed up by a recent Online Computer Library Center (OCLC) report which showed that across all age groups, the library brand is steadily associated with books (see Figure 3). Secondly, architecture has its own unique value, but what is inside of the library must be more important to a community than the outside.

Beyond the United Kingdom, public libraries have been under-funded and under-resourced for a long time. Gomez et al. (2009) found that in Eastern Europe and Eurasia, after more than a decade of reduced budgets, public libraries are seen as 'Irrelevant due to lack of current information, leading to a weaker perception of public library value'. In Latin America, public libraries were seen as places only for academics. In South Asia, public library development is hampered by poor infrastructure and poor information and communications technology (ICT) in particular. A lack of national policy to promote better ICT infrastructure impedes public library relevance in many countries. The Public Libraries 2020 programme highlights that every year 100 million people visit their public library in the European Union. This is not telling us enough, because it is at a time when 73 million adult Europeans, or 1 of 5, is functionally illiterate (publiclibraries2020.eu).

In academia, big changes in the last decade have been in the areas of online learning, scholarly communication, digital preservation, research, managing electronic resources with constrained budgets and no equitable e-book model. The open-access movement, the growth of repositories and data management have been mostly positive, introducing new roles for librarians. This has been evident in the increasing demand for data management roles. 'Big deals' with publishers have fired up much debate among librarians and publishers (Fister, 2014), and challenges have been set to introduce new paradigms for purchasing periodicals (Suber, 2006; Osorio, 2012). The library as a space has had a complete rejuvenation. Off-site warehouse storage of books and materials has become a trend in academic and national libraries (Shenton, 2004). This is freeing up library spaces with the concentration shifting from collection to people and process, including meeting rooms, group areas, study spaces and technology equipment.

OCLC has reported that education and libraries is reaching a 'tipping point', and three forces have converged to cause this tip: consumer behaviour, advanced technology tools and economic incentives (see Figure 4). This tipping point is changing how librarians and educators work and presents new challenges for the profession of librarianship. How librarians respond to this challenge will be key to the evolution of the profession into the future.

School librarianship appears to be the worst-hit sector. It has not managed to reach maturity even in countries where it is mandatory for schools to have a library. The struggle of school librarians everywhere continues. Their plight is more difficult than other sectors of librarianship. The unfortunate reality is that school librarians find themselves competing against educators for resources. This is a competition that librarians are never going to win. Education will always stand on its own two feet as a valued, respected, stand-alone societal good. Despite its long history and despite the evidence to show that school librarianship improves student learning, librarianship as a discipline has not evolved sufficiently to be counted as an equal alongside education.

In health science librarianship, the trends have been new roles for librarians, including embedded or blended librarians, working as part of clinical and multidisciplinary teams, informationists and data scientists. A focus has been on moving outside of the confines of a library and working in outreach roles with research teams, working with biomedical data, and working as clinical librarians, again as part of the clinical team, providing information at the point of need. Librarians have had to completely change what they do to remain critical to the mission of their health centres and hospitals. Despite this, many hospital libraries have closed and librarians have not been replaced where they have retired. In the United States, the Medical Library Association reported that 30% of libraries have had their staff downsized. Of the 189 responses received to a hospital library status report, 28 staff members lost their jobs and 24 libraries closed (MLA, 2013). In European countries severely affected by the global recession, such as Greece, the under-development of hospital libraries has downgraded the important contribution of medical librarians (Kostagiolas et al., 2012). Trends that affect hospitals and health systems naturally affect health science librarians and technology has had a huge impact on medicine. There is a steady growth in mobile technology usage among clinicians who expect and need information to be available to them in the palm of their hand. In hospitals, this can present many challenges with ICT infrastructures blocking library-subscribed databases and social media sites.

**FORCES OF CHANGE**
· · · · · · · · · · · · · · · · ·
Markets tip when
**3 factors** come into alignment:

1. Consumer Behavior.
2. Effective Technology.
3. Economic Incentive.

**Figure 4**   OCLC graphic 2. Reused with permission from OCLC. *OCLC, At a Tipping Point: Education, Learning and Libraries*, 2014.

No matter what sector of librarianship, all libraries and librarians are experiencing unprecedented change in three big areas culminating in constant disruption:

1. Disruptive technology – such as emerging technologies, big data, mass digitization, growth of e-publications and decline of print.
2. Disruptive economics – the global financial crisis of 2007/2008 is continuing to have ramifications for librarians and libraries.
3. Disruptive consumer expectations – people are more likely to use a major search engine to start their research, regardless of what rich data are provided through library websites.

We are living in a culture of convenience in which people expect instant information results and will not waste time to wade through pages and pages of static data. Libraries are challenged to make their online pages and physical spaces more engaging, appealing and, above all, convenient. The digital transition has moved libraries into a period in which homogeneity is commonplace and most services are shared or centralised. In the analogue era, libraries were localised and diverse, mirroring their communities and control was localised.

We are living in an era in which the daily mantra is 'doing more with less'. The global economic downturn has had an immense impact on all communities, readers and libraries, with the effects on-going and the long-term implications still unknown. Marr and Creelman (2014) provide a strategic overview of how not-for-profit and government organisations can effectively manage this economic predicament. Some ideas from this and other areas of strategic management are captured in Chapters 7 and 8.

## What do we do now?

Speaking in 2008, Brewster Kahle answered this question by saying to an audience of information school students in Michigan that we need to build open library services. According to Kahle, this could be achieved in three steps: (1) digitise the library and most of the archives, (2) provide free access to public domain and (3) loan the rest.

The cost of digitising books was 10 cents a page or $30 a book. He illustrated how this could be done in 10 years. The Internet Archive, which Kahle founded in 1996, now preserves 20 petabytes of data – the books, webpages, music, television and software of our cultural heritage – working with more than 400 library and university partners to create a digital library that is accessible to all (archive.org).

Open library services certainly represent an ideal that librarians aspire to. The advent of the open-access movement has been a transformative development for librarians. It has led to repositories and new, enhanced roles for librarians. It is one of the six areas of ethics in librarianship outlined by the International Federation of Library Associations and Institutions (IFLA).

Librarians need to look to thought leaders in their profession. If we look to the past to one of the great thought leaders of library science, to Dr Ranganathan's five laws of library science formulated in 1928, here we will find some leads on where to focus our attention for the present and for the future.

# Books are for use

Today's interpretation of this is that literature or content in all of its formats is for use. Librarians focus must be on the visibility of content and the connection of that provision with the library. For example, there is not much point in purchasing third-party apps for research content if the vendor will not brand that it is provided by the library. That connection must be made, or libraries will be completely bypassed. The content is now co-created and co-built, librarians are creating content on blogs, on Wikis, on YouTube, in classrooms, with three-dimensional printers, on virtual learning environments, and in the literature, including systematic reviews. When this content is created by a multi-disciplinary team such as a librarian and a teacher, a librarian and a clinician, a librarian and a social worker, a librarian and a human resources manager or a librarian and a lawyer, then we are beginning to see that content is for use. Librarians embedding makerspaces in their physical libraries are taking this law to the next level.

# Every reader his book

Think about user satisfaction with content. This is where special librarianship comes to the fore. Acquisitions librarians, special collections librarians and rare book cataloguers carefully select resources and make them discoverable with the reader in mind. The systems librarians, emerging technology librarians and electronic resources librarians build the technical architecture to enable ease of connection between readers and resources. Librarianship has moved a step further and expanded the connection to include patron-driven acquisition, in which the reader is empowered to have a say in the selection of content.

# Every book its reader

This translates roughly to a user needs analysis. Every reader is different and has distinct needs. Librarians have to respond to readers needs by finding out what they are. This is the starting point for librarians. Once needs are established from a reader base, a library must respond in an innovative and thoughtful way. Customer service has an important role to play in achieving this as well as quality in librarianship. Librarians need to make every interaction with a reader count.

## Save the time of the reader

This is more true today then Ranganathan could ever have possibly imagined when he wrote this law back during the first third of the twentieth century. This is the library's value proposition. One of the main values that all librarians bring to the reader is that they save them valuable time. When that time is translated into a cost, because we know that 'time is money', librarians can always show a good return on investment. Librarians save clinicians time when they need information to make a decision based on evidence about a patient. Librarians save teachers time when their students need additional reading and learning material and a space that is free to learn in. Librarians save lawyers time when they need to find a case from the archives to inform a big trial. Librarians save the taxpayer time by providing them with free Internet access and assistance when filling out their tax returns in a public library. Librarians save the researchers time when they need to locate an important full-text paper that is not available anywhere online. This is a unique quality of librarianship, and it is one that is often not seen and taken for granted. This is where librarians need to be more vocal about the value-added proposition that they bring to their organisations and their communities.

## Library is a growing organism

This law is as true today as it was in 1928. The library continues to evolve and grow. Any library that does not will not survive. The test of time and technology has shown that libraries that respond to change and that adapt and evolve will thrive. This book will highlight some of the ways that libraries and librarians are responding to change, showing their value and making themselves more visible to readers and stakeholders.

What we need now is transformative librarianship. Some examples of transformative librarianship, which is captured by a willingness to change, are highlighted in Chapter 9. We need leadership and we need librarians to become leaders. Leaders will have to come from existing librarians in the short term and a new generation of librarians in the longer term. Librarians of all ages and all levels of experience need to learn from each other and share best practice. They need to share their fears and hopes, but most importantly they need to share their dreams. A vision for the future must be a shared vision – one that will embrace change and catapult the value of librarians into the next century. The paths to transformative librarianship are beginning to take shape, and leaders are emerging. Putting in support structures for new librarians is proving to be effective in shaping new leaders. For example, participation in a new professionals group set up in one Australian university was shown to be a catalyst in developing potential leaders (Leong & Vaughan, 2010). It is a rocky road that lies ahead of us, with plenty of speed bumps and even the likelihood of some fines. It is important that we focus on the road ahead and not get distracted with disruptions. The temptation for taking shortcuts is high when resources are low and we feel like we are running out of gas. However, now is not the time for switching on the autopilot. Librarians need to belt up, step on the gas and take their place in the driving seat toward a new destination.

In the course of my work as a systems librarian in the health service, I occasionally provide tailored training to groups of health care professionals. In the spring of 2015, I collaborated with an external agency in the delivery of an evidence-informed practitioner training course. This was given to social workers who work with children and young people in extremely challenging situations. After delivering my 'Finding the Evidence' lecture, at which I talked about open access, evidence-informed practice, the Patient-Intervention-Comparison-Outcome (PICO) method for framing a research question and illustrated examples of finding evidence for social work, adding to the body of evidence and making it available in a repository, one of the presenters who is an educator spoke to me afterwards. She said, 'You're not really a librarian are you?'. 'Actually yes, I am a librarian', I said. Her response was 'But you're much more than a librarian…' She paused… 'You're more like a knowledge manager'. I recall that this type of conversation has cropped up repeatedly during my work. A consultant paediatrician said to fellow librarians and I that he felt we had an 'image problem'. It was to do with the fact that we called ourselves 'librarians'. He preferred 'informationist' or at least 'clinical librarian'. This is more to do with people's preconceived perceptions of librarians than the profession of librarianship itself.

I remember having lunch with a hospital manager who had lost her only hospital librarian to a career break. The librarian had not been replaced because of a recruitment embargo. She spoke highly of her. She said to me, 'But she was so much more than a librarian'. I asked her what she meant. She explained how the hospital librarian worked closely with clinical teams, how she practically wrote the hospital corporate plan and how she was a strategic thinker. Of course, I know that this is what librarians do, but managers do not. They do not know what librarians do. We are invisible. We have an image problem, and we have a visibility problem. Knowledge management is one way forward. Improving visibility is another. Visibility is about key stakeholders understanding what the librarian does and placing a value on their work. People have perceptions about librarians that are almost impossible to change.

The stereotypical librarian, the image of which is reinforced by the media and by popular culture, is hard to change. From the timid spinster Mary in *A Wonderful Life* to the stern, bespectacled, cardigan-wearing librarian in *Monsters University*, librarians are held in a negative light. Shaffer and Casey (2013) found that librarians in world cinema were mostly portrayed negatively with some exceptions. Although the profession is recognised, it is largely misunderstood. Librarians must challenge the stereotype and avoid getting relegated to the shelf amongst a dusty collection of books.

This leaves librarians with a choice. Keep the job title as 'librarian' and adopt quality improvement processes and a visibility improvement plan (VIP) to increase visibility, impact and value. Or rebrand to a 'knowledge manager', 'knowledge librarian' or 'information specialist' or whatever brand stakeholders value and understand. As Wheaton and Murray (2011) have pointed out, 'The survivors will be the ones that remember that they are in the knowledge business. Just as the core mission of a railroad is to enable the transfer and exchange of goods, a library enables the flow of knowledge – plain and simple'. Whatever labels a librarian wishes to adopt and as long as they remain true to their profession by adhering to the values and ethics of librarianship, it is ultimately the visibility of the profession that will determine its success.

The ethics of librarianship are outlined by IFLA's Code of Ethics (2012) and encompass six key areas:

1. Access to information
2. Responsibilities toward individuals and society
3. Privacy, secrecy and transparency
4. Open access and intellectual property
5. Neutrality, personal integrity and professional skills
6. Colleague and employer/employee relationship

Librarians need to lift the lid on their best kept secret and talk about what they do and share what libraries have to offer and what it takes to be a good librarian. Librarians are great at sharing best practice with each other through the literature, through social media, on blogs and Twitter and on Wikis. However, they are not so good at sharing this with the broader community, by publishing outside of the field of library and information science (LIS) and by partaking in conferences outside of LIS.

If you ever wondered what a librarian does, then you are invited to step into the shoes of a librarian in the first chapter to find out what it is like. You will be challenged to take on the role of the librarian in turbulent times and to prove your worth and value and increase your visibility to your organisation.

The experience of various librarians is brought to the fore in a series of 23 case studies that were conducted in 2014/2015. They are highlighted in Chapters 2–6, in which librarians talk about their roles and how they are responding to change and increasing their visibility, value and impact. Librarians were interviewed who work in academic, special, health, school and public library roles.

Chapter 7 examines the current state of play with regard to library and librarian visibility. Librarians are encouraged to take a snapshot of their own current visibility. It will empower the librarian to take stock and reflect upon current visibility using methods to engage with stakeholders and readers. Finding out what their needs are and how they perceive the value of library and information services is necessary to remaining relevant in the future and concentrating resources on value-added library and information initiatives.

Chapter 8 includes a VIP, which focuses on having a vision for the future. Librarians need reflective time to think about where they want to go and how they are going to get there. The vision will benefit from the collective input of readers, stakeholders and library staff by gaining buy-in and a sense of shared ownership of the library's future. Management and scientific techniques such as strategic planning, change management and implementation science are built in to the VIP.

Chapter 9 details progressive examples from the LIS literature about strategies that work to increase the visibility, impact and value of librarians and libraries. Librarians must keep an eye on the future to stay relevant in the present. This is achieved by doing what comes naturally to librarians – reading literature, keeping up to date through colleagues and virtual networks, spotting trends, future gazing and scenario building.

Finally, the future will be discussed as one that has many possible outcomes. Librarians have a strong role in the future, but that role needs to be defined and shaped and librarians need to be brave enough to embrace transformative librarianship as 'A Big Opportunity'.

## Note

**Public Libraries 2020**: This is run by the Reading & Writing Foundation, a Dutch-based organisation, with the aim of structurally solving illiteracy. They work with public libraries to internationally extend this goal. See http://www.publiclibraries2020.eu/.

# Step into the shoes of a librarian

**1**

*Empathy is about standing in someone else's shoes, feeling with his or her heart, seeing with his or her eyes. Not only is empathy hard to outsource and automate, but it makes the world a better place.*

**Daniel H. Pink**

Your mission, should you wish to accept it, is to step into the shoes of a librarian, to increase your visibility and impact and to convince those around you of your value and worth. You have five options. You can choose which type of librarian you would like to be: a school librarian, a medical librarian, an academic librarian, a public librarian or a librarian working in a specialised setting. Your skills include critical/analytical thinking, advanced search and retrieval of information in all formats, teaching, information technology, interpersonal skills, communication and research methods. Depending on the speciality of the librarian you choose to be, additional skills make up your repertoire. You will be given a scenario of adversity depending on the type of librarian that you choose to be and you will have three options to determine which path you will take. Remember, your mission is to overcome hardship, improve your visibility, impact and value and save your job!

## Background

It is another hot day. The library is unbearably stuffy. You've been asking the maintenance department to see if they can do anything to get some air into the place for weeks now to no avail. It's only when it is coming up to summer that it becomes a real problem. You have a pile of books waiting to get re-shelved and a few dozen new emails in your inbox. There is a flashing icon on your computer screen. It's the online 'ask a librarian' chatbox. Someone is looking for help. They have forgotten their password to the digital library. You click on the icon to respond and just as you are beginning to type a response your screen goes black and then shuts down! Well, this is just typical. You didn't even have time to get the person's email address to contact them. You have to contact the information technology (IT) department. You have no choice but to ring the helpdesk. You put the phone on speaker because you know this is going to take a while. The automated voice booms out 'Thank you for calling the computer helpdesk. Did you know that you may also email your query to the support team at compdesk@mail.com? You are now position...(wait for it)...10...in queue'. You decide to get some coffee and leave the phone on speaker. The morning has not gotten off to a good start...

If you choose to step into the shoes of a school librarian, then go to the heading 'School' below. If you choose to step into the shoes of a medical librarian, then go to the heading 'Medical' below. If you choose to step into the shoes of a public librarian, then go to page 3. If you choose to step into the shoes of an academic librarian, then go to the heading 'Academic' below. Finally, if you choose to step into the shoes of a librarian working in a specialised setting, then go to page 3.

## School

As a school librarian, you have bonus skills in how to teach children literacy skills, including information literacy and digital literacy. It's the last week before the summer break, and the school principal calls you into his office. He says that, regretfully, because of government cutbacks, he doesn't think he has a job for you in September. You are working in a school that is designated by the government as educationally disadvantaged. He tells you that several other school librarians in the area have been given a similar fate. He gives you a week to come up with a plan to save your job. If you decide to drop everything and get working on a plan, then turn to page 22. If you decide to call a meeting with the other school librarians, then turn to page 24. If you decide to concentrate on applying for jobs elsewhere, then turn to page 24.

## Medical

As a medical librarian, you have additional subject knowledge of the health sciences. The director of finance at your hospital sends you a memo. He wants to cut your budget by 50% and redeploy your only library assistant to the admissions office, which is severely understaffed. He wants to see value for money or your budget will be cut even further. He is familiar with an online clinical point-of-care tool that he thinks will be sufficient for the information needs of the medical staff. He is proposing that you are redeployed to the human resources (HR) department in the hospital. He has seen the library's annual report and looked at the key performance indicators reported for the library's performance for the past 6 months. The memo alludes to the fact that the clinical director has his eye on a room in the library that he would like to make into a meeting room. The director thinks that the library may remain open un-staffed with swipe access for health care professionals, but he is willing to give you 24 h to come up with a response. If you decide to analyse the key performance indicators (KPIs) of the library service and annual report and re-draft them, then turn to page 26. If you decide to lobby consultants in the hospital, then turn to page 30. If you decide to draft a 'gap analysis' plan that shows what would happen if this scenario was lived out, then turn to page 31.

## Academic

As an academic librarian, you have excellent research skills. You currently work as a reference librarian. The director of the library has decided that the reference desk is no longer viable. The usage statistics have been consistently dropping. The number of reference queries you receive on the reference desk has been decreasing for the past 2 years if not longer. She wants you to come up with an alternative plan within a week that she will consider. She has made it clear that you will be moving to another department in the university if the plan is not valid. The department she has in mind is computer services. If you decide you are determined to keep the reference desk and will fight to keep it, then turn to page 15. If you decide to plan an alternative to the reference desk, then turn to page 13. If you decide to transfer to computer services, then turn to page 16.

## Public

As a public librarian, you are shrewdly aware of local and national politics. The town council has decided that your public library will close in 6 months. This will occur in tandem with three other public libraries in your area. Each public library has received a letter indicating the reasons for this, which include the recession and cutbacks in all local authority services. You have to come up with a plan to save it. You have until the end of the week to produce a plan. If you decide to contact the other three public librarians in your area and decide on a collective strategy, then turn to page 9. If you decide to lobby the local government with the other public librarians in your area, then turn to page 12. If you decide to come up with a cost-neutral solution involving community volunteers, then turn to page 12.

## Special

As a librarian working in a corporate setting, you have advanced business management skills. You manage the corporate information library and work on your own. It is Monday morning, and the management team has just come out of the boardroom where their monthly meeting is held. A half an hour later, you receive an email. It is from the director of your division – corporate intelligence and research services—who sends you an email to tell you that he thinks the library and your position are under threat. The email reads as follows:

---

Pat,

At the management team meeting this morning, the library came up for discussion. It was relayed to me that 'everything is now available on the Internet' and the library and librarian is a 'luxury that we can no longer afford'. Because I am impressed with your work over the past year, I decided to request that they re-consider and allow an additional month before making a final decision. I urge you to come up with a plan to make your value more evident and the library more visible to management. Please get back to me Friday with your ideas and outline.

Regards,
Bob
Director of Corporate Intelligence and Research Services

If you decide to do a business case to save the library and your job, then turn to page... If you decide to embark upon an intensive marketing and promotional campaign, then turn to page... If you decide to shut down the electronic library and remove all access to online resources that you have created, then turn to page...

## Special librarian

You decide that a business case is what is needed. You've written at least 20 of these in your 2 years at the firm, so you call up a business case template. You spend 2 days getting fresh references to justify the business case for keeping the library. You include a balanced scorecard, and you align the case to the strategic plan of the company. You show how the mission of the library is aligned to that of the organisation. You outline the financial returns that the company receives by having the library. You include testimonials from two recent employees that you assisted with research queries. The case is now four pages long, and you wonder if you should ask Bob for feedback at this stage. It is now 3:00 p.m. on Thursday, and Bob is expecting the plan on this desk first thing in the morning. If you decide to continue with the case on your own, then continue reading below. If you decide to ask Bob for feedback now, then go to page 5.

## You decide to continue on with your business case

You are rapidly running out of time, and Bob looks extremely busy. He seems to be on a video call. You think that the case you are making is shaping up pretty well. You designed the business case template, and it is used by all departments in the company. You decide to include this fact as a note in your case. The case is now five pages long. You know that the company usually likes short reports that are no longer than two pages but you feel it is impossible to do justice to your work in such a short report. You are fairly satisfied with your work, so you email Bob a copy and go home.

The next day Bob drops into the library. 'Got a minute?' he asks. 'Of course', you reply. 'I think the case is ok but too long, and I'll have to synopsise it for the management team. I'm going in there now for the meeting, so I'll let you know the outcome as soon as I can. Thanks for your work on it'. Your face falls. You have a sinking feeling about this. You knew it was too long, but you know that Bob can very succinctly summarise things. The morning drags on. Bob shows up again. He doesn't look too enthusiastic. 'I'm afraid it's not good news, they are still planning to close the library. I'm afraid they weren't convinced by the business case. There were too many uncertainties there and not enough data or feedback from staff. I'm sorry but I'm going to have to give you notice'. You have failed your mission. The business case produced was strong on strategy but lacked any creativity and input from staff. You failed to make your value and that of the library visible to management.

## You decide to ask Bob for feedback

Bob says that he can only spare 10 min because he is about to join a video conference, but he will read your plan. He says he will drop you an email if he gets around to it. You return to your desk and answer some of the emails that have been piling up in your inbox. A new email arrives from Bob. It reads as follows:

---

Pat,

It's a good case, but I do not see any mention about you—the librarian. The case is for saving the library. I'm advising you to include something about your qualifications, skills and the difference you make. Keep it short and to the point. Four pages is too long. SOTMG.

Talk tomorrow,
Bob

---

You take on board the feedback. He wants you to talk about the value of the librarian. This is tricky. You include your qualifications and list all of your services. You include some of the more challenging research questions for which you helped source information. You look for research on the topic. There are some articles about the value of libraries, but not so many that are applicable to a special library in a corporate setting. You find a survey from an article by Reynolds (2013) that looks like one you will be able to use in your company. It looks at the impact of the corporate information unit in a specific setting. You include it as one of your deliverables if the business case is approved. You find an article about marketing in the age of technology (Satell, 2013). It refers to looking at three metrics to capture the essence of a business: sales, awareness and advocacy (see Figure 5).

You think about these three metrics in relation to your corporate library. The brand of the corporate library in your opinion is recognised and strong. People in the company know on the whole what to expect from your services. It is possible that

**Figure 5** Metrics triangle for business.
Reused with permission from Greg Satell:
Digital Tonto 2013.

the management team is not fully aware of everything that you do or the extent to which you add value to other departments in the company. Sales is not applicable to the library in the sense that you are not selling anything, but the library or your work as a librarian possibly contributes to increasing sales of company products. One example of this is the research that is performed on emerging markets and business opportunities, which is usually sourced by you or you provide summaries of the latest market analyses. This is something that you will add to your plan. Awareness of the library is high. You measured this last year in a survey in which you asked, 'Have you heard of the corporate library?' and 68% of respondents had heard of the library. On the advocacy side, you have not done much to advance this. It would be fairly easy to find some corporate champions amongst current users of the library to champion your cause. This is something you didn't have time to do before. You build this into your business case as an area you will grow in the third quarter of the year. Loyalty to the library is something you have not yet measured. You also incorporate this into your plan. These are all areas for future development and research. You hope that this will be enough. You include your budget and forecast for the coming years. The cost of databases and ejournals are all increasing. You will need a budget increase to keep all of the resources that you have. Inflation is part of the market economy, and you have no influence over price increases in electronic resources. In comparison to other departments in the company, you do not think the library budget is large.

You are suddenly interrupted by a sales executive who is looking for a product description sheet for one of the product lines that is due for launch this spring. You ask 'can you come back in about 20 min? I'm just in the middle of something'. 'Is it anything I can help you with?' he asks. 'I seriously doubt it', you think to yourself. 'It's actually a business case for retaining the library, I do not think you can help, but thanks for the offer'. The sales executive picks up on your negative tone but ignores it. 'I'll give you one piece of advice—think of it as a sales pitch—and as you know I've practised enough of those in here in the library! Focus on your unique selling point (USP). Good luck with it'. He leaves you to it. You remember his sales pitches. In your opinion, he came across as pushy and made you feel most uncomfortable. He was usually talking about a product that he knew very little about but sounded like an expert. If anyone asked him a technical question, then he would say that he'd have to refer them to the technical team. You found it tedious. There was no way you were accepting any advice from him! You are the USP of the library, but you cannot very well put that forward as a case. That's it. You've done enough for the day. You have managed to get your business case shortened to three pages. You email a copy to Bob, leave the library and forget all about the sales executive's request for the product sheet.

The next day the sales executive is attending a sales meeting that Bob is also attending. The product that he was looking for information on from you yesterday comes up as an agenda item. Bob asks him if he is up to date on the product specifications. He says that he is waiting for you to get back to him, he had called back to the library, yesterday but you weren't there. Bob makes a mental note of this. Later that day,

Bob attends the management team meeting. The library and your business case are discussed. Management feel that you are not very approachable, and there have been a few cases where people have needed access to the library but it was closed. They decide that from a financial point of view they will have to let you go. They see some merit in your business case, but the majority of it is about things you are planning to do in the future. They think that some of this should have already been in place. They are going to continue to have a library with open access, and they ask Bob to transfer the procurement of electronic business resources to another member of his team. You have failed your mission. The management team does not consider your contribution to the company as being core to their business strategy and view the library as 'nice to have' but not essential. You didn't outline your USP, and you didn't use adequate business language in your case. You have not succeeded in convincing them of your value and the impact that you have on business operations in the company. You have failed your mission.

## *Special librarian (option 2 from start)*

You decide you have not done enough to increase your visibility to management. This is an area that has been neglected. You come up with a marketing action plan. You decide to put it into action because time is of the essence. You know one member of the management team, Dan, who is the head of business operations, so you decide to keep an eye out for him in the building. You spot him in the staff canteen during the coffee break. You approach him and ask if he would mind if you joined him. He is amenable. You chat about several things, and then you broach the subject. 'I was wondering Dan, would you consider doing a "return to the shop floor" day in the company? This is when senior managers spend a day working in departments on the ground'. He seems interested. He explains that this was introduced at his previous job and it was very successful. You ask him if he would be the manager to return to the shop floor of the library and spend a morning at your desk. He likes the idea. It's scheduled for the following week.

Dan decides to extend the return to the shop floor idea beyond the library and into each of the seven departments of the company. They rotate the managers so that Dan and the head of marketing spend half of a day in your shoes. They gain a real insight into your work, and they find it impossible to answer a lot of the queries that you receive. They attempt to find answers using Google and a few other search engines and business directories, but they fail. People are asking for books on specific subjects. They are not familiar with the best books in different subjects, and they bring out a pile of books that are mostly unrelated to the topics that people are looking for help in. By the end of the day, they have a new appreciation for your skills and the electronic resources that you provide. The marketing manager says he will help you with a proactive marketing plan to tailor some of your research services to other employees in the company. The plan seems to have worked. Bob passes by the library and smiles in. He knows you've done a good job, but the management team just needed to see it.

The following month, the library comes up for discussion at the management team meeting. Bob doesn't have to say much. Dan and the marketing director start singing your praises. They decide to give you a 5% salary increase. They found that the return to the shop floor day increased collaboration across the whole company, and to them better collaboration means better business. They realise they have not been valuing your contribution to the business at all. They throw in a bonus of €3000 in addition to your pay increase that Christmas. Good job! You made yourself visible to three key stakeholders in the company and helped them to understand the work that you do by giving them the opportunity to sit at your desk and manage your work for a few hours. It paid off! Congratulations, you have succeeded in your mission.

## Special librarian

You are going to shut down the electronic library. Let's see how people like that. If they think 'Everything is on the Internet', then let's see how people find information without access to full-text business resources, ebooks, business journals and market reports. It takes you 2 days to properly shut down all access. People are not happy. You start receiving complaints, but not that many—not as many as you had anticipated. You are getting worried. Bob comes in. 'What happened to my password? I cannot login to anything anymore'. You explain your strategy. He doesn't like it. He suggests that you document the complaints and switch the access back on. You have no choice. Everything is back up and running. You've received three verbal complaints and five emails in 10 days. It's not really enough. That's all you have. You put together an alternative plan to save the library and your job, but you've run out of time. It includes the complaints received. You hand it to Bob on Friday in advance of the management team monthly meeting. Bob reads it. He is not terribly impressed. The tone is defensive and the examples given will not speak to management. The language is business-like, but it is not strategic enough. The usage statistics are healthy and demonstrate that electronic resources are being heavily used and are cost-effective. However, there is no evidence or data to show that the library service and in particular the employment of a librarian is having a positive effect on the user. This is an area that is lacking in the business case. Bob was not in favour of your strategy of cutting off the electronic information services with no prior warning to users. He understands the idea, but he thinks you handled it with poor communication skills.

Bob goes to the meeting and explains your business case to the other members of the management team. They have the same concerns as Bob. They decide that the job of the librarian is superfluous and ask Bob to give you your notice. They feel that the contracts department will be able to continue the corporate subscriptions to the electronic business resources that are valuable, and they will outsource training in business intelligence research tools. After the meeting, Bob gives you the news. You have been let go. The key stakeholders in your company gave you an opportunity to prove your value and impact on the organisation and increase your visibility, but you failed. You have failed your mission.

## Public librarian (option 1 from start)

You make phone calls to the other three librarians in your area and arrange a meeting the following evening. The meeting goes well. You jointly decide that a co-ordinated approach is required. You agree that an urgent town meeting is necessary. You need to rally all of the support possible from the local community. Each librarian is going to organise a town meeting in each of the four towns in the area. Librarians from other sectors in the area, including school, hospital and academic, are all going to be invited. The approach to each town meeting will be locally replicated. Councillors, the general public, borrowers, school children, parents and the active local community groups are all on the invitation list. Any group that uses any of the libraries are added to the list. There are many. The list is growing.

You set up a Facebook page with a campaign to save the public libraries of the area. The computer services staff and library assistants agree to maintain the Facebook and Twitter feed with regular updates. The school, hospital and academic librarians in the area are all using social media to support the campaign. The Library Association is contacted, and the president offers his support. He is going to attend two of the town meetings, which will be held in the public libraries, which all have good-sized meeting spaces. The community is becoming united in this collective effort. The reason this is working is because the public libraries are valued in the locality and the librarians have done extensive work in increasing their visibility and raising the profile of their value to their local communities and disadvantaged in society.

You realise you need a vision to keep the libraries open. Ideas are generated at the town meetings. Local business people prove extremely helpful and innovative. This is an area of the community that possibly has been overlooked by some of the libraries.

The plan puts a focus on the economic, social and cultural value of the public libraries to the community. This has to tie in with the current government strategy and with the overall plans for public libraries in the country. A few different strands inform your campaign. On the economic side, you are going to replicate the model of a recent winner of 'CILIP Libraries Change Lives award', in which public libraries offered space for business meetings and training for budding entrepreneurs.

On the social side, you are gathering testimonials from the community groups who have been using the public library to host events and meetings, including the local active retirement group, parents and toddlers group, schools, youth literacy group, lone parents, business start-up group and creative writing group. These are positive examples of social inclusion. On the cultural side, you have gathered feedback from attendees at cultural events hosted by the library, including a photography exhibition, local history lecture, health promotion lecture series, read-a-thon, visits from local authors and a storyteller event.

You compile the evidence for the value and impact that the public libraries have on individuals and groups in the community. You extract qualitative data and run a comparison with the previous year to show that the usage and activity are increasing all of the time. Your social media presence is very strong with 10,000 followers. You include the ranking of the public libraries in your region in terms of benchmarking with other public libraries in the country. Feedback from users and nonusers is used to inform new directions for the library, including digital collections and the use of space in the library. You have qualitative data to demonstrate your value; for example, that a minimum attendance at homework clubs three times a week for school children led to better school attendance and grades as reported by local schools and parents. Another example is improved digital literacy as shown by adult learners attending digital literacy tuition given by librarians. The 'silver surfer' club has been very successful with local retired people in the community.

You know that from the council's viewpoint there is probably a 'bottom line' that they will need. They are struggling for money, and there is a severe housing problem in the area. The council has been tasked with making savings of €50m in the next 2 years. You decide to offer a partnership with the town council and free up a librarian's office for the housing division staff. It will require some re-design, but it may just work. You include a plan to provide reserved access for housing staff to one of the meeting rooms in your library and access to the Internet and laptops. The academic library offers to work with public libraries in both of your towns and the housing division staff in partnership. The academic library has access to lecture halls and advanced technology laboratories, which they will make available during out-of-term hours. The plan is shaping up well.

The librarians are now deciding if they have done enough and what the next step is. One of the librarians, Laura, thinks that a meeting with the town council and the librarians should be set up. The other two librarians think that you have all done enough and that the plan should be sent to the council as is. They feel that the plan is robust and there is no need to go in person to meet the council. If you decide to side with the two librarians, then go to the end of page 11. If you decide to agree with Laura, who wants to arrange a meeting with the council, then continue reading.

You agree with Laura about meeting with the town council. There is a disagreement between the librarians. You eventually convince the other two librarians that you need to go and meet with the town council as a collective group to make your pitch. Laura knows one of her local councillors and manages to arrange a slot at the upcoming town council meeting. The day of the meeting arrives. It is beginning to feel like an episode of *Dragons Den*. You remember that figures are important. You have flashcards with you. You have practised mock pitches. However, nothing could prepare you for the town councillors. They seem to know everything about each of the public libraries before you get to the second point on your flashcard. They are quizzing every detail and every point or claim that you make. They want numbers, and they want evidence of values. They want to know how libraries can save money, not cost more money. They ask about volunteers. You are ready for that question. You have a policy in place for volunteers that effectively works. Your head is reeling from the intense bullet-like attack. Laura begins to fidget. One of the other librarians is moving from one foot to the other every time she makes a point. You finish with your ultimatum: 'Do you want to live in a place where we nurture our young; we encourage the unemployed; we include people of all colour, gender, race and ability; and we open our doors to create a public space for all to have an opportunity to learn, to engage with their community and to reach their potential? Or do you want to live in a community where all of those opportunities are only available to the elite? That is the difference that a public library makes'.

This was met with some nods of approval. With that, the council asked if you could give them some time to come up with their decision. They ask you all to wait in the adjacent room. Twenty minutes later, a councillor joins you. He says that there will be conditions, but the plan you have put forward is viable and he is delighted to tell you that the public libraries will remain open for business. Success! You have accomplished your mission of saving the public libraries and the jobs of the public librarians. A collective informed effort bringing together key stakeholders and public library users from the community assisted you in your mission. Forming partnerships with the academic community was a good move. Showing the councillors that the public librarians had a shared vision for going forward and beating the cuts was a positive force. You have proven your value to society in your area and to the local community. Your visibility is high. Well done!

## Public librarian

You have all done enough with the plan and decide to send it to the town council in advance of their monthly meeting on Thursday. Public libraries are on the agenda of the meeting. Only one of the councillors has read your submitted plan. The others did not have time to read it in detail. They only have 5 min left during the meeting to discuss it because other items, such as finance, have taken up the majority of their time. The councillor who reads the plan thinks it has merit, but he is a lone voice. The others say that public libraries are costing too much to run and they will make instant savings in the budget by closing them. This is met with general agreement. A vote is taken. The following day, you and the other three librarians are sent a copy of the minutes of the meeting. The decision has been taken to close all four libraries. Laura was right; you should have made your case in person. The well-thought-out plan was not suffi-cient in saving the public libraries and your jobs. You have failed your mission.

## Public librarian (option 2 from start)

You convene a meeting with all other public librarians in the region. Together, you decide that your only hope is to lobby local councillors and politicians to defend the public libraries in the area. You have a 5-year strategic plan that was agreed with the town council. They are re-neging on this! They agree to an hour meeting with the public librarians from the region. You have an opportunity to convince them that the libraries are worth keeping. You start off with a strong opening, but you can feel your voice quiver and you wish you'd invested more time in presentation skills training. Another librarian steps in, but she speaks defensively. She talks about the history of the public library and how it has always 'been there'. She suggests that reductions should be made from other departments in the local council but not from the library. You find your voice again and plead that keeping the libraries open is 'really, really important', and it is given that it is a 'public good'. You are not having much luck. This strategy of self-belief in the importance of the public library is not going down well with the town councillors, who have nothing but budgets to balance and cuts to make. You have failed in your portrayal of the value of the librarian and the public library. A decision is taken. All public libraries in the region are closed within 6 months. You have failed your mission.

## Public librarian (option 3 from start)

You know that this decision is all about money. You want to keep the library open, so you think that the best way to do this is through an appeal for volunteers. You launch a campaign locally and put posters up in the town appealing to 'Save your public library—volunteer'. One month later, you have a mixed group of 10 volunteers willing to 'serve'. You take their names and commence the volunteer recruitment procedures that you have in place for taking on volunteers. This takes another few weeks and some volunteers have dropped out for one reason or another. You still have five vol-unteers, and they are eager to help out. None of them are available from 9:00 a.m. to 5:00 p.m., so there is a mixed rota drawn up. The opening hours are going to have to carry on as normal, but the staffing structure is going to be chaotic. You are intending on keeping your job and that of one more librarian, and you are going to have to let your two library assistants go. This is what goes into your plan that you present to the town council. They are intrigued by the idea of volunteers. They agree to pilot this for the next 2 months at your library. Two months later, you and your librarian colleague receive notice of termination of employment. The library is kept open with volunteers running it. A year later, the library is in chaos, books have been stolen and there is no crowd control. The town council closes all libraries in the area. The use of volunteers to replace experienced library staff failed. Having a public library without a qualified librarian was unsuccessful. You failed to demonstrate the importance of your qualifications and experience of running and managing a public library. The town council only saw savings by using volunteers, which is why this initially appealed to them. After that, they had no case to keep the library open. You've failed your mission.

## Academic librarian (option 2 from start)

You see this as a great opportunity. You've been thinking that the reference desk is not working any longer. The number of reference queries that you receive has been steadily declining, and this has been something that has been on your mind. Students do not seem as keen to come up to the desk and ask questions anymore. They seem to be always walking around with their heads buried in one electronic device or another. You have recently come across some research articles about online reference. You remember reading an article by Zhang and Mayer (2011) about 'Getting into the users' space'. It was about using a proactive chat reference software and embedding the chat into online spaces that people with information and research needs would habitually use. Some of the benefits of using trigger-initiated chat in online reference were outlined. This is backed up by Gilson's (2011) research that finds that users often find virtual reference more convenient. Aguilar, Keating, Schadl, and Van Reenen (2011) also reported that establishing a virtual service desk 'increased the accessibility and visibility of the library to "meet the users where they are" in an electronic environment'. This is exactly the type of research that your library director will approve of. The university has its own virtual learning environment (VLE), but the 'ask a librarian' online chat is not available on the VLE. You decide to write out a one-page executive summary detailing your vision for a new online proactive chat service including the elimination of the reference desk.

You are going to replace this service and become a 'roving librarian'. You are going to have a T-shirt made with a message reading, 'Need help? Just ask, I'm a librarian'. You've seen this type of approach being used in the retail sector, particularly in hardware stores and in computer stores, and do not really see why it wouldn't work in the library. You do not wish to remain static at your desk anymore. Cason Barratt, Acheson, and Luken (2010) found that the roving model was well received by students. There is evidence to show that students are still intimidated by a reference desk in a library and sometimes find it difficult to approach librarians behind a desk. You also include an option of having a laptop or tablet and a type of pop-up stand where you plan to pop-up in various areas around the campus; for example, in the student residence halls, in the various restaurants, in the student book shop, in the sports hall you are going to be available during the campus tour and outside of the entrance to the library. You plan to embed the new reference software into the VLE, the main homepage of the university's website and the library subject guide pages. You've involved the subject librarians in this decision, and they are on board. This is an opportunity to try out the 'embedded librarian' role that is being talked about in the LIS literature.

There is some literature that found that users still attach importance to a physical desk for queries (Gratz & Gilbert, 2011). In particular undergraduates prefer some face-to-face time with a librarian (Ismail, 2010). To combat the lack of a physical reference desk, the pop-up reference will go some way to increasing the physical visibility of the reference desk or stand. You decide to talk to computer services. They have an information desk. They come up with an idea from the restaurant business. It entails offering students a portable pager that they can take with them. The student can roam within the library or building. The IT staff will text you to tell you that a student requires assistance and when you are free you notify the computer desk. Then, the IT staff will make the pager vibrate or light up, which notifies the student that there is a librarian free. You can meet back at the computer services desk with the student and start the reference interview. The IT staff has developed an app for this that can also track user preferences and will be able to provide you with useful data about your reference queries and activity. Your one page is looking smart and is full of references to recent literature with examples of the roving or embedded librarian and the success of the proactive chat model.

The next day, you meet with your boss and talk her through the plan. She seems keen. She likes the idea of the pop-up reference but isn't too sure about the T-shirt. She agrees to give it a go. Working in conjunction with computer services is particularly important, and she is bowled over by their readiness to engage with you. She says she will give you 6 months to see if it works. Success! Six months in and your reference queries have trebled compared with the previous 6 months when you had the reference desk. The students are responding well to the pop-up reference stand, and you've received thousands of likes on your Facebook page, where you put up a photo of your new T-shirt. The 'page a librarian' service has gone down very well with the students, and they refer to it as the 'buzz a librarian' service. Students are recognising you now, and they've even asked you to give a presentation at one of their student union meetings.

Your boss is delighted. It has been so successful that she is considering hiring another reference librarian. She has also spoken to staff at the computer services desk who are fielding some of the questions from students that do not require a librarian's input. She read about Dempsey's holistic approach to reference (2011) and convinced the computer services department to allow students to staff their desk at certain times to answer some of the queries that do not require a computer specialist or librarian. You have proven your value, increased your visibility and made a real impact to your key stakeholders—your library manager, your fellow librarians, computer services and most importantly to students.

## Academic librarian (option 1 from start)

You've always worked at the reference desk. This is what you know and enjoy. You know that the numbers of questions you receive from students are steadily declining. You decide to come up with a marketing plan. You just have neglected to do any promotion or marketing. That must be what the problem is. You need to market yourself and the reference desk. Maybe you could make it more attractive looking and less intimidating. You should probably tweet more and fix the library's Facebook page—there is not a lot of new content on there. You decide to do some research. That's the thing. You are looking for examples where the reference desk is working well in academic libraries. The most recent literature talks about the changing landscape of the reference librarian and adding value at the desk (Solorzano, 2013). It is all about change. You're not sure about this. You start looking at literature around marketing. The seven Ps. That's it! Your product must be the reference desk. You decide to include a makeover of the desk in the plan. Your price—well, it's not going to cost too much money, but you include a small budget. Your promotion—well yes, you need to promote the reference desk. Place (i.e. where to position the physical reference desk)—you decide perhaps it should be moved nearer to the entrance of the library. Participants—these are the students and you do not think you have time to get their feedback, so you will put a paragraph in the plan to do an online survey. Physical evidence—that is the physical reference desk that you are determined to keep, but you will revamp it. Process—you may introduce a more streamlined process for capturing reference interviews. Therefore, you begin to put together a plan titled 'Marketing the Reference Desk'. You work on this for the rest of the afternoon and fill the plan with ideas backed up by examples in the literature. You couldn't find any about marketing the reference desk, but you did find some about marketing the reference service, so you think that is the next best thing.

You outline a marketing plan that includes a revamp of the reference desk. You suggest using a different area in the library near the entrance with a smaller stand-up desk and stools. This will make it look more modern. You are going to do an intense marketing campaign by having a launch of the new reference area, and you've asked the subject librarians in the university to tweet about it to generate some attention from their student followers. They are also going to highlight it on their subject portals. The web services librarian has agreed to update the Facebook page and highlight the new reference area. You are going to include the desk and make yourself available during the campus visits for new students to the university.

You take your marketing plan to the director of the library at the end of the week. She is impressed that you've come up with a marketing plan, but she is disappointed that you have not engaged with any students about their views or needs. You have no student input or feedback at all. She doesn't see any real change to the physical reference desk or the reference service. Marketing might boost your profile temporarily, but it is likely to lose momentum again. Marketing should be an on-going activity, not just a reactive time-limited approach to boosting a service. The computer services department is badly understaffed and needs someone with your IT skills. You are transferred. Your value as a reference librarian was not adequately conveyed to the director, and although she saw that you might temporarily increase your visibility, this was not an adequate vision for reference services. Unfortunately, you have failed this mission.

## Academic librarian (option 3 from start)

You decide to transfer to computer services. What is the point in stating the value of your role to the director of the library if she hasn't seen your contribution or impact at all until now. You know that the number of reference queries you were receiving was falling and that a lot of questions you did receive were not even related to the library. People were looking to book rooms or find out where the computer laboratory was. You weren't really needed there anymore. The director must be right. You meet in her office on Friday. She asks you for an alternative plan. You say that she should either get rid of the desk or put a student on it. There is no need for you to be there anymore. You will move to computer services. She is visibly disappointed. She thought that you had good qualifications and skills that were not being effectively used in the reference area, but she was hoping that you would come up with an alternative plan. She was not expecting you to give up so easily. With such a lack of enthusiasm or willingness to innovate and change, she has no choice but to let you go. You have failed your mission. You now report to computer services. After 1 month you resign. The computer services department was not for you.

## Medical librarian (option 1 from start)

You go back to your desk and decide to analyse your KPIs and annual report. You know that the data are there and you have testimonials from three senior figures in the hospital—the clinical director, the head of nursing and the manager of the paramedic service. The evidence is there, so you cannot understand why this is happening. You know that your library assistant will gladly move departments. She has been complaining to you for years about the layout of the library. She feels it is not in keeping with the times. There is no Wi-Fi access, and there are stacks and stacks of books. Although the journals have mostly gone electronic, the library is still looking like a traditional library with rows of books, newspapers and medical and nursing newsletters. The carpet is worn, and the rows of computers are outdated. There are noticeboards everywhere. However, you do not think it is your fault. After all, you've been sending up the annual report year in year out, and you've made a case to get funding to get better computers, but this has never been approved.

You like the comfort of having all of these excellent medical textbooks around you. The data show that the books are being used. Wait. If you look closer at the data, then you see that approximately 3000 items are checked out each year. That figure used to be much higher. The downloads of full-text articles are impressive. Given that you have 10,000 items in the library, 3000 checkouts is only 30%. Maybe the library assistant had a point. You're fed up. You do not feel valued. Your energy levels are running low. The HR director never really understood what the library was for or what you do. He always passed the budget, but it was diminishing year after year. However, 50% is really too much. How are you supposed to run the library on such a little amount? You library assistant Angela offers to help. She also offers you a coffee and an energy bar. If you decide to take your library assistant up on her offer and involve her in compiling your response to the director, then go to the second paragraph below. If you decline the offer and continue to update the plan alone, then continue reading below.

You update the plan with more current data and come up with a response that strongly defends your position. You meet with the financial director the next day. You say that you are willing to concede that your library assistant be moved, but you say that you couldn't possibly transfer to HR. Your qualifications are in library and information science and this would be unacceptable. You insist that as a librarian you need a private office. This is what the standards for hospital libraries say. The HR manager mentions that he has received complaints that you are often 'hidden away in your office' and that staff are not sure if you are available or not and sometimes feel like they are interrupting you. He has also received complaints about the library door being locked while you were in your office. Although doctors were ringing, you wouldn't answer the phone, but he doesn't say this to you, he wants to give you a last chance. You try to explain your value to the HR manager. You talk about how you are providing an evidence-based service, you are regularly compiling current awareness bulletins to clinical and nursing staff and you list all of the services that you have on offer. You can see his eyes glazing over, particularly when you are explaining in detail the many lists of electronic resources and bibliographic databases that you procure and provide. He clearly does not understand the language or jargon that you are using. This feels like déja vu. You've been here before. He stops you mid-sentence and says, 'I was really hoping that you could have come up with an alternative. The clinical director is supportive of the space and the service that you provide, but he needs a meeting room. The hospital is running out of options. I'm afraid I'm going to have to ask you to report to HR from Monday morning onward'. Your heart sinks. He still doesn't get it. You feel that all of the work you have done has been invisible. HR you think? No, you do not see yourself fitting in there at all. By Monday you hand in your resignation. Despite what you considered were your best efforts, you have failed the mission.

You decide to leave your misgivings to one side and involve your library assistant, Angela. Despite her recent lack of motivation, she never takes it out on customers of the library and has always received nothing but praise from health care workers in the hospital. You explain the situation to her. She suggests you put a sign on the door and close for the rest of the day to work out a plan. Although you hesitate, you eventually agree. You get a renewed vigour boost from the energy bar. Despite the dire circumstances, she seems to have perked up. She goes over to the filing cabinet and pulls out a file labelled 'library redesign'. This was something she brought up with you last year and at the start of the year that you dismissed. It required so much change!

Her plans included transforming the librarian's office into a meeting room; removing several library stacks and having an open plan area in the library; and recycling all of the 10 computers that were lined up along the wall in a row, along with the printers, which mostly no longer worked. In their place, she suggested buying 10 tablets and having these pre-loaded with ebooks and other content and being made available for loan in the same way as books. She had read about this at another hospital library and saw that it was proving a big hit, particularly with the doctors. 'But there is no way we can afford that', you say with a defensive stance. She had a response ready: 'I've already spoken to one of our suppliers—at least earlier this year—and they are happy to sponsor the tablets as long as they have their logo on them'.

'Ok, that sounds reasonable, but what about my office? I mean, I am *the librarian*. It even says so on the door!' You are particularly annoyed that your office is going to be taken over. 'I'm afraid you are going to have to face facts. Would you rather be in an office in HR? Because that is your only other option. Come on David, it is make or break time. This is our last chance'.

She has included in the plan that your office is made into a meeting room and that the room is booked for your exclusive use on the first Thursday of every month. You agree that this is a good idea, because you know that usually on Thursdays there are not too many committee meetings. You decide this might be a good day to offer consultations to hospital staff, who are working on difficult cases or need collaboration on research projects. The compromise is that the sign on the door will now read 'Library Meeting Room'. Together, the both of you work on a plan, you do out the costings, which are minimal and point to hospital libraries in the region and internationally who have successfully re-imaged their spaces and outline the outcomes they have achieved. You include things such as a coffee machine, a new carpet and a universal charging station. You feel like you are both getting a little carried away, after all, the finance director was talking about a 50% cut, not increase! You plough ahead with the ideas.

You check the US Medical Library Discussion List for ideas. You remember people talking about this recently on the list but had dismissed it as not being applicable to you. Other medical librarians have come up with some interesting ideas. They include a free book cart where you can offer older textbooks after weeding the collection (this is particularly relevant for your collection); a comfortable lounge area or massage chairs; vending machines for food and drink; pet therapy, where a dog or cat is made available to staff for a walk or to stroke to reduce stress; electronic portals for each department in the hospital; a self-service area with scanner, printer, laptop and self-checkout of books; a history of medicine section and some general books of a non-medical nature. These medical librarians had some incredibly innovative ideas. You come up with a plan to incorporate some of these ideas, particularly the self-service checkout area and the free book cart. You think that the facilities department in the hospital might consider putting in a vending machine, and they may cover the cost of a new carpet. You are going to apply for a grant from the Medical Library Association for the self-checkout scanner. It's been a long time since you've applied for a grant, so you feel confident that you have a reasonable chance of being successful.

You happen to have a Jack Russell dog called Sam and are considering bringing him into the library at lunchtime on Wednesdays. He is a lively little dog and is sure to go down well with the medical residents. Your library assistant thinks you have 'lost the plot' at this stage. The two of you are laughing at the thought of it. The time is racing on. It's now 6:00 p.m., and Angela realises she really has to go home to her family. You thank her most sincerely. Before she goes, you ask if she would consider accompanying you to the meeting tomorrow. She enthusiastically agrees. She hands you a book. 'Do me a favour David, if you are not too tired, then please read this before you go to sleep. I'll see you tomorrow'. The book she has given you is *Who Moved My Cheese?* You know of it but dismissed it as a corporate gibberish. You only bought it for the HR department, who never seem to read anything other than the *Harvard Business Review*. Anyway, you do not want to lose the positive feeling that you've just had, so you take the book and finish up the plan and presentation you were both working on. Just as you are switching out the light the clinical director walks in. He wants to warn you about the potential of you moving to HR. You tell him you are aware of the situation and are going to make changes. You tell him that you and Angela are going to give the library a long overdue make over. He asks about the meeting room. You say, 'It's yours, except for the first Thursday of every month. How does that sound?' 'Excellent', he says. You part ways and he wishes you the best. He knows you are meeting with HR tomorrow. He decides to drop by to the finance director's office before he finishes his shift.

The next day you feel prepared. You have read the book *Who Moved My Cheese?* and realise the hidden message Angela was trying to give you. You understand that it may be too late. The makeover of the library and other changes should have been done over a year ago. In a last-ditch attempt, you've brought your dog Sam with you. You ring the quality manager of the hospital on your mobile phone to ask if it is ok to bring a dog with you into the Academic Centre building where the library is. Because this building is separate from the main hospital, he thinks it should be ok as long as the dog is kept under control. Angela is ready with laptop under her arm. She also has a rolled up poster under the other arm. She seems surprised to see Sam, but gives him a friendly pat. He licks her hand. 'I've got some sketches of a new library space based on what we talked about. I hope you're ok with that?' 'Great', you say.

You walk up to the director's office. You know that he likes dogs because he has a photo of himself and his wife walking on the beach with a golden Labrador on his desk. He's surprised to see Sam, but gives him a pet. He listens to your ideas as Sam licks his palm. Angela is great. You both give an enthusiastic presentation using language that he is familiar with. He says that the clinical director stopped by last evening and now that he has heard your plans he is going to make changes and tweak the budget but reduce it by just 10%. He needs you to generate revenue and has some ideas for this. Well done! You've made your case with the help of your library assistant and Sam. You've proven the value of the library and library staff, and you've shown that you are not afraid of change. You've increased your relevance to the hospital, and you've heightened your visibility to two key stakeholders—the clinical director and the director of finance. You've also shown leadership and the importance of teamwork, collaboration and the value of the library assistant. You have successfully accomplished your mission.

## Medical librarian (option 2 from start)

You decide your only hope is to lobby as many of the consultants and key people in the hospital as you can find. They are extremely busy, so you get a notebook and start walking around the corridors of the hospital to try to get signatures and support. First stop—haematology. The consultant is busy with inpatients and cannot be disturbed. His secretary says she will pass on the message and assures you that she will do her best. The next department is paediatrics. There are numerous consultants there who know you. They all sign the petition and emphasise that the meeting room is required. You acknowledge their sentiments. You move to the canteen. There are a few people there that you recognise. You gather 10 more signatures, including the cardiologist who is well respected. They are more than happy to sign. You feel enthused about the support you are receiving.

The issue of the meeting room keeps coming up in the conversations you are having. You are determined to hold onto your office. You are trying to find the clinical director, but he is at a meeting. You go to the director of nursing. She is very pleasant and gives you some ideas. She feels the library space needs to change. Although she supports books, she thinks that the stock is possibly out of date and not being used as much as it should be. She suggests a re-design with fewer or no books and more technology. You thank her, but you are not convinced. It's getting late, and you've got three pages of signatures—approximately 100 signatures. Not bad for a day's work you think. You turn off the lights in the library and make your way home. Twenty minutes later, the clinical director goes to the library to find that you're not there. He leaves a note to say:

'Sorry I missed you today. I hope you will consider offering the meeting room for clinical use. As you are aware the hospital is under pressure to perform, and accommodation and space are at a premium. I have some ideas for the library and re-use of space'.

The next day you go notebook in hand to the director of finance's office. He is eager to hear your response. He has spoken to the clinical director earlier. You display the signatures and he seems impressed. He asks you about using your office as a meeting room. You disagree. He asks you about changing the space and whether you have any ideas. You say that you could weed out some of the older stock and make some space but you need all of the stacks that you have. He's unfamiliar with the terms 'weed' and 'stacks'. You are using jargon. He interprets your lack of commitment to a re-design of the library as you being closed to change. The director of nursing and clinical director spoke to him with innovative ideas for the library. It seems you have not taken into account what your main stakeholders want and need. He decides that you would be of better use to the hospital and to him in HR. He cannot afford to keep someone in your salary in a library that is not providing enough return on investment. Unfortunately for you, he tells you that you have to report to HR on Monday morning. To him your role and value as a librarian is invisible. You have failed your mission.

## Medical librarian (option 3 from start)

You decide to do a gap analysis. This is not as easy as you anticipated. You want to show that the organisation will not perform to the best of its potential without you or the library. You begin to imagine the library without you or Angela, your library assistant. Although it seems cold, you can imagine the clinicians and nurses gathering in your office, having meetings. The books would be free for all, so that means they would probably be taken and not replaced. The shelves would eventually become empty, and the hospital facilities department would remove them. The library is suddenly a big, open space with tables and chairs. You picture the hospital staff sitting there, working on their tablets and smartphones and having conversations about cases. It is suddenly their space. How can you relay this as potentially disastrous to the director of finance? What is it that you do? What value do you add? How can you relay this in a gap analysis… you do some research.

You talk to Angela, who isn't surprised at the upcoming fate. It's not as if she hasn't been asking you to change the space for over a year now. She helps you with the drawing. The space doesn't seem that bad. You are beginning to panic and cannot concentrate. You scramble to get statistics. You are able to put together some data. For example, you can point out that if you weren't there hundreds of articles would no longer be available. You can show that this would cost the hospital more money to purchase on demand because you get good discounts being a library in good stead. Of course, they will have access to this point-of-care tool, which all of the doctors rave about, so they will be happy with that. Perhaps some of the older clinicians will grumble that the print copy of the *Lancet* is no longer available. They will probably just buy a personal subscription. You have data to show the number of clinical queries you do a month, the number of books loaned and the number of readers. You have helped several teams with systematic reviews, but you realise you are not acknowledged on any of them and you are not listed as a co-author. After all that work that you did! All of the articles you sourced and screened… and you have no evidence to back it up.

You've delivered training sessions to hundreds of medical students and nurses over the years. You only have numbers. You have nothing to demonstrate whether the training led to better outcomes. You have nothing to show patient outcomes. You had good intentions to try Marshall's (Marshall et al., 2013) methodology in the hospital and try out one of her surveys on hospital staff. You decide to at least cite her research in your gap analysis. It is a pity that you didn't get around to doing that study. It would have been so useful now. You have no recent testimonial. Your last staff survey was 3 years ago. There have been many staff changes since then and many new residents in the hospital. It's not your fault, you think. You need more staff. You need more support. You've been trying to do things as best as you knew how. You take Angela's drawing and thank her. You close up the library at 5:30 p.m. and head for home with a heavy heart. A few minutes later, the clinical director arrives at the library, which is closed. He has swipe access. He leaves you a note that reads, 'Sorry I missed you today. I hope you will consider offering the meeting room for clinical use. As you are aware, the hospital is under pressure to perform and accommodation and space are at a premium. I have some ideas for the library and re-use of space'.

The next day you see the note and grit your teeth. You are not giving up your office. You've worked in this hospital for 12 years, and this is how they are treating you. You bring the drawing and the gap analysis to the director of finance. You start talking statistics. You feel because he is a numbers man he must respond well to this. He doesn't understand 'clinical queries', 'ILLs', 'document delivery', 'information literacy', 'full-text' and something about being 'embedded'. The only two things that resonate with him are Angela's drawing, which he likes, and cost per download. He decides that the hospital cannot afford to be paying for journals without your involvement in procurement. Therefore, he has decided from a value for money point of view that his decision to move you to HR still stands. You can continue with the procurement of electronic content and the point-of-care tool from there as well as taking on a new HR role. He thinks Angela should stay in the library and will be able to keep it running with her new design. You adopted a defensive stance and showed an unwillingness to change. Your value as a qualified librarian is invisible to a key stakeholder—the director of finance. You have failed your mission.

## School librarian (option 1 from start)

You've decided to start reading some material and find out from the literature how other school librarians have overcome this hurdle. You find yourself exasperated by the forthcoming doom and scramble to find literature. The library is particularly busy this time of year, and the students are constantly coming in asking for help with their exam preparations. You are running out of time. You find some studies that show that school librarians make a difference. If you decide to make an appointment with your local councillor, then continue reading below. If you decide to continue looking for more research, then turn to page 23.

## School librarian (continued from above)

You contact your local councillor and make an appointment to see her on Thursday. She agrees to meet with you at her offices at 10:00 a.m. You've informed the principal that the library will be closed that morning. Thursday comes and you convey your arguments to the councillor to defend your position at the school, including highlighting the importance of the library for education and improving literacy skills for children attending the school. You highlight the gravity of the situation and insist that time is of the essence. You point to the evidence in other countries that making it mandatory for schools to employ a professional librarian is achievable. The councillor is aware of the importance of education to people and particularly in this electoral area. She takes your concerns seriously and promised to raise it with the Minister for Education. You ask her if possible to contact you again before Friday to see if there is a positive outcome you can relay to the principal. She promises to ring you later that afternoon. At 4:30 p.m. later that day, you still have not heard anything from the councillor. You decide to ring her. You get through and she apologises, but she couldn't get to speak to the Minister. She says she will do her best tomorrow and wishes you the best of luck with your meeting with the principal. She says that she endorses your position and will send you an email to state the same. You gather the three studies you've found and summarise a two-page plan for tomorrow's meeting. You receive an email with endorsement from the councillor at 4:45 p.m. You go home with a heavy heart.

## School librarian

Friday comes and the principal invites you to his office at 10:00 a.m. You go with your two-page plan and an email of endorsement signed by the councillor in hand. The principal is impressed with your evidence-based summary and the email. However, he says that it may not be enough. He says he will do his best. He is expecting a call from the Department of Education later that morning, and he will let you know the outcome by lunchtime. You go back to the library and hope for the best. You've spent 2 years building up the place to be a respite for children and a welcoming place for all to explore, learn and engage. You are dreading the lunchtime bell, but you have not given up hope yet. The principal walks in at 1:30 p.m. He doesn't look happy. 'I'm so sorry, but I did all that I could. I'm afraid I cannot keep you on next year'. You have not succeeded to demonstrate the value of your role as a school librarian or the impact that the school library has on the mission of the school. Your plan and approach have failed.

## School librarian (if you've decided to continue doing research from earlier)

You continue searching for relevant research and you find another five articles (Gildersleeves, 2012; Kuon, Flores, & Pickett, 2014; Lance, 2001, 2012; Slee, 2014) that will help you make your case to the school principal and board of management of the school. You highlight a research instrument from an article by Small and Snyder (2010) that you will use going forward to measure your impact. You start writing up your plan, and you hope to present it to the principal on Friday. It is now 4:00 p.m. Thursday, and the plan is 15 pages long. You feel that you've done as much as you can in the time frame. You shut the library door and head home.

The next day, the principal invites you in at 10:00 a.m. to hear your plan. You convey your plan in as much detail as you can, highlighting all of the evidence and data that show that having a professionally qualified librarian running the school library is key to successful learning outcomes for students. The principal is leafing through the 15-page document and finds it a little difficult to follow. He is looking for a summary that will explain to him in a brief outline what the main points are. Unfortunately, you have not included one. He says he has a call with the Department of Education shortly, and he will let you know the outcome by lunchtime. You return to the library, and you meet some of the students in the corridor. They want to know if the library is going to open. They follow you down and you open up and let them in. Shortly later, the principal arrives. He shakes his head and apologises that the department did not have a favourable response. He thanks you sincerely for all of the work that you have done and wishes you well in securing another job. You have failed your mission.

## School librarian (option 2 from start)

You put a sign on the library door 'closed until further notice'. You text all school librarians in the area whom you know well and arrange an emergency meeting. They are all willing to come to your library because you are the most centrally located. They have all received similar notices from their principals. At 3:00 p.m. the meeting is held. You collectively decide that you will need to lobby local politicians and get children attending the school, their parents and the teachers to support you. The local councillor is known to one of the librarians, so she agrees to make contact with them. Another librarian suggests that they accumulate signatures from all students at every school as well as teachers to 'save our librarian' and 'save our library'. You suggest that signatures of parents are also collected. Time is of the essence. The school secretaries are contacted and agree to help with contacting the parents. The principals are informed of the lobbying and agree that it is a good idea. You contact the president of the school library association and ask her for a letter of support. The president goes a step further and suggests that a protest march is staged outside of the House of Parliament. This rallies the school librarians into action and a protest is arranged for the following evening.

Announcements are made in each of the schools across the public address system about the protest and signatures. Students, teachers and parents are on board. The next day, the local councillor, 500 students, parents, teachers and the group of librarians arrive at the House of Parliament and stage a powerful protest. Over 1000 signatures have been gathered, including mainly signatures of school children. The librarians are furiously tweeting about the event and the banners read 'Save our librarian'. The media pick up upon the march and suddenly the protest is on the 9:00 news that evening. It has been a huge success. The next day all of the principals receive a directive from the department to continue the employment of the school librarians. Well done! You've succeeded in collaborating with several key stakeholders and involved the main beneficiaries—school pupils—to help fight your cause. You and your profession are now fully visible! You have successfully accomplished your mission!

## School librarian (option 3 from start)

You are fed up constantly having to justify your existence. This is a new low. You've been given such short notice; it doesn't seem fair. You feel as though you've given a lot both personally and professionally to the school and enough is enough. You start to look for other jobs, but there are no library jobs listed in the best library vacancy websites, at least none in your country. You gather your draft annual report that you had been preparing and ensure you have outcome measures highlighted, including an increase in digital and information literacy among students and greater integration and cultural diversity awareness. You include testimonials from students that you've gathered during the year. You go through the annual report in detail with the principal that Friday. He is impressed with what you have accomplished with the students in the school. He is disappointed that you lack a plan, but accepts your position. The principal has no choice but to email the annual report to the department and await their outcome. It is not surprising that the representative from the Department of Education decides, on the basis of the annual report, that the job will no longer be viable for the coming school year. The principal wishes you good fortune in seeking a new job. You have failed in your mission of increasing your visibility.

## Notes

SOTMG    Abbreviation used in emails or test messages meaning 'Short of time, must go'.
CILIP    Chartered Institute of Library and Information Professionals (UK organisation)
STACKS   Set of shelves usually in a library where materials are arranged or classified in
         a specific order.

# Case studies: visibility of academic librarians and academic libraries

**2**

> *I do not think, sir, you have any right to command me, merely because you are older than I, or because you have seen more of the world than I have; your claim to superiority depends on the use you have made of your time and experience.*
>
> **Charlotte Brontë, Jane Eyre**

Interviews were performed in person or by using Skype at different times between 2014 and 2015 with the librarians listed in the case studies that follow. The librarians were chosen because of their high visibility internationally or within their country or speciality. For example, one public librarian interviewed was the recipient of the UK 2014 'CILIP Libraries Change Lives Award' and one of the school librarians won the 2013 'School Librarian of the Year' award from the School Library Association of the United Kingdom and Ireland. Two of the librarians have been occasional lecturers at the School of Information and Library Studies at University College Dublin. One of the librarians is the former president of the Library Association of Ireland. Finally, one of the health librarians runs the world's most popular librarian Wiki (HLWIKI International) 2015. Most librarians who were interviewed are working in Ireland and the United Kingdom, with some librarians from Australia, Canada, New Zealand, Finland and the United States.

All librarians interviewed are working in a period of economic strain. Resources are scarce, and there is increasing pressure to demonstrate impact, value and visibility of their profession to employers and in some cases the public. The role of the librarian has evolved and changed substantially in the last 10 years, and the experience of the librarians interviewed demonstrates this. The librarians interviewed are all working in their organisations for a minimum of 12 months. Most have been working in the same organisation for more than 7 years. They are asked to rate themselves on a scale of 0 to 10 as to how visible they feel among firstly key stakeholders and secondly readers or users of their services. Visibility is explained to the interviewees as how key stakeholders and readers know who they are and what they do on the one hand and understand and value what they do on the other. All state that they had a low visibility score at the time of their appointment and report an increase in their visibility over time. The methods that they use to increase their visibility is detailed together with tips for librarians in their special areas of work and tips for librarians who are new to the profession of librarianship.

Each librarian and each library have its own personality. The personality of the librarian is usually reflected in the library and the service that is provided. These case studies provide an insight into the personalities of librarians and the real work that they do. They reflect upon their visibility within their respective organisations and share stories and tips on how that has been improved over time. Overwhelmingly, the librarians individually express the need to move outside the library and the importance of being seen outside of the library.

An area in which all librarians agreed was the importance of online visibility of either the librarian or library as a service. There was unanimous agreement that this was extremely important in an increasingly technical and Internet-dependent society. Another area where there was commonality was in the advice given by the librarians interviewed on how to increase visibility. All librarians said it was important to get out of the library. To be physically seen outside of the confines of a physical library was perceived to be important for raising awareness about the librarian and to help others to gain an understanding about the work that the librarian does. Getting outside of the library also helps raise the profile of the librarian in the organisation.

The first set of case studies is from interviews with librarians working in academic or third-level education institutions. Each study is presented using a template that sets the context of the organisation where the librarian works by outlining its mission and that of the library, the online visibility of the same and a few key facts about the organisation. The five librarians interviewed include a subject librarian, a liaison librarian, an emerging technologies librarian, a systems librarian and a librarian in a managerial role as head of services. The librarians are based in Ireland, the United States and Finland. Interviews were held in person and via Skype during 2014.

Much research exists that demonstrates the positive value and impact that academic librarians and libraries bring to their institutions and readers. Professional library associations are taking a leadership role in pursuing research into this topic. For example, in North America, the Association of College and Research Libraries (ACRL) in conjunction with other partners has sponsored a 3-year project called Assessment in Action: Academic Libraries and Student Success (AiA). This is due for completion in 2016. The project is documenting successful contributions that librarians and libraries make to students success. The projects are open for other academic libraries to locally reproduce.

A snapshot of recent literature demonstrating the value of academic librarians and libraries to their organisations and readers is summarised in Table 1. For a

**Table 1** **Research demonstrating the value of academic librarians and libraries to readers and organisations**

| Value/impact indicator | Research/evidence |
| --- | --- |
| ROI (return on investment) and positive CBA (cost benefit analysis) | Pan, Ferrer-Vinent, and Bruehl (2014), Pan and Fong (2010) and Luther (2008) |
| Improved information literacy of students | Pan et al. (2014), Oakleaf (2010) and Bowles-Terry (2012) |
| Student attainment via eresources use and book borrowing | Cox and Jantti (2012, 2013) and Stone and Ramsden (2012) |
| Increase research output and increase research profile and reputation of university | Tenopir, Volentine, and King (2012) and Rin and Rluk (2011) |

comprehensive list of references, the University of Huddersfield in the United Kingdom has a Library Impact Data Blog with a useful online bibliography of impact studies that is part of a JISC Activity Data Programme.

# Case study 1: subject librarian in engineering, mathematics, business, social science and philosophy working in reader services

| | |
|---|---|
| Name: | David MacNaughton |
| Organisation: | Trinity College Dublin, University of Dublin, Ireland |

Founded in 1592, Trinity College Dublin is the oldest university in Ireland and one of the oldest in Western Europe. It has some 17,000 international students, 92,000 alumni and 2860 members on staff. It sits in the city centre of Dublin and has cobbled stone squares, and the building is modelled on the universities of Oxford and Cambridge. It ranked seventy-first in the world university rankings in 2014. The library contains 5 million volumes and famously houses the Book of Kells.

## Mission of the organisation

Through our research and teaching, we engage students and society in the quest for knowledge, seeking to achieve excellence in all we do, and responding with creativity and imagination to the challenges and opportunities of a shared future (Trinity College Dublin, 2009).

## Mission of the library

The library supports the learning and research needs across all disciplines of the college; it is a major research library of international repute; it provides services to a wide range of external users and institutions; it contributes to the development of creative initiatives in information provision and its exhibitions of manuscripts and other treasures attracts hundreds of thousands of visitors to visit the Old Library each year.

## Online visibility of the library and subject librarian

| | |
|---|---|
| Library website: | https://www.tcd.ie/Library/ |
| Subject librarian webpage: | https://www.tcd.ie/Library/support/subjects/business/ |
| Institutional repository: | http://www.tara.tcd.ie/ |
| Facebook: | https://www.facebook.com/tcdlibrary |
| Library electronic newsletter: | http://www.tcd.ie/Library/about/newsletters/folio/ |
| YouTube: | https://www.youtube.com/user/TrinityLibrary/videos |
| Twitter: | https://twitter.com/tcdlibrary |
| | http://ie.linkedin.com/pub/david-macnaughton/54/634/589 |

## Background and current role

The subject librarian David MacNaughton has worked in Trinity College Dublin Library for 9 years. He is one of a team of subject librarians. When he first started, there were 13 subject librarians. In 2014, that number has been reduced to approximately 9.5 FTEs (full-time equivalents). Similar to everywhere in the public sector, there are fewer staff members. The main role that the subject librarians have is to act as the principal liaison between academic faculty and the library. That includes things such as how librarians can make collections relevant to courses, or getting new books for courses, ordering journals and databases for research purposes and making the library holdings relevant. Budgets have also been reducing. Budgets are allocated to each school on an FTE basis with some exceptions. For example, in the subject area of law, books tend to be much more expensive than some other disciplines. Some disciplines are more heavily reliant on electronic resources such as pharmacy; therefore, he explains that the budget would be larger for electronic material than for print for this department. An important part of David's job is to correctly spend his budget and troubleshoot any issues that may arise around collections with other librarians in the college.

Another main role subject librarians have is advocacy and being 'that visible person', getting out into the classrooms and into the curriculums. Promoting library services and showing library resources to students is important. All of the checkouts and downloads are counted so the subject librarians promote the use of printed and electronic resources and make academics and students aware of the range of resources they have access to. David also allocates time to one-to-one tuition and assistance directly to both academics and students. Visibility is pertinent to David's role.

In terms of visibility, David feels he rates a 7 with key stakeholders, in this case senior management within the library (Table 2). The library has recently appointed a new librarian and college archivist, Helen Shenton, who is very supportive of the subject librarian role. She has assisted in the promotion and visibility of subject librarians to faculty in the college. In such a large organisation, there are naturally conflicts and competition for budgets between all departments such as reader services, special collections, and collection management. David feels that overall the subject librarian role is valued within the university. The subject librarians are well known throughout the university, they are at assistant librarian grades, which is not a management grade. David is unsure how visible subject librarians are to the higher level of management in the organisation.

Among students, David scores high in terms of visibility. Just last week, he says that he stood up in front of approximately 1000 students, in different sessions, introducing himself and the library services. There were two sessions consisting of 300 business economic and social studies (BESS) students and a further two sessions comprising 200 engineering students. He is also running new courses for postgraduate students and many generic courses and walk-in courses.

His visibility with certain students is very high, and he scores an 8 or a 9 with economics and political science students, but he reports a slightly less score with engineering students – perhaps a 6 or a 7 (Table 2). He finds that visibility can be very subject dependent because the way in which people engage with the librarian or library vastly differs. For example, in his experience, in the area of physics and chemistry, people are slightly more resistant to engaging with the library.

When David first started, he reported a score of 7 with people in charge or key stakeholders. He feels he scored much the same as he does today. What has dramatically changed is what the subject librarian does. This has changed significantly in the time he has worked there. The role of the librarian has expanded in the last 10 years to include teaching and research. Some older colleagues may have somewhat resisted this evolving role. They would not see teaching as a role of a subject librarian. They would gather reading lists, manage budgets, acquire resources, and maybe give one or two talks a year. In terms of the students, he feels that the subject

**Table 2  Self-reported visibility rating of librarian at time of appointment versus today**

| Visibility rating at time of appointment: where 0 = invisible, 10 = highly visible | | | | | | | | | | | |
|---|---|---|---|---|---|---|---|---|---|---|---|
| With key stakeholders (library management) | 0 | 1 | 2 | 3 | 4 | 5 | 6 | **7** | 8 | 9 | 10 |
| With staff/students | 0 | 1 | **2** | 3 | 4 | 5 | 6 | 7 | 8 | 9 | 10 |
| Visibility today (9 years after appointment): where 0 = invisible 10 = highly visible | | | | | | | | | | | |
| With key stakeholders (library management) | 0 | 1 | 2 | 3 | 4 | 5 | 6 | **7** | 8 | 9 | 10 |
| With staff/students | 0 | 1 | 2 | 3 | 4 | 5 | 6 | **7** | 8 | 9 | 10 |

librarians are much more visible to students now. Subject librarians in the college have much more face time with students now than before. A simple thing such as his email inbox being full with emails from students confirms this. The visibility dilemma of the librarian is that the more visible you are, the more this perpetuates itself. David says that in terms of visibility, there is a balance to be struck between being physically and virtually available for students. He states, 'If you hide away in this age of communication and technology and rely on tweeting, then you are not visible'.

## Most successful way of increasing visibility?

David feels that getting into the curriculum was a turning point in terms of improved visibility. Subject librarians initially gave talks to the freshmen, but now training is becoming more advanced, tailored and personalised. The training is also orientated toward research. The library is running many courses now. For example, he has been asked to give a lecture to all first-year engineers on citation and plagiarism. He also gives training in the product Endnote™, evaluating research papers and managing your academic presence online. The training that the team of subject librarians is now offering is more advanced than in the past. Before, he describes training as 'it was a PowerPoint presentation describing opening hours, reading lists and how many volumes of works are available in the library'. This has been completely turned around. Particularly via engagement with academics, this has been another turning point in heightening visibility. Unless the librarian shows that they can do something for them, they will not seek out the librarian. This means that the librarian has to adopt a proactive approach.

## Value that the librarian brings to the organisation

When asked about what value he brings to the organisation, he shares that he has helped many people over the years individually and in groups with their research. He says, 'I offer a high-quality, "cherry on the cake" type service. I do not just answer emails, I sit down with people, spend an hour here and an hour there, with students'. The support structures are not there because the academics are extremely busy and there is an increasing student population. He says it is difficult to quantify the value that he brings. However, he has received hugely positive feedback, and some days he is very content that he has added value, particularly during the busy academic year.

## *Do you use any formal method of measuring and/or reporting your impact?*

The subject librarians collect anecdotal information and feedback forms on courses and training that they give. There is also an annual report of the library, which includes a mention of the work of subject librarians as well as other librarians and departments. The feedback that is received is used to inform future training and developments. Although the feedback is anecdotal, David says, 'I do not think that the lecturers would be asking me back year after year if the students weren't satisfied'. Sometimes lecturers attend library lectures and then they ask him back to do more sessions.

## *Challenging scenarios*

David is not part of the management team of the library, so although the library has seen challenging times, such as the library budget being slashed, he is not in a position to fight for more because he is not part of the management team.

### Top tips for academic librarians to increase visibility

David offers some no-nonsense advice for academic librarians, including 'Pick up the phone. Don't hide in your office'. He says librarians should identify new staff, introduce themselves and perhaps ask them out for coffee. When pushing library services, use the approach of 'this is going to make your life easier' (e.g. citation and plagiarism is a big issue for all academics). Using Endnote™ and referencing is a key area where librarians assist academics and use their skills to teach and improve education in this area of information management. David says that academics run the college, so librarians have to get in with them. He says, 'You need to be a "people person" in this job. You have to like dealing with people. You have to like solving problems. You have to be visible; you have to go the extra mile with people. You cannot sit at a desk looking completely unapproachable'. David feels that if a librarian is interested in programming, then they are best suited to a systems or cataloguing role but not other areas of librarianship. Librarians cannot be full of dread when someone approaches them or sends them an email. Librarians have always been educators and have to be visible in that role.

### What do you think of the 'embedded librarian' model, in which the librarian is part of a multidisciplinary team, doing all of the things she may have done in the library but the physical library is no longer there, she is now part of this team?

David thinks that the embedded librarian is the ideal model. However, given the present staffing situation, it would be impossible to implement. For example, the subject librarian for nursing involves a lot of teaching and tends to be a much embedded role. However, it is important to balance this with the role of academics – who would not wish to see their role diminished in any way. There is still some convincing to do with academics about the value of the embedded role. Librarians are not invited to curriculum meetings. They are not currently at the same table, but that may change.

David has spoken at some committee meetings on specific agenda items but is not on the committee. This is a cultural feature of how the organisation presently works. It is traditional. He has not been formally invited.

## How important is it to be visible to users in an online environment?

David admits he is unsure about this. He thinks that the library website is important. People are increasingly doing podcasts and videos. He thinks it is important but not as important as people were imagining it to be a few years ago. In his experience, the face-to-face contact with people works better. The library conducted a library review a few years ago and asked a question about Twitter and Facebook, and the response from students about the usefulness of information from the Twitter and Facebook page was extremely low. Emails seem to work better. They have a library Facebook page and a couple of 1000 people like it, but he says 'Nothing ever happens on it aside from a few Likes'. The web librarian maintains the content. David doesn't use Twitter.

## Advice to new people into the profession of librarianship?

David says that it is very important to make a good first impression. Don't have a fixed idea about what librarians do. Be open. If you see a project, then run with it. He mentions Niamh O'Sullivan (who is also interviewed, later in the book) as being a really good example of someone who is good at this. Don't shy away from new directions. For example, do not say things such as 'that's not library related'; embrace new ideas and new challenges. Top management are looking for people who will get involved and be engaged. Don't be afraid to fail. A lot is to do with people's personality. Some people in librarianship can be quiet. It is important to be able to go up and talk to people and introduce yourself. Meet people for coffee. Don't sit at your desk and Tweet all day; go out and meet people. Be sociable, and then they will remember you. David recently met two new academics for the first time for coffee and spent about half an hour chatting to them about general things and he knows that they will remember him and recognise him when he meets them again. He wasn't talking to them about library service, he was just having a general conversation.

## Where do you see the subject librarian in 5 years?

David attended the Librarians' Information Literacy Annual Conference (LILAC) in 2013, and he took from the conference that the name of the role of the subject librarian has changed. The description 'subject librarian' is now considered old hat. There are now evolving roles such as teaching support librarians and research reference librarians. What it comes down to is that libraries still need staff to 'get out there and speak to students'; therefore, regardless of what the description of the job is, a lot of what the librarian needs to do is to connect and engage with people *in person*. This type of engagement cannot be done online, at least not to the same degree, in David's opinion. He worries that there is an idea even among some librarians and managers that videos may be created and students can click into content and learning and that is sufficient. According to some research he has been reading, students do not like libraries and librarians invading their social spaces – such as Facebook and YouTube – which are social spaces for them and their peers. Libraries are seen as an authority, and when they have social media sites such as Facebook this does not always appeal to students, according to David.

We talk about Florida Polytechnic University (Library Journal, 2014), which recently opened a new bookless library, with a library team of just six staff. David sees this as akin to 'the end of the world'. In his experience, there is very little support there for students. There is an assumption that everyone learns in the same way through technology and by self-direction, but this is not the case.

### What is your favourite thing about being a librarian?

David likes the one-to-one interaction with people. To him that is critical. When someone comes up to his desk or sends him an email, he likes this contact. He *says*, 'I get to meet some really interesting scholarly people from America and all over the world. If I can get them going on their research or point them in the right direction, they are hugely appreciative. Then I feel that my job is worthwhile'.

## Case study 2: emerging technologies librarian working in an academic medical library

| | |
|---|---|
| Organisation: | Norris Medical Library, University of Southern California, Los Angeles, CA, United States |

The University of Southern California (USC) is a private research university. It was founded in 1880 and was ranked as tied for 25th place in national university rankings in 2014 by the *US News & World Report*. The academic year 2013/2014 had a student enrolment of 41,000. Undergraduates study in the College of Letters, Arts and Sciences.

### Mission of the organisation

> The central mission of USC is the development of human beings and society as a whole through the cultivation and enrichment of the human mind and spirit.

The Norris Medical Library is located on the Health Sciences Campus, northeast of downtown Los Angeles and 7 miles from the University Park campus. The library contains 168,185 volumes and receives 1935 current periodicals. The library serves the Keck School of Medicine, the School of Pharmacy and the Independent Health Professions, including the Departments of Biokinesiology and Physical Therapy and Occupational Science and Therapy. The Health Sciences Library (HSL) system comprises the Norris Medical Library and the Wilson Dental Library, which is located on the University Park campus.

## Mission of the library

According to the library's strategic plan 2007/2008, the mission is outlined as follows:

HSL, composed of the Norris Medical Library and the Wilson Dental Library, provides information support for USC Health Sciences faculty, students and staff. HSL services are designed to anticipate and be responsive to the individual's information needs for teaching, learning, research and health care. In addition, HSL serves the health science information needs of the USC University Park campus community and provides limited access to our resources and services to the general health care community and the public.

## Online visibility of library and librarian

| | |
|---|---|
| Norris Medical library website: | http://www.usc.edu/hsc/nml/ |
| Librarian's page on website: | http://www.usc.edu/hsc/nml/lib-information/libn-bios/wu.html |
| Library blog: | http://norrislib.wordpress.com/ |
| Subject guide: | http://norris.usc.libguides.com/profile.php?uid=24250 |
| Linkedin: | https://www.linkedin.com/pub/jin-wu/21/779/162 |
| Twitter: | http://twitter.com/norrislib |
| Slideshare: | http://www.slideshare.net/JinWu1/ |
| Facebook: | http://www.facebook.com/pages/Los-Angeles-CA/USC-Norris-Medical-Library/81470694233 |
| YouTube: | https://www.youtube.com/user/NorrisLib |

## Role in the organisation

Jin Wu is the emerging technologies librarian. The former title for the librarian was 'web services librarian'. The previous position focused on web development and web maintenance. The position was modified because the library saw the increasing need for technology responsibilities outside of just the web. They required a person who could think broadly, not just about the Web, but about technology in general. For example, mobile devices are really trending, and this is a huge growth area for librarians. Jin does a lot of web work, and she is also the chair of the Emerging Technologies Committee for the

USC Campus Library. She evaluates technology solutions for the library. She actively participates at the reference and instruction department of the library. She attends their weekly meeting. She believes technology has a purpose: 'You cannot just bring a new technology to the library without any purpose; it must have a purpose'.

## Visibility at time of appointment

The role was a new position when she first started the job. When Jin applied she was a reference librarian in Connecticut. When she saw the job advertised, she said, 'That's amazing, that is something I've always wanted to do'. So, she applied and was thrilled to get it. She finds attendance at the reference and instruction department meetings really useful. This is because she can see the problems that the librarians come across and she listens to the difficulties and tries to think of technical solutions. Sometimes she provides her opinion and sometimes they will brainstorm as a group. They look at what other libraries are doing or try to come up with a way of doing things better in the context of technology.

Jin rates her visibility as a five when she first started her job because it was a new role and she had to build up her visibility. It usually takes a couple of years to build up your presence, and she had to work at this and do some outreach. She was also trying to figure out what to do in her job. Once she started to build up a connection with people then this helped her to reach out to the community and expand her visibility and usefulness to them.

## Visibility today

On a scale of 0–10, she rates herself as 8 with key stakeholders of the library, including the library director. With users and students of the library, she rates her visibility as 7 out of 10 (Table 3). She attributes this to the 4h a week that she works at the reference desk and gets the opportunity to interact with students. She also teaches workshops about new technologies. She teaches two categories of workshops. One is a 'Technology Lunch Series', which is a lunchtime lecture where faculty and

Table 3 **Self-reported visibility rating of librarian at time of appointment versus today**

| Visibility rating at time of appointment: where 0=invisible and 10=highly visible | | | | | | | | | | | |
|---|---|---|---|---|---|---|---|---|---|---|---|
| With key stakeholders (decision-makers, library director) | 0 | 1 | 2 | 3 | 4 | **5** | 6 | 7 | 8 | 9 | 10 |
| With staff – students and academics (users of the service) | 0 | 1 | 2 | 3 | 4 | **5** | 6 | 7 | 8 | 9 | 10 |
| **Visibility today (5 years after appointment): where 0=invisible 10=highly visible** | | | | | | | | | | | |
| With key stakeholders | 0 | 1 | 2 | 3 | 4 | 5 | 6 | 7 | **8** | 9 | 10 |
| With staff – students and academics (users of the service) | 0 | 1 | 2 | 3 | 4 | 5 | **6** | 7 | 8 | 9 | 10 |

students are invited to attend. The lecture usually covers a new or popular technology where the librarians feel that students and faculty may want to keep up to date with. The library provides lunch such as pizza and water and people come and get updated. The other class that she teaches is called the 'Technology Workshop'. This is more intensive and usually lasts 3 full hours. People will come to the class with a specific problem and she shows them how to solve it. Software programs and tools that she teaches include Advanced PowerPoint™, tools to edit photos, Adobe Photoshop™ and data analysis tools. She usually teaches these workshops by herself. The workshops are not part of the curriculum, but they are needed and students are very interested in them.

## What has been your most successful method of increasing your visibility over the past 5 years?

Jin says there have been a couple of successful ways of increasing visibility. For her, it is all about interaction. She says there are three ways of increasing your visibility as a librarian. Firstly, interacting with other librarians at work has been very helpful – to have a true and genuine interest in other librarians work and to talk to them and see how they approach new technologies and what they are doing with them in a library setting. Secondly, working with the reference librarians who are the frontline librarian, has been extremely beneficial for Jin. Jin sees her role as finding new ways to help library patrons.

By working on the reference desk, she gets to interact directly with students and finds out how she can help them on a practical level. This connectivity to real students in real life – not just online – is important. This is something that David MacNaughton also highlights as being important for academic librarians. Interacting with students on a one-to-one basis is important for improved visibility and to ensure a real impact that a librarian can have.

When she works at the reference desk she directly helps students. She says often they do not know that the library has an emerging technologies librarian – herself – so once they realise she is there and at hand to help out, they ask for help installing apps on their mobile phones or help with software functionality or hardware problems. She often deals with usability issues with apps on mobile phones and teaches students how to more effectively use them. She has a name card and students will sometimes spread the word about her and this works. They tell others, 'There's this person in the library, who can help with technology problems' and people come on foot of that word-of-mouth messaging.

The third way is interacting with the professional librarian community. Jin volunteers for one of the chapters of the Medical Library Association (MLA) in the United States. She serves as a member of some of the MLA committees and was the Web Committee Chair of the MLAGSCA, an MLA chapter. She also volunteers to do peer reviews for some papers in conjunction with the MLA: 'This type of professional contribution also helps to build your presence, makes you visible to the community. People know you and know what you do. When something comes up, they think about you and want you to contribute'.

## What value have you brought to the organisation?

'A lot of times I do not see my value as direct. I'm not directly involved with patrons apart from the 4 h a week I do at the reference desk. Therefore, my value as an emerging technologies librarian is to create an innovative and forward-thinking environment in the library – to always encourage people to learn about new technologies in their daily lives. Even with cataloguers and reference librarians, I can bring value to them by encouraging them to try new technologies that may help their workflows'. Her value is more evident in what she brings to the library as a whole and to her library colleagues as opposed to patrons. Adopting new technical solutions in the library is the other key value that she brings to the organisation. She helps people do work more efficiently or help them to communicate better. It is an accumulative process with an accumulative effect. She says, 'There is no "auto set" button for my value'. She also creates content for the Web, which she states has its own value but she sees her main value as the accumulative influence that she brings to people in the organisation to adopt new technologies.

## Does the library have any formal way of measuring and reporting impact?

Jin's position is a tenure-track faculty position that requires her to have an annual eval-uation or appraisal with her immediate supervisor. The tenure process in the United States requires this. She has an annual, 3- and 6-year review. In 2015, she will undergo her tenure review. This process helps her to be reflective and think about her job and evaluate what she is doing and keep track of her progress.

## Have you ever had a challenging scenario where you had to prove your value or worth to the organisation and how did you respond? What worked/did not work?

Part of her job is to discover new technical solutions. She used another library man-agement system in a previous library position. She found that this was a very useful system. When she started her current job, a different system was in use that she did not find user-friendly. Therefore, she suggested that the library think about changing the library system for the online catalogue. At the time, she talked to the head of catalogu-ing. However, it turned out that the system she was thinking of changing to was too expensive and the library could not afford it. However, she didn't give up. The clunky catalogue interface was still on her mind, and she knew she that needed to change it.

Two years later, when the library website was re-designed, she decided to bring the topic up again for discussion. She suggested it was an opportune time to update the library catalogue in conjunction with the new library website. Therefore, she was able to reinvestigate the library management system. It turned out that the price had come down because it was 2 years later. She gave a demonstration to all of the librar-ians of the system to show to them that it was a promising product. Eventually, that product was pursued and she was successful in implementing the product that she originally wanted to get for the library. She says, 'Just never give up. If you believe that something is good for the library or the organisation, then keep bringing it up, a few months later or a few years later. Technology is always advancing, and as it advances the price drops'.

She often comes across products she thinks are 'awesome' but can be met with remarks such as, 'it is too expensive' or 'it is too complicated for us'. However, Jin says her job is to be 'that constant reminder' and to keep telling people that they need to move forward and that the library needs to always be on top of technology solutions.

## Top tips for academic librarians to improve impact and visibility?

Jin thinks about her first job, which was as a reference and instruction librarian. She spent 2 years doing this job. She feels that this helped her immensely to do her current job as an emerging technologies librarian. The reason that this helped her is because it helped her to understand people and what their needs were. She sees programmers and web services librarians, but she feels that some of them do not have the same connection with people and do not fully understand people's needs from technology. To know what users are looking for and what they want helps her to do her job better. You can be a cataloguer who doesn't interact with patrons or a librarian who does the 'back-end' office job and never goes out of the office. However, Jin feels it is very important to find a way for all librarians to interact directly with patrons. Only then will they increase their visibility and ultimately affect users: 'That is where you will find opportunities and that is how you will find out how to do your job better. If you keep to yourself, doing what you are doing behind the scenes most of the time, then you will have no opportunity to make yourself visible'. Her tips are

- Go out of the library.
- Get out of your comfort zone.
- Talk to patrons.
- Get involved with other librarians.
- Tell people what you are doing, and talk about the value of your job.

Don't think, 'Oh, other people do not understand what I'm doing'; do think 'I'm going to help people to understand what I'm doing'. Maybe they do not understand what you are doing because you never explained it to them. Maybe you never shared your passion for your job with them and never told them how awesome your job is.

Having a mentor within or outside of your organisation is really helpful. This is especially useful if you are new to the profession where you may start off being clueless. Having an experienced mentor is invaluable. They can help you and give you guidance.

## Do you think the embedded librarian/liaison librarian/librarian in context is the future for academic librarians?

Jin feels the term 'academic librarian' is too broad of a term to be able to answer this question. Different academic libraries serve different populations, undergraduate, postgraduate, etc. However, in her experience in their library, they have a liaison librarian to the medical school, the pharmacy school, the occupational therapy department, and a clinical librarian position. This is a model that works at her library and it is effective. Jin says, 'The liaison librarian to the school of pharmacy whose name is Amy did such a good job that all of the pharmacy students keep asking for her. Every time there is an online reference chat, they say "Hi Amy", although it may be a different librarian online'. The liaison librarian helps students to identify the librarian and to know who they are so in this sense it does heighten the visibility of the librarian. It helps students to build a personal connection with the librarian. In her library, it has helped students to have an identified 'go-to' person and Amy is a good example of this. Jin feels there is great value in having an embedded or liaison librarian because it builds connections between librarians and students in a more meaningful and direct way than a general librarian could ever do.

### How important is it for the librarian to be visible to users in an online environment?

'Most libraries nowadays have some kind of online presence using Facebook™, Google Plus™ or Twitter™'. Jin's library has a Facebook™ page, but they have found that their patrons are not that interested in interacting with the librarians online. Because of this, they do not waste too much time using Facebook™. However, the library has a blog and that is very well received. This is used as a communication channel to reach out to people. When the library website was re-launched, the blog was given a very prominent place on the website and people go to the Blog and see what is new in the library. It is very important for the library to be visible on the university website and for patrons to know what is going on in the library. Most of the students are graduate students or have faculty positions. They are extremely busy and she feels some probably do not interact with their own family or friends online so the librarian can hardly expect them to interact with her online. Whenever they use the online service, the librarian tries to give them as much information as she can.

### What has been the most successful method of increasing visibility in an online environment?

The library blog has been the most successful.

### Where do you see the emerging technologies librarian in 5 years?

'I really enjoy what I am doing right now. I can see the role becoming more challenging. The library's role is ever-changing'. She has done a lot of research and she sees part of her job as working in the library, but the other part is doing research. She is definitely interested in doing more research in the future and hopes her role will evolve in this way. She is interested in how users interact with libraries online and doing more research in this area. This is particularly interesting now in an evolving information environment. Mobile devices are a definite trend, and she can see that the usage of the library's website from mobile devices is increasing. She has statistics and data on this area, so she wants to do more research on that.

Inside of the library, she wants to bring more technology solutions to the library but with a purpose. Every year she looks at a few new solutions, but it doesn't always lead to an implementation nor does it need to. She is a big believer in 'you should have a purpose in whatever you do'. Keeping up to date with new technologies is always going to be important.

She wants to help other people in other libraries and collaborate more. She wants to collaborate with other librarians in other communities to build up a better picture of research and generate richer data. This will help others and help the profession as a whole.

## What is your favourite thing about being a librarian?

'I have more than one thing! To me personally, I am a big fan of lifelong learning and this is why I love my job. I am working in a higher education environment and am constantly surrounded by students, faculty, physicians and librarians. I feel that they inspire me to learn more. I am a very self-motivated person and always like to learn new things and new technologies. To me this is fun. It is important to do something you enjoy doing. I can bring this motivation to other people. If I had to name just one thing, I'd say it is definitely constant learning. This makes me feel fulfilled. I'm always learning and helping other people. It makes me feel that I am becoming a better person, intellectually or in a challenging way. I never feel like I am doing the same job every day. I feel like I am growing in this position'.

# Case study 3: liaison librarian working in an academic library

| Name: | The librarian interviewed chose to remain anonymous. |
|---|---|

She has worked in this academic library for 1 year. Her role is as to act as a liaison with any of the colleges, schools or academics at the university. She has an important communication function and acts as a primary contact point for all issues (e.g. a collections issue or a marketing issue). Academics contact her initially and then she may refer them on to another person in the library (e.g. someone in collection development or perhaps the repository manager). Her main responsibility is for teaching and learning. She runs several classes including information literacy, information skills support and some in research support. The library has a dedicated team for research support but sometimes she assists with queries from academics around research. She is involved in a lot of reference work and support work – both for students and for staff. She is the liaison for 10 out of the 50 schools at the university.

The key stakeholders were defined as management within the library and management or senior figures of the university (i.e. people who could make decisions about her role). The librarian defined her current visibility as 6 of 10, with key stakeholders in her organisation. She defined visibility with students as 5 of 10 (Table 4). Her

**Table 4 Self-reported visibility rating of librarian at time of appointment versus today**

| Visibility rating at time of appointment: where 0=invisible 10=highly visible | | | | | | | | | | |
|---|---|---|---|---|---|---|---|---|---|---|
| With key stakeholders (management of the library/senior figures) | 0 | 1 | 2 | 3 | 4 | **5** | 6 | 7 | 8 | 9 | 10 |
| With students | 0 | 1 | **2** | 3 | 4 | 5 | 6 | 7 | 8 | 9 | 10 |
| **Visibility today (1 year after appointment): where 0=invisible 10=highly visible** | | | | | | | | | | |
| With key stakeholders (management of the library/senior figures) | 0 | 1 | 2 | 3 | 4 | 5 | **6** | 7 | 8 | 9 | 10 |
| With students | 0 | 1 | 2 | 3 | 4 | **5** | 6 | 7 | 8 | 9 | 10 |

reasons for determining this score had to do with the role that she has within teaching and learning. She felt that teaching and learning did not have the same high profile in the organisation as something similar to research assessment. It was not as 'hot of a topic' or not as high up on the agenda. Teaching and learning is a type of 'bread and butter' area of work for librarians in academic settings, similar to collection development. These are areas that are 'always there in the background' but not necessarily highly visible.

The reason for determining a score of 5 with students has to do with the fact that she felt the visibility of the library in general is low with students. The library is low on their list, although this would depend on the individual. The broader area of library services is low on their list of priorities. Students associate the library with books. Therefore, students see the value of the library in terms of 'getting books for an essay' and 'getting information for an assignment'. Other services the library offers such as training on the ethical use of information, information management and information skills are services that the students do not necessarily associate with the library and that side of the library service is invisible.

## How to increase visibility?

With students, it is an on-going process and one that she would like to think that she 'is chipping away at'. She is doing this through the provision of information skills classes. Making face-to-face contact goes a long way to increasing visibility. The library has an outreach and marketing unit that the librarian feels they are 'lucky to have'. This is a great help in terms of raising the profile of the library to students.

'In terms of stakeholders outside of the library, getting into their spaces of work helps a lot. Getting out of the library space and embedding yourself into other areas of work helps increase visibility. For example attending education conferences, teaching and learning conferences all increase the visibility of the librarian. Getting yourself onto their agendas and in their terms of engagement. Find out what their strategies are and their priorities are and align yourself to those. Try to position yourself in terms of what they are looking for and to their needs and get out of the library more'. She concedes that it takes time for people to get to know your name and who you are. Joining committees and attending departmental meetings helps to increase awareness about the role of the liaison librarian.

When she first started, her visibility score was 'very low' with students, but not quite zero. Nobody knew who she was and they did not have her contact details. She has spent the last year gradually building up her profile. She has found that a lot of students that didn't take her classes last year are asking to take them this year and she has made lots of new contacts. She is confident that this shows she has done a good job of promoting herself and the services she can offer.

## What has been your most successful method of increasing your visibility?

'Being involved in school and college committees. This gives the librarian an opportunity to share news about the library, to promote the library and to advocate for the library and it is a very captive audience. It is also an opportunity in a place of academics, teaching staff and researchers where the librarian may be seen as one of their peers as opposed to "someone in the library". This removes an identity problem that a librarian might have when at times librarians are perhaps seen in a "library box". This is the most valuable channel to build relationships and get to know people and to become known as a contact point for the library. It also helps to get the library message out there and sell it'.

## Value the librarian brings to the organisation

The librarian is happy that she brings an evidence-based approach to what she does. This is perhaps a different approach to what has been previously done in the organisation. Some librarians use their extensive experience as a primary decision-making tool. The librarian who is new to the profession felt that she didn't have that luxury. She also has a preference to looking toward the evidence in terms of best practice to shape what she does and inform her practice. She has an evidence-based approach to everything that she does – including projects that she works on and her teaching role, and she shares this approach with the teams that she works with. She likes to encourage other people to adopt this kind of thinking – evidence-based librarianship. Having spent some time in health sciences in a previous role she said that this influenced her going forward in her career. Working in a health science environment leads you to develop a certain mind-set and it is hard not to take that forward into practice.

## The value and impact of the library service to the organisation

The librarian thinks the library has a very positive impact on the organisation as a whole. Sometimes the impact isn't necessarily visible, but it would definitely be noticed if it was not there. 'Perhaps librarians need to think of the library in those terms sometimes. If it was taken away tomorrow, the university would have a very difficult time continuing on with things like accreditation, quality reviews; students would have no books, no spaces and no resources. The library is heavily involved in activities right across the university (e.g. teaching and learning), the librarians work with many academic programs in an embedded way and they have very strong links with departments who wish to develop special collections. The repository helps greatly in the promotion of research – the library has a strong impact in a wide range of areas right throughout the university'.

## Does the librarian use any formal method of evaluation for reporting her impact?

This is an area that the librarian is currently working on with her team. They have recently begun to use a new method of tracking and recording teaching and learning sessions and feedback around that. They are trying to move into a more formal area of assessment in terms of formal assessment of learning. It is a complex area to try to capture information like that so they are trying to do it in a planned and structured way. They are currently building relationships with the various schools where there might be an opportunity to look at things such as rubrics or pre- and post-tests. At the moment, they do not have any impacts recorded. Across all areas of the library, there is pressure and expectation to account for what one does and to show and demonstrate value and impact and everyone in the organisation; not just the library is feeling that pressure. This percolates to every aspect of the service; for example, transactions at the reference desk are recorded in an online system that can be tied in with general university metrics. They are trying to do this in an integrated way with areas such as student registration. There is an analytical basis there. The repository is very active in terms of metrics such as downloads and visits, etc. However, the librarian feels that the repository metrics are in a sense an easy one to measure. An 'achievements of the year' document is produced, and the library produces its own report. The former is more of an outreach tool that is not necessarily designed for higher management. It is really for users. It will introduce different resources and detail new library services. Library management are given an opportunity to feed into university-wide policies such as the strategic plan.

## Challenging scenario

In a previous role, she recalls a challenging scenario involving a cut in serials. Budget cuts came, and the librarian had to significantly cut back on serials. She could foresee it was going to be a problem and potentially a very negative issue for the library. The approach that she took was to be as open as possible, to communicate effectively and to be completely transparent about the issue. She set out the situation in very clear terms, she openly communicated with all parties that would be affected and asked for their opinion, explaining the reality of the situation and saying that 'doing nothing is not an option'.

The journals just had to be cut. She did receive some negative reactions that were to be expected. However, on the whole, people were broadly tolerant of the situation. They understood the situation and accepted it and had to make the best of it. She asked them to rate the journals and decide which ones they needed to keep most. Of course, they 'didn't want to let any journals go' given an opportunity to be stoic about it. What makes challenging issues a bit easier is the challenging climate that we have at the moment. Everyone is in a challenging circumstance at present and it is continuing in most organisations given the economic situation we are in. People are more accepting of this; therefore, the journal cut became an easier sell and less of a negative message in a way. However, if the right approach isn't taken, then it is not so easy to overcome the negativity. Using the relationships that she had built up with staff and being open and communicative was a good approach she found in that instance. For example, if she had come up with a list without consulting people, there would have been very different outcomes.

## Top tips for academic librarians to increase their visibility and impact?

'Move out of the library space and the library mind-set as much as possible!'

'Get yourself into your user's space and your user's mind-set instead. Stop thinking of yourself as "the library" and start thinking about what you can do for your stakeholders. Package yourself and the services that you offer in a way that is of direct value to people rather than having a list of services for people that they do not necessarily see the value of. Showcase benefits to people and then they will understand your value. Try and get yourself physically into their space. Go to academic conferences or conferences that your stakeholders go to. Write for academic journals and attend seminars that academics attend. Physical networking and building relationships that way is important. There is a lot to be said for face-to-face networking and making personal contact. If you get to know people that way, then they are more likely to consult you in the future. Stop talking about the libraries so much and the library as a place. Talk more about the librarian and the skill set that they bring and begin to think of ourselves in this way'.

## Do you think the embedded librarian or liaison librarian is the future for academic librarians?

'Ideally, yes. But the reality of the situation is that with staffing levels being so low and in decline it is not a sustainable model. "I would love to do more embedded work, but if everyone took me up on this offer, I wouldn't be able to cope! It is about getting a balance". Doing as much embedded work as you can with the resources that you have. It is definitely the best approach for the teaching and learning role in terms of capturing "teachable moments" and getting to students when they need the help the most. However, there are questions over the sustainability of it. It is certainly an ideal model, but it is not necessarily a realistic one with current resourcing levels'.

'There are a lot more social learning spaces and collaborative learning spaces in academic libraries now. If librarians got to this ideal scenario, then our profession would be a lot more visible and therefore more valuable to people'.

## How important is it for the librarian to be visible to users in an online environment?

The librarian feels this is really important. Librarians ideally need to be visible to people in person and online. Some people prefer learning online; some people will never be on campus to interact with the librarian in person. 'Developing a suite of online learning supports and having an online presence is incredibly important for any academic librarian. Every library has a website with online tutorials and online help; most libraries have an online presence in the Virtual Learning Environment (VLE) (e.g. Blackboard, that kind of visibility) – especially when most students use online information as their single source of information – if the library didn't have any presence there, then the students are never going to see the library.

I think most librarians would agree that in addition to the physical presence, you do need the online presence. In terms of "absolute visibility" and demonstrating impact – getting your ideas to management – then face to face is incredibly important'.

## Where do you see the academic librarian in 5 years?

'Moving into more specialised areas, specialised areas of expertise, more high level. Working more in the research support area, data management, emerging technologies, more embedded roles, moving ourselves up the value chain by offering higher levels of expertise. More data librarians or technology librarians and outreach librarian roles'.

## What is your favourite thing about being a librarian?

'Connecting people with the information they need can be a very rewarding experience. I derive a great deal of satisfaction from helping people to do what they do – research, learning something new, writing an assignment – better as a result of being able to find the best or most appropriate information available to them. It can often make a small, but important, difference'.

# Case study 4: systems librarian working in an academic library

| | |
|---|---|
| Name: | Niamh Headon-Walker |
| Organisation: | Institute of Technology Tallaght, Dublin 24. Ireland |

The Institute of Technology Tallaght Dublin (ITT Dublin) is a relatively new organisation and was established as a higher education institution in 1992. The student population is 3700 and it has a staff of 400. The Institute comprises a school of engineering, business, humanities, and science and computing.

## Mission of the organisation

The mission of the Institute of Technology, Tallaght is to be the centre of higher education and knowledge creation within South Dublin County and its environs, to broaden participation in higher education in the region, to be recognised as a leader in supporting research and commercial innovation and to assist in the advancement of the economic, social and cultural life of the region (Institute of Technology, Tallaght, 2014).

## Mission of the library

The library supports the institute in terms of its teaching, learning, research and development goals. Through its learning resources and knowledge, it also gives individuals the life skills necessary to play an active role in society and the workplace.

## Online visibility of library and librarian

| | |
|---|---|
| Library website: | http://library.ittdublin.ie/ |
| Library app: | https://www.libanywhere.com/m/302 |
| Facebook: | http://www.facebook.com/pages/Library-ITT-Dublin/131669563534418 |
| Subject portal: | http://library.ittdublin.ie/screens/hum.html#.VD0crWddVlM |
| Institutional repository: | http://arrow.dit.ie/itt/ |
| Library blog: | http://libraryittdublin.Blogspot.ie/ |
| You tube: | https://www.youtube.com/user/TrinityLibrary/videos |
| Twitter: | http://www.twitter.com/LibraryITTDub and https://twitter.com/AnLeabharlannai |
| Linkedin: | ie.linkedin.com/in/niamhwh |
| Slideshare: | www.slideshare.net/Niamh1/presentations |

The systems librarian Niamh Headon-Walker of ITT Dublin has worked here for 12 years. She looks after the web services, the library management system and all of the add-on systems that have subsequently evolved. She also works on the library desk one late night and some Saturdays. This equates to a maximum of 3 h a week, but she finds this very useful for finding out things from users about the systems that may not work correctly. She comes across technical problems that need to be fixed. She also has a humanities liaison role. She supports information literacy training with senior staff and research consultations from the humanities department are routed to her. This can include queries in relation to stock control. There is not a huge budget for books but she forwards on new acquisitions to the department to keep them aware of what's new in their field.

Her organisation is small and people tend to know each other. For example, the registrar knows the librarian by name. There have been three different presidents in her time there, and they all knew her by name and would have said 'hello' to her. The incoming president might not know her as much, but for them to know what her role is and understand what she does, she would see this as a totally different issue. She explains that on a personal level, she considers that key stakeholders know her so she would score 10 on the visibility scale, but with regards to her professional role she would score 3 or 4. In terms of students, many of them know who she is and she sends out messages on the VLE, which includes a picture of her beside the message so she is instantly recognisable. However, because her role is 'systems', she feels that this role is fairly alien to most people. She recalled that once a Human Resources manager asked, 'Sure, what does a systems librarian do?' and when she started to explain her role, the eyes began to glaze over but in the end they did admit 'Ok, we actually *do* need you'. It's a split thing – people are aware that she is there, people might say hello to her in the corridors of the Institute and she would have 'no idea who they are'. In terms of people recognising her and knowing her, she would rate a 6 or a 7, but in terms of people understanding her role she would rate a 3 or a 4 (Table 5).

Niamh explains that it is said that a 'good manager is one who can be absent and the whole thing runs', so when she took maternity leave and was not replaced, 'the whole thing ran'. She explains that 'it ran' because she had good, robust systems in place and she had people trained in doing maintenance work. However, when she returned to work, she had just 3 weeks to do three system upgrades. So although things ran and

**Table 5 Self-reported visibility rating of librarian at time of appointment versus today**

| Visibility rating at time of appointment: where 0=invisible and 10=highly visible | | | | | | | | | | | |
|---|---|---|---|---|---|---|---|---|---|---|---|
| With key stakeholders | 0 | 1 | 2 | 3 | 4 | 5 | 6 | 7 | 8 | 9 | **10** |
| With staff – students and academics (users of the service) | **0** | 1 | 2 | 3 | 4 | 5 | 6 | 7 | 8 | 9 | 10 |
| Visibility today (12 years after appointment): where 0=invisible 10=highly visible | | | | | | | | | | | |
| With key stakeholders | 0 | 1 | 2 | **3** | 4 | 5 | 6 | 7 | 8 | 9 | 10 |
| With staff – students and academics (users of the service) | 0 | 1 | 2 | 3 | 4 | 5 | **6** | **7** | 8 | 9 | 10 |

on the surface everything looked perfect, underneath there were a lot of cracks. For example 170,000 records had to be updated (edited, deleted). The system ran, but there was a large backlog. If it had gone on for another 6 months, then she felt there would have been serious issues. There were several critical incidents while she was on leave in which support was sought from vendors in the United States. She wasn't replaced because there is a recruitment embargo in place and it was said that her role was not considered 'unique'. This is despite the fact that she is the only systems librarian on the staff. Another librarian at the same grade had to take on her duties while she was away, as well as their own job, which wasn't possible.

She said that the way people interact with the library service is with 'the book', the 'library assistant on the desk' or the information literacy team goes out and delivers training, but her role is specifically invisible. This is because it is a 'behind-the-scenes' job. The only place where she has visibility or an understanding of her role is within the library community. If her name comes up at a library meeting or conference in Ireland, then someone will know it because the library community in Ireland is small but also because she is 'out there'. People contact her by email, and she will respond giving them advice or explaining how she got around a systems issue.

When she first started the job, she judged her visibility with key stakeholders as being a 10 because they were all part of the interview panel who gave her the job. In terms of the students, she felt it was 'definitely zero'. She feels it has certainly improved over time. When she first started, her role was very 'library management systems' oriented because the system in place did not have the full suite of modules, it had circulation, a basic Online Public Access Catalog (OPAC), interlibrary loan (ILL) and basic serials. Everything else had to be implemented. She remembers implementing the Z39.50 interfaces, which they still have. They are still used by students and by library staff downloading Machine Readable Cataloguing (MARC) records.

Sending out messages on Moodle has increased her visibility with the students. The sessions that she does with people undertaking dissertations and theses also helps increase her visibility; for example, one-to-one sessions with someone who might be stuck trying to do a literature review (e.g. a member of staff doing a PhD). Research methods is another area in which she would give consultations. The things that work are providing a good service directly to teaching staff and communicating effectively with the students.

## What value have you brought to the organisation?

Within the Institutes of Technology, Niamh is one of the longest serving systems librarians; therefore, her experience spans the full implementation of the Millennium Library Management System. She has developed ancillary services as she is given some freedom to do the systems end of things in the library. She defines her value in terms of a gap analysis. If she wasn't there, then the institute would not have a room booking system, the Website might not be to the level that it is, there might not be a resource discovery layer, they might not have a LinkResolver – there is a whole list of technologies that she has campaigned to get and been successful in getting them added on to the library service. Although they do not have a physically large stock, their virtual stock is large. The virtual stock is made available through several layers, which she has put in place. If the role of the systems librarian was not in the institute, then she says 'it would be like something out of the 1980s!' There might be an OPAC, but if there is nobody there to develop the services and systems and manage their integration, then they would be left behind. Over the years, she has re-designed the website to be in line with the overall institute's website, it has been rebranded and a responsive design was developed. She has integrated subject blogs; for example, she has a humanities subject blog, she has pulled in RSS feeds into the site and used JavaScript to pull in information from eight different humanities sources to create a humanities news section. She has set up blogs for the engineering liaison librarian and the science and computing librarian. She has shown them how to maintain them; however, she feels if she wasn't there, then the blogs would not exist. There are many auxiliary tasks that she does that are not seen.

For example, the exam papers are on the library server. The exams office send them to the library on the day of the exam, library staff physically scan them in to a PDF file and they become attached item records in the Millennium system, which means students can access exam papers through their library account. She doesn't think the exam papers would be online if the library hadn't taken on this work. She had a development role 10 years ago where she would have taken on big projects, but now she is working on more specialised projects.

## What impact has the library service had on the organisation?

The library service has been essential to the organisation getting delegated authority to the PhD level. There was intense examination of the quality systems in place for this. She has made the library staff manual into an online Wiki using Google Sites. This saves library staff time from trying to find sections of a manual housed in a separate work space at the back of the library. She has plugged Google Analytics™ into the Wiki so she knows that staff use it and she can monitor this. It is really useful for desk procedures and how to load catalogue records, etc. The Wiki is visually very different from the website and it is instantly recognisable. All staff have access to amend it and keep it up to date. She enables people to use technology by giving all staff access. For example, the cataloguer can edit the authority file procedures directly on the Wiki. If people are allowed to edit it, then they are more likely to use it and find it useful. She says that the online room booking facility that she implemented using LibCal has also really helped the organisation.

## Does the library have any formal way of measuring and reporting impact?

The systems librarian creates an annual review statistics file that is loosely based on the Global Library Statistics group of indicators, which is based on ISO 11620. There are budgetary control systems in place that report back to the financial controller, and the library also contributes to the institute's annual report. The institute librarians have a base set of indicators that they use to compare and contrast performance (e.g. a decision to use counter statistics for consortia packages etc.).

## Have you ever had a challenging scenario?

Niamh has not experienced a challenging scenario as of yet. However, the institute is due to merge with another organisation and become part of the Dublin Institute of Technology, so she feels that challenges are ahead of her in the very near future. She is not sure where or what her role will be in 2 years; there is a lot of uncertainty about this at present. Much of this is out of her control, but she is hoping that she will end up 'doing something interesting'. Part of the reason she has not faced too many difficult situations she feels is because she is working in a young organisation. It is only 22 years in existence. The culture has not developed into a hierarchical place and has not been slowed down by this. For example, she was asked to teach a module at University College Dublin without a great deal of notice, and within a week she had received sign-off from the Registrar and Institute Librarian to allow her to do this. This is the type of organisational culture that frees librarians and employees up to expand their role. The organisation is young and small and everyone knows each other; challenges such as redeployment or loss of employment have not arisen. There is a flexible culture in the organisation and a good deal of 'give and take'. There is a type of 'clan culture' in place in the sense that it is family oriented and people look out for one another.

## Top tips for systems librarians in an academic setting to improve impact and visibility?

'Tune in to what academics are doing. It is very easy to sit at your desk with your blinkers on and just "be the systems librarian". If you sit in a corner at tea break and put your head down, if you do not network, if you do not communicate outside of the library, then you are never going to have any visibility. Blogging helps'. Being involved in the humanities area has helped her to increase her visibility outside of the systems side of things. Library support road shows are a good way of increasing visibility in the staff canteen or in the foyer. All staff go out with laptops, posters and stands about the library. This is important because there will always be nonusers or people who feel they are nonusers. Then they might realise that they are getting into a full text article because of the library or the exam papers. 'It is important to realise that "we do not work in a vacuum", and not to be siloed. If you let yourself work in a vacuum, then you are going to become invisible and irrelevant'.

The Student Union President knew Niamh from giving the Information Literacy (IL) talks and approached her while she was outside the building during the summer time. He had a few suggestions about the library website. She feels that because of her visibility he would never have approached her like this otherwise. It was good feedback; sometimes there is no need to do mass user surveys. They partake in LibQual every 3–5 years, which takes care of the big issues. However, by having an informal structure, they can solve problems quicker.

### Do you think the embedded librarian is the future for academic librarians? ('embedded' meaning outside of the library, with no need to physically be in the library)

'I think it will eventually mellow out to a cross-over. At the moment this seems to be a buzzword alongside problem-based learning. A medium will be found. You still need to have the library time. If you become too embedded in a team, then you may lose sight of any library service you are trying to provide and you lose contact with developments happening in the library world. It is very easy to get "sucked in" to a discipline. Some people in academic libraries are more like academics than librarians and they are becoming researchers; some people who are librarians are suited to that role.'

If your role as an academic librarian is a supporting one, then you need to be aware of developments in librarianship. The library as a space will continue to exist. The library as a brand will continue to exist because it has been around for more than 1000 years. The 'learning resource centre' thing was tried and failed because nobody knew what it was. It diluted the brand. People know 'library', 'books', 'information', 'assistance' and 'a place to sit down and read'. People will always need a space to sit down and read irrespective of what they are reading on. They will always need assistance to find information. Highly trained paraprofessional staff can fill this role. We do not necessarily need the embedded librarian for this. Group work has mushroomed in the last 10 years. The use of space in the library over time has changed completely; for example, one meeting room was used for people who needed to use assistive technology. Now that is integrated into PCs everywhere across the campuses. The furniture colours are integrated from the logo of the institution.

### How important is it for the librarian to be visible to users in an online environment?

Niamh feels in her case that the users do not care; they just want it 'to work'. Users probably want to know that there is a librarian and a human is behind the service. There is huge usage of the website. Niamh is able to reel off statistics with ease. She explains there was over 277,000 accesses last year and 880,000 page views. There have been 18,000 unique visitors in the last 4 months since they put in the responsive website. The number of registered library users is 5000. There were 77,000 exam papers downloaded from the system. It is assumed that the service will be there, that is will be high quality and it will work, but nobody thinks about 'who does it?'

### What is the most successful method of increasing visibility in an online environment?

She has worked hard at her social media profile so that if students or academics Google her, professional related sites will come up in the results. Pictures of her at social events such as barbeques do not come up – Linkedin, Blog and Facebook come up – the ones that appear in search engine results are all in relation to her professional role. She knows that people will get a professional contact if they look for her online. People do not understand the systems part of her role at all. 'Systems' as a title puts people off; they do not understand it. She feels, 'If it was "online development", then people would be queuing up with ideas'.

## What advice would you give to new entrants to the profession?

'Given our current environment, it is important for librarians to publish, network, attend free training where available and attend events organised by the Library Association of Ireland'. Niamh advocates that new entrants to librarianship need to attend events. Their presence will mean that people will see their face and know that they are motivated. Perhaps a recruitment agency will notice a new librarian by reading something they have published. She also advises travelling to build up experience and to publish.

## Where do you see the systems librarian in 5 years?

There will still be a systems role, but it may be labelled differently. There will be much more to the job than the responsibility of the library management system; this is already happening. There will be systems administration of many other types of systems – at least seven or eight different systems. There are now a cadre of experienced systems librarians, so there will be big opportunities; SaaS and PaaS and cloud services will have a role. In particular, any software that is seen to save money – research profile management system will come to the library – it is an expanding role.

Niamh thinks that it is dangerous to have one person in the systems role; a library ideally needs an entire technical team. In the absence of a team, there should be another librarian available to shadow the systems role.

## What is your favourite thing about being a librarian?

'My favourite thing about being a librarian is the feeling that what I do can make a difference, even for just one person. That's what makes it feel like it's worth my while to remain as a librarian'.

## Case study 5: head of services at University of Eastern Finland Library/Kuopio University Hospital Medical Library

| | |
|---|---|
| Name: | Tuulevi Ovaska |
| Organisation: | University of Eastern Finland |
| Background: | In 2010, two Finnish universities, the University of Joensuu and the University of Kuopio, merged to form the University of Eastern Finland. With more than 15,000 students registered in 2013 and 2800 members of staff, it is one of the largest universities in the country. The university was ranked 24th in the 2014 QS top 50 under 50, which is a ranking of the top universities under 50 years old (topuniversities.com). It offers courses in more than 100 different subjects. There are three campuses, and the library has facilities on each campus in Joensuu, Kuopio and Savonlinna. |

## *Mission of the organisation: (University of Finland, 2014)*

> The University's strategy 2015–2020 outlines its vision, mission and values as follows:
> **Vision:** We are an internationally attractive university that seeks to find interdisciplinary solutions to global challenges.
> **Mission:** We are an international, multidisciplinary and student-centred university. Our high standard of research and appealing academic offering build the competence base of the future.
> **Values:**
>
> - Freedom of science, teaching and learning.
> - Transparency and courage.
> - Responsibility and impact.

## *Mission of the library*

> The library is described in its online brochure as follows:
>   The University of Eastern Finland Library is an internationally recognised pioneer in the field of library and information services. The library is a public scientific library, the services, collections and facilities of which are open to all.

## *Online visibility*

| | |
|---|---|
| Library website: | http://www.uef.fi/en/kirjasto |
| Institutional repository: | http://epublications.uef.fi/ |
| Facebook: | https://www.facebook.com/ueflibrary |
| Blog: | http://ueflibrary.wordpress.com/ |
| Youtube: | https://www.youtube.com/user/UEFLibrary |
| Twitter | www.slideshare.net/tuulevi |
| | www.researchgate.net/profile/Tuulevi_Ovaskafi.linkedin.com/in/tuulevi |

Tuulevi Ovaska is Head of Services at University of Eastern Finland Library/Kuopio University Hospital (KUH) Medical Library. She is responsible for the library services for the hospital and its clinicians as well as medical, dental, public health, ergonomics and exercise medicine students and researchers. She describes it as 'somewhat complicated' in that they are in between being a faculty library and a hospital medical library. It is a joint library of two organisations – the university and the hospital district. She is Head of Services for the KUH Medical Library and the information specialist/librarian with teaching responsibilities for undergraduate and postgraduate students.

Tuulevi is essentially working in two organisations. Among her key stakeholders she rates 7 out of 10 on the visibility scale. Among users of the library, she feels she rates very high – 9 out of 10 (Table 6). She feels highly visible to her users because she interacts with them and sees them all of the time. She works in a relatively small unit in the university. Although Tuulevi is a manager, she says, 'I'm not the kind of manager who stays in their office all of the time and never sees anyone'. Sometimes she works on the reference desk and she teaches a lot. She meets with users in different groups. Users are able to recognise her face and her name. She runs many online courses in which students do not necessarily see her but they know her name from taking the courses. Among the stakeholders it is a little more difficult because there are almost two sets of stakeholders in the two organisations. However, given that Tuulevi has worked there for 10 years, she has built up relationships with people in the university and has got to know people.

When asked what the most successful methods of increasing her visibility were, she noted the following:

- Not sitting in my office or even in the library, but doing outreach.
- Offering to attend meetings in the hospital – to teach or train or to help to give answers in a type of embedded role.
- Embedding library services into the work of others in the hospital or users of the library.
- Pushing the library agenda, particularly if there are changes coming in the curriculum. Keeping the library in the minds of management.
- Being proactive and speaking up if it there is an opportunity to say something about the library or services provided. Not thinking when it is too late, 'Oh, I should have said something about the library'.

Tuulevi has good support from the library director, who she describes as being 'very active' with good skills for communicating with stakeholders. The director started just

### Table 6  Self-reported visibility rating of librarian at time of appointment versus today

| Self-reported visibility rating at time of appointment: where 0 = invisible and 10 = highly visible | | | | | | | | | | |
|---|---|---|---|---|---|---|---|---|---|---|
| With key stakeholders | 0 | **1** | 2 | 3 | 4 | 5 | 6 | 7 | 8 | 9 | 10 |
| With staff/users of the service | 0 | **1** | 2 | 3 | 4 | 5 | 6 | 7 | 8 | 9 | 10 |
| **Self-reported visibility today (10 years after appointment): where 0 = invisible and 10 = highly visible** | | | | | | | | | | |
| With key stakeholders | 0 | 1 | 2 | 3 | 4 | 5 | 6 | **7** | 8 | 9 | 10 |
| With key staff/users of the service | 0 | 1 | 2 | 3 | 4 | 5 | 6 | 7 | 8 | **9** | 10 |

before Tuulevi, and she says that he has helped to increase the visibility, positioning and profile of the library and the work that they do within the university. The work that he has done has increased everyone's importance in the library, which is very positive.

## Value that the librarian brings to the organisation

Medical, dental and other students have much better information literacy skills because of the instruction and training received from Tuulevi. Many of the hospital staff, clinicians and nursing staff would not have some of the skills that they have now acquired through direct teaching provided by Tuulevi. She feels that she has done a good job at increasing the visibility of the library services and promoting the work that the library staff do given her management position.

## Impact that the library brings to the organisation

The medical library as a physical space offers a place for students to do individual study or partake in group work. Students and staff also can find someone in the library who can offer them assistance if they need it, such as information retrieval.

## Is there a formal method of measuring and/or reporting library and librarian impact?

The library has an annual report and annual budget negotiations. In the former, key statistics and numerical data are brought to the negotiations to demonstrate the value and impact of library services. There is a quality management system in place for this type of data reporting in the university. There are standards in Finland for this. This university was one of the first universities in Finland to have a regular quality audit.

## Challenging scenario

Funding is received from both the universities and the hospital, and Tuulevi recalls a situation when it was her second year in charge when the budget negotiations were extremely difficult. Looking back, she thinks perhaps it may have been a test of her ability as a 'new person' to see if she could prove the value of the library for the money required to run it. Management were trying to reduce the budget, and she was able to give numbers and scenarios of what would happen if they did not give her the budget. It was difficult, but she managed to keep the budget the same as the previous year.

## Top tips for academic or health science librarians to increase visibility

'Go to the customer or user; do not wait for them to come to you'.

## How important is it for the librarian to be visible to users in an online environment?

Tuulevi feels this is very important. She says this becomes more and more important with new generations who seem to be online all of the time. 'It is not as important for people who are from the "analog era". It will be more important to be where the users are and they are online more and more. It may change overtime. We do not know if it will still be Facebook or Twitter in 5 years, but regardless of what the platform will be, you have to be where your users are. If they are online, then you need to be online'.

## Most successful method of increasing online visibility?

The library has a space on the university website, it has a Facebook page, a series of YouTube videos and a Blog. Tuulevi also uses Twitter. She feels that the website is not as useful as it should be because the content management system is not particularly flexible. She describes the website look as 'boring'. At the moment they are trying to re-vamp it to make it look a bit more inviting. The Facebook page does not have a huge number of followers, but those who are following it are mostly students. The YouTube channel is relatively new, but they do receive many views because of the information contained in them is very practical (e.g. how to upload ebooks to your devices). Of all of the online outlets that the library has, Tuulevi thinks the blog is possibly the most visible and successful. It attracts many readers. Most of the online pages are in Finnish, and some pages are in English and Finnish. She feels that there should be more in English but it can be difficult to persuade people to write in English because they can be shy about doing that. An English native speaker proofreads entries on the website, but they do not have someone to do that for every blog entry. This means that they will live with some mistakes in the English entries, and she feels that people will understand.

## Do you think the embedded librarian/librarian in context is the future for health librarians? [Note: Embedded librarian refers to a librarian who does not necessarily need a physical library to do their job. They can work in a research team or health care team independent of the library.]

Tuulevi has a mixed opinion on the role of the embedded librarian. The embedded librarian could be a future for some librarians, but not for everyone. Not everyone wants or needs to be embedded.

## What is your favourite thing about being a librarian?

'I always say I love my job. I think for me it is captured as "the satisfied customer". When you succeed with something, such as if someone calls you and says, "Oh I have a problem with Refworks – or something similar, and you say that you will come and help them, and you help them in person. Sometimes they will say "That's magic!" or "You're an angel". This for me is the satisfied customer'.

**Figure 6** Word cloud of tips for academic librarians to increase their visibility.

On the basis of responses from the five academic librarians to the question 'What are your top tips for academic or systems librarians to increase their visibility?' the following word cloud was produced (see Figure 6).

## Summary

Based on the five interviews with academic librarians, the following tips and strategies emerged for academic librarians to improve visibility, impact and understanding of their value:

1. Be visible in an online environment, such as a library website, blog, etc.
2. The library should have an inviting, exciting website that is attractive to students.
3. Don't sit in the library all of the time; get out more and mingle.
4. Socialise with academics; approach them for an informal coffee or chat and get to know them.
5. Get information literacy and other Library and Information Science (LIS) subjects into the main curriculum.
6. Assess and evaluate teaching and learning and report upon outcomes.
7. Get involved in committees on campus.
8. Advocate for librarians.
9. Have a professional Internet image and maintain a social media profile.
10. Try blogging and Twitter.
11. Don't underestimate the power and importance of face-to-face meetings with students and academics; try to make this a regular part of your working day.
12. Publish your research and findings; share best practice.
13. Spend time in the classrooms.
14. Go to the customer; do not wait for them to come to you.
15. Outreach is an important activity for increasing visibility.
16. Keep up to date with developments in librarianship, teaching and learning.
17. Be visible in the users' workspace, such as the VLE.
18. Have an open and flexible approach to working with students and academics; take on new projects where feasible.

19. Get involved in reference work or direct contact with students.
20. Tell people about your role and be open and share your enthusiasm for your job – it is contagious.
21. Try giving lectures during lunchtime, and offer lunch to students where possible.
22. Get involved in your professional library association.
23. Contribute research to the LIS community and to the academic community.
24. Keep up to date with emerging technologies and seek to answer what purpose they might have in a library or learning environment.
25. Attend education, teaching and learning conferences. Give a presentation or poster if possible.
26. Seek a mentor.
27. Maintain a professional social media profile.

# Notes

Library Impact Data Project. JISC and University of Huddersfield. Library Analytics Bibliography See https://library3.hud.ac.uk/blogs/lidp/project-outputs/library-analytics-bibliography/ Accessed 07.03.15.

Trinity College Dublin Strategic Plan 2009–2014. 2009. Dublin: Trinity College Dublin. P.V Available from https://www.tcd.ie/about/content/pdf/tcd-strategic-plan-2009-2014-english.pdf Accessed 01.10.14.

See Helen Shenton's TEDx Talk "Collaboratories and bubbles of shush – how libraries are transforming" Available at https://www.youtube.com/watch?v=pHdlWQ28gE8 Accessed 07.02.15.

Florida Polytechnic Bookless Library See http://lj.libraryjournal.com/2014/08/academic-libraries/new-florida-polytechnic-unveils-bookless-library/#_ Accessed 02.10.14.

Interdisciplinary Solutions: University of Eastern Finland Strategy 2015–2020. Joensuu: University of Eastern Finland. Available from http://www.uef.fi/en/strategia Accessed 07.10.14.

See http://www.topuniversities.com/ for rankings of universities worldwide.

Library Analytics Bibliography is available at https://library3.hud.ac.uk/blogs/lidp/project-outputs/library-analytics-bibliography/.

# Case studies: visibility of school librarians and school libraries

*What a school thinks about its library is a measure of what it feels about education.*

**Harold Howe**

Before delving into the visibility of a selection of school librarians, the international context for school libraries with particular reference to Ireland is set. A brief overview of literature on the impact of school libraries and school librarians is described. This is by means of a background to the case studies and to give the reader some context of the environment of school librarianship.

In Europe and the rest of the world, legislation on school libraries varies. Very few states or countries (e.g. New York, Sweden) in the world make it mandatory for publicly funded schools to employ a school librarian or even have a school library. This continues despite the growing international body of evidence to demonstrate that school libraries and school librarians have a positive impact on student achievement. In the United States, Keith Lance has been performing research on school library impact since 1993. Significant research has been produced internationally that demonstrates school library impact on student learning and achievement. See Table 7 for a snapshot of just some of the published research that demonstrates the impact of a school library or school librarian on student learning and achievement.

In Europe, school libraries are generally not required to produce evidence of their impact or value (Marquardt, 2008). Only 60% of public schools in the United States have a school library staffed by a state-certified school librarian and 8830 public schools have no school library (American Library Association, 2014). In the European Union (EU), the data on school libraries are of a patchwork nature. Some limited data are available from Eurydice, which looks, among other things, at how reading is taught in Europe. This report mentions libraries, however the focus is on national and public libraries and professional associations in EU countries with little mention of school libraries.

Evidence has shown the link between schools that employ librarians and higher reading scores. According to the Library Research Service report,

*Schools that either maintained or gained an endorsed librarian between 2005 and 2011 tended to have more students scoring advanced in reading in 2011 and to have increased their performance more than schools that either lost their librarians or never had one.*

*Lance and Hofshire (2012), p. 3*

Table 7 **Mapping literature demonstrating evidence of impact of school library or school librarian on student learning and achievement**

| Reported finding of impact of school library/librarian | Lance and Hofshire (2012) and Lance, Welborne, and Hamilton-Pennel (1992) | Todd and Kuhlthau (2005) | Baxter and Smalley (2003) | Callison (2014) and Callison et al. (2004) | Burgin, Brown, and Bracy (2003) |
|---|---|---|---|---|---|
| Improved reading | • | • | • | • | • |
| Improved information literacy | | • | • | • | |
| Improved learning and evolution toward inquiry | • | • | | • | |
| Better scores on standardized achievement tests | • | • | • | • | • |

The latest benchmark set by the European Commission for education includes fewer than 15% of 15 year olds should be under-skilled in **reading**, mathematics and science by 2020 (European Commission, 2009). The latest Programme for International Student Assessment (PISA) scores shows that the top Organisation for Economic Co-operation and Development (OECD) countries for reading in Europe include Finland, Ireland and Poland (OECD PISA, 2012). If reading tests are to be improved, then more school librarians will need to be hired right across the EU.

The International Federation of Library Associations (IFLA)/UN Educational Scientific and Cultural Organisation (UNESCO) school library manifesto of 1999 states that: 'The school library provides information and ideas that are fundamental to functioning successfully in today's information and knowledge-based society. The school library equips students with lifelong learning skills and develops the imagination, enabling them to live as responsible citizens'. Governments and school library associations are encouraged to adopt this manifesto by IFLA.

The same manifesto is unclear about the nature of the qualification needed to be a school librarian. It simply states that, 'The school librarian is the professionally qualified staff member'. It is uncertain what qualification is deemed relevant. This ambiguity is played out across the world and weakens the plight of the school librarian as a profession to evolve or to have a solid future. In some areas of the world (e.g. Australia), school librarians are called 'teacher-librarians' and are required to be qualified teachers as well as qualified librarians. The school library was shown to help

## Table 8 Ireland Department of Education and skills allocation of funding to primary schools for the purchase of books

| Primary[a] | Rate per capita |
|---|---|
| Allocation to DEIS[b] schools for books (enhanced) | €21 |
| Allocation to non-DEIS schools for books | €11 |

[a]A minimum grant is paid to small primary schools based on an enrolment of 60 pupils.
[b]Delivering Equality of Opportunity in Schools (DEIS) launched in 2005 and is a policy instrument to address educational disadvantage; 852 schools are included in the programme. These comprise 658 primary schools (336 urban/town schools and 322 rural primary schools) and 194 post-primary schools.
*Source:* http://www.education.ie/en/Parliamentary-Questions-and-Debates/Parliamentary-Questions-2014/DEIS-April. pdf.

students to develop a focus and define learning tasks. The teacher-librarian helped students' information literacy skills, including a better understanding of the curriculum (Hay, 2006). In other areas (e.g. the United Kingdom), there is no requirement for a school librarian to have a library qualification.

The three school librarians interviewed all work in secondary-level schools in Ireland. They cater for students between the ages of 12 and 18 years. School librarians in Ireland are somewhat of a rare species. The Education Act of 1998 does not make any reference or provision for school libraries. The Local Government Act (2001), which governs public libraries in Ireland, is the only legislation that includes a provision for school libraries, 'A library authority may make such arrangements as it considers desirable for the provision of library services to any other library authority, public authority or other body (including a school) or by any such body to that library authority'. The public libraries in Ireland receive a capitation grant for a school library service for primary schools, which covers the purchase of approximately one book for every three to four pupils every year. At the post-primary level, there are very few librarians employed, or indeed libraries.

The Department of Education and Skills allocates per-capita funding for primary and post-primary schools for the purchase of books as outlined in Tables 8 and 9.

In 2002, an important library initiative was introduced for school libraries in Ireland supported by the Minister for Education. It was the Junior Certificate School Programme (JCSP) Demonstration Library Project. Eleven school libraries were set up and were staffed by professionally qualified librarians. The JCSP support service commissioned research into the impact of the project. The result of this was the publication of a report, *'Room for Reading'*, which stated the following:

> ... the findings demonstrate over and over again, that well stocked, well managed school libraries, with access to books through structured library programmes that are directed towards the learning needs and interests of even the most reluctant and hesitant readers, can have impacts that are very significant.
>
> Haslett (2005), p. 131

Since then, an additional 19 schools have joined the project. This highlights the importance of research to provide evidence of the impact of school libraries. Indeed,

**Table 9** **Ireland Department of Education and skills allocation of funding to post-primary schools for the purchase of books**

| Post-primary | Rate per capita |
|---|---|
| Allocation to DEIS schools for books (enhanced) | €39 |
| Allocation to non-DEIS schools for books | €24 |

*Source:* Schools Division – Financial Department of Education and Skills Circular letter 0046/2013. Available at http://www.education.ie.

research and evidence to promote the value of any type of library or librarian is generally vital for the growth of librarianship. Furthermore, a follow-up research report was published, '*More than a Room for Reading JCSP Demonstration Library Project*', which specifically addressed the research question, 'Does a professionally staffed school library have a longitudinal impact on the educational aspirations, experiences, and outcomes of adolescent students who attend schools that are located in "disadvantaged" communities?' (Henefer, 2007, p. 4). Through triangulated methods combining qualitative and quantitative research instruments, the research found that:

- Most JCSP graduates believe that their experiences in the school library have made a difference in terms of their literacy skills, their educational achievements and their self-esteem and confidence within an academic context.
- More than three-quarters of student respondents indicated that the library had helped them to feel more confident in their information seeking.
- In the students' opinion, the different services and resources available in the JCSP libraries have contributed meaningfully to the work they have done in school. With the exception of library-based clubs and activities, on average, 76.1% (N = 172) of the student respondents indicated that they had been helped in their school work and studies by the library service, with a particular emphasis on the role of the librarian (82.7%) and the electronic resources available in the library (86.7%).

The research concluded that, 'It is clear from the data that the presence of a professionally staffed library has had a meaningful impact on the educational experiences of and outcomes for the majority of JCSP students' (p. 31).

In addition, the research demonstrated that students, through their engagement with the library and librarian, saw themselves as readers and showed that they used their public library and the school library. This indicated that formal library services were playing a part in their lives.

The evidence is overwhelming, but school libraries continue to be under-funded and under-staffed everywhere from Shanghai (Lo, 2014) to Cape Town (Hart, 2014). Is this a visibility issue? Demonstrating evidence through research and published reports has led to increased support for school libraries and for the employment of school librarians. This has been shown by the success of the JCSP project in Ireland. Documenting the impact of the school library and school librarian is essential in maintaining funding and resources for school libraries going forward.

The first two case studies are based on interviews with two school librarians working in JCSP school libraries in Dublin and Waterford, Ireland. The third case study is of a librarian working in an all-girls secondary-level Dominican college in Dublin. The librarians were selected because they have all worked a considerable length of time in different libraries and different jobs. In addition to this, they are all well established in their current roles with vast experience of running and managing school libraries. One of the librarians is highly visible, having won the School Library Association's Librarian of the Year Award in 2013. This award is open to all school librarians working in the United Kingdom and Ireland.

# Case study 6: school librarian in secondary (second-level) school for boys

| Name: | The librarian chose to remain anonymous. |
|---|---|

The first case study is of a school librarian working in a school classed by the Department of Education as disadvantaged (Delivering Equality of Opportunity in Schools (DEIS)) in the capital city, Dublin. The school librarian chose to remain anonymous. This study is based on an interview held with her in June 2014. The aim of the study is to demonstrate how this librarian brings value to the environment around her and the school that she works in and to investigate the level of visibility that librarians have in different school settings and look at how this can be improved. Visibility was explained to the librarian as how key stakeholders and users see, understand and value the role of the librarian (i.e. what the librarian does).

The school library is part of the 'JCSP Library Project'. The library is open 8:00 a.m. to 5:00 p.m. Monday through Friday including during lunchtime. Students have time-tabled, scheduled classes that take place in the library. Because it is a disadvantaged school, the main focus is on improving literacy and numeracy levels with the students. The librarian has worked there for 6 years.

## Visibility

When asked on a scale of 0–10 how visible the librarian currently felt to her key stakeholders, she answered 9 of 10 (Table 10). The librarian indicated that her key stakeholders were the management of the school, including the principal. The reason for her high score is based on the very positive feedback she has received via the monthly meetings with the principal. The principal has shared responses from teachers and parents with her, who have all been enthusiastic about the work she is doing and the library that she runs. There is a structured process in place for performance measurement, which includes a monthly report that is sent to the Department of Education and is copied to the management of the school. She has scheduled meetings once a month with management of the school, and even if these do not always happen every month, the report is received by management.

## On a scale of 0–10, how visible do you feel in your organisation to your users (i.e. teachers/students)?

The librarian answered a 7 or an 8 (Table 10). She explained that teachers and students see the library as 'somewhere to go'. They see it as somewhere to hang out after class or when school is over, but they do not necessarily see the other values of it. For students, it is 'somewhere to come and do my homework'; it's not necessarily 'somewhere where I do my research' or to learn something new.

She says, 'I think they kind of take it for granted, that it will always be there. Like if you come here at lunchtime students will be hanging around, chilling out and using it a bit like a youth club rather than a library, which I see as a positive thing because so many of the students come in to use it. But they see it in a different context of a library to how a librarian might see it'.

The space is not necessarily used the way a librarian might intend it, but she doesn't see this as a negative thing. She explains that between 6 and 8 students might come in at lunchtime and sit and chat, but in the morning up to 20 students might come in and sit and do their homework, which is structured. Lunchtime use of the library is seen by students as somewhere to go and hangout that is nicer than the alternatives such as the school hall.

## How do you think you can bring those scores up to a 10?

'I do not know how you would do it with management. Everything is reported back to them. It is just sometimes a bit like the students, they take you for granted, they know that you are there and you are getting on with things. They are happy enough with what you are doing and they understand what you are doing'.

The librarian thinks that students need something more structured to improve the usage of the library for intended purposes, such as homework clubs or book clubs. When they come in, the librarian teaches them how to use the library, how to find information on a particular subject and how to search for something in a book or on the Internet. She aims to improve the lunchtime system and give it a bit more structure. She specifically intends to introduce book clubs with the students.

### Table 10  Self-reported visibility of school librarian

| Visibility rating at time of appointment: where 0=invisible and 10=highly visible | | | | | | | | | | | |
|---|---|---|---|---|---|---|---|---|---|---|---|
| With key stakeholders | 0 | 1 | 2 | 3 | 4 | **5** | 6 | 7 | 8 | 9 | 10 |
| With teachers and students | 0 | **1** | 2 | 3 | 4 | 5 | 6 | 7 | 8 | 9 | 10 |
| Visibility today (6 years after appointment): where 0=invisible and 10=highly visible | | | | | | | | | | | |
| With key stakeholders | 0 | 1 | 2 | 3 | 4 | 5 | 6 | 7 | 8 | **9** | 10 |
| With teachers and students | 0 | 1 | 2 | 3 | 4 | 5 | 6 | **7** | 8 | 9 | 10 |

## When you first started the job 6 years ago, what would your visibility score have been with key stakeholders?

The librarian rated herself as a 5 on the visibility scale with key stakeholders when she first started (see Table 9). She explains that, 'They had no clue what to expect, there was no school library or school librarian ever in the school before'. With students, she rated her visibility as a 1 or 2. At the time, the students did not understand the library or what it was for.

## How did you make the library work? How did you improve your visibility score and what were the most successful strategies?

To improve her visibility with management, things such as going to meetings and acting on the feedback from the reports submitted monthly made a difference. If she was going to do something or introduce a new service, then she would ask for input from management. She produces an annual development plan and involves management in what goes into the plan. Instead of the librarian dictating what services she intends to provide, she pitches her ideas to management and asks them for their opinions on the suitability and how successful they thought those strategies might be. When management were involved from the start, they knew what was happening; therefore, they understood her role better. Even what might seem trivial to some ended up being an important method of engagement; for example, including management on decisions such as what colour to paint the school library walls – those details were important. This is a good example of active engagement with key stakeholders.

When she first started, the librarian conducted a survey for students and teachers. She put the survey in each of the teachers' pigeon holes and asked them questions such as what would they like to see the library being used for, what kind of books would they like and what did they think was important for the school library. She performed a similar survey with the students. The librarian felt it was very important to go to the staff room at every single break time and every single lunchtime when she first started to make herself visible to all of the teaching staff. She continued this for the first year and made a conscious decision not to be 'hiding away in the library'.

After her first year, she needed to be physically present in the library during lunchtime because the library door was deliberately left open to allow students to come in and use the library space if they wanted to. It was important for the librarian to be available for students during the lunch hour so that if they came in and asked for a book or a DVD, then she was physically there to help them. If they needed help with homework, then she could do research on the computers and students slowly began to understand the role of the library, feel comfortable with the space and they soon started to feel ownership of the library.

A couple of times, the librarian brought students with her to do the stock picks, which was very successful because they would brag to others that 'I picked that book', which was an important part of the ownership. Furthermore, when they are involved, the librarian is getting stock that the students really want. The librarian said,

*I'm in my thirties, I do not know what a 14-year-old boy wants to read and I'm not sure that I want to know!*

## What value do you think you as a librarian have brought to the school?

When she first started, there was no school library, so she has brought a library to the heart of the school. She helps the students with research. She helps them with the research projects that the students are given as part of the curriculum. From a professional point of view, school librarians have done a lot of research on how best to get boys to read in terms of literacy development skills and literacy programs (e.g. the Better Reading Program, which is a U.K. program). The librarian brought those skills to the school, which were not previously there. In addition, the availability of the librarian is extensive and important for the students. She is there from 8:00 a.m. to 5:00 p.m. whereas teachers are in classes teaching from 8:45 a.m. to 4:00 p.m. The librarian is available for students for an extra amount of time each day, which makes the service more accessible to students.

## What impact has the school library as a service had on the organisation?

'If you talk to any of the teachers, they will say it is an essential part of the school'. The librarian works with the primary school, which is on the same grounds as the secondary school and the students from the primary school come in once a week to use the library. Any events that happen in the school take place in the library. For example, some graduations take place in the library. Graduations take place for transition-year students (i.e. those students in their fourth year of secondary-level school) and JCSP graduation also happens in the library. Parents of the school pupils are present for the graduations, which gives the parents an opportunity to see the library.

### Formal assessment

The librarian tests the reading and numeracy skills of the students at the beginning and end of the year to see if there is any improvement. This is a mandatory reporting and assessment requirement of the Department of Education. The department wants to see an overall improvement. In general, the reading age of most students improves every year. There are also statistics recorded, such as how many people come in at lunchtime, before school and after school; what activities they are doing while in the library; and how many contact hours the librarian has with staff. There are 30 schools in the JCSP project, and each school has to provide a monthly feedback report, which feeds into an annual report. The department can then benchmark the schools. Librarians are open to sharing their data and sharing ideas and experiences of what works and what does not work.

A 2-day conference is held each year at which school librarians in the project share their data, ideas and information. This is a niche area, which means they can improve their progress and share best practice. In schools, students get bored. Therefore, it is important to introduce new activities. 'It doesn't matter if it is a public or a private school, students do not have a long attention span and get bored quickly, so it is important to be creative and introduce one or two new things each year'.

## Can you think of any challenging scenarios as a school librarian and what strategies worked or did not work?

The librarian did suffer from job insecurity. She states that after working there for 6 years and she is now going into her seventh year that it is only just now that she is being made permanent in her job. She is still awaiting her physical official contract. It has been a temporary role up to now, which meant it was August to August. Every year she had to prepare for the worst in June, in case she would not be there the following school year. She had to put together a plan each year in case the worst happened and her contract was not renewed.

The school gives the space to the JCSP project, and everything is owned by the project, which simply means if the librarian goes, then the project can bring a van to the school and pack up everything and go, but thankfully, she says, this has not happened.

The Department of Education recognises that the school library requires a professionally qualified librarian to run it. It cannot be run by a teacher or volunteer. If the librarian's contract is not renewed, then potentially the library goes back to the Department of Education.

'We ran a campaign with politicians to be made permanent, but that got us nowhere'. She described a campaign that the school librarians held a few years ago for a Contract of Indefinite Duration (CID) that in the public sector if you work there for 4 years you should be made permanent. This is similar to the way that a teacher, with over 3 years of continuous employment with the same employer, is made permanent. Secretaries and teachers got permanency but librarians did not. They lobbied politicians and went to the Minister of Education only to be sacked on the national news, who confirmed live on air, 'I'm just going to confirm, the contracts will not be renewed'. That was 4 years ago. The school librarians and their principals joined forces to lobby. The Minister and Department of Education were contacted. They decided that they needed to get parents, teachers and students collectively involved. Two days later, the minister backed down and claimed to have been quoted 'out of context' and proceeded to announce that the school librarian contracts would be renewed for another year. The students from several of the schools sent postcards in support of their librarian and library to the minister, and that made a big difference.

This particular example emphasizes the importance of the voice of the customer, in this case students, who can be a powerful force for advocacy for school librarians. Another important voice is that of a key stakeholder – the school principal. One school principal at another school in Dublin gave an interview with a local newspaper heralding the importance of the continued employment of the librarian, stating, 'We consider it [the library] to be a hugely important part of school life and the work of the librarian is essential' (Twomey, 2010). Around the same time, there is evidence from parliamentary debates in Ireland that the issue of supporting continued employment of school librarians was raised by another key stakeholder – a local politician (Upton, 2010).

## What are your top tips for school librarians to increase their visibility and impact?

'You have to go to the staff room; you cannot sit in the school library. You have to make yourself physically visible. If people do not see you, then they do not know who you are. You have to be fairly easy going and welcoming and go with the flow, especially in a school library. Be positive. If you are grumpy, you are never going to survive in a place like this. It is important to be open to new ideas. You have to be creative, think on the spot and come up with new ideas all of the time because students will quickly get bored. Once students get bored, they lose interest and they will stop coming to the library'.

'Every year we try to have different events; we run rap workshops, which are poetry and literacy based. We have storytellers and seanchaí (traditional Irish storyteller) that come in. For Maths day I got a Magi-mathician to come in – this is someone who does all magic but through maths. Another year we had a juggler come in who explained the whole concept behind the motion of juggling and why it works and how sometimes it doesn't work. Stuff like this, which grabs the interest of kids and adults alike, can really work well'.

'Another event is "make a book"; this year, we did "return from the dead" with a zombie who was returning from the dead. One group did all of the art work and another group made up stories to go with the art work. It is important to get kids to be 'hands on' and bring out their creative side'.

## What tips would you give new entrants to the school librarian profession?

'They need to talk to the previous people who have been in this role. They need to network and share ideas'. When she first started, she had never worked in a school library before, so she talked to other school librarians to find out what worked and what did not work. She also suggested that school librarians should look up school library websites and look at their activities.

In 2014, the school principal put up a page on the school website on the library. This is very important in terms of visibility and impact for parents. They check the websites for events that all happen in the library. It is also good for attracting new students into the school because they have a library. She has approximately €15,000 per year to spend on stock and to take people out and bring people in.

## What is the most read book in the library?

The most popular book is the *Guinness Book of Records*. The librarian feels that this is a 'boy thing'. In terms of a storybook, it is *Diary of a Wimpy Kid*. All of the big reference books are popular with boys, including *Ripley's Believe It or Not* and factual books. 'If you look at my fiction section and see how shiny and new the books are, it is clear that the students prefer fiction to non-fiction'.

## What is your favourite thing about being a school librarian?

'I love the variety in the job; there is never a dull moment and one day is never the same as any other and the interaction and craic you get from kids is just fantastic. To see kids grow and improve every day gives me a great sense of achievement'.

# Case study 7: librarian working in a secondary school for boys and girls

| | |
|---|---|
| Name: | Hilary Cantwell |
| School: | St. Paul's Community College, Waterford, Ireland |

The second case study is of a school librarian working in St. Paul's Community College, a school that is included in the DEIS Action Plan for Educational Inclusion, which was launched in May 2005 and remains the Department of Education and Skills policy instrument to address educational disadvantage.

The school librarian is Hilary Cantwell, who is well respected in her profession. She is highly visible, having won the prestigious School Library of the Year award in 2013, which is awarded by the School Library Association and covers entries from the United Kingdom and Ireland.

## Mission statement

St. Paul's Community College is a multi-denominational, co-educational school providing an inclusive learning environment for all.

We recognise and respect each student as an individual, embracing various learning and teaching styles and aspiring to encourage each student's unique skills and talents.

St. Paul's Community College encourages the involvement of parents through home school contacts and through the involvement in the development and growth of the Parents Council.

| | |
|---|---|
| School website: | http://www.stpaulswaterford.ie/stpaulswaterford/Main/Home.htm |
| Library website: | http://www.stpaulswaterford.ie/stpaulswaterford/Main/Library_Home.htm |
| JCSP website: | http://www.jcspliteracy.ie/index.php |

This case study is based on an interview conducted using Skype in October 2014.

## The role of the librarian in this school

It is a school library and part of the JCSP. The JCSP Library Project was launched by the Minister for Education in 2001. Eleven schools initially participated in the scheme, with a further 19 joining the project. From the beginning, each school library was staffed by a professionally qualified librarian. Each of the librarians received intensive training by the JCSP support service in literacy and language development specifically aimed at teenagers who are at risk of underachieving.

Libraries in the JCSP programme are creative learning spaces specifically aimed at increasing literacy and numeracy levels. In addition to being open from 9:00 a.m. to 5:00 p.m. Monday through Friday, the library is also open lunchtimes as well as before and after school. The current librarian has worked there since 2006. The remit of the librarian is to provide students with access to appropriate books and resources, which will positively affect their learning experience. The job of the JCSP librarian is to reach out to students who might not consider themselves readers.

The library follows the JCSP model, which prepares students for the Junior Certificate Examination using a profiling system. A student profile is a positive record of what a student has achieved and can do. Central to the profiling system is personal and social development and the improvement of basic skills. This profile system is supported with the use of learning statements; these describe an area of knowledge, a concept or a skill. It states that a student knows, understands or can do something.

Hilary has worked in a variety of different schools in Ireland in areas of varying socio-economic advantage. Before that, she worked first as an indexer and then at the New York Public Library. All of these experiences have shaped her approach to her job today. JCSP is currently part of the Professional Development Service for Teachers (PDST).

## Visibility to key stakeholders

When asked on a scale of 0–10 how visible the librarian currently felt to her key stakeholders, she answered 8 (Table 11). The librarian said her key stakeholders were management of the school, including the principal. The school has had a change of management in the last 2 years.

## On a scale of 0–10, how visible do you feel in your organisation to your users (i.e. teachers/students)?

'JCSP school libraries are very welcoming spaces'. Hilary feels that she is lucky because she has an exceptionally large room and everything is on casters, which makes the space extremely flexible. The remit of JCSP is 12- to 15-year-old students. She works more intensively with first and second years, helping with the transition from primary to secondary school, subject classes, extra-curricular activities and homework club. The students see the library as a bright and inviting place to be. Not all JSCP libraries will have the same layout, but they all strive to be warm, welcoming and creative spaces.

She can become slightly less visible to students who are in exam years. In Ireland, this is in the third and sixth year, when students sit their Junior and Leaving Certificates – the state exams. During those years, the students come to the library specifically to do homework, project work and revise for exams. They are aware of other activities going on in the library, but unfortunately the focus of those years is exam oriented. They do still like coming in and wish and often plea to attend events planned for first and second years. There is a transition year in the fourth year of secondary school, and Hilary has a lot of interaction with students in this year. The transition-year curriculum is very much project based, providing many opportunities for group and independent learning in which the library plays an important role. The scope of the transition year allows teachers to be more creative in their teaching practice. Hilary feels that the education system in Ireland has in some cases hampered the ability of teachers to be creative because of the emphasis on the state exams. However, with the proposed new Junior Certification, this is changing. It is an exciting time to be involved in education.

Contact with students picks up again when they enter the senior cycle (fifth and sixth years). Students have things they need to do. Hilary can relate to them at a deeper level. Students at this age 'are focused on learning how to drive'. Students can still be divided into two groups: those that read for pleasure and those that see themselves as non-readers.

It is vital to continue to tap into their extra-curricular interests. Hilary is adamant that her printer and computers always work. The library supports all of their course-work. Students in the 6th year become nostalgic for their first year and recall stories about the library, events they attended in the library, projects they participated in, JCSP Make a Book Project authors and storytellers they have met. She feels the students definitely know who she is, and she has a high profile with them, rating her visibility at 9 out of 10 (Table 11).

**Table 11** **Self-reported visibility of school librarian**

| Visibility rating at time of appointment: where 0=invisible and 10=highly visible | | | | | | | | | | |
|---|---|---|---|---|---|---|---|---|---|---|
| With key stakeholders | 0 | 1 | 2 | 3 | 4 | **5** | 6 | 7 | 8 | 9 | 10 |
| With teachers and students | 0 | 1 | 2 | 3 | **4** | 5 | 6 | 7 | 8 | 9 | 10 |
| Visibility today (8 years after appointment): where 0=invisible and 10=highly visible | | | | | | | | | | |
| With key stakeholders | 0 | 1 | 2 | 3 | 4 | 5 | 6 | 7 | **8** | 9 | 10 |
| With teachers and students | 0 | 1 | 2 | 3 | 4 | 5 | 6 | 7 | 8 | **9** | 10 |

## Challenging the traditional image of the stereotypical librarian

Hilary says that there still is an outdated perception about librarians, both among adults and students. People think perhaps that working in a library must be a really easy job to have. Librarians perhaps reinforce that image, including Hilary, because she says, 'I am sitting in a bright inviting room probably one of the nicest rooms in the building and it's calm. I appear to have lots of time to listen to students and teachers coming in and out of the space. I could be pounding away on the keyboard trying to catalogue, write reports, create posters, search for resources, buy stock, support a teacher's CPD, plan library classes or catalogue new resources. Students and teachers are not aware of the amount of organising and administrative work involved in managing a library'.

School librarians work hard at academically and culturally enriching students' school experiences. 'I like students to experience music, theatre and books outside of their frame of reference; read books that they might not opt to choose to attend or read. I ask them to give things "a try". I explain that to have an informed opinion, you have to experience it at least once'.

On the basis of this theory, she is the only adult that the students are allowed to say 'no' to. She says some students are cautious around her. Libraries are for handing out books, so why does she have a rapper in the library? She encourages them to speak out to have their opinions. The boundaries are slightly different between librarian and student and teacher and student. Students call her by her first name.

## When you first started the job 8 years ago, what would your score have been with key stakeholders?

She rates her visibility with stakeholders as 5 out of 10 when she first started. There were librarians in the school before her who were all popular. The teachers would often quote to her what former librarians might have done. She says she appears to be laid back in her approach; despite appearance, she is 'highly organised'. she wants students to come through the door and use the library.

With students, she says she rated 4 out of 10. She said she was initially seen by students as 'just another adult with a pulse'. She describes it as a 'slow build', and it can take a long time to build up your visibility in a school. The librarian is under much pressure in terms of statistics and performance measurement. She has to use systems that record statistics, including promotional activities. She feels that libraries are so much more than those simple statistics such as 'how many books were read today' or 'how many people came through the door'. The softer outcomes such as relationship building, which take time, are arguably more important and are more difficult to qualify or quantify. However, over time, students and teachers have gotten to know her and at times they are surprised that she comes up with good ideas.

Although school librarians work on their own (at least in Ireland), she feels that they probably have more interaction with all adults in the school than anyone else. They 'bridge a lot of gaps'. For example, she might say to a teacher, 'Do you know that a colleague of yours is doing a very similar project but is looking at it from a different angle?' She has a bird's eye view of what is going on in the school. This particular point is true for many types of librarians, particularly public librarians, who have an ear to the ground and are in touch with what is going on in their communities. She says that she is a 'generalist'; she likes to know a little bit about a subject, but she may back off if it gets too technical – 'I like to know the keywords'.

Librarians are not shy and quiet individuals. 'Librarians can be assertive'. She says, 'Personally, I play the quirky card'. She can be sometimes found in unusual places in the school. She always asks direct questions.

### How did you make the library work? How did you improve your visibility score, and what were the most successful strategies?

Hilary can turn up anywhere in the building. She says she can be found sitting in the middle of the woodwork room. It's important to get out of the library. She says her 'audience' teenagers are under pressure to be 'perfect'; therefore, it is important that adults model behaviour that confirms that it is sometimes good to take chances and opportunities and to be yourself. For example, the physical education teacher will recruit her to participate in a Zumba dancing class when they sense students are reluctant and inhibited.

The teachers do not have the same freedom that she has in her role. The biggest thing that teenagers get from the library aside from support with school work is being able to ask for things. She does not know all of the students and is inclined to get to know the naughtier ones, or the more colourful ones. However, she is constantly looking for the shy, retiring student, who might talk to her about an event in the library.

If that student approaches her about an event or comes to one, then she feels that is a measure of her success.

## What value do you think you as a librarian have brought to the school?

The award she received in 2013 heightened her visibility as well as that of the JCSP library project and the school. There are good working relationships between the schools and the education community in Waterford. She says that the public library 'is wonderful' and very supportive of her. She feels that if you are a librarian then you can connect organisations that might not otherwise have done so. This type of connection can help organisations share ideas, barter skills and do things better.

She feels that she brings a 'bird's eye view' approach to everything she does. She says that she does not approach a topic from just one perspective. Interestingly, this echoes what Jane Burns said in her interview about approaching the medical topic from an educational perspective – something the clinician had not thought of.

Hilary recalls that she used to have the teachers do a 'Dewey hunt', which would connect different sections such as history and social science. She feels that school librarians are at the forefront of education, and she likes experimenting with new ideas. She is very open to new things. She is going to run a soapbox competition. She is encouraging the students to rant; on the other hand, the teachers have a more conservative view, but she is less restricted in her approach. It is a slow process in which she might expose a teacher to a new idea. They may not take it in the first year, but gradually they come on board. She feels that the staff does value her.

She feels a duty to keep up to date with technical skills. She feels librarians are constantly looking to learn, and she does not mind going on courses and learning in her own time. The nature of the business of librarianship is to continue learning. In the JCSP project, the librarians are constantly pushing the boundaries and are very excited about the new Junior Certification curriculum that is coming to Irish education. 'Librarians are very adaptable and flexible by nature, and the industry of librarianship has gone through so many changes that we have to be able to embrace change. If we revert to the stereotype that they keep imposing on us, nobody will notice us'. For example, if someone approaches a librarian, then it is important to put everything down, listen and even if there are no resources that match the person's request, you have to be able to think quickly on your feet and offer them something. Her advice is to 'ensure that they leave with something'.

## What impact has the school library as a service had on the organisation?

Waterford has the highest rate of unemployment in Ireland. It has been severely affected by the recession. There is only one book shop remaining in Waterford city. There are three public library branches in the city. There is one small public library located near the school. The other two branches are on the far side of the city, where the school community would not migrate into. The centre city has been ravaged by the recession, and people are more likely to go to a retail park than into the city. She feels that having her in the school has probably brought more life to the school. She has lunchtime activities, including a darts club, film club, and girls' club.

She has a homework club after school where she could have up to 28 students in attendance. She recalls that people initially came in just to use the computers. She told them a white lie and said that the Internet connection was not working. Suddenly, they then began to play chess and puzzles, and they were using Legos and being social with each other. They also use the computers to code or play 'scratch', but usually it is to do something constructive. They make films. A big priority is to provide a social learning space. In Waterford, for that age group, there are not too many places for teenagers to hang out. When they go home, they retreat to their bedrooms and into a virtual world via the Internet. Occasionally, students may fall asleep in class due to a lack of sleep. This is because they spend hours late at night playing computer games at home; therefore, Hilary is careful to avoid feeding their addictions to games. She is a big advocate and follower of Bridge21, which is an approach to collaborate social learning based at Trinity College Dublin. It is based on the Scouting movement.

## Formal assessment

Statistics are centrally collected; the librarian compiles a monthly report. Several case studies are done as well as tests for group reading for first-year students. The first-year students are tested twice and then annually until they reach their third year. A correlation is then made between predictions and how they perform in the Junior Certification exam. The statistics are sent via the JCSP co-ordinator and reported into the Department of Education. Their aim is to improve the educational experience, attrition, attainment and progression through the system. In 2002, there were still students dropping out before and after their Junior Cert. However, in 2014, there was nowhere for them to drop out to. Alternative education programmes such as YouthReach, have become much harder for students to get into. Students are staying longer in school, but sometimes school is not for them. They might not be performing well, but if they have an interest in something, then the librarian tries to tap into that. She feels if they are developing socially with their peers, then the exam deficit can be addressed. JCSP is for students who are lagging slightly behind.

However, sometimes she has students who may need a specialized intervention; for example, some need a '100 dot-a-sight' word to be done with them. She taps into an interest that a student might have, and eventually they do some work with her and she liaises a lot with the teachers. She is on a first-name basis with the students, and she does not have discipline issues. It is a different environment. Librarians plod the neutral ground and stand up for students.

## Can you think of a challenging scenario as a school librarian and what strategies worked or did not work?

Budgets are centralised and are allocated from Dublin. The JCSP librarians are employed at a Grade VI level in the public service. They are responsible and accountable for a large budget. Sometimes it can be challenging to make sure that it is spent on the library and not something completely outside of the library. The librarians are accountable for the budgetary spend; therefore, she has to ensure that the budget is allocated according to the remit of the JCSP library project. There is a significant lack of understanding about what a librarian does; for example, 'Teachers think that we take books out of a box and pop them on the shelf. They do not realise that they have to be catalogued, classified, labelled and correctly shelved'. She has some students that help out in the library. The best training she received was in the New York Public Library. She says they have some 'quirky things'. She remembers returning to Ireland from New York and says, 'I came back talking about edging shelves, nobody in Kilkenny Public Library knew what I was going on about'. The library in Kilkenny was constantly getting flooded, so they spent their time pushing the shelves back against the walls to avoid water damage.

Students are eager to help and they love organising the 'Eye-Witness Guides' together. They should be in subject order, but the students put them all together. Hilary says 'What can you do except smile?' Hilary has a hardbound volume of Dewey that the students find fascinating, particularly the younger students. Firstly, they look it up on Amazon and find out that it is a really expensive book. Then they try to catch her out by asking her if she put the right classification number on it.

## What are your top tips for school librarians to increase their visibility and impact?

'Don't sit in the library'.

'Be bolshie'. If she does not have a time-tabled class, then she gets out of the library and brings things with her. She does things such as asking the students to pull four books from the fiction section and read the first few lines of each book. She would then ask them if she found them interesting. She feels that when students arrive in secondary school they do not come with many literacy skills.

## What tips would you give new entrants into the librarian profession?

'You have to buck that trend. You have to be that person that is curious and get to know people in your organisation. People will not come to you, they are very busy'. She puts things in people's mailboxes. If people ignore her, then she says 'I wear them down, until eventually they will notice what I do. I woo people, I will not go as far as to say I seduce them, but I get to know what people are interested in and send them information that I think they will find useful'. She does not leave her name beside the information in the mailbox, but other teachers see her placing things there so they know it is coming from her. 'People know that we are there. They will come and find us when they need us, but sometimes they do not even know that they need us, but they do need us'.

'Get out there and have a visible presence – there are so many ways to do this. In the early days, librarians used to labour over signs and posters, but now there are more interesting ways to heighten visibility, like Blogging, tweeting and emailing'.

## How important is online visibility for the school librarian?

'Being online is very important'. She is not allowed to have a Facebook page. The JCSP project has begun tweeting. She feels that every time she goes to a meeting about the school website she is thinking, 'sure no teenager is ever going to look at that'; however, teenagers are choosing what school they will go to now, so there is more competition. There are always questions about who is going to maintain the website in schools. There is a suggestion that because she is the librarian and is sitting next to a computer and a phone that she could take this role on. It is important not to take on everything.

## What is the most read book in the library?

Hilary has 7000 books in the library. Everyone from 0 to 99 loves the Guinness book of records! A funny book that may not be the most read but is the most 'travelled' book (as it can be found in different locations around the library) is called *Hair in Funny Places*, by Babette Cole.

The students are influenced by popular culture. Graphic novels, Manga and anything Japanese is very popular. The boys are more influenced by the look of the book; if it has a red or pink cover, then they will not be seen with it. The girls are not as bothered by this.

The poet Colm Keagan has made several visits to the library. He has appealed to the student's sensitive side. On his recommendation, the boys would have no hesitation in reading a book. Role models, particularly male role models, are important to promote reading among boys.

'Non-fiction can be a way of getting boys to write. Both boys and girls like humour. There is a jokes encyclopaedia that is very popular. They like an injection of information – this is the culture we are living in. People do not make time to read. Peer recommendations work. When children are initially learning to read, they are competitive; they see the progress that they are making and the new words they are learning. Between the ages of 12 and 16 years, they can fall out of love with reading. They read text books for long periods of the day. These textbooks can be challenging to read and they may be on a subject that a student is not particularly interested in so they may perceive reading negatively and something "they have to do". The library is a non-judgemental environment. It is not uncommon for senior students to seek out titles they have read numerous times of which they have a positive, less stressful time association with; for example, Roald Dahl and Dr Seuss are favourites among all students'.

There is little acknowledgement that students are in fact constantly reading and reading in lots of different ways using various devices. Language and its use have also changed. We must remember that the students we teach have a different frame of reference. Shortening and blending words are all accepted in their social circles; however, we need to remind them that this language may not get them the marks they need on their English exam.

'There is much emphasis on technology within the education sector. We must remember it is only a tool for teaching, learning and presenting the information we wish to convey'. Hilary has 20 tablets in the library where students can complete assignments and access the Internet.

However, Hilary has built in to the school week periods when students are encouraged to solve their information needs in other ways using the collection and using the teacher and student expertise in the building. The library is a community space; therefore, it hosts and facilitates various events such as school quizzes, X-factor and some that are a little more unusual such as the Reptile Zoo.

## About school librarianship

Hilary would worry about someone coming into the area of school librarianship with little professional experience. She herself had lots of different experiences before taking up her job as school librarian. The New York Public Library provided her with a great frame of reference and prepared her for working independently. She does not think that it is an easy path to take immediately after having graduated with a library qualification. It is good to have a mentor – someone who can inspire and model best practice. This is not always possible in a school setting because the librarian is usually working alone in the library. It is important to join professional organisations, such as the School Library Association in the Republic of Ireland (SLARI), and seek out support networks. Hilary thinks it is important for people working in an educational sector to be lifelong learners. In Ireland, the opportunity for librarians to be promoted in schools is limited. The JCSP project team is supportive, and there is very good collaboration among colleagues.

## What's your favourite thing about being a librarian?

'The variety and the flexibility of the job'. Her manager is a librarian and understands and trusts what she does. Every library and every librarian has his or her own personality. She has freedom and she enjoys that. 'It is a very creative space to work in. You have to be a strong person to work solo, particularly in a big organisation. You can retreat behind the librarian desk, scanning and shelving books and answering questions. But it is more important to be the librarian asking the users you serve what they need from the library; how you can support their work, interests and professional development'. Hilary is continually learning from other librarians, teachers and students. Interaction with different groups and their perspectives is important for informing best practice.

## Taking credit

'Our innate nature as librarians is that we are collaborators. We do not always take the glory or credit for things, not that we seek glory'. Presenting library policies and plans came up in discussion during a School Library Association conference that Hilary attended. School librarians admitted to frequently giving their policies and plans to other members of staff to present to management and in some cases to the school board. This is not good practice.

## Threats to the profession

In Ireland, there is a scheme called 'Job Bridge'. This is a national internship scheme in which a person lacking experience or returning to the workforce may apply for a 6- or 9-month internship. They are paid an allowance of €50 per week in addition to a social welfare allowance. It is intended that after the internship the employer may offer a paid position. The scheme has been in place since 2011, and although participation in the scheme has been linked with progression to employment (Indecon, 2013), this has not been evident in librarianship. A private school that became a public school recently advertised for a librarian under the Job Bridge scheme. Although some schools may think that the Job Bridge scheme is a good solution to filling the position of librarian, it is not. In the library, as in all aspects of education, there needs to be continuity for students.

In England, librarians are not always employed as school librarians. Teachers who wish to stay in the educational sector are being used instead. Although the employing of teachers may seem logical, it is not good for the profession. It muddies the water. Library and information science is a science – information needs to be organised, managed, disseminated and even created. In summary, people are very enthusiastic about and supportive of the JCSP library project.

# Case study 8: school librarian in secondary (second-level) school for girls

| Name: | Martina Kealy |
|---|---|
| School: | Dominican College, Glasnevin, Dublin, Ireland |

School website: http://www.dominican-college.com/

## Mission statement

> Inspired by our motto, *Veritas*, we strive to realise each individual's full potential in a Catholic environment.

## Library aims

- To support the curriculum and the work of teachers and students.
- To promote reading and researching for pleasure and information both electronically and in hard-copy format.
- To ensure that students learn how to use the library enabling them to become independent researchers.

Martina Kealy has worked in the Dominican College in Dublin, Ireland, for some 5 years. She previously worked in medical libraries and freelanced as a cataloguer. The school was first established in 1883 and is a Roman Catholic school for girls. She has 7500 books in her library collection and 16 iPads. There are 705 teenage girls in the school in 2014. Martina's main role is to manage and run the library on her own. It is a solo job. Since she started there, she has trained two library prefects in the school who 'help her out' in the library. The sixth-year girls (aged 17) apply for posts as prefects in the library. They have to do an interview with the year head teacher and explain why they think they would be suitable to work in the library. Their job is defined by the librarian, who teaches them how to shelve books in Dewey order and how to issue and discharge books.

It is very convenient for the librarian to have the two prefects to help out, especially if she has to attend a seminar or if she is absent from work because of illness or any other reason. The librarian also has an informal arrangement in which transition-year students (fourth year) also help her out in the library. Working in the library is one of the 'work experience' options that students may avail of during their fourth year of school, known as the 'transition year'.

Sometimes the librarian will have two transition-year students who help out in the library. This is really useful, particularly during very busy times such as lunchtime. They would come in for the second part of their lunch break. It can be challenging to try to keep the noise level down in a school library according to Martina, but having two students there helping out in the library makes a big difference to her. The sixth-year students help out during lunch breaks, whereas the transition-year students might help out at other times of the day because their school year is more flexible.

## Visibility score

On a scale of 0–10, Martina felt she rated as a 10 for her visibility with key stakeholders and with teachers and students (Table 12). It is a public school, and there has always

**Table 12  Self-reported visibility of school librarian**

| Visibility rating at time of appointment: where 0 = invisible and 10 = highly visible | | | | | | | | | | |
|---|---|---|---|---|---|---|---|---|---|---|
| With key stakeholders | 0 | 1 | 2 | 3 | **4** | 5 | 6 | 7 | 8 | 9 | 10 |
| With teachers and students | 0 | 1 | 2 | 3 | **4** | 5 | 6 | 7 | 8 | 9 | 10 |
| Visibility today (6 years after appointment): where 0 = invisible and 10 = highly visible | | | | | | | | | | |
| With key stakeholders | 0 | 1 | 2 | 3 | 4 | 5 | 6 | 7 | 8 | 9 | **10** |
| With teachers and students | 0 | 1 | 2 | 3 | 4 | 5 | 6 | 7 | 8 | 9 | **10** |

been a tradition in the school of having a library, so 'by tradition, the library has always been visible'. The OECD statistics on literacy show that teenagers are reading less now than years ago. This has helped to increase the profile and visibility of the library among key stakeholders. Everybody in the school gets involved in a reading drive – the DEAR week (Drop Everything And Read) – that means that not just people in the library but every single person in the school, including the principal, the school secretaries and the maintenance staff, literally drop everything for 40 min a day for 1 week and pick up something to read during that time. They will read a book or a magazine, and it may include any parent that is waiting in the reception area. This activity encourages students who do not like reading to try it for a change. Therefore, the promotion of the library as something that enables literacy has increased the visibility of it.

## Activities to increase visibility of the librarian and library

Other activities that have helped to increase the visibility of the librarian and library have been author visits. The Irish author Anna Carey, who writes novels for teenagers, came to the school and was able to talk to the teenagers about the library and recalled funny stories such as a time when she got stuck in a chair. The teenagers enjoyed this and were enthusiastic and asked the author many questions. They had all been encouraged by the librarian to read the author's book, *The Real Rebecca*, before her visit for them to get more out of the visit. She says, 'I'm also Mrs. Lost Property, which is a useful way of getting to know the kids'.

Martina likes that her job is very varied. 'I do all of the normal library tasks – circulation, cataloguing, purchasing books and journals, paying invoices, finding information and answering queries. I also show the students how to use the OPAC and how to find a book, etc.'. She says that there is also another dimension to her school library job. She can get involved in general school activities by supervising small groups of students in the library. She sometimes does paired reading on a one-to-one basis with students with reading difficulties. She also supervises online typing in the library with a small group of students.

The librarian organises 'Bring a Book, Buy a Book', pioneered by the charity St. Michael's House. Fundraising can be fun, and fundraising drives are always welcome by the school. The students really enjoy this and it gives them an opportunity to bring in some books from home. There are also other opportunities to get involved with wider school activities, including helping with the school musical, providing an appropriate library display to go with it and judging the talent contests as well as promoting interests of one's own (e.g. mental health and its awareness). She is also available to listen to teenagers who are having emotional problems that they might not verbalise otherwise. In these cases, the issues are always passed on to the Care Team in the school and dealt with in a sensitive way. Just being an observer of the students in the library can be an advantage to the staff.

The librarian would also rate her visibility with the students as a 10 (Table 12). The school time-tables library classes, in which a teacher would bring her class to the library for a reading class. This makes the library very much a part of a student's day and a part of their education. Any student, no matter what year they are in, would be able to direct someone new to the school to the library and would know who the librarian was. Even before a student starts in the school, they are given a tour of the school that includes the library during an open day. The librarian is there during the evening time of the open day to show the group of potential students around the library. This means they become familiar with it even before they formally begin their first school term.

The tradition of the Dominicans centres on education. The ethos of the school supports the library as a place of learning. The Dominicans support the education of women. The Dominicans always believe that education and reading in particular empowered women with information, which was important for their lives and their freedom and justice.

When Martina first started 5 years ago, she felt her visibility would have been much lower – about a 4 for both students and teachers/management (Table 12). The reason she gives for this is because she had not previously worked in a school library and she was not familiar with all of the different ways to promote the library in a school (e.g. the DEAR initiative). Any activity that the librarian engages with always helps to promote her work and the library.

## Tips for increasing visibility

Anything to do with literacy helps increase the visibility of the librarian. A few years ago the librarian acquired several iPads for the school library. She had a role in educating the students about technology and the difference between the various methods of accessing information in the physical and virtual environments. The teachers also helped out with this. If the students are given a project to do or an essay to write, then the teachers will ask them to cite at least three sources. They are not allowed to just cite Internet-based sources. They would need to cite a book and perhaps a journal (e.g. *National Geographic* or a history of Ireland journal or *BBC history*). These sources are all indexed in the catalogue. The students are taught how to look up the index and how to cite references. The school library has an OPAC, but the students are able to look up references themselves. The history teacher in particular emphasizes to students the importance of using the catalogue and learning how to cite and read different sources to inform their work. They also have access to newspapers and some databases such as JSTOR and Scoilnet.

## Value of librarian to the school

When asked what value she has brought to the school as a librarian, Martina felt that she is regarded by the students as 'not a teacher', which was a good thing for her and for them. The students regard her as 'an alternative person', particularly if there was a problem that arose and they would go in and talk to her. 'I'm like one of the safety valves in the school', and she can act as a conduit to refer students on to either a counsellor or a year head depending on what the issue was. 'Every child needs a safety valve – it's like a way out'.

## What impact does the school library have on the school?

The fact that the school library still has 7500 books is good. The fiction section is particularly popular in the school. The school library does not get much funding anymore because of all of the cutbacks during the recession. The librarian has had to get creative and collaborative. She has made arrangements with the local public libraries in the area to put in place a book donation scheme. Public libraries are seen by the librarian to still be in receipt of healthy budgets from the government, but school libraries are not. Public libraries pass on relatively new books – perhaps just 2 years old – both fiction and non-fiction, to the school library. This is the only way the librarian can presently restock her shelves.

'Keeping a library in a school definitely promotes a love of reading'. If the physical library with paper books was not in the school, then the librarian felt that reading would diminish or even disappear. Students could still use a public library, but it is more of an effort when they are under time pressure. They have lots of homework to do and particularly during an exam year their time is precious. When a library is there on site this enables reading and study. The books are tangible. Teachers can build the library into the education programme; they can walk in with an entire class and use the space. This promotes a love of reading. That is not to say that we do not or should not use technology. Students come in to the library and sit and look up information using iPads.

## Methods of reporting impact

The librarian uses her library management system to record and report usage statistics to the management of the school. She always shows statistics around the DEAR week, the week before and after it where there is usually a peak in borrowing books. There is always a big run on the books during this time. The library management 'Heritage' system includes a statistical module that she uses to report usage. There is no formal requirement for the librarian to issue an annual report to management. However, she does produce a report and hands it to the principal at the end of each school year.

## Challenging scenario

The challenging scenario for the school librarian is being told that there was no money to buy books. Her response was to get in contact with local librarians in her area and seek advice and help. The students also helped and took it on board. The sixth years in particular helped out and brought in collections of books and donated them to the school library. The librarian sent a message to the sixth years to say if they had any books at home that they no longer wanted, then they might consider donating them to the library. This received a very positive response, and the books were in really good condition. Martina contacted the Department of Education to find out about funding for school libraries. She was told that the money is going into publicly funded libraries, not publicly funded school libraries. They see public libraries as being open for students to use. Private schools are different because the parents are paying fees; some of the fees go toward funding those libraries and salaries. Public schools are very different.

## What are your top tips for school librarians to increase their visibility?

'To keep encouraging literacy and literacy programs. Sometimes there are students in the school who come to the library during periods where there is a subject they do not take such as foreign national students who do not take the Irish language as a subject'. When such a student comes to the library, the librarian has an opportunity to offer the student one-to-one tutoring (e.g. assisting with reading and paired reading). This is where the librarian sits down with the student and observes them reading. If they happen upon a word that they do not understand, then the librarian explains the meaning of the passage where it occurred. This also helps students with dyslexia. The student might also come across a word that she cannot pronounce, and then the librarian would highlight the word within the sentence and help them with the pronunciation. The librarian would ask them, 'What do you think it means?' and have a dictionary beside them.

## What advice would you give to new entrants to school librarianship?

'I think you have to keep it vibrant, keep things fresh, and introduce new ideas all the time. Keep thinking of new ideas. We have things like poetry competitions which go down well. We have prizes and little gifts; our prefects get gifts at the end of their term. The kids work really hard, and it is good to acknowledge that and to offer an incentive. Especially when I have no help for getting books back on the shelves during the day,

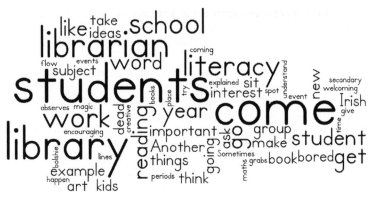

**Figure 7** Word cloud of tips for school librarians to increase their visibility.

the prefects really help a lot. It is great to have students that understand the shelving system and they are enthusiastic about helping out'.

### What is the most read book in the library?

The *Hunger Games* series are the most popular books. The girls are extremely interested in fiction, more so than the non-fiction books.

### What is your favourite thing about being a school librarian?

'My favourite thing about being a school librarian is that I am working in a school! Being part of the school staff means that you are very much part of the teaching team. So, the interests, education and welfare of the students (in this case, teenage girls) is a priority. Above all, being able to talk to and encourage teenagers is a privilege every day'.

On the basis of the responses of all three school librarians to what their top tips would be for new entrants to the profession of school librarianship, the following word cloud was produced (see Figure 7).

## Summary

On the basis of the interviews with the three librarians working in secondary school libraries in Ireland, the following summarises their tips for improving impact, value and visibility of school libraries and librarians:

1. Promote the library as a means of improving literacy.
2. Try the DEAR initiative 'Drop Everything And Read'.
3. Train students to be library prefects (or similar); it gives students a sense of responsibility and can be a big help to the librarian.
4. Reward students with little gifts while adhering to school policy.

5. Invite local authors to come and speak to the students.
6. Use paired reading and capture its outcomes.
7. Demonstrate the impact and value of the library with evidence of improved literacy and/or numeracy skills.
8. Formally report impact through existing reporting structures in the school.
9. Link in with teachers in the school and invite them to time-table classes in the library.
10. Make the library a visually appealing and attractive place for students to spend time in. Talk to them about the space and involve them in its layout. Get flexible furniture if possible.
11. Adopt an inclusive engaging approach with key stakeholders – communicate your plans and involve management in decision-making about the library.
12. Have flexible opening times; if possible, be open early and late.
13. Offer to host school events in the library (e.g. graduations).
14. Set up clubs for students for different days of the week or during lunchtime (e.g. homework club, book club, chess club, film club, coding club, darts club).
15. Keep the book stock and information technology equipment up to date and in good working order in the library.
16. Host interesting events (e.g. invite storytellers or mathimagians) to bring learning to life; run competitions, talent shows or quizzes.
17. Be creative and host workshops (e.g. poetry or rap workshops).
18. The school library should be open during lunchtimes.
19. Involve the students as much as possible (e.g. in performing book buys/stock picks, helping with shelving books, writing book reviews, setting up clubs, reviewing technologies).
20. Develop links with other libraries and librarians in the community (e.g. public, academic libraries etc.).
21. Network with other school librarians in the area.
22. Have a library presence on the school's website. Ensure that it is an interesting and dynamic site to visit.
23. If someone comes in to the library looking for assistance, then drop everything and help them.
24. Don't be grumpy; have a positive attitude.
25. If you are new to the role of school librarianship, then talk to other librarians who have worked in this area before and get ideas from them and learn from their experience.
26. Be visible always as a member of the staff, interested in all aspects of the students' education.
27. Keep an open mind. Be willing to create new initiatives for student advancement.

# Notes

**Craic** an Irish term used to describe fun.
**BRIDGE21** Bridge21 is an education programme based in Trinity College Dublin. It is designed to support an innovative 21st century learning environment within schools on the basis of a learning model for second-level education that is: Team-based, technology-mediated, project-based and cross-curricular. See more at www.bridge21.ie.
**Fizzbook** is an optimized wireless device that pre-loaded with educational software.
**JSTOR** is a not-for-profit site founded to help academic libraries and publishers. http://www.jstor.org/.

**Scoilnet** is an online portal to support the continuing professional development of teachers in Ireland. It includes more than 11,000 resources that are handpicked by teachers for their relevance to the curriculum. The website is available at https://www.scoilnet.ie/.

**Scaffolding system** See more about this system online at http://www.learnnc.org/lp/pages/5074.

**Youthreach** is a Department of Education and Skills official education, training and work experience programme for early school leavers aged 15–20 years in Ireland. It offers young people the opportunity to identify options within adult life and provides them with opportunities to acquire certification. See more online at http://www.youthreach.ie/.

# Case studies: visibility of public libraries and public librarians

# 4

*There is not such a cradle of democracy upon the earth as the Free Public Library, this republic of letters, where neither rank, office, nor wealth receives the slightest consideration.*

**Andrew Carnegie**

Public libraries are arguably what the general public immediately think of when 'library' or 'librarian' is mentioned in a conversation or on the news or media. Public libraries have a huge role in defining, delivering and shaping the 'brand' of librarianship to the world. Arguably, every other type of library will only ever see a specialist strata of society pass through its doors (i.e. a doctor, scholar, lawyer or chief executive officer [CEO]). The exception to this is perhaps school libraries, but most are grossly under-funded and are much less prevalent than public libraries. Public libraries are funded by central governments and are an essential component of democratic societies. Although recessionary times see a peak in the use of public libraries, they ironically receive severe cuts to resources during those same times. Like other areas of librarianship, public libraries are under threat and have lost funding and staff over the years. However, what is even more important than that is how they meet that challenge, what image public librarians and public libraries portray and which services they offer – this is crucial to the visibility of librarianship in the minds of the everyday citizen; therefore, it is crucial to the future of the profession.

Research showing the value of the public library and public librarian to society is plentiful. Much is in the form of grey literature such as annual reports produced by public libraries and their local authorities or county councils. However, there are peer-reviewed articles available and a snapshot of this is highlighted in Table 13. This is by no means an exhaustive list, but it shows value indicators of public librarians and libraries in the area of social, health, economic and community well-being.

Methods used in public library research to measure value will be highlighted for use by other librarians later in this book. The use of research to inform practice and current level of visibility will be discussed in more detail in Chapter 7.

Five public librarians are interviewed. Three are from Irish public libraries, one is from the United Kingdom and one is from Australia. Two of the Irish librarians work in the Dublin City Council and the other Irish librarian is a county manager of Wexford County Libraries in Southeast Ireland as well as a former president of the Library Association of Ireland (2011–2013). The English librarian is a principal librarian and part of the management team at Northamptonshire, in the East Midlands of England. The librarian based in Australia is starting to a new job in another public library as a

Table 13 **Research demonstrating evidence of the impact and value indicators of public libraries and librarians to society**

| Impact/value indicator | Research |
|---|---|
| Enhanced social inclusion, including alleviation of rural isolation and civic engagement | Benstead, Spacey, and Goulding (2004), Lockyer-Benzie (2004) Hicken (2004), Forcier, Rathi and Given (2013) Gomez, Ambikar, and Coward (2009) |
| Improved health – books on prescription, self-care, education, empowerment, improved health and well-being, therapeutic environment with positive influence on mental health | Furness & Casselden (2012) Linnan (2004) Ingham (2014) Brewster (2014) |
| Community lifeline during emergencies and natural disasters, building community resilience | Carlo Bertot, McClure, and Jaeger (2008) Veil and Wade Bishop (2014) Welsh and Higgins (2009) |
| Enhanced knowledge sharing and building social capital | Veil and Wade Bishop (2014) Forcier et al. (2013) Varheim (2007) |
| Return on investment (ROI) | Svanhild Aabø (2005, 2009) Griffiths et al. (2004) |

Systems and Resources Coordinator at Brimbank Libraries in Victoria, Southeast Australia. Two of the five librarians have won national awards. One has a highly acclaimed personal blog and is one of the editors of the open-access journal *In the Library with the Leadpipe*. The librarians were interviewed in person and using Skype in 2014 and 2015. They share their opinions of public libraries in their environments and talk about their visibility, impact and reporting structures. All five librarians are in management positions and highly visible within their profession.

# Case study 9: county librarian at Wexford county council public libraries, Ireland, and a former president of the Library Association of Ireland (2011–2013)

| | |
|---|---|
| Name: | Fionnuala Hanrahan |
| Organisation: | Wexford County Council |

Wexford has a population of 145,320 (Census 2011) and is located in Southeast Ireland. There are four main towns in Wexford. The council employs approximately 780 staff, providing a range of services primarily for the residents of Wexford, Enniscorthy, Gorey, New Ross and the surrounding rural hinterland areas.

## Mission of the organisation

The council's Corporate Plan 2004–2009 states their mission as follows:

> To improve the quality of life of the people of Wexford by representing the interests of citizens and customers and providing services to meet their needs (Wexford County Council, 2004).

## Mission of the library

> To promote change and social justice through access to knowledge and information.
>
> Wexford Public Library Services are provided by Wexford County Council, the local government authority of Wexford County. We provide access to informational, educational, cultural and recreational library materials and services in various formats and technologies. We aim to be responsive to the public library needs of our community and to uphold the public's freedom of access to information.

## Online visibility of library and librarian

| | |
|---|---|
| Library website: | http://www.wexford.ie/wex/Departments/Library/ |
| Oral history podcasts: | http://www.wexford.ie/wex/Departments/Library/OralHistoryPodcasts/ |
| Flickr: | http://flickr.com/photo.gne?id=14647248933 |
| Linkedin: | http://ie.linkedin.com/pub/fionnuala-hanrahan/20/a72/8b1 |
| Facebook: | https://www.facebook.com/Wexfordlib |

**Library:**
The library employs a staff of 60 and there are 8 library facilities in the county.

## Role of county librarian

The county librarian of Wexford is Fionnuala Hanrahan, who has worked there for 17 years. She is an advisory officer and reports to a director of services within the council who in turn reports to the chief executive/manager. The county librarian is positioned on the third level in terms of the organisational hierarchy. She is a member of an executive team that consists of the heads of departments across the local authority. She has a managerial role and is responsible for the development of three key areas: libraries, archives and the arts. She acts as the library leader for the organisation in these three areas.

## Visibility vis-à-vis policy-makers in the county council

In terms of structure, the county council is made up of 34 elected members and is divided into four municipal districts. The librarian indirectly serves the council. She submits a monthly report to all committees and, depending on the agenda, there are some meetings at the council level that she attends. Supporting the council, there are Strategic Policy Committees (SPCs) that combine nominees with sectoral interests and public representatives. They come together to look at areas of policy. The county librarian serves the SPC. She occasionally attends municipal district meetings together with the local librarian as a support to them and to offer a broader political context to the work that the community librarians are doing in the district.

The librarian is very supportive of local achievements, strengthening national developments and plans for national progress.

## Visibility through internal and external co-operation and collaboration

Internally, for management, Fionnuala ensures that she co-operates fully with the Human Resources, Finance and Information Technology (IT) departments in the council. For service development, local authority departments that are particularly good partners include the Environment, Community, Economic Development and Arts Departments.

Fionnuala is a member of the Library Development (LD) within the Local Government Management Agency, a new organisation in Ireland that replaced the former Library Council/An Chomhairle Leabharlanna. The LD has a national remit; it is responsible for rolling out a 5-year public library development plan.

The Library Association of Ireland supports her in her role, and she previously held several senior positions and has been active throughout her career. She is a board member of Age and Opportunity, a national organisation in Ireland promoting positive ageing. She does this in her personal capacity, but the council supports her work there.

## Strategic areas of public library service provision

Information, learning, heritage and culture are the four areas that are core to the library service in Wexford. She would consider her role reasonably strong in the area of culture and very strong in the areas of learning and information.

In the area of heritage, there are many facilities in Wexford (e.g. facilities with a tourist heritage remit). The library is involved directly and indirectly in activities related to heritage. However, she feels that the role of the library in the area of heritage is probably the least visible because of the nature of organisational structures serving heritage in the council.

**Table 14** **Self-reported visibility rating of librarian at time of appointment versus today**

| Self-reported visibility rating at time of appointment: where 0 = invisible and 10 = highly visible | | | | | | | | | | |
| --- | --- | --- | --- | --- | --- | --- | --- | --- | --- | --- |
| With key stakeholders/librarians — 0 | **1** | 2 | 3 | 4 | 5 | 6 | 7 | 8 | 9 | 10 |
| With staff/users of the service — 0 | **1** | 2 | 3 | 4 | 5 | 6 | 7 | 8 | 9 | 10 |
| **Self-reported visibility today (16 years after appointment): where 0 = invisible and 10 = highly visible** | | | | | | | | | | |
| With key stakeholders — 0 | 1 | 2 | 3 | **4** | 5 | 6 | 7 | 8 | 9 | 10 |
| With key staff/librarians — 0 | 1 | 2 | 3 | 4 | 5 | 6 | 7 | **8** | 9 | 10 |

## Visibility to key stakeholders and librarians

Because there has been a very recent change of Chief Executive and change of Director of Services, Fionnuala finds it difficult to rate her visibility to key stakeholders at present. There has also been structural change in the council with the creation of the sub-county municipal districts. At the beginning of 2014, she would have rated an 8 or a 9 with key stakeholders, but right now she says a 3 or a 4. She feels that there is much work to be done with recently appointed politicians and with colleagues who are new to the positions in the organisation. She feels she rates an 8 in terms of her peer group – other librarians and managers in the service (Table 14).

Regarding the media and general public, she considers it more important that they know and liaise with local librarians. She attends events and launches in support of local librarians, who are the liaisons to the public. She occasionally plays a more participatory role if there was a strategic purpose, which might occur once or twice a year. Likewise, politicians, who are responsible for policy and service support, need to get elected. If there is a 'glory moment', then it should be theirs – she does not need to get elected, but clearly councillors and parliamentarians do.

## Visibility at time of appointment

Fionnuala started in the job 16 years ago in November 1996 and felt her move, which involved a demotion, from the capital city of the country, Dublin, to Wexford may have been a topic of conversation before she started. From a professional point of view, Fionnuala rates her visibility score at the time of her appointment low, scoring a 1 out of 10 for users and stakeholders (Table 14).

## Building up a public library service countywide

In 1998, just over 1 year after she started her job, Fionnuala had a stroke of luck. There was a bicentenary commemoration of a revolutionary period of history, a rebellion of 1798. At the time the library services in the county were under-developed. She decided to develop a three-strand programme in which the library could contribute to the bicentenary commemorations. The three strands were heritage, community and finally the library held a once-off celebration of French culture. The latter was a peculiarity of the time because the Tour de France – a major cycling event – happened to be passing through the community of Wexford that year.

## Heritage

Heritage was a strong starting point to build upon. Wexford Studies was already developed because it was the only service that could be built up with minimal funding. Because of its strong foundation, local studies in Wexford formed the platform for library development going forward. It was the libraries' biggest strength at the time. Fionnuala saw this as an opportunity and developed and delivered a programme around it. Following from the 1998 commemoration, opportunities were identified to digitize local resources. Because the key stakeholders in the community were interested in heritage, Fionnuala strengthened the heritage sector of the library service, responding directly to community needs. Heritage was expanded into the education sector and curricula.

## Infrastructure

Community building could only advance with good infrastructure. There were no computers in any of the libraries in 1996; therefore, a technical project began. Automation became a priority for Fionnuala. Library staff had been 'longing for automation', and this project was an opportunity to up-skill. Public Internet access services were introduced while a library management system was being put in place. There was a national movement at the time that allowed for the creation of additional posts and promotional opportunities. This gave staff a considerable boost and strengthened their motivation. Services to primary schools and improvements in literacy were key areas that were developed. From poor facilities and poor base, after investment, more extensive services were becoming visible.

## What value as a librarian do you bring to the organisation?

As a manager, Fionnuala says 'I try to bring an information focus to everything I manage'. For example, she looks at the information side of every agenda item that goes to the Executive Team in the organisation. She likes to know how social media is being used in the organisation. She encourages e-publishing. The library is involved in formal publications that the council produce. The library has good visibility within the organisation on this front. She is hoping that the library will influence the communications function in the organisation and within that, the website, which is in need of re-design, and social media. The website is currently run by the IT department that reports to the finance officer.

## Impact of library service on the community in Wexford

Fionnuala says that, 'The library is the public face of the council. The council recognises that the library does a lot of work in the area of community development. The Housing and Economic Development Departments within the council recognise the library as a "front of house" service to local communities. They can use the library as a channel to deliver or advertise particular types of council services'. The librarian feels that the library service is an element in the council in which relatively little money is spent and where the local authority has achieved a positive reputation.

The library is 'trotted out' as an example to the public of good value when things such as new taxes are being introduced. For example, in 2013 a domestic property tax was re-introduced. Public libraries have been seen as a 'good news story' for local authorities and an example of a good return on investment for the public.

## Measuring impact of the library service

A 5-year library development plan is required by legislation, adopted by the council. This includes assessment and measurement elements. It breaks down into annual business plans and reports. Therefore, Fionnuala is responsible for a significant amount of formal management reports that are submitted to the council. Each District Committee receives a monthly events programme in advance. In addition, annual and monthly reports for those areas are sent to each of the four districts. A bi-monthly report is submitted to the council, and a contribution is provided for the chief executive's report to the council. Thematic policy reports are sent to the council via the SPC.

A monthly budgetary report is forwarded to the Director of Services. The librarian has one-to-one meetings with the director.

There are five national service indicators that the library has to respond to each year. The central government produces a comparative table that is based on the five service indicators. Under the new public library development plan (Department of the Environment, 2013), international standards and benchmarking are being introduced.

Quantitative statistics are compiled for internal management purposes such as borrowers, items loaned, attendance at events and feedback from the public at events. A public electronic survey is performed each year on e-literacy resources. Depending on service development needs, a particular theme would be looked at in detail over a couple of months. Each of the libraries produces an annual report that is based on the strategic objectives of the 5-year development plan with targets and goals for the coming year.

## Top tips for public librarians to increase visibility and impact

Fionnuala's tips are to

1. Look at your core responsibility and apply this to the environment in which you operate.
2. Identify core areas where you are most likely to achieve *quick wins* and succeed. Prioritise them.

3. In terms of people, there are the ones who are perceived to be in charge and there are people who are *actually* in charge. It is essential to identify *the achievers* and work with them – but only so far as it applies to your own role.
4. Choose what you are going to volunteer for very carefully. Although you want to be recognised as someone who is committed and responsible, you need to volunteer for services that align with your own service and your own information agenda. Volunteering should be strategic. The contribution that you make should not be predominantly administrative; it should be centred on development.

## What is your general opinion of the use of volunteers in public libraries?

'Choose people with care. The most successful volunteers in Wexford are those with a good level of education and with a commitment to a particular project where they have expertise. The project needs to be finite'.

## What do you see changing in the public library as a space and function in 5 years?

'A good public library facility will be sufficiently spacious that it operates as a community space. It gives people who may share an interest the opportunity to come together as well as allowing people to use the space at an individual level. In Irish communities, there is still a requirement to give people quiet study space and community gathering spaces. It could be to celebrate something locally or to engage in an on-going activity. Public libraries are being used as a "congregating space for celebration". Community education is the biggest growth area'.

'The area of adult continuing education and group learning is particularly successful in Wexford. The power that the library has for people is in part that they are surrounded by information resources, rather than meeting in another community space (e.g. a local hotel). The power that the library has is the librarian – a qualified information expert who can assist with the discussions the groups may be having in the library'.

Some upcoming projects involve e-learning for groups. In late 2014, the library was involved with a MOOC (Massive Open Online Course) project with Trinity College Dublin. This is potentially a huge growth area for public libraries – having groups of people supporting each other through online learning. Fionnuala says, 'The element of "browsing and borrowing" will continue despite the growth in electronic information resources. It will be interesting to see what happens to published materials as they are already much less accessible than they used to be'.

## The importance of online visibility for public libraries

Fionnuala says, 'Online visibility is increasingly important as the public become better educated. In Wexford Libraries, there is a focus on digitisation of local information. A lot of existing material has been digitised and the library has created e-resources. The older population is very interested in local studies; however, they also have the least digital literacy skills. Newly elected councillors who have joined the council are more e-literate than their predecessors. There is a balancing act in terms of making the library visible and accessible in an online environment to those in the community who are e-literate and those who struggle with technology. In local communities, the power of the individual is still very strong. People are still more likely to ask each other for information. The library has a critical role in the education of people in using e-resources. On the one hand, you are trying to make people independent from an information point of view; on the other hand, you are trying to encourage them to come together in groups as social animals to use e- and print resources'.

## Have you faced any challenging scenarios and how have you dealt with them?

Fionnuala shares two different scenarios: one in which she was successful and one in which she was not so successful. First, there was a partnership initiative between the trade union and management to roll out library services within the council. As part of this, she set up a staff library in the council. A grant was obtained to develop the staff library during the Celtic Tiger years (2000–2004) in Ireland. The aim was to assist staff with poor literacy skills or those who lacked a mentor. Two members of staff were working on the library and an extensive needs assessment was performed. One member of staff was assigned full time for 1 year before the library opened. It was a 1-year contract post, renewed. This was an unheard-of resource because projects are usually planned within existing resources and staff are acquired one or only a few days more before a library is due to open. As the service developed, senior management was trained in information skills and e-learning was a big component of the staff library. Three years later, central government scrutinised staff numbers organisation-wide, and the recurring post stopped. The post was lost and with it the service. The service turned from a proactive into a more passive reactive service.

Since then, Fionnuala has tried to reinstate the post by handing a business case for the position to every new director and chief executive, but she has been unsuccessful to date. The timing never seems to be right for this. She says that she has a perfect location in mind for the library at the back of the council's headquarters staff canteen.

Her second and more successful example was that of setting up a business information service (BIS). In public libraries in Ireland, there is one BIS in Dublin and one in Belfast (Northern Ireland). There is no business information centre delivered from rural public libraries. This has been a pet project since 2005, and Fionnuala had applied for every grant, scheme or application possible to get the project going. In 2012, a first, purpose-built, county library was opened in Wexford and people saw what a modern library could be. The director at the time was responsible for economic development; therefore, when the new library opened, Fionnuala saw it as an opportunity to push for the BIS. They commissioned a piece of research into a BIS in 2013. Resources in terms of business information were selected, but the staff expertise in the business information has to grow. The director agreed to pay for licensed business databases and some promotional material out of his budget and his support is continuing. To date, this initiative is on target and successful.

Her tip for managing challenging scenarios is to 'never give up'. She says 'You might have to take a step back, call it something different, re-invent it, but if you really believe in something, then never give up'. Three libraries opened in 3 years in County Wexford and in 2007–2012, all of the libraries were all brought up to a good standard. The county library was the last to open. All of the planning and preliminary work bore fruit in a rush.

Her managerial tips include, 'start talking about a project 2 years before you need it and by the time you action it, it is understood, accepted, normalised and owned by the decision-makers'. It is their project – which she says "is fine" – as climate and politics count. Employment and enterprise are so important to councils now given the recession. Timing is critical. Anything that the library can do to aid those two strategic areas – employment and enterprise – helps the authority and local communities overall'.

### Advice to new professionals

1. 'Librarians can get bogged down in operational issues. Once you are competent, you have **got to network**. It is about judgement. Judging what meeting is worth going to, who are the key people to talk to, influence or impress and making sure that you do this.
2. It is absolutely essential that you deliver. Librarians should be ambitious, but realistic. It is always wise to have a contingency plan because things may go wrong. You are better off publicly saying 'I'm going to do A', but then delivering A++.
3. Once you network, deliver and operate strategically, networking can be refined. You will find that people will start coming to you'.

### What is your favourite thing about being a librarian?

*'Influencing change!'*

## Case study 10: principal librarian information, advice and digital services and overall manager for Northamptonshire central library, United Kingdom

| | |
|---|---|
| Name: | Carl Dorney |
| Organisation: | Northamptonshire County Council |

Northamptonshire has a population of 691,952. It is reported to be the fastest growing area in the United Kingdom and the population is set to increase to 774,832 by 2021. There are 36 static libraries and 2 mobile libraries in the library network.

Northamptonshire Libraries and Information Service (NLIS) is part of the Customers, Culture and Place Division within the Public Health and Wellbeing Directorate of the council. The overall budget for 2013/2014 was £4.5 million with an income target of £806,000.

## Vision of Northamptonshire county council

'Proud to make Northamptonshire a great place to live and work'.

*Source:* Northamptonshire County Council Plan 2012–2016. Accessed 02.11.2014.

## Mission of Northamptonshire central library

To provide service that makes you smile.

## Online visibility of library and librarian

Library website: http://www.northamptonshire.gov.uk/en/councilservices/
Leisure/libraries/visit-your-library/ListLibraries/Pages/
Northamptonshire-Central-Library.aspx

Facebook: https://www.facebook.com/northamptonshirecentrallibrary/info

Twitter: https://twitter.com/Library_Plus and
https://twitter.com/CarlDorney77

Pinterest: http://www.pinterest.com/libplus/

Linkedin: https://uk.linkedin.com/pub/carl-dorney/8a/358/923

Carl Dorney's role is quite diverse and covers a wide range of areas. He is the principal librarian for Information, Advice and Digital Services. His responsibilities are countywide. He is the lead on information provision for the whole county. In terms of the 'advice' part of his job description, he explains that this is his role in delivering the 'front face' of the county council. This relates to library walk-ins and assisting people with daily library transactions and things such as 'blue badge' applications. They have just completed training for staff on debt and money management. This means that all staff are able to handle low-level enquiries about debt because this is a key problem in the community at present.

### Visibility to key stakeholders

Carl says that he feels visible to the councillors who make up the cabinet; he has deliberately tried to make himself and the library service visible to them. The library has had a strategy on the table for the past 4 years to prevent closures. The library has reported heavily on the strategy to the cabinet as often as they can. The cabinet has a quarterly economic report and the work that the library has done with the business

**Table 15 Self-reported visibility rating of librarian at time of appointment versus today**

| Self-reported visibility rating at time of appointment: where 0 = invisible 10 = highly visible | | | | | | | | | | | |
|---|---|---|---|---|---|---|---|---|---|---|---|
| With key stakeholders | 0 | 1 | 2 | 3 | 4 | 5 | 6 | **7** | 8 | 9 | 10 |
| With staff/users of the service | 0 | 1 | 2 | 3 | **4** | 5 | 6 | 7 | 8 | 9 | 10 |
| **Self-reported visibility today (20 years after appointment): where 0 = invisible 10 = highly visible** | | | | | | | | | | | |
| With key stakeholders | 0 | 1 | 2 | 3 | 4 | 5 | 6 | 7 | **8** | 9 | 10 |
| With key staff/users of the service | 0 | 1 | 2 | 3 | 4 | 5 | 6 | **7** | 8 | 9 | 10 |

start-ups and job creation always feature in this report. Carl says you have to 'chip away all of the time, and sound like a scratched record'. He says that they always invite the portfolio holder and the cabinet members to all of the events that the library holds. The tactic is to help to keep the library in their minds at all times. The cabinet have a large remit and they are seeing different people all of the time so it is essential that the library keeps plugging its importance. The library sells the message that 'it is a solution to a problem or problems' to improve its visibility.

He rates the library as an 8 with stakeholders (Table 15). Winning the CILIP 'Library Saves Lives' award for 2014 was a huge achievement and helped to put his library on the map. However, he says there is 'always more to be done'. Other factors can also cause the library to disappear slightly. At the time of writing, the council is facing another massive spate of budget cuts that is happening right across the United Kingdom. This means the council have other budgetary concerns on their minds, but Carl is adamant that he will continue to plug away at 'pushing the library as a positive message' and continue to plan for what the library hopes to achieve.

He says 'The more we can show the impact of libraries, the safer they'll be'. If the council recognise this, then the library is more protected when cuts come. He explains that the chief executive is a real champion for libraries and he is fairly visible to him. He is a person who has always seen libraries at the heart of the council's strategy, which is a big help. The libraries deliver frontline services on behalf of the council so they are a good fit. The library has moved into a new directorate called 'Health and Well-Being', and Carl feels there is some work to be done with that directorate to improve visibility of the library services. This is a new playing field for the library and it is difficult to get grounding in it, because other than the 'holistic well-being' that libraries inherently give, they are not used to libraries being part of their world. Carl says he has to start from scratch with this directorate.

## Visibility with readers/users

With users, Carl says it is difficult to rate librarians visibility with users. Personally he started out his career as a library assistant working on Saturdays. He has worked there for 20 years. He has worked his way up to being a professional librarian. People who walk in have always called all staff 'librarians', and they do not differentiate between professional and para-professional staff. From the point of view of the specialist services that the library offers such as the business services, the librarians are more visible in this scenario because business people see librarians as specialists. This makes librarians more visible to them and they trust librarians. They are happy to take what a librarian might say or recommend as a good source of information. There is still wide visibility for professional librarians in the eyes of the public. The difficulty is that everyone that uses the library tends to use it for a specific purpose and in their minds, that's what it does. The librarians are doing lots of different things for many different audiences. However, if you ask someone what their library does, they will usually just tell you about one specific thing that affects them and their position. This makes it difficult to make everything that the librarian or library is doing visible to everyone.

Carl rates the librarians in the service as a 7 overall on the visibility score with the public (Table 15).

When he first started, he was on the frontline and his visibility did not 'enter his circle of concern'. Twenty years ago, the public libraries were different and offered a traditional service. It has changed radically since then. Nobody was too concerned about the libraries back then, unless they were being threatened with closures. They were nice, quiet places where you could sit and read a book or borrow one. The professional services were much less visible then. Everyone that came into the library assumed they were talking to a librarian. A lot of what the librarian did 20 years ago was not front-facing. The only exception was enquiry work on the desk. The librarians were mainly occupied with stock room work and backroom office work and of course none of that is seen by the public. Unless a librarian is front-facing, the public do not see the work that the librarian does.

## What has been your most successful method of increasing visibility?

Carl's experience comes from the Enterprise Hub project for which he won a CILIP award in 2014. He says it is all about 'making yourself a player' and gaining people's confidence in you. When the library started the Hub project 2.5 years ago, the library was not offering any business services at all. The British Library was just starting to work on their Enterprise Hub project, but Carl's library was 'too small-fry' to be included in that project. However, they knew that there was a gap in the market in their area; therefore, it was a case of 'we'll find the partners in the area, we'll talk to the relevant people and we will prove that libraries are the best place to deliver this and that **we absolutely can deliver this**'. This echos Fionnuala's sentiment to aim for an 'A++' type service and to deliver on promises made.

It is all about convincing stakeholders, be they internal or external, and gaining their confidence and trust. Very often it is the partners that help with this part of the project. Partners can see where libraries can do things that *they* cannot. For example, the library can offer 36 different local contact points for enterprise partnership that the partners could not possibly deliver themselves because they are all based in one small office. The partners immediately saw the potential of the library. Training was delivered by professional information advisers so that librarians had an opportunity to learn a subject that they could then go on to deliver. Everything gets reported back – how many businesses have started up, how many people the library has seen in relation to the project, how many job-seekers attended the jobs' club, etc. This is combined with anecdotal evidence (e.g. their stories are collected and their journeys are followed). All of this can be time-consuming, but Carl says 'it is absolute gold dust, because without this, how do you prove your worth?' They have built up the evidence of the impact that they are having with this project, which makes it much easier to get buy-in going forward from stakeholders.

Nobody knew at the beginning of the project whether it would take off or not, and it has been much more successful than was anticipated. It is a good example of librarians being willing to take risks and running with projects. It has given the librarians confidence to think about branching out into other or new areas such as intellectual property. Three staff have been trained in this skill, and they are hoping to launch a patent library in 2015. Therefore, the project has led to new things. People may not have taken them seriously at the beginning, but now the library has a proven track record. The award is a testament to this. Carl says he has to continue to shout about it though.

## What value do you think you've brought to the organisation as a librarian?

'This is a tricky question'. Carl explains that his first professional role was 13 years ago. When he trained to become a qualified librarian, the training he received at Loughborough University was traditional and based on a different information world than that which exists today. He says a lot of what he learned on the course were things he was already aware of having worked a long time in libraries. He picked up a lot of these skills through practice. What he does today, involves much more people management, working with partners and negotiation – these skills are ones that librarians traditionally didn't have much opportunity to gain or to train in. Previously librarians were doing the same role for a number of years and didn't have much opportunity to evolve or learn new skills.

The skills that Carl brings as a librarian are experience and transferable skills. Personally he says that he has capitalized on partnership working and that has really aided the organisation. The library is at extremely low capacity so that nothing can be delivered as a solo operation. Interestingly, none of the roles of either library staff or librarians in the service are called 'librarians'. Many are called 'programme co-ordinators'. Carl manages 2.6 FTEs (full-time equivalents) who are programme co-ordinators on his team. All three of them are professional librarians. They all work interchangeably on the business, web services, communication and information side of the library. They are using traditional information skills and the roles that they are in warrant this. Their job titles as programme managers are so-called because that is what their primary role is – to co-ordinate various programmes. There are other roles in the service such as a programme co-ordinator for bequests and giving, who works on income streams for the long-term sustainability of the library. The co-ordinator's background is in charity work, she is not a trained librarian. However, Carl explains that these are the correct skills for that particular job.

## Impact of library service on the organisation

Carl's team recently held an event on economic well-being in the library. There were several speakers, including a representative from the British Library. The chief executive of the council was there and re-iterated that the library service was absolutely essential for him in delivering his council strategy. Hardly any of the other services have public-facing staff anymore because the council has had to pare down staffing. The council relies on the library service to deliver the 'front door' to the county council. There is nowhere else that people can come in and ask for help. The council has a call centre and a website, but not everyone in the community is comfortable with or able to use these options. The library has a role in helping these people in the community to become digitally fluent and confident and to convert them to people that are comfortable and happy to use the Web. The next time they come in they may be able to go online and access council services themselves. This has to do with budgets; that is, as the budget decreases, new ways of delivering services are being looked at.

For the past 5–6 years, the library has been central to the changes that the council has brought in. Carl says he is fortunate that the CEO is on board. He has spoken to colleagues in other parts of the United Kingdom who are trying to introduce similar Enterprise Hub projects, but they find that they are met by partners who will not take them seriously or councillors who just do not want to know. They cannot get backing from the council offices or their local CEO. Carl says that much depends on the personalities involved and timing. Campaigns are worth doing, but if there is no buy-in from the senior level, there is not much hope of success.

## Measuring impact of the library service

The library has a corporate scorecard with key parts indicating deliverables based on the council's strategy. This is reported upon each quarter. The library is also included on the economic quarterly report that goes to the cabinet because of the work they are doing for local businesses and job-seekers. Carl explains that very little of what is reported is what one would associate with traditional library roles. They have high income targets that are monitored. The library also reports on issues, visits and traditional statistics.

Every year the library applies for the Customer Service Excellence Standard, which is an independent standard. The library has achieved this standard for 18 years running. One of the items that they are only partially compliant on is benchmarking. There are no library standards for benchmarking for public libraries in England. He remembers this being muted some years ago, but it dropped off of the agenda. This makes it very difficult for Carl to compare his service with other authorities in England. However, it is difficult because every authority might have a different focus. His authority is focusing on economic impact; another might be focusing on well-being. This makes benchmarking difficult.

## What is your general opinion of the use of volunteers in public libraries?

This features heavily in the library strategy. They have always had volunteers in the public libraries, but it was mainly to deliver the 'home library service'. Books were taken out to people who were housebound. Other than that, volunteers were not really used very much. However, Carl says that they realised they would have to make better use of volunteers if they were to deliver upon the range of services that they needed to. They decided to focus their volunteer structure on 'added value'. They had 33 volunteer roles in 2014. There are 800 volunteers in the database, and they hope to double this to 1600. The volunteers add value to the library as a service. For example, some do 'meet and greet' for people who visit the library. However, they do not do any activity that would be a role of library staff. They might run things such as 'rhyme time', and there are young volunteers who help out with children's activities and events. There are volunteers who do gardening. There is a 'Friends of the Library' made up of volunteers who help out with fundraising for the library. Carl feels that they have become more a part of the team now than they have been in the past. They are in the staff canteen and engage with staff. At the beginning, library staff felt threatened, but now they are happier with the situation because they realise that they cannot do the added extras that the library offers without the help of the volunteers. The policy has been that there would be at least one paid member of staff in each of the libraries at all times. The volunteers are there to assist, but they do not replace the jobs of librarians.

All of the libraries have self-service. This was imperative because of the changes coming from the council. Carl knew that if library staff were stuck behind a desk doing issues and returns and stamping books, then they could not deliver on the other services the council had in mind for libraries to roll out. It was an 'invest to save' initiative to put in the self-service kiosks.

Part of the customer advisor role is to coach and mentor volunteers. They are involved in the recruitment process, training and making sure that the volunteers have a good experience. The key to retaining volunteers is to offer them a good and valuable experience.

## Where do you see the public library in 5 years?

Carl and the library services manager attended the CILIP Annual General Meeting (AGM) in 2014. William Sieghart, who is doing the library service review in the United Kingdom, was at the AGM. He found that the picture is grim for public libraries in the United Kingdom. Some public libraries have been given over to communities to run; there are so many cuts that some are being severely run down. Carl feels that much of the network is gone and it will be extremely difficult to turn this around. The review may be a case of too little too late. William would like to see a model of best practice that is based on work that Carl's library and others such as Suffolk are doing. He would like to see this being rolled out countrywide.

## Online visibility for public libraries

Carl sees this as absolutely essential. He admits that this is not something that he was very good at until a couple of years ago. The team that he manages has revolutionised their social media presence, which was non-existent before. This has been built up, and they have one library Twitter account, but they made the decision that each library would have its own Facebook page. Each of the communities is local with local needs that vary. They have control of their own pages and events that are going on locally. They have received hundreds and thousands of 'likes', some have received many, others have not. It is slowly taking off. The library has never had a marketing budget; therefore, social media has really helped to promote events and activities. It is also a great way to crowd source and obtain volunteers. It has been very important.

The library has put a chunk of its budget into online resources; therefore, it is essential that the resources are used and promoted online. The library website is a small part of the county council's website, which has meant that Facebook has become even more important for increasing visibility. The council's website is restrictive regarding look and feel, and the library is not permitted to have its own website. The council has a corporate look and feel. The library has gotten around this dilemma by having a Facebook page and making it look vibrant and inviting. They can put lots of images up using Pinterest and Facebook, whereas they cannot put them up on the library's webpage. They can put links up on the library webpages, but they do most of this through Facebook.

## Challenging scenarios

Carl says that the council recently announced that they have to find an additional £41 million in savings in 2014, which is a huge amount of money. They are looking at everything. He thinks back to 2010 when they had a threat of eight library closures. Rather than going with the closures, they did some consultation and came up with a strategy to save the money that was needed over a 4-year period without closing any libraries. The strategy meant working in a different way.

They had to restructure and in 2013, and £300,000 was cut from the staffing budget. They changed the role of the library assistants who were already doing more and more of the 'front-facing' council work anyway. They deleted the role of library assistant and replaced it with one of 'customer advisor'. Carl says this reflects the work that they are doing better and it is at two grades higher than that of library assistant. It has become more about the customer. They are no longer 'an assistant to a library', which was about a building and about books; they are now an 'advisor to customers'. That was a key change for them as a library and as an organisation. This was a key strategy for them, which they had to deliver on. They are about half way through the strategy, and Carl says that they are on course. Although, it has been very challenging, it has meant that the closure of eight libraries was kept off of the table.

In the past, libraries have always come in on or under budget. Any excess gets swallowed up by another department. Thus, regardless of whether you are achieving your targets or making savings, if the council comes back looking for further cuts, then it can be extremely difficult to make a case to oppose this.

### Advice to new professionals to increase visibility and impact

'Traditionally, people going into librarianship were not very good at selling things. This is something we have learned to our cost. It is about believing in what you've got to offer; a public or special library service is an amazing thing. It is an amazing resource, but nobody is going to shout about it but you. There is always word of mouth, but that will be people talking about the bits that they use; they will not be talking about or highlighting all of the services and things that are on offer. It is about getting out there. Public libraries never get TV coverage but try to get radio coverage at any opportunity and press coverage – it has a far wider coverage than anything else they have tried. Get more savvy about how you do market yourself; do not be afraid to do it'.

'You cannot do this from within the library. You've got to get out there and talk to people and form partnerships. Talk to stakeholders, talk to people who are not using the library. They are important too'. As Bill Gates, founder of Microsoft said, 'Your most unhappy customers are your greatest source of learning'.

### What is your favourite thing about being a librarian?

'I think you go into public libraries for one of two reasons: One you either love books or two you love information and helping people. It has always been the information and people side that has driven me. I have always loved learning and the information side of it, but actually it is about helping those people and knowing that you've made a difference to their lives. We get people coming into libraries asking all sorts of questions, from all sorts of backgrounds. In some cases you know that you are the only person who is going to speak to that person that day. It is the people element and the tendency to want to help people that I enjoy'.

## Case study 11: librarian working at Dublin city public libraries, Ireland

| Name: | Sheila Kelly |
|---|---|
| Organisation: | Dublin City Council |

The Dublin City Council serves a population of 527,612 and is a gateway to the greater Dublin area with a population of 1.273,069 (Census, 2011). Dublin is the capital city of Ireland and is located in the east of the country. The council employs approximately 5500 staff, providing a range of services primarily for the residents of Dublin City.

## Mission of the organisation

The Dublin City Council's Corporate Plan 2010–2014 states their mission:

> To drive Dublin forward as a creative and sustainable city and be a place where family, community and the economy can prosper together.
>
> *Source:* Dublin City Council. (2009). Dublin City Council 2010–2014 corporate plan. Dublin: Dublin City Council.

## Mission of Dublin city public libraries

> We will maximise opportunity for all – individuals and communities – through guided access to ideas, learning, literature, information and heritage resources supported by cultural programming.
>
> *Source:* Dublin City Council Public Libraries development plan 2012–2016.

## Online visibility of the library and librarian

| | |
|---|---|
| Library website: | www.dublincitypubliclibraries.ie |
| Library blog: | www.dublincitylibraries.com |
| Facebook: | https://www.facebook.com/DublinCityPublicLibraries |
| YouTube: | https://www.youtube.com/user/dubcilib |
| Flickr: | www.flickr.com/photos/dublincitypubliclibraries |
| Twitter: | https://twitter.com/dubcilib |
| Netvibes: | http://www.netvibes.com/dublincitypubliclibraries#Home |
| Vimeo: | http://vimeo.com/dubcilib/videos |
| Pinterest: | http://www.pinterest.com/dcclibraries |
| Slideshare: | http://www.slideshare.net/dubcilib/presentations |
| Delicious: | http://delicious.com/DublinCityPublicLibraries |

Dublin City Council library services are the largest public library service in Ireland and attract over 3 million visitors per year. There are 24 library service points in Dublin City Council, including branch libraries, a central library, a mobile library service to homes, schools and other institutions in the city. There is a prison library service to eight of the prisons in Dublin and specialist services include a business library, a learning resource centre, local studies and archives, a music library and a corporate staff library service. The library staff of the council is 289.7 (FTEs) on the basis of figures from 2011 (Source: Dublin City Council Workforce Plan 2010-2014. Dublin: Dublin City Council, May 2011. http://www.environ.ie/en/LocalGovernment/ PublicationsDocuments/FileDownLoad,27321,en.pdf).

Two librarians are interviewed separately who work as part of the library management team of Dublin City Council. They are Sheila Kelly and Anne-Marie Kelly. Sheila is interviewed first.

Sheila Kelly is one of the nine divisional librarians employed by the council. The divisional librarians make up part of the management team of the library services. Her remit is Continuing Professional Development, Equality and Diversity and the library prison service. Sheila started work in 1979 as a library assistant and gained a professional qualification and worked her way up to the management team of the library. She says simply, 'It's been my life, really'.

In terms of visibility, she rates herself as 5 with key stakeholders in the organisation (Table 16). These are the councillors. Although she is part of the management team, she does not have the job of reporting directly to councillors.

She does not feel that she is personally visible to users of the public library service at present, although she feels very connected to them via the branch libraries. She is no longer working in a front-facing job and does not work in a branch library. However, she feels that the library as a service is highly visible to users. Previously in her career, she managed a local branch library at Pearse Street, and she feels that she would have rated 10 as the local librarian at that time in her career. For example, she is now based at the Pearse Street Library, and anytime she walks out of the building she runs into someone she knows or who recognises her from her time as branch librarian.

### Value as a librarian to the organisation

Personally and professionally, Sheila claims that 'I am always on the side of the underdog'. Although she is not a big sports fan, she would always support the underdog

### Table 16 Self-reported visibility rating of librarian at time of appointment versus today

| Self-reported visibility rating at time of appointment: where 0 = invisible and 10 = highly visible | | | | | | | | | | |
|---|---|---|---|---|---|---|---|---|---|---|
| With key stakeholders | 0 | **1** | 2 | 3 | 4 | 5 | 6 | 7 | 8 | 9 | 10 |
| With staff/users of the service | 0 | 1 | 2 | 3 | 4 | 5 | 6 | 7 | 8 | 9 | **10** |
| Self-reported visibility today (35 years after appointment): where 0 = invisible and 10 = highly visible | | | | | | | | | | |
| With key stakeholders | 0 | 1 | 2 | 3 | 4 | **5** | 6 | 7 | 8 | 9 | 10 |
| With key staff/users of the service | 0 | 1 | 2 | **3** | 4 | 5 | 6 | 7 | **8** | 9 | 10 |

in a game. She would be up for the losing team. She feels this is why she chose the career of librarianship. She says, it wasn't about the books, although she adores books, it was really about equality. She says, 'the desire to progress equality is a driving force in my life'. She saw the value of the library and the role that it could play in people's lives from early on in her career.

## The impact of the library service on the community in Dublin city

There is economic and social impact. This is something that needs to be measured and reported upon. Sheila uses the nine grounds of the Irish Equality Act of 1998 to try to determine part of the social impact that the public library service has on the community it serves. The nine grounds include discrimination on the grounds of gender, civil status, family status, age, race, religion, disability, sexual orientation or membership of the Traveller community. Sheila explains that the library also includes grounds of educational disadvantage and cultural disadvantage. They take a lifecycle approach and look at the impact of the public library service on people at different stages of their life – from toddlers to the elderly. In the last few years, the impact of the library service on unemployed people has become more important because of the high unemployment rate in the country.

## Proving value

What drew Sheila's attention to measuring the impact of public libraries on people in this way was when she made a submission for an $O_2$-sponsored Ability Award in 2010. At that time, she was explaining that the libraries were 'great' and that they were doing a great job at inclusivity, but the response that she got was, 'Ok, well prove it!'. This challenge led Sheila to begin to realise how important hard evidence is to prove the value of libraries and the work that librarians do. She started to collate reports of impact several years ago. She asks each of the branch libraries to collect impact stories or testimonials from library users as well as quantitative evidence of impact. She collates customer service reports, including compliments or any negative feedback that they receive.

## Successful ways of increasing visibility: through community outreach

Ways to increase visibility that were successful for Sheila include collaboration. In particular, she explained that local partnerships within communities have helped to make the library very visible to people living in the local area. She gives the example of urban towns in Dublin such as Ballymun and Ballyfermot, where the branch libraries play a big part in the social element of the people living in those areas. In both of those towns, poverty and social exclusion are high. Partnerships built up with external groups in these localities have helped to raise the visibility of the library there. Sheila says that the library management team is encouraging the librarians to go out into the community more and to be more proactive about engaging with people in the community. They are compiling community reports; however, she feels that sometimes librarians get 'trapped inside' and it is important to play an active role in outreach activities. There is more emphasis today in having librarians out in the community, visiting local centres and schools and talking to people. Public libraries have a huge community role to play.

## Getting to know people in different communities

Different communities develop different relationships with their local librarian. Sheila has worked in the Ballyfermot and Pearse Street branches of Dublin City libraries. Both communities adopted different needs. She has worked in areas of advantage and disadvantage and says that she has a *really strong connection with the city'*. She says that to this day she can walk down the main street of Dublin City, O'Connell Street, and meet someone who might recognise her from years ago from when she was working in one of the city's public library branches. She explains that when you work in a public library, you can get to know people, particularly people who use the public library on a daily basis.

When she started out in 1979 as a library assistant, she felt very visible and very connected, particularly with the stock, which she says she 'loves'. She still loves to shelve books. She had a good familiarity with borrowers at that time. She says she would have scored a 10 on the visibility scale with borrowers when she first started. Library assistants do not have many opportunities to be visible to key stakeholders; therefore, she did not feel very visible to them when she first started out. This has changed now since she has moved into management.

## Most successful way of increasing visibility: building the evidence

One way that Sheila increased her visibility was by entering the library for an award. In 2010 she wrote two submissions for the Ability Awards, which were set up by Caroline Casey, an Irish social entrepreneur. Writing the submissions forced her to demonstrate evidence of the value of the library. She was successful in both submissions. The awards were for the category of learning, development and progression. She says that the awards meant a lot to her. Even applying for the award in the first place was a good learning experience. She says that it taught her the 'best lesson of my life: we need to look at *impact*'. Now she says if a councillor rings up and asks, 'What is the library doing for older people?' she is ready with an impact story and evidence to show the impact that the library is having for older people in society. These impact stories are collected quarterly and reported in an annual report. The libraries have a system in place now for this, and the branch libraries acknowledge the need to measure impact.

They have collected an enormous amount of anecdotal evidence about the quality of the service that is based on people that use the service and appreciate it. They have very loyal customers. Some of the impacts that are documented are very indicative of the value that the library makes to society. The fact that people have taken the time to write their views down is important.

## Impact of the library service on the organisation

'The library is the public face of the council. Increasingly, councillors have come to appreciate that fact'. It is a service that has loyal, appreciative customers and councillors will see the advantage in that. It is a good news story for councillors. It is a win–win situation. They were looking at the budget for 2015, and they have done well compared with other departments in the council. The recession has seen an increase of 30% in usage of public libraries throughout Ireland (Local Government Management Agency, 2012). Globally, there is a huge increase in the use of public libraries in recessionary times (Rooney-Browne, 2009). Sheila does not attribute this solely to the fact that there is increased unemployment; she feels that there is more value placed on a free service. Furthermore, they have fought very hard to keep the service free to readers. Some local authorities charge a membership or joining fee, but Dublin City Council libraries have remained free. This can be an equality issue.

## Formal reporting of impact

There are quarterly reports and an annual report. The council has a 'Social Inclusion' office and a social inclusion officer to whom Sheila submits reports.

## Challenging scenarios

The ban on public sector recruitment has affected the service. It has meant that people in administrative positions have had to be moved out into the front line. The impact is that they have lost administrative support in the offices, but the frontline service has to be prioritised. The libraries are driven by customers. They have introduced radio-frequency identification to identify books, and it is planned to be in place in all of the branches. This frees up staff from more routine and mundane tasks. The advantage of this is that they have seen an increase in the quality of customer service provided by library staff. Self-service has been put in place in five branches, but some people are still a little slow to use it and prefer the human contact with library staff. She compares it to the way some people do not like to use the self-checkout systems in supermarkets such as Tescos.

Sheila says there are still some people including stakeholders who simply 'do not get libraries'. She is firmly convinced that if you use libraries as a child that you will use them for the rest of your life. She says, 'I can tell immediately people who have used public libraries as a child and those who have not. There is still some persuading to be done she feels with the "unconvinced"'. For example, it can be difficult in meetings with councillors at times when they argue that they desperately need more housing or that there is a big homelessness problem in the city. This is another reason that Sheila collates the impact stories because it helps make the value and impact of public libraries to people in society real to councillors. These stories help councillors understand that libraries are in fact contributing to a better quality of life for people and can have a positive influence on their lives. The aspect of building communities appeals to councillors.

## Top tips for public librarians to increase visibility and impact

Get out into the community – just get out and about – take cognisance of your own value. Understand that there is a business case for building up evidence of your value. Take showing impact and value seriously – understand that this is a serious part of your job as a librarian. It can be used as a safety buffer. It can also enhance your reputation. Community outreach is an important part of the job. Go out and meet people in the community. In Dublin City libraries, there is a city and community housebound service where books are brought to people in their homes who cannot come to the library. The most successful community partnerships are in Ballymun and Ballyfermot. Mother and toddler groups are particularly successful. Sheila likes to encourage mothers and fathers to bring their children to the public library from a young age.

## What is your general opinion of the use of volunteers in public libraries?

Sheila has no objection to the use of volunteers. She would not like to see a situation in which librarians were replaced by volunteers. There is a place for volunteers. In some areas of the country, there are community public libraries that are run by volunteers, and she feels that readers are not getting the full-quality customer service that they would be getting if professional librarians were involved. The corporate value and the experience that library staff members have and the value that they place on the service is not in equal measure with a library service led only by volunteers. Anyone can stand on the street and hand out books, but that is not a 'library experience' that communities deserve.

## Public library as a space in 5 years

Sheila says, it is important to have a vision for public libraries of the future. She thinks because of the changes in technology that it is possible that public libraries will *'lose customers to Kindles'*. She says that they have not properly sorted out their ebook offering in the libraries because it has been problematic. There will always be a need for a community to have a place to meet and socialize. There is a new city library in Parnell Square due to open in 2018, and the library management team is looking at that to try to determine what the needs of the city will be. Space and access and whatever technology evolves by 2018 will all have to be taken into account. Whatever products and services are available, they will have to be relevant to people and the space will have to be promoted. People will always need public spaces.

## Online visibility for public libraries

Sheila says, 'As a user myself, I would have used a lot of online library services myself. And I can see the value of it'. At the moment, there is a big value in archiving and digitization of collections and making them available online. In Dublin City, they have made photographic collections available online, including photographs of Dublin during James Joyce's time when he wrote *Dubliners* in 1914 and the city's pubs and streets at the beginning of the 20th century. People would not have previously had access to these collections. Content creation and accessibility of unique digitized content potentially has great local and national value.

The library service has made a big effort to engage with social media platforms and have a good profile on the Web. Sheila says that the blog has given library staff a chance to write and to bring out their creative side. That opportunity to be creative was not there before, and this is an interesting and important development. This has been particularly empowering for library staff working in some of the branches, who at times can feel isolated from the centre. Flickr, the blog and using social media tools have helped to connect library staff and help them all to have an online profile and to feel more connected and part of a team.

They have 'awful problems' with the IT department in the council, which is a common complaint in all types of libraries. They cannot access YouTube and so many other websites. IT focuses on security, and the library focuses on freedom of information, access to content and access for all – there is a clear clash of cultures there.

They would love to have their own website, but they are not allowed. The site is a space within the site, and this means that the content is condensed and not as prominent or as easy to access as it potentially could be. It is frustrating because the council has a highly skilled webmaster, but he is curtailed in his ability to expand the website and access content. Sheila says at times she finds it hard to reconcile this because the library has huge allegiance to the council, but this barrier remains. 'Their focus is security – ours is freedom of information – there is bound to be a clash!'

## Advice to new professionals

Develop an awareness of the value of the library service. Take feedback on board, good and bad, and take responsibility for acting upon it. Have a vision and have a passion for librarianship. Sheila says she was inspired by librarians when she first started as a library assistant, who imbued her with a passion for librarianship and a vision for the future. Her managers showed leadership, and this impressed upon her the value of the profession of librarianship from an early point in her career. Back then, they did not need reports; they had fought and fought for libraries from early on. She understood their fight and took it on board.

## What is your favourite thing about being a librarian?

'The public! The public part of it. For me it's the public and the books...'.

# Case study 12: librarian working at Dublin city public libraries, Ireland

| Name: | Anne-Marie Kelly |
|---|---|
| Organisation: | Dublin City Council |

   Anne-Marie Kelly is one of the nine divisional librarians used by Dublin City Council. The divisional librarians make up part of the management team of the library services. Her remit is in development and marketing section. She has been in this role for 2 years. Overall, she has worked in the council for some 26 years.

## Role in the organisation

Anne-Marie is responsible for a team of people who co-ordinate and promote library events. The team works to support the objectives of the business plan. She coordinates a team of people who are responsible for the promotion of library collections. The events are tailored to animate the collections. Her remit is to support the objectives of the business plan: the role of the library as a centre of culture is one element of this, preserving the record and memory of the city is another. Events are linked into reader development initiatives; therefore, she is always conscious that the underlying brief of the library is connected with the printed word, visual world and information. Her role is dual-fold. Anne-Marie with her team organises events and programmes on the one hand and promotes them on the other.

## Self-reported visibility

Anne-Marie says her visibility with key stakeholders rates as 5 out of 10 because she has only been in her current role 2 years. She hopes to see this improve with time.

**Table 17 Self-reported visibility rating of librarian at time of appointment versus today**

| Self-reported visibility rating at time of appointment to current role: where 0=invisible and 10=highly visible | | | | | | | | | | |
|---|---|---|---|---|---|---|---|---|---|---|
| With key stakeholders | 0 | 1 | 2 | 3 | 4 | **5** | 6 | 7 | **8** | 9 | 10 |
| With staff/ users of the service | 0 | 1 | 2 | 3 | 4 | **5** | 6 | 7 | **8** | 9 | 10 |
| Self-reported visibility today (2 years after appointment to current role): where 0=invisible 10=highly visible | | | | | | | | | | |
| With key stakeholders | 0 | 1 | 2 | 3 | 4 | **5** | 6 | 7 | **8** | 9 | 10 |
| With key staff/ users of the service | 0 | 1 | 2 | 3 | 4 | 5 | 6 | **7** | **8** | 9 | 10 |

She works as part of a larger team. Her managers link in with key stakeholders in the council. The managers would attend strategic committee council meetings (Table 17).

In Anne-Marie's case, she feels that all senior librarians who are divisional librarians know her. She presented at the assembly, which is a continuing professional development event for council library staff that meets each quarter. She regularly sends out emails to keep the management team and librarians aware of new programmes. She considers that her team is visible. She rates her visibility as 7 out of 10 (Table 17).

The visibility of the library as a service to the public is explained by Anne-Marie as having several strata – it is visible to those who use it. For people who do not use public libraries, Anne-Marie feels that they would have to be Internet savvy to identify where the library services are. She says that her team does as much as they can to promote the library via social media. They have a dedicated team of two people – a senior librarian and a librarian – to develop the website and Dublin City Public Libraries' web presence. The web unit and the development team are responsible for the city council's library website, and they have a role in promoting events through the site.

In terms of printed material, the library produces brochures of programmes that are delivered to all library locations, councillors area offices and to other organisations, but the public would have to come in to the main library to get a copy.

## When you first started, would the visibility score have been less?

Her role has developed over the last 2 years, but in terms of visibility, it remains the same as when she was first given the brief. There is recruitment embargo at present, and one person left her team last year and was not replaced. The work that this person did had to be taken on by her and the team, which inhibited the development of some plans. She was unable to launch into the marketing and promotion as much as she had hoped. However, now the team is sorted out, and she hopes to rectify the marketing end of her role.

## What has been the most successful way to increase visibility?

The effective use of email has helped, and giving presentations at assembly meetings has helped. The assembly meetings are a gathering of librarians for an afternoon once every quarter with a continuing professional development slant. They bring in invited speakers (e.g. a literacy expert and the divisional librarians make presentations on particular things in which they are involved). In 2013, Anne-Marie presented and took the opportunity to introduce herself and her role to the rest of the librarians in the organisation. She had not met some of the staff members in several years, and some new and younger staff had since joined who she had an opportunity to meet. She wanted to make all of the librarians aware of what events were in the pipeline and to get the statistics up to date. Not all librarians can make the events all of the time, but it is a good way to bring people together.

## What value do you bring to the organisation as a librarian?

Anne-Marie feels that she is very self-motivated and conscientious in her role and always has been. Because of her commitment to public service, she feels this helped her in succeeding in her current role.

## What impact has the library service on the organisation?

The library service is valued by council management because it is a front line service that provides venues for delivery of culture, information and arts programmes to local communities. Anne-Marie gives an example of the 'one-city one-book' award-winning event, which has been running since 2006. It won a local government award in 2009 in the category of Arts and Culture. It encourages people to read a designated book during the month of April each year that has a connection with the city. The author of the book is usually from Dublin or the subject of the book has a connection to the city – past chosen books include James Joyce *Dubliners*, Bram Stoker's *Dracula* and Jonathan Swift's *Gulliver's Travels*. It helps that Dublin has produced some of the best writers in English literature and that Dublin is one of the four of UNESCO's cities of literature in the world. The latter is because of a successful bid by Dublin City public libraries in 2010. The International IMPAC literary award is also administered by Dublin City libraries. The award is a prize for a single work of fiction and brings together libraries from 120 cities in 44 countries.

The Dublin Festival of History is another big event for the council that was launched in 2013. As Anne-Marie explains, there is a huge appetite for history from the public.

She and her team are responsible for organising events for Spring, Bealtaine, Summer and Autumn programmes in the libraries and reports that they have been well attended. Over 30,000 people attended events in 2013. On average, there were 35 people per audience in attendance, which is good considering venue size. Anne-Marie comments that attendance alone is not enough to measure the value of the event. She collects comments from attendees to build up a picture of the value that attendees gain from attending. In 2014, there was a focus on the mental health zeitgeist. This is a greater societal issue in Ireland in 2014, and Anne-Marie has organised taster sessions on what people can expect to gain from alternative therapies. For example, she says, some people may not have €100 to spend on a yoga programme, but they may attend a session in the public library free of charge to find out more about the benefits of yoga – how it can calm the spirit – because people use their local library to find out information about maintaining a positive mental health. Anne-Marie is exploring the longer lasting effects of the events she hosts; she does not want them to be a 'flash-in-the-pan' type of initiative. She would like people who attend events to gain something positive that may have a good influence on them for their lives.

## Do you have a formal way to measure impact?

Customer feedback forms are gathered in every branch and statistics are collated. At the end of every quarter, there is an analysis made of key performance indicators (KPIs). The KPIs she gathers are in relation to events. There is an annual report that is required by the city librarian from each branch librarian. The city librarian reports to the SPC at the council level so the report is a mandatory requirement. The library management team and library staff in 21 service points progress the goals detailed in the policy of the libraries own business plan 2012–2016, 'What is the stars?'

## Have you experienced any recent challenging scenarios and how did you react?

In 2013, one of Anne-Marie's team members left; although this was challenging, she feels that 'you just have to get on with things'. Attendance to events during that year increased by one third. 'If there is a challenge, you just have to work harder. It can be hard going for a while. The spinoff of this is that it causes you to evaluate the things you do more carefully'. As a person in a leadership role, Anne-Marie says, it is important to have time to think and reflect. This reflective time is key to learning how to be more effective and how to develop the library service. She says that she would like people to have a value-added experience and this requires time, thought and effort.

## Top tips for public librarians to increase their visibility and impact

In public libraries, it is important to attend meetings and to meet up with branch managers where possible and go to other networking events in the council and beyond. This is huge in terms of visibility. Advocating for library services at the council level is done by all library management teams when the opportunity presents itself.

Anne-Marie recently had a chance to advocate for the library with a manager of the recreation and amenity section of the council. She worked on a design brief for brochures for Spring, Summer and Autumn programmes, and the council manager was impressed with them to the degree that he enquired if she could also do similar brochures for the whole Culture Recreation and Amenity Department. The more visible your service is even in the production of brochures, the more attention you attract, and this can cause a spiral effect, which is good on the one hand, but you can end up getting even more work to do.

However, advocacy is a good way of increasing visibility. Advocacy is achieved through networking and through 'products' such as the brochures or tangible things by which you can demonstrate what you are doing in a practical and real way.

## What is your opinion of the use of volunteers in public libraries?

Anne-Marie says, she has no problem at all with volunteers working in public libraries. She worked in the United States where patrons were working in public libraries. There are many things that volunteers could do that add value; for example, withdrawing of stock, which can take up a lot of library staff time. Once there are guidelines in place, then it would be useful. Volunteers can have a lot to offer. Anne-Marie says, she is never threatened by extra people coming in as she thinks that (a) I'm going to learn something, (b) they are probably going to do something that we do not have time to do and (c) it frees up staff to do the things that they really need to get to. This is a positive experience for the public. It gives volunteers an opportunity to develop transferable skills. Anne-Marie feels that public librarians need to be generous toward volunteers.

Sometimes younger volunteers may need more direction, but it really depends on the person and their skill set and attitude. She took on volunteers in 2013 to assist with some events and says it was a positive experience.

It is not great if there are qualified librarians hanging around looking for work, but Anne-Marie would approach it by looking for an optimum team in place first before taking in any volunteers. She would not see any volunteer replacing the skill set of a librarian because it is 'just not feasible'.

## Where do you see the changes in 5 years in public libraries?

Anne-Marie sees public libraries being denuded of materials to the extent that most things will be digital. It will be similar to the scenarios in the film *Robot & Frank*. We will have these centres of culture frequented by members of the public looking for an experience. They will be coming to centres for an experience. People will participate more in book clubs and film clubs, and we will attend author talks to share experiences with others. That is how Anne-Marie envisages some of the trends in public libraries going. People will come to look at exhibitions, to obtain job-seeker skills – the kind of programmes that people need to get them from A to Z in life. These skills and experiences will be available in neutral civic spaces. It is something that is badly needed for every generation for every age group. She does not see libraries regressing; she sees them growing and evolving. She feels the value they bring to communities is ever important regardless of the age that we live in. Just because the book may no longer be a printed material does not mean that public libraries will subside; in fact, quite the opposite.

### How important do you think it is for the public library to be visible in an online environment?

'This is how it is going. Everybody I know is online, from every age group'. Anne-Marie recently saw via Twitter that an 80-year-old woman saw an event about knitting in one of the public libraries being advertised on Twitter and wanted to attend. She had been an avid knitter her whole life, and she had written an article that was published in a Sunday newspaper asking why people were complaining about knitting clubs. She had written how she attends a knitting club in her local public library every Thursday and she found it fantastic. She said that it keeps her going and she has arthritis in her fingers but the knitting helped her. This is how people are accessing information no matter what age they are. It is imperative for libraries to have high visibility on the Internet for the general public and through the use of social media, Twitter, Facebook, etc.

### Which is the most successful online method of increasing visibility?

Anne-Marie feels that the Twitter feed is currently the best way to promote events happening in the library and to quickly reach a wide audience. Particularly when people have not booked in or are at last minute, Twitter can be a fast way to contact people and get the message out there.

There is no app for the library website; in fact, most libraries do not have apps. She feels this is a growth area and libraries are going to have to start looking at developing apps. If people cannot get information on their phone, then they may not be too bothered about accessing information via a website that is not mobile friendly.

### What advice would you give to new entrants to the profession of librarianship on increasing their value, impact and visibility?

'To maximize impact it is essential to join committees. Be out there. Make sure that you are going to assembly meetings and networking. Entry-level librarians should

sign up for work that is not part of their normal routine. There are plenty of opportunities for work out there'. Anne-Marie suggests that librarians seeking employment
could perhaps contact public libraries with ideas that they may have for public library
events. This would convey their interest in the profession.

## What is your favourite thing about being a public librarian?

'It is just the connection with people. I think that you need to have a connection with
people more than you have a connection with books'. Anne-Marie says that she has
seen through the years people who are very intelligent, who are good communicators
who love books but perhaps do not have the spirit or connect with the public. Some
librarians, admittedly a few, fail to see that the public deserve the utmost in professional customer service. It is essential for every librarian to offer professional service –
from the small kid that comes in to the frail elderly person. It is important to deal with
the public in the right manner, such as speaking softly to an older person and trying
to excite a child into learning something new – all of these things are key. If you have
a way about you in which the public is at the heart of what you do and to be civic
minded about your job, then you will be a good librarian. She thinks anyone can learn
this people skill.

# Case study 13: information management and Kew librarian at Boroondara, Victoria, Australia

| Name: | Hugh Rundle |
|-------|-------------|
| Organisation: | Boroondara Council |

Boroondara is situated in the inner eastern suburbs of Melbourne, Victoria, Australia.
Boroondara Council serves a population of 170,553 (Census, 2011) and is responsible
for more than 150 services, from family and children's services, traffic regulation,
open space, youth facilities, waste management and community building to matters
concerning business development, planning for appropriate development and ensuring
accountability for the council's budget. The council employs approximately 783 FTE
staff. The area is culturally diverse and affluent, with income levels for individuals
and households higher than the metropolitan Melbourne average. Forty-five percent of
Boroondara households have an income in the top 25% for Victoria.

## Vision of Boroondara council

The City of Boroondara's vision is to have a vibrant and inclusive community
with an outstanding quality of life.

## Mission of Boroondara council

The council's publication 'City of Boroondara Annual Report 2013–14 (2014) states their mission:

> The City of Boroondara will provide services, facilities, support and advocacy to enable our community to further its sense of place and connection.

## Objective of the council for Boroondara libraries

> Provide innovative and proactive library services, which respond to the community's diverse and changing leisure, learning and information needs.
>
> *Source:* City of Boroondara Council Plan 2008–2013.

## Online visibility of the library and librarian

| | |
|---|---|
| Library website: | http://www.boroondara.vic.gov.au/libraries |
| Library blogs: | http://boroondarabookends.blogspot.com/; http://aboutthebooks.blogspot.com/; http://boroondaratellingtales.blogspot.com/; |
| Facebook: | http://www.facebook.com/pages/Hawthorn-Australia/City-of-Boroondara-Library-Service/7905992206 |
| Twitter: | http://twitter.com/BoroondaraLib |
| Tumblr: | http://boroondaralibraries.tumblr.com/ |
| Instagram: | http://instagram.com/boroondaralibraries |
| Enewsletters: | http://eepurl.com/cwK1; http://eepurl.com/dOlcs |
| Hugh's blog: | www.hughrundle.net/ |
| Hugh on Twitter: | https://twitter.com/hughrundle |

Boroondara library services are expanding with the opening of a new co-located library and community centre at Ashburton in November 2013. The library website is currently part of the council's website, but the 2013–2014 annual report includes a plan for a stand-alone website for the Boroondara library service. The service employs service 71.2 FTEs (2004) and operates five service points. A home library service is provided to residents who cannot physically visit the library because of age, frailty or disability. Services and facilities are provided at all branches for people with disabilities. At the time of this interview, Hugh had just finished up at Boroondara library, where he worked for 14 years. He talks to me about his time there. He is due to start a new job as systems and resources co-ordinator in another public library service, Brimbank, the following week (February 2015).

Hugh's substantive position in Boroondara was in a hybrid role. He was a manager of an individual branch library and he looked after IT systems across five branches. Most states in Australia have multiple libraries within a service. Hugh also looks after the information services team. He says that this team would have been called the 'reference' team 10 or 15 years ago. They rebranded as the information services team and started performing additional programs. He was in this position for 2.5 years. He started off as a library officer, and he was supported to perform his library qualification and had approximately 10 years of experience in different librarian roles.

In terms of visibility, Hugh rates himself as very visible, scoring 9 out of 10 with key stakeholders in the organisation. These are the councillors and decision-makers.

In his job, he spent the majority of his time in the 'backroom'. He did a front-desk shift approximately once a week. He rates 4 out of 10 with readers and users of the service because of his position, which did not deal directly with readers. All library staff members, with the exception of the manager, do a shift on the desk at least once a week; this helps increase the visibility of staff to patrons and informs library services by keeping in touch with readers. The librarians all do at least three shifts a week on the desk. This includes people in systems roles. He says, 'It's crazy to have people in systems roles who do not interact with people. Arguably, they should have more time with the public, because the systems role is becoming more and more important'.

When he first started, he feels he was not very visible and would have scored a 1 or 2 for key stakeholders and a 5 for library patrons (Table 18).

### Table 18  Self-reported visibility rating of librarian at time of appointment versus today

| Self-reported visibility rating at time of appointment: where 0 = invisible 10 = highly visible | | | | | | | | | | | |
|---|---|---|---|---|---|---|---|---|---|---|---|
| With key stakeholders | 0 | 1 | **2** | 3 | 4 | 5 | 6 | 7 | 8 | 9 | 10 |
| With readers/ users of the service | 0 | 1 | 2 | 3 | 4 | **5** | 6 | 7 | 8 | 9 | 10 |
| Self-reported visibility today (14 years after appointment): where 0 = invisible and 10 = highly visible | | | | | | | | | | | |
| With key stakeholders | 0 | 1 | 2 | 3 | 4 | 5 | 6 | 7 | 8 | **9** | 10 |
| With readers/ users of the service | 0 | 1 | 2 | 3 | **4** | 5 | 6 | 7 | 8 | 9 | 10 |

## What has been your most successful method of increasing your visibility?

Hugh feels that he made an unconscious decision early on to get involved with the wider council. Hugh says that Boroondara is a well-resourced local government organisation that is smart about staff training and supporting employee development. They gave him paid time off to get his degree and become a librarian. They have internal courses available to staff. They make opportunities available across departments in the council for staff to have an input, and Hugh made sure he got involved in those staff engagements. 'Inevitably, what happens is, you become known as the person who is happy to do that. So you get more opportunities to do it. It doesn't hurt if you are interested in that kind of thing, to get the reputation as someone who is willing to do it'. He feels that made him visible outside of his own department which was important for the library as a whole.

The organisation has almost 800 staff members, and a lot of the libraries are offsite. Most staff members work in the same location, but he was 10 km down the road at the branch library. He got to know people working in other departments of the Council by attending training courses and cross-departmental staff days.

The Staff Representative Committee (SRC) was particularly useful. The SRC was a way for the council to engage with staff. Many senior people, including directors who are just one level down from the CEO, attended those particular meetings. They were in effect the executives of the organisation. At the time, he felt that he probably underestimated the importance of the meetings, but later in his career he came to realise that they all knew who he was.

He feels that anyone in a systems or IT role, by the nature of the job, must be visible to other people in the organisation. 'You have to be talking to other people, because if you do not, it's impossible to do your job well. I had to have a strong relationship with the IT department, and I had to make sure that it worked'. He initially found that difficult because there had been a 'very bad' relationship with IT before. For example, things were done behind their backs, and then librarians would wonder why IT would not let them do anything. He made good connections with IT and also helped other departments make connections with IT. He says, 'I'd worked there for 14 years, you'd have to go out of your way to not interact with other people'.

## Value as a librarian to the organisation

'Generally speaking, librarians are of a type – we are interested in helping the community, we want to give people access to information. This is particularly true of public libraries. If you are not interested in helping people who perhaps have not had the best start in life, you are probably in the wrong job. That sort of interest in making sure that everyone in the community has as close to an equal opportunity as possible'. He feels that this is part of the reason that he is going to a new position. He is going to an area of Melbourne that is a lot less well off, and that was something that he was interested in. He describes Boroondara as a great place to work, but it is a fairly privileged community and after a long time working there, he was interested in working in an area less privileged. He feels that he is not exceptional in this regard and that this could generally describe nearly everybody who works in public libraries.

He has a keen interest in the open access (OA) movement and has been following the development of OA in academic and special libraries. He thinks he has been following this more closely than perhaps the average public librarian might be. He is interested in open source software and taking those conversations forward into public libraries. He says that the discussions about OA thus far have been very focused on academia for obvious reasons. He sees it from a different viewpoint and thinks that 'OA could resolve a bunch of other problems that we all have'. However, he is not sure that all of the dots have been joined up.

For example, there are a lot of issues around digital rights management (DRM). 'You say "ebooks" to the average public librarian and it's like you've just sworn at them! Because the situation with ebooks is so diabolical. It sounds so straight-forward to funders. They are like "Why do not you have all of these ebooks now?" and you have to explain, "Well, actually there are about 17 steps in between saying 'I'd like to read that' and actually being able to read it"'.

'OA just makes all of that go away. There are a lot of accessibility ramifications around open access'. The idea of providing access to citizens and people who do not work in universities appeals to Hugh. He feels that there are huge opportunities for public and academic libraries and librarians to work together on this issue. He says 'Once you unlock that door, all kinds of things can happen, like getting the public involved in research'. He finds it a really exciting opportunity and wonders why more people are not talking about this.

## What impact has the library service had on the community at Boroondara

Hugh says, 'Boroondara is an interesting place. I think there's a bunch of patrons that most public librarians would recognise, like people who are really down on their luck. Sometimes there are in the building because it is the only warm place to go or it's a place with air-conditioning. Often they are there because it's the only place they can send an email. There are still lots of patrons like this. On the other hand, Boroondara has just become a million-dollar municipality. The average house price in Boroondara is now *1 million* Australian dollars. It also had a lot of rooming houses. There are still homeless old people around and affluent people trying not to rub shoulders with them, so it's an unusual place'.

Hugh describes two main types of patrons. 'People who really need the library, their life would be quite miserable without it. It's a place to just hang out and not be bothered and be expected to buy another coffee or whatever. They get reading material they couldn't otherwise get, they get access to the Internet. Then there are these other patrons who are very demanding but you couldn't really say that they *needed* the library. However, they are really appreciative of the library and they are happy to provide funding for the library. They see the library service as the "crown jewels" in a way. It is the one council service that the constituents do not begrudgingly pay for. People come and say "At least I get something for my rates money"'.

'They can all buy their own books and they all have cable and Internet at home but they like the library for the social experience. They like it because we can provide them with reading devices. One of the things Boroondara has prided itself on is getting in the new bestsellers at the same time as they hit the bookshop'. He feels, 'In one sense it is crazy to prioritise that because, who cares, you know? But at the same time, that was what was important to a very important set of our library patrons. That was the thing that was going to keep them happy to provide lots of funding to the library. If that funding meant that an old homeless man could go and sit in the corner and not be bothered, then it is probably a small price to pay'.

## Do you have any formal method of reporting impact?

One of the things that Hugh is keen on and the older he gets the more interested he is in is not measurement per se, but measuring things that need to be measured. Looking from afar, he feels that they are pretty lucky in Australia at the moment (e.g. in comparison to public libraries in the United Kingdom). The United Kingdom and the United States to some extent had this problem with measuring many things, but they are not particularly useful things to be measuring when somebody knocks on the door and asks, 'Well, how do you justify your existence?'

A big part of his role was being responsible for all of the statistics. He was interested in this area, and he was more aware than anyone else in the library service that the things that were used to judge their performance were 'Completely insane, and some of them are becoming even more ridiculous'. The state government in Australia has just brought in several standard measures for public libraries. Statistics were always measured through government state departments. The public libraries network decided what was going to be measured and passed on the information. Now, the state government said, 'No, this is what you are going to measure, the measure is this and the way you calculate it is you divide this by this, etc.'. Different libraries previously calculated measures in different ways so they were not comparing like with like.

Therefore, they now have some standardised measures, which Hugh thinks is great, but because they have to bring it down to the lowest common denominator, they have done things such as measuring loans per member of the population. They are only counting physical loans because they know that everyone can count those. Just as physical loans are becoming less important, they are saying that is the only thing that can be measured. He says, 'It is slightly ridiculous'.

Hugh provides statistics to the council, which is internal. They were measuring things in which nobody was sure what exactly was being measured. 'All anyone cared about was "Is this number bigger or smaller than last year?"' Hugh had to rework the measurements so that they were meaningful. He found the process 'very painful'. The reasons why libraries are really important are the very things that are difficult to measure. 'If we are looking for funding and we are able to say things like "the community benefit of the library is X", then it's very difficult for someone to argue with that. But, if you are saying things like this is how many things we loaned out and this is how many people came through the door, who cares? So, areas like general well-being is very difficult to measure'. It is difficult to measure the societal impact of the public library such as homeless people that use the library.

## Can you tell me about any challenging scenarios you faced as a librarian and how did you deal with them?

'Dealing with the public involves facing a challenging scenario every day. The challenge is change over time'. Originally, he was in front-of-house roles, where the challenges were things such as 'guys wanting to punch each other up and people screaming at you because they do not want to pay their $4 dollar overdue fine. The way you deal with that is you remain calm and not get personally involved in their angst and talk them down'. The training he received in the public libraries helped with these situations. 'Sometimes the best thing to do is to not say anything and let people vent. The biggest problem is when they vent in front of other people as it gets embarrassing for them about 10 min later when they realise they've just had a tantrum. It's not great for everybody else either'.

In a management role, he was the person that those people got referred to. 'Sometimes this is easier, because people just want to be referred on to someone more important. Then you just re-iterate what the librarian had already told them and it usually goes smoothly'.

He has also found himself in difficult situations with senior management and local councillors at times. The councillors are very responsive to their community. They have very high expectations and want all complaints resolved. He was writing several responses on behalf of councillors or the CEO. There is a different skill set involved here, and he needed to be extremely careful about the way he worded responses. Every email that any employee writes can be accessed through freedom of information, which comes with a responsibility. For example, if someone wrote a letter to the mayor complaining about a 5-dollar fine, he might have to write a response. He would also have to explain to the councillors why it was an unreasonable complaint and what the library policy was. It takes a different skill to deal with those situations.

## Is Australia facing any cuts and closures in public libraries?

Hugh says that Australia more or less managed to dodge the economic recession of 2008 and afterward. 'In a senior role in a public library in Australia you would be *nuts* not to be looking at what is happening to public libraries in the UK and to an extent the US. Inevitably that could easily happen to us'. That is part of the reason that Hugh became interested in the measurement area of public libraries. 'Why would we wait for the Australian economy to collapse and then suddenly we might be under scrutiny'.

In Victoria they have a new state government since November 2014. One of their key policies is to cap the extent to which local governments can increase their rates. Local governments are funded by property rates or land taxes. These are paid annually plus state government grants. The new government policy is that these taxes cannot be increased any more than inflation. However, costs are going up more than inflation. Sometimes a project will get funded for a year and costs go up, but the amount that they fund remains the same. It is a small indication of how easily a situation can change very quickly. There are going to be some difficult decisions to be made because of this change. 'So it is important to prepare in the good times. Get some good measures and good stories together for when you need them'.

## Top tips for public librarians to increase visibility and impact

'You need to get a Twitter account *immediately*. I always encourage librarians to start a Blog'. He admits that he has not been great at keeping himself up to date; there was a lapse of approximately 6 months since his last post. 'If you are a public librarian who wants to have any kind of influence over anything and you do not have a Twitter account, you're mad. And even if you do not want to have an influence, but you just want to know what's going on, you need a Twitter account'. He says 'People think I'm exaggerating or I'm crazy sometimes, but Twitter is *the best professional development tool I have ever used*. It is incredible. Famous VIP librarians are on Twitter, and you can chat with them and discover they're just normal people'. Hugh has found Twitter to be amazing. His blog has been really effective at making him visible to an extent that it surprised and even horrified him. It has made him highly visible to the librarian community and to a small extent to others outside of this community.

Two years ago, he had a new manager at Boroondara and he had fortnightly one-on-one meetings with the team leaders and the manager. At his first meeting with her she declared that she knew all about him because she read his blog. This made him say to himself, 'Oh my God, what did I say?' This is an indication of how external influence became an internal influence. He tries to be careful not to talk too much about specifics at work in his blog. He likes to talk about the profession in the blog – what libraries should be doing or not doing and what librarianship is all about. However, this helped his new manager to know where he was coming from and how to work with him. This was an unexpected outcome from the blog. He initially started the blog because he was not in a position of power and he did not have opportunities to frequently go to conferences, but he was passionate about the profession and wanted to get his thoughts out there. The blog enabled him to do this.

## How would you advise new people into the profession of librarianship on increasing their visibility?

'I would advise them to do exactly the same, to get on Twitter and start a blog. It is even more important when you are new to the profession because nobody knows you yet'. Hugh had been a librarian for approximately 5 years when he started his blog. As a consequence of this, he contributed to a chapter for an American Library Association (ALA) publication and this got him onto the editorial board of a library journal, which never would have happened if he did not have the blog. The blog gave him the confidence to write the chapter, and things flowed from there. 'Visibility for new professionals is in some ways more important because you have to differentiate yourself somehow'.

In Australia, there is usually an organisation running events that are open to new graduates. The Australian Library and Information Association (ALIA) is the national organisation and there is a state-based ALIA group in each state that runs strong social and information events for new graduates. He says, 'You've got to go to these events, you are nuts if you do not go. You have to force yourself to talk to people that you do not know'. That is one of the values of Twitter. Before he had a Twitter account, he would go to conferences and hope he might get to talk to people. Because he had a Twitter account for a year before a conference, he interacted with other Australian librarians on Twitter and he would go to the conference and meet those people in person. You have background on them and know what they are interested in, which helps. He finds that the online and the offline in combination are highly effective.

### How important is it for librarians to be visible in an online environment?

'It's crucial. This is an information profession. I would put it to this extent, I'm at a level where I am interviewing people for jobs. If somebody doesn't have online visibility, if I Google you and nothing comes up, if I cannot find any social media account, if I cannot find a website or even something like a Tumblr account, if I cannot find anything, I would have serious reservations about whether you are somebody I'd like to hire. It's not because I think Twitter is cool. This is an information profession. If you do not understand the value of having online visibility or do not have the nose to know that when I look for you, your accounts come up rather than somebody else, then I would wonder. If you do not have your own landing page for everything about you, then it's not that you will not get the job, but it certainly doesn't count in your favour to be invisible online'.

### What is your most successful method of increasing your visibility in an online environment?

'Twitter'.

### Where do you see the public librarian in 5 years?

Hugh jokingly asks if I mean the *successful* public librarian, which of course, I do. 'My ideal public librarian in 5 years will be much more confident. Perhaps this is because I'm hanging out with lots of people from the UK who are pretty depressed at the moment! There is a lot of negativity. There seems to be two camps at the moment. On the one hand, there are those saying "Oh my God, libraries are so amazing and the best thing ever, why doesn't everybody recognise us for our amazing genius!" Then there is the other camp, which is people saying "Oh everything is stupid, we are all losing our funding, why cannot we all just go back to the way things were before". I'd like some middle ground there'.

'I think that librarianship is extremely exciting, and there is a lot we can offer the world. But we need to live in the real world as well. It's not just neo-liberalism that is willing libraries to change and modernise, there are actually good reasons why librarians are asked to justify their existence based on measuring their effectiveness. We cannot just complain about neo-liberal governments forcing us to put a number on everything. I do not actually think it is that unreasonable to expect you to measure your effectiveness and then to see whether we are actually effective. If you measure your effectiveness well, then you perhaps receive more funding rather than maintaining the funding that you currently have'.

'In 5 years' time, hopefully librarians will be confident about their role in the world. They will be leading developments in publishing, leading developments in the organisation of information in a digital context. I'm really hoping that we are going to get a bit more of this type of leadership'.

'Rather than librarians getting caught up thinking that Google is evil or we need better discovery layers, I'd like to see us taking control and knowing what we want and developing ourselves so that we have the skills to deliver that. If you think about it, this is what librarians were doing 100 years ago and somewhere along the line we kind of got lost. We seem to be expecting other people to resolve our problems for us'.

'The profession is in need of a confidence boost. It's like when animals sense defensiveness, they take control. The decision-makers of the world can sense this. They can sense when someone is being defensive and not confident. You've got to say, "No, what we are doing is important and we know what we are doing".

## What is your view of the use of volunteers in public libraries?

'Yes, we have volunteers in Australian public libraries, it can be quite a sensitive topic. In Boroondara, there was a consistent but slightly conflicted policy. It didn't change in 14 years'. Hugh explains that, 'Boroondara is like the blue ribbon seat for the conservative party, who are called the liberals, in Australia. It's like the home of liberal economics'. The library service had a policy in which volunteers should not be brought in to replace someone who is getting paid to do a job, so the use of volunteers was limited. There were four areas where volunteers were taken on. There was a home library service for house-bound people. Professionally trained and paid librarians made the selections for home delivery, and volunteers delivered the books. Volunteers were also used for an English conversation club. This was an informal club. They were very picky about the use of volunteers; for example, they had to have teaching qualifications. It was strict in that they were interviewed like people would be for a job. There was a long list of people who wished to volunteer on the English conversation club. There are many retired teachers in Boroondara, which perhaps accounted for this. The club met for an hour once a week. This was not a replacement job.

The third area was a computer-surfing seniors training programme in which seniors taught other seniors computer skills and volunteers were also used for this. They also had some students who volunteered from private schools who had to do some community service. In other library services in Australia, similar scenarios are used for volunteers. It is not like areas in the United Kingdom where some libraries are run completely by volunteers. Hugh finds that type of scenario pretty insulting. There is nothing close to that scenario in Australia. He says, 'Nobody is interested in that. The councils recognise that if you are running a service, you need to pay staff to run it and you need to have professionals running it. I think that it is more likely that things would just get shut down. Some of the rural libraries in Australia, which have very large areas to look after with minimal residents and lots of roads to maintain, might be open 1 day a week. Rather than having it open 3 days a week by volunteers, it is open 1 day a week with professional staff and that seems to be the attitude in Australia'.

'There are particular things you work well with volunteers. However, the idea that volunteers save you time and money is a false economy. For example, the English conversation club had six volunteers. There was one person per branch and one as a back-up person. One staff member had to look after this club, arrange the event and train the volunteers. It can quickly reach a point where it is better to pay a member of staff or hire someone. It's impossible to run large projects long term in a sustainable way with volunteers alone. While we can all get up in arms about de-professionalisation, but on the other hand, on a practical level, it is just stupid'.

## What is your favourite thing about being a librarian?

'It's probably related to something my manager said at my farewell speech, which was very nice of her. She was talking about technology, and I'm really focussed on how we can use technology to improve people's lives. A big part of my role and what I talk about on my blog is about the use of technology in libraries. I'm very uninterested in new technology just because it's new and it's shiny. I'm always interested in how this is going to affect peoples' lot. The thing that I really like about being a librarian is being involved in that space that is very 'of the moment'; it's digital technology, it's the online world and all of these start-up staff and the stuff that people love to think about; politicians like to talk about how they are going to make all of these things happen in their country. But we get to look at it from the perspective of "what are the possibilities here to improve the lives of ordinary people and communities generally"'.

'We do not think about "how is this going to improve my election prospects or what is this going to do for the economy or how much money am I going to make from buying shares in this start-up?" We get to look at the perspective of how are we going to improve the lives of people in a community generally in a non-market sense. I find that really exciting. In some ways it is limiting, but in other ways it is much less limiting. A bit like the DRM and open access issues. From a commercial publisher's point of view, there are exciting opportunities in digital and online information, but at a certain point they are limited because they have to make money, whereas librarians are completely unlimited. We can just look at technology and see an amazing opportunity and we do not care if we do not make any money. We can take it to a much further extent'.

The public librarians interviewed shared their tips for increasing visibility; these are captured by the word cloud in Figure 8.

**Figure 8** Word cloud of tips for public librarians to increase their visibility.

## Summary

On the basis of the experience of the public librarians listed in the case studies, the following lessons have been learned to improve the visibility, impact and value of public libraries:

1. Have a vision for the future of public libraries.
2. Keep an eye on emerging trends and technologies.
3. Be strategic – align services and deliverables to the mission of the county council.
4. Be proactive and engage with the local community outside of the library.
5. Co-operation is important – both within the council and with external partners.
6. It is crucial to deliver upon your promises; this enhances your reputation and value.
7. Find out who the real decision-makers are in your organisation and develop links with them.
8. Develop strong links with the local community and its key stakeholders.
9. Find out what the needs of the local community are and build a library service around those needs.
10. Gather impact stories and anecdotal evidence of value.
11. Demonstrate the social, cultural and economic value of public libraries.
12. Measure cultural or social impact (e.g. the effect of events held in the library on people attending). To do this, try focus groups, interviews or surveys.
13. Show the economic impact of the library in how it helps job-seekers and local businesses.
14. Report impact and value through formal annual reports. Use reporting structures within the council to report upon the library achievements.
15. Take advantage of social, cultural and economic events happening in your area (even things such as the Tour de France).
16. Have a policy on the use of volunteers in public libraries.
17. Have self-belief and believe in the mission of the library.
18. In tough times, keep going and be relentless about your promotional messages.
19. Have a strong social media presence and build a library app.
20. Ensure the library website is accessible on a mobile device.
21. Apply for awards – it is both a learning process and an opportunity to demonstrate impact by gathering evidence of the value of the library service.

22. Share best practice as a means of continuing professional development (e.g. give presentations at assembly meetings/Continuing Professional Development (CPD) events).
23. Be an active advocate for the library at council meetings and whenever possible.
24. Maintain open communication with peers.
25. Be civic-minded.
26. Invest in tangible library products (e.g. events brochures).
27. Collaborate with other librarians in academic, school, health and special settings in the community.

## Notes

**Wexford Equestrian Centre:** See https://www.youtube.com/watch?v=SflzctTmS_c
**Tour de France:** A major international cycling event. See http://www.letour.com/.
**Blue Badge:** BlueBadge is a scheme by the U.K. government to make it easier for disabled people to park near their desired estination. See https://www.gov.uk/blue-badge-scheme-information-council.
**UK Customer Service Excellence Standard:** See http://www.customerserviceexcellence.uk.com/.
**Caroline Casey:** A social entrepreneur from Ireland. See Caroline Casey's Ted talk at https://www.ted.com/speakers/caroline_casey, which helped put Ireland on the accessibility map.
**Ability Awards:** See http://theabilityawards.com/case-studies/2010-category-winners.
**Future new public city library in Dublin:** See http://www.parnellsquare.ie.
**Dublin City Libraries' online photographic collections:** See http://dublincitypubliclibraries.com/image-galleries/digital-collections.

# Case studies: visibility of health science librarians and libraries

> *We do not get a chance to do that many things, and everyone should be really excellent. Because this is our life. Life is brief, and then you die, you know? So this is what we've chosen to do with our life.*
>
> **Steve Jobs**

Health science librarians work in diverse settings, including hospitals, clinical teams, academic health centres, consumer health libraries and in data management research teams, to name just a few. The roles for health science libraries have evolved tremendously, in part because of the fast pace of change in health care generally, the political frameworks that governs health and because of the rapid advances in technology, which globally impacts health systems. Understanding the health care environment where librarians work is one of the key competencies outlined by the U.S. Medical Library Association (MLA) that is needed for health science librarians to excel.

The value of health science librarians and libraries to health care has been identified by librarians working in this sector as an area needing constant research and monitoring. In 2013, the U.S. MLA put out a call for librarians to become involved in systematic reviews on selected areas of health science librarianship to find the evidence to support their value and impact. To date, several reviews have been published with more underway. The body of evidence to demonstrate value is strong in health science librarianship. A snapshot of recent research is outlined in Table 19. Evidence-based practice was a movement that originated in medicine and has been translated to health science librarianship. Evidence-based librarianship is important for all areas of librarianship in terms of proving value and demonstrating impact. It is applicable to school, public, academic and special areas of librarianship, which could all benefit from the health sciences approach.

Five librarians were interviewed who all work in health care settings. They include librarians working in the United Kingdom, Ireland and Canada. Three of the librarians work in hospitals, one works in a palliative care setting and one works in a specialist health organisation – the national blood transfusion service. Interviews were held in person and via Skype during 2014. The interviewees include a librarian, a research officer, a clinical librarian, a reference librarian and an e-resources librarian. All of the librarians interviewed are well respected within the profession and have heightened visibility. The three countries where they are based have all experienced recent economic recession, and this continues to impact upon budgets and staffing in medical libraries and hospitals.

**Table 19**  **Research demonstrating evidence of impact/value indicator of health science library or librarian on health care**

| Impact/value indicator health science librarian/library | Research |
| --- | --- |
| Save health professionals time | Perrier et al. (2014) |
| | Marshall, Morgan, Klem, Thompson, and Wells (2014) |
| | Marshall et al. (2013) |
| | Weightman and Williamson (2005) |
| Aid evidence-based clinical decision-making | Perrier et al. (2014) |
| | Marshall et al. (2013) |
| | Marshall et al. (2013) |
| | McGowan, Hogg, Campbell, and Rowan (2008) |
| Positive impact on quality of patient care | Marshall et al. (2014) |
| | Marshall et al. (2013) |
| | Sievert et al. (2011) |
| | Brettle et al. (2011) |
| | Aitken, Powelson, Reaume, and Ghali (2011) |
| | Weightman and Williamson (2005) |
| | Janke and Rush (2014) |
| | Wagner and Byrd (2004) |
| Reduce patient length of stay | Marshall and Sollenberger (2013) |
| | Banks et al. (2007) |
| Reduce adverse events/ medication errors | Marshall et al. (2013) |
| | Marshall et al. (2014) |
| | Brettle et al. (2011) |

In the United Kingdom, the Labour government announced a 10-year plan to be put in place from 2015 to 2025 that sees a promise of £2.5 billion to fund the National Health Service (NHS) and social care service. However, in 2014, the NHS was in its fourth year of saving £20 billion and NHS England is expected to find savings of £30 billion by 2020–2021 (Allsop, 2014). In Canada, the federal government allocates funding to the provinces and territories to deliver health care. The Canadian government has announced $36 billion worth of health care cuts to come into effect after 2015 (Canada needs a Health Care Accord (2014, April)). In Ireland, government funding for the public health system was cut by €3.3 billion between 2009 and 2013 (Thomas, Burke, & Barry, 2014).

In addition to the economic circumstances, societal changes in Western countries have changed radically in the past decade in terms of how people engage with information. The technological society continues to evolve and change, and librarians are well positioned to play a strong role in guiding people to reliable health information. With 72% of U.S. Internet users reported to have looked online for health information in 2013 (Pew Research Centre, 2014a), health science librarians have a valuable role to play in directing people to sound consumer health information online. One way they achieve this is by creating and participating in spaces and environments for knowledge creation about patient information.

Between 2012 and 2015, the Health Information and Libraries Journal published a set of articles highlighting trends in different countries and continents in health science librarianship, and this is a useful source for reflecting upon how this discipline has evolved, what the major challenges are and how to move the discipline forward. The authors include working librarians with extensive experience and the series brings together a collective voice of health science librarian practitioners, which is a valuable real-life insight into the achievements, work, challenges and hopes of this professional group over a decade.

The first of the case studies is a solo librarian working in a palliative care setting in Ireland.

## Case study 14: librarian working in a palliative care setting

| | |
|---|---|
| Name: | Joanne Callinan |
| Organisation: | Milford Care Centre is a provider of specialist palliative care and services for older people in the mid-West of Ireland. Milford Nursing Home was established in 1928 by the Little Company of Mary. In 1977, nine beds within the nursing home were allocated to palliative care. In 1998, it became a Company Limited by Guarantee and has grown substantially since that time. In 2007, it became the first facility to be accredited for palliative care and nursing home care. |

### Mission of the organisation

The website (www.milfordcarecentre.ie) of the organisation outlines its mission and values:

'To provide the highest quality of care to patients or residents, family and friends, both in the areas of palliative care and services to the older person, as envisaged by Venerable Mary Potter. We strive to live our core values of

| | |
|---|---|
| Justice | To be rooted in integrity, honesty and fairness in all that we do |
| Compassion | To seek to understand and to care for all with compassion |
| Respect | To treat each person as a unique and valued individual |
| Communication | To be open, honest and sensitive in all of our communications |
| Accountability | To provide a professional service that uses resources economically, efficiently and effectively' |

## Online visibility of library and librarian

| | |
|---|---|
| Library website: | https://www.milfordcarecentre.ie/education_library.html |
| Linkedin: | ie.linkedin.com/pub/joanne-callinan/37/93a/a46 |
| ResearchGate: | www.researchgate.net/profile/Joanne_Callinan/info |
| Slideshare: | http://www.slideshare.net/hslgcommittee/evaluation-of-bibliotherapy-joanne-callinan-hslg-2013-23513185 |

Joanne Callinan is the librarian based at Milford Care Centre and has worked there for 6.5 years. In the last 3 years, she has had 3 different managers, each with a different take on the role of library and information services and the librarian in the organisation. This managerial change was followed by organisational change that brought changing priorities and changing directions. Changing organisational structures is not uncommon in health care organisations.

When she first started in her position, it was a clean slate – a greenfield site in the sense that there had never been a librarian there before. She reported to the head of education, research and development in the organisation. Her manager was 'extremely positive' about the library. Her job was funded because of two key influences: her manager's belief that a professional librarian was needed by the organisation and the Department of Health 'Report of the National Advisory Committee in Palliative Care', which had as one of its recommendations that specialist palliative care services should employ a librarian. 'Specialist services should also have the following staff available full time, part time or with regular sessions: librarian' (Department of Health, 2001, p. 60). This approach to creating jobs for librarians based on evidence or recommendations from an expert group published in a report is echoed further in this chapter by another librarian working in a specialist organisation – the Irish Blood Transfusion Service.

Joanne's role is extremely varied, and she does not work full-time hours. When she first started, she had a more 'traditional librarian' role in that she was cataloguing items, loaning out material, doing literature searches and providing inter-library loans. Now, some 6 years on, she is still doing some of those things, but not loaning out as many books as in previous years. She is unsure about this development: 'I'm not sure if this is a good thing or a bad thing. People still walk by and associate the library with books, and it is hard to break down that stereotype'. She claims there is greater awareness about her role and the fact that the library also has journals and access to databases helps build up her visibility. She applied for a grant in 2010 and was successful. The Irish Hospice Foundation awarded the grant, and she put it toward setting up a bibliotherapy service for the bereavement support service.

Her role has evolved over the years, and because she reported into the education department of the organisation, there was a big focus on education, research and training. Her manager was putting together a proposal to obtain funding to support a distance education program online, and as part of that they were looking to appoint a project officer to develop, deliver and evaluate an e-learning program to support candidates doing the distance learning course. The position was advertised internally, and the librarian was successful in obtaining the post. She then worked as an e-learning project officer 1 day a week in addition to her normal hours as librarian at the organisation. This is a good example of when it is important to keep an ear to the ground, be aware of what is going on in the organisation, spot opportunities and go for them. The position was initially for 1 year, and the librarian continues to work on e-learning. She did a post-graduate degree in digital media development for education to boost her skill set in this area. Health science librarians will be familiar with this scenario of organisational restructuring, managers changing and generally nothing being completely mapped out in advance. The librarian has experience of writing grant proposals, and she successfully received a clinical research fellowship to conduct research on e-learning in palliative care in Ireland.

When she first started, her visibility score was 5 among users and key stakeholders (Table 20). She feels that her visibility is now raised with key stakeholders and users of the service. The librarian is constantly contacted by management, staff and other stakeholders who are looking for information. She feels that since the national grouping of librarians in Ireland became involved in the National Clinical Effectiveness Committee (NCEC), which is led by the Department of Health, the visibility of librarians working in health care has enormously increased. She became involved in the work of NCEC, and it has boosted her profile within her organisation. For example, consultants in palliative medicine at her organisation were involved in writing a clinical guideline, and because of the work of NCEC, they contacted her as a quality checkpoint to conduct a systematic search. However, when the librarian conducted her search and forwarded a list of articles, they were surprised that there were studies available on the topic. Thus, here is an example in which the value of the librarian is clear. An information gap was presented and filled by the librarian.

### Table 20  Self-reported visibility rating of librarian at time of appointment versus today

| Self-reported visibility rating at time of appointment: where 0 = invisible and 10 = highly visible | | | | | | | | | | |
|---|---|---|---|---|---|---|---|---|---|---|
| With key stakeholders | 0 | 1 | 2 | 3 | 4 | 5 | 6 | 7 | 8 | 9 | 10 |
| With staff/users of the service | 0 | 1 | 2 | 3 | 4 | 5 | 6 | 7 | 8 | 9 | 10 |
| Self-reported visibility today (6.5 years after appointment): where 0 = invisible and 10 = highly visible | | | | | | | | | | |
| With key stakeholders | 0 | 1 | 2 | 3 | 4 | 5 | 6 | 7 | 8 | 9 | 10 |
| With key staff/users of the service | 0 | 1 | 2 | 3 | 4 | 5 | 6 | 7 | 8 | 9 | 10 |

'Our roles as librarians are very broad. It is important to find your niche within your own organisation'. You cannot be all things to all people. At present it is a balancing act between research, library and e-learning. She works on her own. However, there are some volunteers who work an hour at a time some days. Although volunteers have an important role and do excellent work, she feels that it is essential for health care libraries to be managed by qualified librarians.

To become more visible and have more impact, she thinks her best strategy is to cut back on some areas. She feels her current awareness services could be improved. She finds that clinical guideline work takes a lot of time – it can take 4–5 days, then between that and responding to emails 2 weeks of time could be gone. There are problems with the delivery of current awareness bulletins because of restrictions on the size of the electronic mailboxes. Her aim is to develop a blog and make current awareness bulletins more accessible to people that way and more permanent. Email works well, some of the time, but she has concerns about a blog because people may not always visit it. At least with email you know that people receive it.

The organisation is small; it employs approximately 350 people. This makes it easier for her to be visible. She contacts heads of departments with up-to-date information. She likes to get information to all of the target groups. She says there are always people in her organisation who immediately 'get what I do' and they will always seek her out for information needs. 'They are not afraid to ask for help'. However, it is important to be inclusive and not spend all of your time doing something for one person. Visibility is on-going; it never stops. It is important to be responsive and to seek out opportunities. Sometimes you are sought out, but if you are ahead of the game, then you can seek out the ones you want. The role is slightly 'outside of librarianship', but this does not really matter as long as you are meeting the needs of the organisation. Information needs are very broad.

## Value of the librarian to the organisation

In terms of value to the organisation, as a librarian having a mixed skill set is important; traditional librarian skills are also relevant. However, she feels that her real strength is that she has conducted research herself and probably could not do her job without having immersed herself in research. Things such as reference management help, as well as e-learning and her experience of working on systematic reviews. In terms of the library as a service, she feels it probably needs to have more impact, but can health care libraries ever have enough impact? 'I do get worried when people aren't borrowing as much'. She thinks that if staff members do not physically see people in the library, then there is a fear that you are not making an impact although this could not be further from the truth. On the basis of her own research, she has found that bibliotherapy services have definitely had an impact on the families and staff who use it (Callinan, 2011).

The Librarian designed and developed an online induction programme for volunteers. This has worked well, but she is still working on getting staff on board. However there is reluctance among some staff members toward e-learning. They are daunted by the prospect. It received mixed reaction from the start. She feels it will really take off in a few years, but in the meantime there is going to be a generation gap for some time to come. The new generation will be the leaders of e-learning in the future.

## Reporting impact and value to management

The librarian regularly sends management information updates relevant to their working areas. She is keen to increase her working hours in the organisation and has prepared reports on activity and impact and made her case to management. She has demonstrated that she has taken on extra workload and was integrated into the education and research departments of the organisation. However, the priority will always be towards frontline patient care in health care organisations. It is very important to measure the library's activity because you never know what is going to happen in the future. She feels it is also important to measure online training and database usage.

## Challenging scenarios

A challenging scenario for Joanne was having 3 different managers in 3 years. Each comes with a completely different perspective on the library and the role of the librarian in the organisation. They have different expectations. This left the librarian with a feeling of insecurity, although it also presented itself with new opportunities.

## Top tips for health librarians to increase their visibility and impact

'You need to know what is going on in your organisation as a whole. You need to find out what people are working on – whether it is policies, guidelines, research. It is not always easy, but you can hear things through the grapevine. If you think that you could play a role; for example, if a department head is developing a policy, they may need literature searching or critical appraisal done. Sometimes people will come to you, but it is best to keep an ear to the ground and talk to people to find out what is going on. Go around and meet people in their workspaces, in their departments'.

'Keep in touch with different groups and spot information gaps. It is not possible to assist everyone, but it is good to know what is going on. Get feedback on literature searches you have performed. Sometimes if you do not hear back from someone having sent results to them you can wonder about what they thought of the service, whereas it is better to get feedback – good or bad – so you can learn from this'.

'Send off lists to heads of departments to ask if any books are needed. There is still a need for books or ebooks, but not for all disciplines'.

## What are your thoughts on the embedded librarian as a future role?

'Embedded librarian being part of a multi-disciplinary team is a possible future for health librarians'. Joanne says that she would love to shadow a clinical librarian (e.g. in the United Kingdom) to understand more about this role.

## What advice would she give to new entrants to the profession?

'Be creative. Librarianship is not the kind of job where you can say "well this is what I do and list a number of things". To be seen as relevant, you have to adapt your role to the needs of the organisation. Some people may not see, for example, e-learning as the role of the librarian, but it is important to try out new things, expand your skill base and become an essential asset to the organisation'.

Joanne feels that working with patients is where librarians could have a stronger role. Public librarians are very involved with their communities, so it would be beneficial if health science librarians could have a more holistic approach to their roles. Involvement with organising or delivering creative writing groups is an area where health librarians could potentially be more involved.

'When you look at statistics relating to patient care in comparison to how many interlibrary loans there are, it becomes very difficult to compete with that'. However, the librarian has an evidence-based approach and published research to show the positive effect of bibliotherapy on clients. She introduced a poetry competition for staff and patients and as part of the Compassionate Community Project, and she linked in with the public libraries in Limerick, who received a seed grant to set up a bibliotherapy section to support the bereaved in the community. The organisation co-hosted an international conference on public health and palliative care, and the librarian and the Compassionate Communities Project jointly organised a poetry corner at the conference on the theme of death, dying, loss and care, with poetry submitted by children and adults from the community.

## What is your favourite thing about being a librarian?

'Every day is different. Every day presents different challenges and there is variety. It is always satisfying when the information you find has an impact on patients and their families'.

The second case study is from a clinical librarian working in University Hospitals of Leicester NHS Trust (UHL) in the United Kingdom.

# Case study 15: clinical librarian working in UHL

| Name: | Sarah Sutton |
|---|---|
| Organisation: | UHL is one of the biggest and busiest NHS trusts in the United Kingdom, incorporating the Leicester General, Glenfield and Royal Infirmary Hospitals. Over 12,000 staff members provide a range of services, primarily for the 1 million residents of Leicester, Leicestershire and Rutland. |

## Mission of the organisation

The trust's website outlines its purpose and values:

> '[T]o provide "caring at its best", and our staff have helped us create a set of values that embody who we are and what we're here to do. They are
>
> - We focus on what matters most.
> - We treat others how we would like to be treated.
> - We are passionate and creative in our work.
> - We do what we say we are going to do.
> - We are one team and we are best when we work together'.
>
> *Source:* http://www.leicestershospitals.nhs.uk/aboutus/. Accessed 22.09.14.

## The mission of the Clinical Librarian Service at UHL

There is no stated mission; however, the website outlines 'what we do' as follows:

> *The Clinical Librarian Service at UHL put research evidence into the heart of the workplace. They attend team meetings and ward rounds to ensure that the evidence is at the heart of patient care and planning.*
>
> *Source:* http://www.uhl-library.nhs.uk/cl/services.html. Accessed 22.09.14.

Sarah Sutton is one of three clinical librarians (CLs) at UHL, and she has worked here for 12 years. She describes her current role as a 'classical clinical librarian role'. Her main role is to assist clinicians to get the evidence they need to care for patients. She is the longest consecutively serving CL in the United Kingdom.

## Online visibility

| | |
|---|---|
| Librarian's profile on NHS website: | http://www.uhl-library.nhs.uk/cl/staff.html |
| CL website: | http://www.uhl-library.nhs.uk/cl/index.html |
| CL library on Twitter: | https://twitter.com/UHLCL |
| CL blog: | http://clinicallibrarian.blogspot.co.uk/ |
| Librarian on Linkedin: | http://uk.linkedin.com/pub/sarah-sutton/3/716/a16 |

When Sarah was first appointed, she felt she scored 0 on the visibility scale with users and key stakeholders. This is explained by the fact that the role of CL was brand new to the clinical areas she was working with and nobody had ever had that position before Sarah. This meant that the concept of a CL was new to people, and Sarah had some work to do to increase understanding of her role, her visibility and the value she could bring to the organisation (Table 21).

Sarah has substantially increased her visibility. When asked how she did increase her visibility and impact, she commented on attendance at clinical meetings as being very relevant. Meetings such as audit and clinical governance were very useful. Initially, she attended ward rounds, which raised awareness of her role. She feels that attending ward rounds was good for gaining subject knowledge and good for helping to get to know clinicians, and the librarian gets to learn about what each department does. However, ward rounds were found overall not to be a very practical use of a CL's time. In Sarah's experience, attending ward rounds does not yield many literature requests; this is for various reasons, including clinicians not wishing to reveal that they do not know something in front of colleagues. Over the years, many activities of the CL team helped increase awareness of the service, so much so that today Sarah feels that she has so many queries she never needs to leave her room again. She has honed her style of delivering search results now to 30–40 results at a time. The only exception to this is systematic reviews, in which all results are sent. She feels that it is very important to send the requestor several key full-text articles. Doing this without the additional barrier of the requestor having to source the articles themselves is a real positive for clinicians. Her repeat business is down to this level of service in her experience.

Today, Sarah reports a high visibility score with key stakeholders and with users (Table 21). She feels that she is perhaps a little better at getting managers to understand what she does rather than users or potential users of the CL service. The reason for this is that she knows all of the senior managers in her directorate, and the clinical directors better than she knows all junior doctors. It is practically impossible to get to know all doctors in the trust.

**Table 21  Self-reported visibility rating of librarian at time of appointment versus today**

| Self-reported visibility rating at time of appointment: where 0=invisible and 10=highly visible | | | | | | | | | | | |
|---|---|---|---|---|---|---|---|---|---|---|---|
| With key stakeholders | **0** | 1 | 2 | 3 | 4 | 5 | 6 | 7 | 8 | 9 | 10 |
| With staff/users of the service | **0** | 1 | 2 | 3 | 4 | 5 | 6 | 7 | 8 | 9 | 10 |
| Self-reported visibility today (12 years after appointment): where 0=invisible and 10=highly visible | | | | | | | | | | | |
| With key stakeholders | 0 | 1 | 2 | 3 | 4 | 5 | 6 | 7 | **8** | 9 | 10 |
| With key staff/users of the service | 0 | 1 | 2 | 3 | 4 | 5 | **6** | 7 | 8 | 9 | 10 |

# Contents

## How do you think you can bring your visibility score up to a 10?

It is difficult to improve on the score because it takes time to provide a good service to particular doctors, and it is not possible to simultaneously market services to all doctors in the trust. She feels that she does her best. She attends meetings whenever she can, uses current awareness bulletins and emails her directorates when interesting new research is published. She finds that the majority of her literature requests come via word of mouth. She rarely does ward rounds. She receives a lot of repeat business. She does try to meet with new consultants, which she finds is helpful.

## Value that the librarian brings to the organisation

The value that Sarah and her team have brought to the trust is 'making access to good evidence easier'. The librarians give clinicians alternatives to Google and Wikipedia, resources that they can feel more confident about. The team has contributed to writing guidelines and research, which they have supported. One specific example Sarah gives is a weekly alert she sends about structured education to the Diabetes Type 2 DESMOND (Diabetes Education and Self-Management for Ongoing and Newly Diagnosed) team. Another team she assists is the Emergency Department Education Team. The feedback from this department was that the Evidence Update (EU) that one of Sarah's team provides to the Emergency Department was the cornerstone that helped to improve the education of the ED team. At one point in the past, the post of the library staff member responsible for the evidence update was under threat. When it was explained to management that this person (a library assistant) was responsible for the EU and that if she was not replaced then the EU would no longer be produced, the post was no longer under threat. Sarah felt that because there was a tangible 'product' (i.e. the EU associated with that job), it made the job more secure. It is also easier to demonstrate impact using something such as an EU, which is delivered directly to staff.

## Value and impact that the library brings to the organisation

The way the library works is to be very supportive and enthusiastic about making access to evidence easy for clinicians. The library has a web-facing Internet site as opposed to an internal intranet. This means that clinicians can get into resources from anywhere in the world, and there is no charge for document supply or interlibrary loans. For example, articles are scanned if it is within copyright law to do so and emailed to health care professionals requesting them. This avoids clinicians having to come to the library to photocopy articles. The whole library is very committed to supporting clinicians' information needs. The library is also delivering good value for money for the hospitals.

## Formal method of measuring and/or reporting library and librarian impact

There is no regular library survey. The library services manager recently performed a focus group that is intended to contribute to the Health Education in England 15-year plan (Health Education England, 2014). The library is also circulating a questionnaire to find out the benefits staff members feel they get from the EU service. The librarians have also contributed some critical incident stories for the Health Education in England research for their 15-year plan; however, there is no annual survey performed. The literature search service does include an automatic feedback option for users, and librarians remind users to send them feedback. The librarians have found that the four questions they use to gather feedback on literature search results were too generic. In one question, the requestor is asked to rate the quality of the results of the search, and this could produce a rating saying that the results are poor just because there is very little evidence on that particular topic, rather than because the librarian had not done a very good search. The library does report statistics on study spaces and number of issues, and a whole host of quantitative statistics to the regional authority and the clinical librarian service contributes to this with statistics on searches completed, training sessions delivered and articles downloaded or borrowed.

## Challenging scenario

The Clinical Librarian Service lost a staff member because she left to take a post at another library. This staff member was responsible for producing the EU (current awareness bulletin) for the Emergency Department. The EU was a good and popular product that was directly linked to the post, and this made replacing the person an easy choice for management of the trust.

When Sarah first started in her job as a CL, she left a full-time permanent job in Further Education and took a 20% pay cut. She felt the position of CL was a very exciting challenge, although it was only a 2-year temporary contract. This meant that Sarah and others in the CL team had to continually make the case to keep the service going. Over the years, the CL team ran several surveys to gather feedback. Another way to reach out was to go around to all of the heads of department, talk to them and ask them how the CL model was going and what improvements could be made. Because of this outreach activity, one of the heads of one of the hospitals wrote a 'really nice letter' to Sarah and copied it to the head of her team, saying that she was 'indispensable to the team'. This came at a time when UHL was putting together a case to extend and expand the role of CLs. This letter – when shown to the right people – enabled the library to extend the role for an additional 2 years. Having a key clinician taking the time to write a letter like this made all of the difference.

## Top tips for CLs to increase visibility

Identify where the roadblocks are for clinicians and try to make their paths easier to information. Then publicise the 'new easier route'. Go to lots of clinical meetings and introduce yourself. Keep introducing yourself to key people in the organisation. Send out global emails with useful information written in a clear and easy-to-understand way. The subject line of emails is particularly important to get right. It needs to get straight to the point because the reader will make a judgement call on whether to read the email or delete it based on the subject line alone. It is important to hook people in with the subject strapline, particularly in health care, because these professionals are very, very busy people. Sarah gives an example of an email subject line she uses when supplying an article. It will read, 'Article as requested: from Sarah Sutton'. When the requestor sees the email, they will recognise her name and know what it is about. People receive many random emails, and they will not bother opening it unless they recognise something useful in the subject line.

Sarah's top tip: 'Try and delight your customer'. Think about what they would like in an ideal world. This goes for all librarians, not just CLs.

## Online visibility

The team at UHL have a blog, and all of their EUs are made available online. The Clinical Information Search Service (CISS) officers, who are part of the CL team at UHL, produce the EUs in collaboration with the CLs and tweet when they become available and tweet relevant news. Sarah helped to set up the blog and the bulletins, but she relies on the team to keep the blog up to date and to use social media to promote new items. She feels that social media does not take a huge effort, but it is another useful way of getting the library message out to users. The trust also uses Yammer™, and also they promote the CL service using this. Sarah is particularly 'proud' of the library website because she feels very confident when she directs clinicians to use it and knows that they will be able to access evidence-based literature from any Internet-enabled device from any location in the world. She receives emails, sometimes from clinicians, who may be doing research from home. She feels that any library without a web-facing access point (website) cannot properly function.

## Advice to new health science librarians?

Make sure you know what your product is. Have your 'lift speech' ready. If you are stuck in a lift with someone and you want to sell your service to them, how would you do this? Have this speech prepared and at the ready. Find an excuse to regularly email clinical groups. This is a very good strategy for increasing your visibility. Sometimes when she sends out the EU, it triggers a request from a clinician and leads to further queries. It acts as a reminder that you are there. Popping up at meetings also is useful. Do a talk or presentation entitled 'What the library can do for you' or 'What's new in the library'. There is always something new to report, and Sarah runs these every year for her different departments.

THE LIFT SPEECH

## Where do you see the CL in 5 years?

There are a couple of possible scenarios. Sarah feels that health science librarians will not survive unless they adopt some of the 'clinical librarian tendencies'. If librarians continue to say 'I look after the books', then this is not going to get anyone excited. It is vital to have a peppy message about 'getting key evidence to clinicians'. Otherwise, you are most likely going to find yourself unemployed. The message has to be sexy.

Another scenario is for CLs to become embedded into research teams and to get involved perhaps full time in things such as systematic reviews and devising search strategies. Another area is getting involved in guideline development, making sure they are correctly titled and indexed. Rather than librarians being a dying profession, Sarah feels that if we are able to explain your skills and demonstrate them to people in your organisation, then Sarah thinks that librarians are actually more employable than ever before. We just need to get out there and flaunt it a bit. For example, if you assist someone who is going to publish an item, then ask for an acknowledgement **as a minimum**. Sarah gives an example of statisticians who possibly provide an overview of statistics or cross check for other authors on a piece of research, and they are always named as co-authors on a paper. On the other hand, librarians may have done hours of searching, retrieval and screening of results but may not be named on a paper. Librarians need to stand up for themselves more, and if a person comes back for assistance with a search, then the librarian ought to say 'I'll help you with this as long as I get an acknowledgement on the paper'. Otherwise, people do not realise the background work that librarians do (e.g. searching, retrieving and scanning abstracts). If librarians do not insist on some type of acknowledgement, then there is a danger that they will end up unemployed because their role in this particular example is invisible to the reader. When a clinician comes back for help on a paper the next time, the librarian may not be there if librarians do not start to get the recognition and acknowledgement for the work they contribute to research.

### Physical library

There was a period of 9 months at the Leicester Royal Infirmary (LRI) hospital when there was no physical library. Sarah's role as the CL based at LRI was not affected by this; the service ticked along nicely. However, there is a need in a hospital for a physical space for people to read. There is a need for some people at a certain point in their career to be able to access books. For 2 years, there was a library at the Royal Infirmary without any books. Users complained very strongly about not having books, and in 2015 a new library with books will be opened. Books still have their place. For example, if Sarah receives a literature request about 'change management', then her advice to the requestor would be to read a book about it because articles will not be enough. Or, she gives an example of locating a picture of a nodule on a lung – which was only possible to find such detail in an atlas of lung imaging. Certain clinical and management questions are better answered by information contained in books.

### What is your favourite thing about being a librarian?

'Helping clinical staff find the information they want as speedily as possible. It's great being able to deliver the "wow" factor. The lovely thing about clinical staff is that they do say thank you and encourage you to feel part of the team'.

The third case study is from a reference librarian working in a biomedical library that is part of a Canadian university that is based in Vancouver.

## Case study 16: reference librarian working in a biomedical library that is part of the Faculty of Medicine at the University of British Columbia, Vancouver, Canada

| | |
|---|---|
| Name: | Dean Giustini |
| Organisation: | Biomedical branch library at Gordon and Leslie Diamond Health Care Centre at Vancouver General Hospital. The university library has 14 branches with 2 campuses. The biomedical branch library is off campus, being located in the hospital. The university consistently ranks in the top 40 universities in the world and had 58,284 registered students in 2013/2014, making it the second-largest university in Canada. |

## Mission of the organisation

The university's website (www.ubc.ca) outlines its vision and values as follows:

> **Vision**: As one of the world's leading universities, the University of British Columbia (UBC) creates an exceptional learning environment that fosters global citizenship, advances a civil and sustainable society and supports outstanding research to serve the people of British Columbia, Canada and the world.

## Values

> - **Academic freedom**: The university is independent and cherishes and defends free inquiry and scholarly responsibility.
> - **Advancing and sharing knowledge**: The university supports scholarly pursuits that contribute to knowledge and understanding within and across disciplines and seeks every opportunity to broadly share them.
> - **Excellence**: The university, through its students, faculty, staff and alumni, strives for excellence and educates students to the highest standards.
> - **Integrity**: The university acts with integrity, fulfilling promises and ensuring open, respectful relationships.
> - **Mutual respect and equity**: The university values and respects all members of its communities, each of whom individually and collaboratively makes a contribution to create, strengthen and enrich our learning environment.
> - **Public interest**: The university embodies the highest standards of service and stewardship of resources and works within the wider community to enhance societal good.

## Mission of UBC Library

> UBC Library advances research, learning and teaching excellence by connecting communities, within and beyond the university, to the world's knowledge.

## The Biomedical Branch Library is part of the Woodward Library. This mission is outlined on the website (woodward.library.ubc.ca) as follows

> **The mission of the Woodward Library at UBC**: Woodward Library partners with the disciplines of engineering, forestry, health and medicine, land and food systems and science at UBC.

## Cont'd

> • We collaborate in research, teaching and learning; build relevant collections; and pro-vide expertise, inspiring space and technology to empower our community to succeed.
> • We provide excellent, responsive service.
> • We continually develop our resources and services.
> • We are a highly skilled and motivated team, committed to on-going professional development.

## *Online visibility*

| | |
|---|---|
| Library website: | http://services.library.ubc.ca/ |
| Institutional repository: | https://circle.ubc.ca/ |
| Search Principle blog: | http://blogs.ubc.ca/dean |
| Twitter: | http://www.twitter.com/giustini |
| HLWIKI international (1000+ pages of content): | http://hlwiki.slais.ubc.ca/index. php/HLWIKI_International |
| SlideShare: | http://www.slideshare.net/giustinid/ |

The reference librarian of UBC Biomedical Branch Library is Dean Giustini, who has worked here for 18 years. Dean is highly visible within the profession of library and information science, particularly among health science librarians. He has his own Search Principle blog and set up HLWIKI International, which was the most popular librarian wiki in 2014 and 2015. He has over 1900 followers on Twitter since joining in March 2008. Dean manages the UBC Biomedical Branch Library at the teaching hospital. Library services and support is provided for UBC faculty, staff and students at Vancouver General Hospital and at St. Paul's Hospital.

At the time of his appointment, Dean scored a 4 on the visibility scale with key stakeholders and with users. Eighteen years later, this score moved up to a 7 for both groups (Table 22). Dean describes the library as 'not as visible as I would like'; how-ever, he feels that as a librarian he is personally very visible because of his online presence. To improve the visibility of the library, he says he needs to be able to hire another librarian.

When asked what his most successful methods of increasing his visibility were, he noted the following:

• Collaboration with researchers
• Speaking at conference and writing scholarly papers
• Maintaining a wiki and social media accounts on Twitter and elsewhere.

**Table 22  Self-reported visibility rating of librarian at time of appointment versus today**

| Self-reported visibility rating at time of appointment: where 0 = invisible and 10 = highly visible | | | | | | | | | | |
|---|---|---|---|---|---|---|---|---|---|---|
| With key stakeholders | 0 | 1 | 2 | 3 | **4** | 5 | 6 | 7 | 8 | 9 | 10 |
| With staff/users of the service | 0 | 1 | 2 | 3 | **4** | 5 | 6 | 7 | 8 | 9 | 10 |
| **Self-reported visibility today (18 years after appointment): where 0 = invisible and 10 = highly visible** | | | | | | | | | | |
| With key stakeholders | 0 | 1 | 2 | 3 | 4 | 5 | 6 | **7** | 8 | 9 | 10 |
| With key staff/users of the service | 0 | 1 | 2 | 3 | 4 | 5 | 6 | **7** | 8 | 9 | 10 |

## *Value that the librarian brings to the organisation*

The value that Dean feels he has brought to his organisation is through his work in helping residents work on grant proposals and research, his contribution to systematic reviews and continuously raising library issues.

## *Impact that the library brings to the organisation*

The impact that the library service has had on the organisation is felt to be difficult to measure. Ideally, Dean would like to measure impact and value of the service in a formal way, as part of a research project.

## *Formal method of measuring and/or reporting library and librarian impact*

Teaching of courses and all in-services of the library are evaluated. Courses are evaluated using pre-test and post-test evaluation of skills and results are shared. Dean is always open to new methods of measuring performance and recognises the importance of this.

## *Challenging scenario*

The library and faculty have been hit hard by cutbacks. The library has a series of measures that have been implemented since 2012 as part of a 3-year strategic plan. The communication of the changes is visible on the university library's website. Two hospital libraries in the region have closed. Dean receives requests from these locations and tries to help faculty and clinicians as much as possible from a distance.

## *Top tips for health science librarians to increase visibility*

Dean has some great tips for health science librarians to increase their visibility:

- Strive for excellence in any small or large project you are involved in.
- Know your users and help them.

- Publish.
- Present.

## How important is it for the librarian to be visible to users in an online environment?

Dean feels that this is very important. He says that librarians do not have to use all of the web tools that are out there. It is useful to focus and pick one or two tools and use these often and well. His most successful method of increasing his visibility in an online environment was by creating an online profile or identity and sharing his stores online.

## Do you think the embedded librarian/librarian in context is the future for health librarians? (Note: 'Embedded librarian' refers to a librarian who does not necessarily need a physical library to do their job. They can work in a research team or health care team independently of the library.)

'In Canada, this concept comes and goes. What is more important is that the librarian has some regular contact with health professionals. It doesn't have to be an embedded role at all'.

## Do you have any advice to new entrants to the profession of librarianship on increasing their visibility and impact?

'Create an online space, use a blog or a wiki and make sure they have a social media presence. Social networking in person should also be done'.

## Where do you see the health science librarian in 5 years?

- Doing more research
- Maintaining print and electronic collections
- Teaching
- Providing expert searches to user groups

## What is your favourite thing about being a librarian?

'I like the people. Medical and health people work hard to make our lives better. I feel honoured to be a small part of it'.

The next case study is about a librarian/research officer employed by the Irish Blood Transfusion Service.

## Case study 17: librarian working in a specialist health library

| | |
|---|---|
| Name: | Niamh O'Sullivan |
| Organisation: | Irish Blood Transfusion Service |

## Mission of the organisation

The Irish Blood Transfusion Service (IBTS) is a statutory organisation. It has several
specific functions that are outlined in detail in a statutory instrument of 1965. It is in
the business of managing a blood transfusion service. The IBTS has its headquarters
in Dublin and has seven other centres around the country.

## Mission of the library

'The mission of the IBTS library is to promote excellence in learning, education and research within the Irish Blood Transfusion Service by providing an
innovative library service for all staff and by enhancing the dissemination of
information consistent with the organisation's value of learning' (Irish Blood
Transfusion Service, 2003).

## Online visibility of library and librarian

ResearchGate:          http://www.researchgate.net/profile/Niamh_OSullivan
Linkedin:              http://ie.linkedin.com/pub/niamh-o-39-sullivan/20/404/878
Slideshare:            www.slideshare.net/Niamh1/presentations

The librarian and research officer of the IBTS is Niamh O'Sullivan, who has worked
here for 15 years, since 1999. Before this position, she worked in various libraries
in Ireland, the United Kingdom and the United States, including public, university,
government and special libraries. Describing her initial appointment at the IBTS
as 'visionary', she feels that her visibility was high with key stakeholders in the
organisation from the outset. The reason a librarian was sought by this organisation
was to ensure that blood transfusion services would be based on the best available evidence and the quality of information provided to staff would be overseen
by qualified information professional. There was much media attention brought to
blood transfusion scandals in the country at the time, and a part of the solution was
the employment of a librarian. Librarians were held in high regard, and she was
employed as a risk aversion strategy to avoid future mistakes. Similar to Joanne
Callinan, Niamh was also employed on foot of a recommendation from a government report – the Finlay Report 1997. She attended the National Blood Users Group
meetings and supplied research and evidence to support decision-making. The users
group brought together leading haematologists together from around the country
and consultants based at the organisation. The purpose of the group was to ensure
best practice on the use of blood in Ireland. This was informed by evidence that the
librarian researched and provided.

What is interesting about the visibility of the librarian in this example is that her visibility changed over time and changed depending on the stakeholder or audience. Although she felt highly visible to her key stakeholders – mainly the chief executive officer (CEO) and board of the organisation – at the start of her appointment, this reduced over time. She was less visible to staff of the organisation when she started the job, but that increased over some years (Table 23). The main reason for the variance, according to the librarian, was because the key stakeholders of the organisation are extremely busy people and only have time for critical bite-sized information at a time, which is what she provides them with.

On the other hand, staff members are interested in information and they are interested in the physical space that the library offers them. The librarian built up her visibility over time, and some of the examples of how she does this should be of interest to other librarians working in specialist areas.

When asked what the most successful method of increasing visibility was, the librarian had two answers: '(1) use humour (2) be on the "side of the staff". In other words, librarians tend to take themselves very seriously; it is a serious profession after all. However, it doesn't do any harm to let loose every once in a while and introduce humour, particularl into promotional activities. Even in a medical setting, which by its very nature is a serious business, humour can go down very well'.

As a neutral entity, the library is seen by staff as a safe place to visit and to spend time in. People can often come into the library if they are upset or need to get away from their desks. They can go into the quiet study area and they know that the librarian or library staff will not be asking questions or judging them. Niamh removed the swipe card access from the library and adopted a true 'open-door' policy. This is contrary to all other offices in the building, which require a swipe to enter them. She ensures that the eight blood centres that are located around the country are included in any library marketing messages. For example, whenever new books are purchased, a list is sent around to all centres with a message to contact the librarian if any books are required, which are then posted down with the vans that are used by the service. By the same token, Niamh is the editor of 'I-ByTeS', which is the staff newsletter for the organisation. To ensure inclusivity, she always collates news from each of the centres in the newsletter. This helps people working in all centres and remote locations to feel

**Table 23 Self-reported visibility rating of librarian at time of appointment versus today**

| Visibility rating at time of appointment: where 0=invisible and 10=highly visible | | | | | | | | | | |
|---|---|---|---|---|---|---|---|---|---|---|
| With key stakeholders | 0 | 1 | 2 | 3 | 4 | 5 | 6 | 7 | 8 | **9** | 10 |
| With staff | 0 | 1 | 2 | 3 | 4 | 5 | **6** | 7 | 8 | 9 | 10 |
| Visibility today (15 years after appointment): where 0=invisible and 10=highly visible | | | | | | | | | | |
| With key stakeholders | 0 | 1 | 2 | 3 | 4 | 5 | 6 | 7 | 8 | **9** | 10 |
| With key stakeholders | 0 | 1 | 2 | 3 | 4 | 5 | 6 | **7** | 8 | 9 | 10 |

part of the bigger picture and part of the whole organisation. In the library, Niamh has incorporated a fiction section and makes daily newspapers available to staff who may not ordinarily use a library. It needs to be a space that is used by staff, there needs to be something in it for everyone. Then it is valued. It does not have to be perfect; it just has to be used.

## The role of the librarian in the organisation

Niamh manages the library service and the research service, and she has a role within internal communications within the organisation. She talks about the importance of achieving a delicate balance in the quantity and quality of information provided to readers:

'You cannot really bombard people with information; you have to thread a fine line between giving people enough information and pestering them too much. The focus of our management team is in the everyday running of the organisation, which means that sometimes they cannot see the big picture (i.e. future-proofing the organisation and raising its profile) – we should be the best practice in blood transfusion and issuing guidelines on this'.

Niamh feels that humour is hugely under-rated; catchy slogans and catchy posters can go a long way in terms of visibility. 'A lot of librarians are afraid to use humour or pop culture because they feel they should be a serious entity and are afraid of dumbing things down'. Niamh has a series of colourful posters she uses for a book amnesty that she organises anytime she needs to encourage users to return overdue books or to 'come clean' about books that have been misplaced. The posters include cartoons such as the Simpsons™ with a photo of Bart Simpson writing, 'I will return my library book on time' on the blackboard and a message saying 'Return any library books you've had too long and no longer require: no questions asked!'.

She emphasizes the importance of having fun with promotional activities:

'You could be the most professional librarian in the world, but if you do not promote what you do in a fun, inclusive way, then nobody will care about what you do'.

Anyone who knows Niamh will tell you that she is a fun-loving person with an outgoing personality and a great sense of humour. Her library reflects this, because she says, 'It's almost like sometimes our library has a personality. People are proud of it, it is a nice space and non-threatening. It's there if people need it'.

## Value librarian brings to the organisation

When asked about the value she as a librarian brought to the organisation, she felt that she brings common sense. There are things that the librarian feels she does that nobody else will do in the organisation. She feels that she does these things because she is a librarian. The things may not be library related at all. She gave an example of new phones that were just recently installed in the organisation. The phones have the ability to search for a contact using the dial pad. She previously had to update the staff contact list on the intranet, but now that they are available via the phone, this task has become redundant. A phone list was previously sent around every month, which was a printout of staff telephone numbers. Now with the phones, it is possible to type in a first name (e.g. Mary) and all of the people whose first name is Mary will appear on the list. However, when the phones were first installed, the librarian noticed that not all of the names were stored in the phone. They had one number for a laboratory where 30 people were working. Clinical staff members were not all in the phones either. This was an information gap. Therefore, this fell into the realm of internal communications, where the librarian has a role. The librarian went through her list of names and high-lighted any that were not stored in the phone. She gave the list to the department in January and 2 months later nothing had been done.

One day she discovered a button on the phone that when pressed brought up all contacts, the first contact was Abbot Laboratories – an external organisation – which she pressed by mistake and hung up. She received a phone call back from someone at Abbot Laboratories who was extremely irate that she kept receiving hang-ups from this generic number and demanded to know who she was. The librarian explained the situation and vowed to get it solved. She contacted the Information Technology (IT) department and suggested they add a 'dummy' contact, 'AAA', at the start so that nobody would be ringing Abbot Laboratories in error. While she was talking to them, she inquired about her 2-month-old query and wondered if they could update the internal contacts.

As librarians, we want information to be correct and accurate. Information gaps like this are a nuisance, and this example demonstrates on a very practical level what value librarians can bring to organisations. It is about showing a bit of initiative, doing what it takes and solving small problems and making information 'right'. Niamh felt that nobody else in the organisation would (1) bother, (2) care (3) or do anything about it. There are many things like that that Niamh 'minds' or looks after in the organisation.

Another example she gives was a monthly email that is sent around to all depart-ments about financial reports. The email contained information to say that the finan-cial report was ready, but no information about how to access it or no quick link into it. In effect, this meant that each head of department receiving this information had to minimise the email, find and open the program on their desktop, login and find the report. Niamh suggested to the person circulating the email that they include a link to the program in the email (which she found by going into the html of the program) and send that around to all department heads in the email as a signature. He thought this was a great idea, implemented it and a few months later came back to Niamh to thank her because there had been a 150% increase in the budget reports being viewed since he had included the direct link.

## What value or impact does the library bring to the organisation?

The value that the library and library staff bring to the organisation is evident in different ways. For example, a training programme is offered in how to search and find quality information and another training session in effective presentation skills. Niamh affirms that there has been a reported improvement in staff members' information-seeking skills and presentation skills since the training was introduced by the library.

The librarian also helps people to get research published. Many of the consultants are involved in peer reviewing for journals, making document supply a popular service that is provided by the library.

The update of the intranet and the newsletter has assisted internal communications in the organisation. For example, Niamh might put up tips for school lunch-boxes on the intranet that staff have commented on and found useful. Or, she had come across a TV programme that was looking for people who have a fear of public speaking so she advertised this on the intranet. Keeping people informed about conferences that are taking place and current awareness bulletins are always popular. This helps people in the organisation to keep up to date on their topic and avoids a sense of panic when they are asked to give a talk at a conference, which regularly happens.

She keeps up to date with topics relevant to blood and blood transfusion. She noticed in the literature several articles were being published on the topic of hepatitis E, so she sent an email around to the whole organisation using really plain language to alert them to the literature. She deliberately avoided the use of any library jargon.

Niamh is creative about her use of email as a communication tool. She says that her emails will often consist of just a question (e.g. the subject line of the email may read, 'Would you like to be kept up to date on hepatitis E?'). She has found this method works well, because if you ask a question, people feel like they should give an answer. In this case, she received 35 positive responses. In the past, she might have put 'new distribution list in the library', which may only have received 15 responses. It is important to be proactive and speaking 'their language'. Getting to where the users are at, bringing the library to users and speaking to them, giving them what they want. 'It is not about giving them what I think I want, it is about giving them what they **really, really want** – a bit like the Spice Girls!' Don't be afraid to 'dumb things down' or, in other words, be very clever. Market using the active voice, ask questions and speak your users' language.

## Do you use any formal method of measuring and/or reporting your impact?

The librarian admitted that this is an area where perhaps she falls down a little. She quotes Albert Einstein: 'Not everything that is counted counts and not everything that counts can be counted'.

'We do not have time to count every operational thing that we do, between queries, the newsletter, document supply and putting items up on the intranet – this itself is highly visible. What we do is seen by others in the organisation'. She informally gathers feedback using surveys and by talking to key stakeholders in the organisation. She uses a balanced scorecard and presents this to her manager to explain what she has planned for the year. There is no requirement from management to supply 'proof' that things are getting done; the activity and impact speaks for itself.

The newsletter particularly improves the visibility of the librarian organisation wide. She cajoles, begs, bribes and flatters people into providing her with content; it means that she has good interpersonal communication skills with people and good working relationships. For example, she barters by helping people out with a query and asking them to give her some content for the newsletter in return.

## Challenging scenario

A fictional challenging scenario was suggested to Niamh in which she might return from a summer break and be confronted with a scenario of being re-deployed to the Human Resources (HR) department in the service. Her reaction was to say that she would be the worst possible HR person imaginable given that her value was not appreciated. 'On the other hand, you have to start by valuing what you do yourself; then you have to start telling people how good you are and repeat this message to several people in the organisation'. Personally, she knows that she is good at her job and if she stops being valued by her organisation she has the confidence to know that she will get something else. Self-belief is important, and you have to be able to tell people what you are good at, play to your strengths and avoid things that are not your strengths.

## Top tips for librarians to increase visibility

'Get less serious, I understand the values of systematic reviews, but librarians are getting too side-lined into this area. Libraries are a service at the end of the day, and you need to promote what you do and you need "bums on seats" if you have a physical library – you need people in the door, using the space. It doesn't matter if they are reading papers, or what they do, as long as the space is being used'. She feels that helping a team with a systematic review is laudable, but it is 'putting all our eggs in one basket'.

## What do you think of the 'embedded librarian' model, in which the librarian is part of a multi-disciplinary team, doing all of the things she may have done in the library but the physical library is no longer there, she is now part of this team?

'This seems to be the model that everyone is celebrating at the moment, but I have my doubts'. She felt that the people in that particular team would hopefully benefit from having a librarian on board and that they would value the librarian and spread the word. 'However, how visible is the librarian in this scenario? Just to the immediate team? If the library is still there, then isn't the profession also more visible? The danger is that the embedded librarian is pigeon holed. The library is a one-stop-shop for information. Questions are encouraged from everyone on any topic, from "How do I spell something in Irish" to "Can you help me with this systematic review?" This is why internal communications have been working with this library. This suits me; in our profession we enjoy a degree of flexibility. Another librarian might step into my shoes and bring different skills; she may not like the communications piece, but she might be great at something else like acquisitions and strategic planning – an area I'm not so good on. She can put her own shape on the organisation. That is what makes this profession so good'.

Niamh quotes from the film *Robots*, where there was a motto, 'See a need, fill a need'. She feels this approach is applicable in a health care environment in which we cannot afford to get too caught up in planning. 'We need to be able to be reactive and be able to divert from the plan. Because a new disease can rear its ugly head and you have to be able to set up alerts for this immediately. This wouldn't have been part of a strategic plan, but when all is said and done, it is highly valued by the organisation and particularly so by patients'.

### What is your favourite thing about being a librarian?

'My favourite thing about being a librarian, in a nutshell, is that I am never bored at work. I learn something new every day and no day is the same. It's a job with scope as it's not a typical desk job and it's anything but routine. When you work with people, changing technologies, and always-new resources, how could it be?'

'I also love other librarians – they are usually intelligent, cultured, well read and open people who bring a myriad of skills, backgrounds and interests to the profession. I network with and meet other librarians at every opportunity, which is very important as a solo librarian and adds greatly to my professional and personal development'.

'Librarians host great conferences and CPD as they always want to learn more and challenge themselves. I feel that I become a better librarian with each passing year as I amass more knowledge and gain new skills'.

'Many of the skills I have developed as a librarian prove very valuable in all aspects of my life whether I'm doing a very complicated search for a user or figuring out the best place to buy sheet grips online'.

'Most of all – I love the fact that my profession supports the freedom to read and we champion the right to access information for all people, regardless of race, creed, religion or economic disposition. Libraries are everyone's university and have been for centuries and I am very proud to be part of such a worthy and democratic tradition'.

The final health science librarian to be interviewed is an e-resources librarian working in the NHS in the United Kingdom.

## Case study 18: e-resources librarian working at Exeter Health Library, which is the NHS library for the Royal Devon & Exeter NHS Foundation Trust Hospitals

| Name: | Pamela Geldenhuys |
|---|---|
| Organisation: | The Royal Devon & Exeter NHS Foundation Trust Hospital (honorary contract with the University of Exeter Medical School). The trust employs approximately 7000 staff members and serves a population of more than 400,000 people in Exeter, East Devon and Mid-Devon. |

## Cont'd

> Over 115,000 patients are admitted, and 450,000 outpatient clinics are held every year, with £370 million a year spent on delivering high-quality acute health care. The trust is one of the first that was created in the United Kingdom. The University of Exeter Medical School is a new school that was formed out of the Peninsula Medical School (a joint collaboration between the Universities of Exeter and Plymouth). The NHS in Devon and Cornwall works with the school to ensure that its services and facilities offer the right environment to support the way doctors are trained in line with the General Medical Council's guidance, 'Tomorrow's doctors'. The trust outlines its vision in the 2013/2014 Annual Report and Accounts (Royal Devon and Exeter NHS Foundation Trust, 2014) as follows:

> **Vision**: The trust vision is to provide safe, high-quality seamless services delivered with courtesy and respect.
> **Values**:
>
> - Honesty, openness and integrity
> - Fairness
> - Inclusion and collaboration
> - Respect and dignity.

The library has a charter (Exeter Health Library User Charter, 2014) which sets out its mission as follows:

## *Mission of Exeter Medical Library*

> To support the provision of high-quality health care in the Exeter and District Healthcare Community by providing access to the knowledge base of health care and by facilitating its effective use.

## *Online visibility*

| | |
|---|---|
| Librarian's profile on NHS website: | https://medicine.exeter.ac.uk/about/profiles/index.php?web_id=Pamela_Geldenhuys |
| Library website: | http://services.exeter.ac.uk/eml/ |
| Library Facebook page: | https://www.facebook.com/ExeterHealthLibrary |
| Twitter: | https://twitter.com/ExeHealthLib |
| Linkedin: | http://uk.linkedin.com/pub/pamela-geldenhuys/21/888/a39 |

Pamela Geldenhuys is the e-resources librarian based at Exeter Health Library. She has worked there since the end of 2009. She co-ordinates electronic resources for the trust. There is national procurement of 'core content', which the NHS purchases centrally and Pamela looks after local subscriptions. She liaises with local and regional bodies. She is a member of the South West Institute for Clinical Effectiveness (SWICE), which provides access to eight bibliographic databases, ebooks and ejournals. They have some funding to procure regional resources; however, there is doubt whether this funding will continue because the remit of Health Education England has changed. Pam says that there is speculation that the funds will go instead towards the national core content. On the one hand, this could be positive because the NHS will have more buying power; on the other hand, local resources may be affected. The library used to belong to Exeter University, but in 2003 it was handed over to the NHS. The library is in the Peninsula Medical School building now adjoined to the new building, Research, Innovation, Learning and Development (RILD). Pam explains that there has been a 'battle' to get nurses on board to use the library. Plymouth and Exeter Universities initially set up the Peninsula Medical School as a joint initiative, but the universities have since split. There are still 3 years left of students who enrolled with the original Peninsula Medical School, and their time must be honoured. After those 3 years, it will only be the University of Exeter Medical School.

The organisation structure is slightly complicated at present. The library caters for medical students in years three–five and their tutors. Most of the tutors are also clinicians in the hospital; therefore, there is a lot of cross-over. The library is not seen as 'an NHS library'. It is referred to as the 'PMS library' (Peninsula Medical School) a rather unfortunate acronym! They have walk-in access to Exeter University's electronic resources which, according to Pamela, 'is excellent' and access to NHS resources. Pamela explains that the Finch report (Finch, 2012) has helped with the access and sharing of resources. There are issues every day with journals, access, link resolvers and electronic resources. She manages the local NHS OpenAthens Link Resolvers, which is the authentication system used by NHS libraries throughout the United Kingdom.

Pamela feels that at present she rates an 8 on the visibility scale in terms of her visibility with key stakeholders in her organisation (Table 24). There are several key stakeholders including Health Education England, South West Education England, the SWICE group and the Clinical Commissioning Groups (CCGs). From a user authentication point of view, the CCGs are a separate group to her organisation, and there is currently no funding for them. It is a bit of a grey area because Health Education England still supports the CCGs, but they only receive access to basic resources from the core content; they do not have access to the wider suite of resources regionally available. She feels that it is a complex situation in that 'they feel they do not need us'. She feels she has high visibility with Health Education England, South West Education England and the SWICE group.

## Methods of increasing visibility

The library has recently become involved in monthly Grand Round meetings at the hospital, and speakers from the publisher providers, including BMJ™ and

**Table 24  Self-reported visibility rating of librarian at time of appointment versus today**

| Self-reported visibility rating at time of appointment: where 0=invisible and 10=highly visible | | | | | | | | | | |
|---|---|---|---|---|---|---|---|---|---|---|
| With key stakeholders | 0 | 1 | 2 | 3 | 4 | **5** | 6 | 7 | 8 | 9 | 10 |
| With staff/users of the service | 0 | 1 | 2 | 3 | 4 | **5** | 6 | 7 | 8 | 9 | 10 |
| **Self-reported visibility today (5 years after appointment): where 0=invisible and 10=highly visible** | | | | | | | | | | |
| With key stakeholders | 0 | 1 | 2 | 3 | 4 | 5 | 6 | 7 | **8** | 9 | 10 |
| With key staff/users of the service | 0 | 1 | 2 | 3 | 4 | 5 | 6 | **7** | 8 | 9 | 10 |

EBSCO™, were invited. Marketing messages on Twitter and Facebook were sent out to promote it, and a stand was set up in the atrium outside of the lecture theatre where the Grand Rounds take place. A demonstration of EBSCO's point-of-care product, DynaMed™ will be done at the start of one of the Grand Rounds. At the end of the year, the SWICE group will conduct a survey to obtain feedback from clinical staff and clinicians about DynaMed and other products such as UpTo-Date™. She feels this has increased the visibility of library staff and the library among clinicians. Apart from that, she feels that increasing visibility has been 'quite a struggle'.

In 2009, when Pamela first started, she feels she would have rated about a 5. She explains that she is new to librarianship, and she initially started out as a library assistant working in the library for 4 years. She came to the profession late in her life. She was less confident when she first started out. She feels there is much more going on now with the university and working directly with clinicians in the organisation of the Grand Rounds has helped. Initially, the library website was popular, but as time has gone on, it is less so. Word-of-mouth marketing and going around to departments in the hospital sometimes works. However, meetings get cancelled all of the time because of other emergencies in the hospital; therefore, sometimes it is difficult in a hospital environment to get good exposure. Her best ways of increasing visibility is through inductions, Grand Rounds and 'getting out there' more. The library will be setting up a space in the staff canteen, which is in the main hospital building, and making this a regular thing once a week.

### What value do you think you have brought to the organisation as a librarian?

Pamela says she is Internet savvy and she enjoys social media. The trust has recently recruited a young reader services librarian who has 10 years of experience in working at Exeter University. She finds that together they make a good team. She finds that she can be faster at doing things, but she brings a wealth of experience and is keen to 'push forward'. The rest of the team are nearing retirement and are supportive, but it makes a difference to have a new younger person in the team. They are looking at setting up an institutional repository and have been in discussions with the Research and Development department. Pamela feels that librarians have to find different things and try them out. She says, 'You have to figure out which things will be more "people-facing" and give you more return. There's no good in just sitting at your desk and doing your job – you have to get out there'.

## Impact that the library brings to the organisation

'BMJ Learning™ is made available to staff via the library, which means that it is becoming more aligned with medical education. Medical education has moved into the new RILD building next to the library building, which has helped raise the profile of the library. If there is any induction of new junior doctors, the library is involved. The library staff have developed personalised induction packs for them, which have "gone down very well". The physical library is geographically removed from the main hospital, which has not been good for the library's exposure. However, the expansion of e-resources has had a bigger impact than the physical space of the library. Now clinicians cannot rush over and grab a journal/paper or book that they may have done in the past, but they can access journals online. At times they forget their logins and will not admit that they've forgotten them until they specifically need something. This even happens with clinicians, where ejournals have been especially bought for them'.

She recalls that one of the orthopaedic consultants becoming rather agitated – Pamela was not in work that day, and he could not remember his login. He came over to the library and it turned out he had not renewed his NHS OpenAthens account. The journal he needed access to had just changed platform, and he was trying to get in using the original username and password, which had expired. It is at times like this that the library service becomes more visible, although perhaps not in a positive way.

## Formal method of measuring and/or reporting library and librarian impact

Pamela produces a twice-yearly usage report using NHS OpenAthens statistics, circulation statistics from the LMS and e-resources usage statistics. The combined results give the librarian a feel for how they are doing and what impact they are having. They performed a large online survey in 2012 and they ran another one in 2014 to determine physical and virtual visits and experiences of the library. They placed coloured cards in the library, which briefly asked visitors who they are and what they came to the library for. This is going to help to give the librarian a picture of impact and user needs. She says it is difficult to get clinicians to fill surveys in, even if it only takes 2 min. In 2012, only 195 people filled in the survey out of 6000; this is despite the fact that they had vouchers as an incentive to fill in the survey. She says, 'It's like the library needs to be there because you need a library.

But it seems people do not seem to need to engage that much with the library in the same way anymore'.

## Can you think of a challenging scenario you've faced and how did you overcome it?

'The library is responsible for the annual renewal purchase of the subscription to a point-of-care tool. Every year the budget is being cut back. This year the journal budget will be cut by £5000. The hospital requires the electronic point-of-care tool – if the library cannot continue to cover the funding – in the future this will have to be obtained from the Medical Director. This draws attention to the library as the provider but not in a good way if the funding falls short. There is a new government tariff that has changed the way the organisation is funded for students, which means another cut. There is a split between education and service. This is why they are doing a survey to try to find out how many people use the library for education and how many use it for services. The library knows that people use the library for both purposes, so it is difficult to break it down like this'.

## Top tips for health science librarians to increase visibility

- Get involved on the ground as much as possible.
- Be seen at inductions and Grand Rounds.
- Give presentations and lectures.
- Develop online visibility on websites, blogs and social media.

## Do you think the embedded librarian/librarian in context is the future for health librarians? (Note: 'Embedded librarian' refers to a librarian who does not necessarily need a physical library to do their job. They can work in a research team or health care team independent of the library.)

Pamela feels that to a degree this could be the future, but that it is a bit of a mixed bag. She believes that there will be a need for more virtual and online presence for librarians. They have one CL who is starting out in that role – she is the library manager of the psychiatric library – Wonford House Hospital Library, which is the library for Devon Partnership Trust. She performs many literature searches for both trusts. A CL in another South West NHS Trust is working on the ward rounds with an iPad, doing literature searches and this is working out very well. One of the ways of the future is to be embedded, but the virtual presence is also very important.

## How important is it for the librarian to be visible in an online environment?

'Things like having a photo of the librarian online and "Ask a Librarian" live chat service are important. This isn't always possible due to bandwidth or restrictions on content'. She feels that if clinicians may be looking for information at all hours of the night and early morning, then an online chat service might be useful. The 'Chasing the Sun' initiative was tried, but it did not have much uptake in the United Kingdom. South America and Australia had a better uptake. 'Twitter, Facebook and a WordPress blog are all worth having as a library'. She is currently looking at Pinterest. Cardiff University Hospital Library is using this and has developed it very nicely with a board for each specialty. She is thinking of setting this up for every speciality with notices, comments and items of interest. Pinterest is getting more like a blog. 'The problem is that there are more and more technologies and platforms available online, and it can be difficult to know which ones to run with. Of those, Twitter seems to be the most popular. The library ran an induction for third-year medical students in September 2014 and did an audience clicker to find out which form of social media they used most often. The answer was Facebook. However, the students will not join the library on Facebook because they do not want librarians to see what they are up to. It is used for personal socialising rather than work. They all have smartphones now, all students and all clinicians'.

### Do you have any tips for new people entering any specialty within librarianship?

- Have a mentor. Pamela has a mentor via CILIP who helped her with her degree and now with her CILIP chartership. She thinks this is very important
- Study under someone in the area you are interested in – whether it is collection development, social media or acquisitions – go and sit and shadow the librarian who is responsible for that area. This is good for personal development and it helps newcomers to decide which area of librarianship they would enjoy most.

### How to you see the role of the librarian evolving in 5 years?

Pamela feels the role will remain pretty much the same because of the financial situation. She is trying to grow the ebooks collection, but this is being met with a lot of resistance. The budget for print books and journals has dropped. She is hoping that Health Education England will purchase a discovery tool. 'The library as a place will still remain. There may be less books and more e-ILLs, but generally librarians are very dependent on the financial aspect. In the NHS, the computers are on Internet Explorer version 7 because a lot of clinical programs cannot work on higher versions of Internet Explorer'.

### What is your favourite thing about being a librarian?

'The Internet! E-resources, people contact, contact with health professionals and learning about better ways of doing things. There is always something new to learn, it doesn't stop. There are not enough hours in the day'.

All librarians working in health care who were interviewed shared tips on increasing visibility, which is captured in the word cloud in Figure 9.

**Figure 9** Word cloud of tips for health science librarians to increase their visibility.

## Summary

Tips for increasing visibility, value and impact of the librarian in health science environments:

1. Keep an ear to the ground in your organisation; find out what is going on and look out for opportunities to get involved in new projects.
2. Perform your own research and publish it. Collaborate with other disciplines where possible.
3. Highlight your searching skills to anyone involved in research. This is particularly important for systematic reviews.
4. Get credit for search, retrieval and screening of literature either as a named author or acknowledgement in published works, particularly for systematic reviews.
5. Develop a current awareness service and product that works for your users. If you are not sure if it is working, then ask them for feedback. Modify the service and product accordingly. Do not call it a current awareness service as this is library jargon. Call it 'Evidence Update' or something similar.
6. Adapt your role to the needs of the organisation.
7. Attend clinical meetings.
8. Regularly report your impact to management.
9. Try incorporating bibliotherapy services.
10. Directly supply some full-text articles to the requestor when possible.
11. Use email effectively; that is, pay attention to the subject line and keep the message short and snappy. Avoid library jargon.
12. Keep in regular contact with clinicians. Regularly use effective communication strategies to contact clinicians.
13. Have a 'lift speech' or 'elevator pitch' ready and regularly update it.
14. Know what your product(s) is and be prepared to explain it using non-library jargon.
15. Have some fun and use humour to promote your profile and the library.

16. Have a strong online presence, complete with photo of the librarian and contact details.
17. Embed online chat with a librarian into clinicians' online websites when possible.
18. Use social media. Find out if your readers are using social media, which platforms they are on and get into that space. Keep in contact via Twitter, Linkedin etc.
19. Present. Present at health, medical, nursing and interdisciplinary conferences. If you prefer not to present, then have a poster at the conference to start out.
20. Hospital librarians should attend and present at Grand Rounds.
21. Network with health professionals in person within your organisations.
22. Introduce yourself to new people.
23. Get to know your readers and their needs.
24. Ask for feedback and act upon it.
25. If you are new to the profession, then seek a mentor through your professional library association.
26. Liaise with key stakeholders and departments within your organisation, including communications and public health.
27. Strive for excellence in everything you do.

# Note

**Compassionate communities**: See http://www.compassionatecommunities.ie/ for more information.

## *Finlay tribunal*

The report of the Tribunal of Inquiry into the Blood Transfusion Service Board, published in March 1997, recommended a new development plan for the BTSB that detailed a major renewal, re-organisation and investment programme for the organisation. This included the setting up of the **National Blood Users Group** (BUG) and the **National Haemovigilance Office** (NHO) in 1999. The appointment of the Research Officer/Librarian, also in 1999, was to provide research support to these two groups and to the organisation as a whole.

**Grand Rounds**: These are an important teaching tool and ritual of medical education and inpatient care, consisting of presenting the medical problems and treatment of a particular patient to an audience consisting of doctors, residents and medical students (Source: Wikipedia).

**Chasing the Sun**: This is an initiative to cater for online reference queries from clinicians working in different time zones in the world. See more at http://health. sa.gov.au.libguides.com/salus.

# Case studies: visibility of special librarians and special libraries

*The only source of knowledge is experience.*

**Albert Einstein**

One of the advantages of librarianship is that librarians acquire a transferable set of skills and competencies that may be applied to diverse settings, organisations and teams. Special librarianship has a long and varied history. Special libraries include but are not limited to law, corporate settings, business, research and charities as well as military, medical and unique organisations. Many librarians working in special libraries may be working as solo librarians. In this case, the need for networking, peer support and contact is ever important. Making yourself visible to other librarians working in special areas of librarianship is key to success and personal and professional growth.

The library and information science (LIS) literature contains examples of librarians and libraries in special settings where the impact of their presence and involvement has contributed to a business or societal value. Compared with public, academic and school libraries, special librarians do not have a concrete or substantial body of evidence to demonstrate their value. Various library associations lead the way by producing documents for librarians on the topic of impact and value. For example, the U.S. Special Library Association makes several impact publications available to members and the International Federation of Library Associations and Institutions (IFLA) Statistics and Evaluation Group have an impact and outcome bibliography available on their website (Poll, 2014). A snapshot of recent literature where value or impact indicators are present for special libraries/librarians is highlighted in Table 25.

It is essential for special librarians to communicate their value in a tangible and visible way to stakeholders. There are many ways of doing this, including the balanced scorecard as a library scorecard as identified by Matthews (2006); return on investment (ROI) based on an information map (Hendriks & Wooler, 2006); using international standards such as ISO 11620:2014 Information and Documentation – Library Performance Indicators and ISO 16439:2014 Information and Documentation – Methods and Procedures for Assessing the Impact of Libraries; or by simply having a whiteboard with visible data showing value as is highlighted by one of the interviewees in this chapter. Whatever the methodology or the means, special librarians need to focus on the end. Special librarians need to be able to measure and show their impact and value not only for their stakeholders to ensure continued funding and support but also for themselves. Being able to track progress and impact informs strategic plans for librarians and enables them to make data-driven decisions, including stopping doing certain things and putting more effort and resources into other activities that offer them and their clients more return.

**Table 25  Research demonstrating evidence of the value of special libraries/librarians to readers and organisations**

| Value/impact indicator | Research/evidence |
| --- | --- |
| Save money, good return on investment | Hye-Kyung Chung (2007) |
| | Australian Library and Information Association (2014) |
| Stay current and up-to-date | Renn et al. (2012) |
| Save time | Botha, Rene, and Van Deventer (2009) and He and Juterbock (2012) |
| Higher success rate in research | Botha et al. (2009) |
| Improve job performance | He and Juterbock (2012) |

Concentrating on delivering services that are reader or user centred is all important, as has been identified by Germano and others (Germano, 2011; Broady-Preston & Swain, 2012). The literature has seen an increase in the focus on a user-centred approach to library services and user experience in particular (Marquez & Downey, 2015). A good place to start for all librarians thinking about impact is with the reader or user. Strategies adopted by librarians in various settings that successfully incorporated user feedback are covered in Chapter 9. Ways of gathering user input and feedback are further explored in Chapter 7.

The following interviews will give an insight into the working lives of special librarians and their approaches to increasing visibility, value and impact.

# Case study 19: librarian working independently as a knowledge management consultant and an information technology librarian at the State of Alaska Court Law Library

| | |
| --- | --- |
| Name: | Ken Wheaton |
| Organisation: | Applied Knowledge Sciences, State of Alaska Court Law Library |

## Mission of the Alaska Court System

The mission of the Alaska Court System is to provide an accessible and impartial forum for the just resolution of all cases that come before it and to decide such cases in accordance with the law, expeditiously and with integrity.

## Mission of the law library

The Alaska State Court Law Library serves the legal information needs of Alaskans by selecting, organizing and facilitating access to legal research resources and court system information.

The main library collection and statewide administration is at the Anchorage Law Library. Library services are available to people throughout the state. There are 16 branch libraries in the Alaska State Court Law Library system. The law libraries in Anchorage, Fairbanks, Juneau and Ketchikan branches are staffed. All other branches are unstaffed.

## Online visibility of library and librarian

| | |
|---|---|
| Law library website: | http://courts.alaska.gov/library/index.htm |
| Applied Knowledge Sciences website: | http://aksciences.com |
| Linkedin: | www.linkedin.com/pub/dir/ken/wheaton/us-38-Anchorage,-Alaska-Area/ |
| Slideshare: | http://www.slideshare.net/kwheaton/2010-sla-km-murray-and-wheaton |
| Facebook: | facebook.com/kenrwheaton |
| Twitter: | @Krwheaton |

Ken Wheaton is currently the information technology (IT) librarian at the Alaska State Court Law Library in the United States. He recently also began working as a knowledge management consultant at Applied Knowledge Sciences. He previously served as President of the Board of Directors at the Pacific Northwest Chapter of the Special Library Association in the United States. He has extensive experience of special librarianship, knowledge management and IT and high visibility within the special library community.

## Background

Ken had a previous role as a knowledge manager in a private company where he worked from 1993 to 2008. He noticed that a lot of corporate libraries were shutting down and that many librarians were losing their jobs. He knew he had to do things differently. He had to be proactive; he spoke to people in leadership positions at his company and became involved in what was really needed for the organisation. He asked questions such as 'Are we getting the right information?' To find out, he performed a needs assessment.

The number one thing that resulted from the needs assessment exercise was communication issues. Communication issues existed between critical departments such as Research and Development (R&D) and the Sales department. He was surprised by this finding because he was expecting to get feedback on things such as database recommendations.

Because of this finding, he decided that he had to adopt a different approach. He performed 'informational interviewing' and networking with different people. 'I had to do a role shift and transition more into knowledge management. This required a much more visible role than in the past. It was necessary to talk with the e-suite to obtain support'. He looked carefully at the information needs and the databases that the library was providing. He analysed the literature searching that he was performing. He found that these needs were best served by outsourcing the service. 'I also trimmed the library annual budget substantially in this transition by doing a detailed analysis of our services and processes. The library staff jumped into more of a knowledge management role. They became involved in strategic planning, situational analysis and developing goals and objectives'. He received support for this change from his supervisor and leadership. 'I also formed one of the company's first cross-functional teams to help make better informed decisions'. Eventually knowledge management was one of four goals and objectives for the company.

He has since left that position to move to Alaska to take up his current position at the State of Alaska Court Law Library. However, he keeps in contact with his former supervisor and knows that the company is still doing well. The systems he put in place for knowledge management and transfer are still in place. One system was a knowledge base for the sales force to use to report back about competitors. He also built a research database detailing what was going on in R&D so that the sales department could track that. 'These systems led to online visibility and are all still in place and operating effectively. I had an advantage of working for a private company wanting to be much more competitive in the marketplace'.

## How visible do you feel with key stakeholders?

'I have found government, just by its nature, to be very bureaucratic and with many silos. Visibility just takes a lot more work. It can be done. It just takes a lot of patience and a lot of time'. Half of his job is involved with working on a team for website redesign and the updating the court's website. This is a team effort, and he feels it helps his visibility. There are many stakeholders involved with the website, and he has high visibility with them. Ken has received an award for his work on making the court website more ADA (Americans with Disabilities Act) compliant in 2010 and for his involvement with a team project for redesigning the site in 2013.

He started working as a knowledge management consultant a few months ago. One thing he has noticed in the knowledge management profession that is missing is knowledge curation. He feels that librarians have those skills. He would like to see

**Table 26** **Self-reported visibility rating of librarian at time of appointment versus today**

| Self-reported visibility rating at time of appointment: where 0 = invisible and 10 = highly visible | | | | | | | | | | |
|---|---|---|---|---|---|---|---|---|---|---|
| With key stakeholders | 0 | 1 | **2** | 3 | 4 | 5 | 6 | 7 | 8 | 9 | 10 |
| With readers | 0 | **1** | 2 | 3 | 4 | 5 | 6 | 7 | 8 | 9 | 10 |
| Self-reported visibility today (6 years 11 months after appointment): where 0 = invisible and 10 = highly visible | | | | | | | | | | |
| With key stakeholders | 0 | 1 | 2 | 3 | 4 | **5** | 6 | 7 | 8 | 9 | 10 |
| With readers | 0 | 1 | 2 | 3 | 4 | 5 | **6** | 7 | 8 | 9 | 10 |

those skills matched within a knowledge management profession. He is interested in progressing skills that he brought to previous positions, such as the corporate librarian role described above. He calls this 'a total transformation, which I understand, not too many people have done'.

He feels that he scores 5 out of 10 with key stakeholders (Table 26). 'Right now, I'm not as visible as I'd like to be, but it is the nature of government bureaucracy. It makes visibility a little harder. It takes more work, you just have to get out there and network and work with people as best as you can. And yes, expect to get your hands slapped a bit'.

## How visible do you feel with readers/users of the library service?

'We serve the Alaska Bar and the State Law librarian and Public Services librarian work mostly with them. They increase their visibility through determining what the needs of the Alaska Bar, law clerks and other related users are'. He feels that he scores 6 out of 10 for his visibility with readers and users of the library at present. He feels that the visibility of the librarians to the general public could probably improve (Table 26).

## When you first started at the State of Alaska Court Law Library almost 7 years ago, how would you rate your visibility on a scale of 0–10 with (1) key stakeholders and (2) readers or users of the library service?

Ken feels that when he was first appointed, he scored a 2 on the visibility scale with key stakeholders and a 1 with users. His visibility has increased significantly over time.

### If you think back over your career, what has been your most successful method of increasing your visibility as a librarian?

'The most successful method has been being involved with team projects. People notice what your skills are. By providing input to teams and working together, people understand your value'.

### What value do you think you've brought to your organisation as a librarian?

As part of a three-member team, Ken currently shares the primary responsibility for the State Court website. He describes his value by way of a gap analysis. 'The website is pretty important. A lot of important things get posted on the website – opinions and all kinds of announcements. There is a self-help centre for the general public. I'd say that I have a pretty important role. If that wasn't there, they may struggle with getting information that might be needed for anyone involved with the courts. Being trained as an information professional means that I bring even more value to that role'.

### What impact has the library service had on the organisation?

The library service is provided to law clerks, who in turn do work for the judges. The appropriate information, legal databases such as Westlaw, the library catalogue and other legal resources are provided to them. Ken says, 'I think the judges see the value right there in the service provided to the law clerks'.

### Do you use any formal method of reporting impact or value?

Ken previously kept all of his data on a whiteboard, and this was highly visible. People could see at any time where they were at and the impact that the library and librarian were having on the organisation. In his current role, it is a little bit more difficult to do with the bureaucratic management style in government. He works with his boss, who works with the senior staff. Visibility is reported upward, in terms of what he does and how he adds value.

### If you faced a challenging scenario to your role, how did you respond?

Being proactive when he was a corporate librarian and being proactive in his current role have been his best way of responding to challenging situations. He finds that it is very important to keep in touch with peoples' needs and making a fundamental change if it is needed. 'Don't always assume that just because you have a service out there, that it is the right one. Keep track of the data. I'm a strong believer in data and the visibility of data. It can tell a story sometimes'.

### What are your top tips for librarians working in special or corporate settings to increase their visibility?

'I recommend getting involved with leadership. Let them know what your skills are and do not try to tell them what they need to do. Try to determine what their needs are. Then try to meet those needs. This may be things like increasing collaboration across teams or departments or building databases that deliver this'.

### Do you think the embedded librarian or the librarian in context is the future for librarians?

'When we implemented knowledge management , it wasn't embedded at first but was soon as it became one of the organisation's four goals and objectives. But yes, it makes a difference if you are embedded. You really have to be part of it to make it go forward'.

### How important do you think it is for the librarian to be visible to users in an online environment?

Ken feels that it can vary. 'It is nice to be available via a chat box or something similar. However, whether this is a requirement, I'm not so sure. The minimum thing that is needed is contact details, a phone number or email to get help'.

### What is your most successful method of increasing visibility in an online environment?

'Promoting online resources and simultaneously working with the person who had been identified as having information needs. Making sure information needs were met. Making data available that were identified via needs assessments works well. Having an option for people to provide feedback is important'.

### Do you think librarians should be visible in social media such as Twitter and blogs – is this important?

Ken says that if the need is there, then yes. He strongly believes that technology is only an enabler. 'You've got to line up the people, the processes and then bring in the technology – only if needed. If you throw a technology out there and think that it's going to have all the answers, most of the time, when you go that route, it is not successful. Look at the people and what they want. Look at the process and how you are going to get them and then ask, "Is technology the answer?"'.

### For new people in the profession of librarianship, what advice would you give them on increasing their visibility and impact?

'I would network, not just within the profession, but within the organisation. Get around and get to know people and what they do. Tell them about what I do as well.

Informational interviewing is a great way to find out who's who'. This is always the way that Ken has got jobs. He has never applied for an open job.

### Where do you see the corporate librarian in 5 years?

'I really think that knowledge management is the future. Information is usually what is written and is the past and in many cases already outdated; knowledge on the other hand is current and has much more value. Because we live in a knowledge economy and that is where the money is, I see the corporate librarian playing very strongly in that role. And being involved in the strategic planning of an organisation is a key role'.

### Can a librarian be a knowledge manager? Can they transfer into that role?

'I think that traditional librarians will either (a) not make it (b) or they will *have to* go into that role. It is becoming more and more a requirement of most organisations. Most organisations have identified the need for knowledge management'. He talks about Toyota as being a good example of a company that is able to effectively manage the knowledge that they produce. 'They are number one. They come back quickly. This is because they know when to go down into the trenches and work effectively as a team. They are very good at managing what they know. More and more companies are going that way. They are starting to see the value of knowledge and leveraging what people know. And what people can learn from each other'.

### What is your favourite thing about being a librarian?

'My favourite thing has been the change in the profession. It has been huge since I've been in it. I remember way back to the card catalogue environment when the emphasis was totally on books. Then came databases. Then you had to get more involved in change management and knowledge management. You had to start learning more about how to write code for websites and SQL. It's been a very good profession in terms of growth. But you gotta be willing to do that'.

## Case study 20: librarian working as an information scientist in the Child and Family Agency

| Name: | Bernard Barrett |
|-------|-----------------|
| Organisation: | TUSLA – Child and Family Agency |

## Mission of the organisation

TUSLA is a statutory organisation in Ireland. The Child and Family Act, 2013, sets out several of its functions in detail, including the following:

- Supporting and promoting the development, welfare and protection of children and the effective functioning of families.
- Offering care and protection for children in circumstances in which their parents have not been able to, or are unlikely to, provide the care that a child needs. To discharge these responsibilities, the agency is required to maintain and develop the services needed to deliver these supports to children and families and provide certain services for the psychological welfare of children and their families.
- Responsibility for ensuring that every child in the state attends school or otherwise receives an education as well as for providing education welfare services to support and monitor children's attendance, participation and retention in education.
- Ensuring that the best interests of the child guide all decisions affecting individual children.
- Consulting children and families so that they help to shape the agency's policies and services.
- Strengthening interagency co-operation to ensure seamless services responsive to needs.
- Undertaking research relating to its functions and providing information and advice to the minister regarding those functions.
- Commissioning services relating to the provision of child and family services.

## Online visibility of library and librarian

| | |
|---|---|
| Tusla website: | http://www.tusla.ie |
| ResearchGate | www.researchgate.net/profile/Bernard_Barrett |
| Linkedin: | https://ie.linkedin.com/pub/bernard-barrett/3/ab9/654 |

Bernard Barrett is an information scientist based within the Child and Family Agency, who undertakes research and systems analysis within his role as research officer. Bernard formerly worked as a librarian and is the only professionally qualified librarian working at his organisation, which is called the Child and Family Agency. This agency was set up at the beginning of 2014 as part of a governmental restructuring of the Irish National Health Service. Before this, he worked with the mental health directorate in the local and national health system in Ireland. He has extensive experience in working in health libraries and previously held the position of Chair to the Irish Health Science Libraries Group, a section of the Library Association of Ireland. His role is presently information scientist/research officer.

## Current role

Although it is difficult to encapsulate everything that he does, his primary role at present is as a Local Systems Administrator to the pilot of the National Childcare Information System (NCCIS). In addition to that, he has been asked to get involved with records management and archiving. He is frequently asked to evaluate different databases. In 2014, he will be evaluating a database to capture information about violence against women and domestic abuse. A lot of his work can change depending on priorities, and he is often asked to assist with research and writing of guidelines, policies and reports. The organisation is new; therefore, there are lots of administrative pieces that continue to have a settling-in period.

When first appointed, Bernard felt he scored a 0 to both stakeholders and staff as the role was completely new. Today, on a scale of 1–10, Bernard would consider himself to score a 9 with his key stakeholders (Table 27). He presently reports to the Area Child Care manager, and he finds it is important to be able to relate to social workers. He has been pinpointed to work with regional and national staff. He is also writing and involved in the accreditation of national fostering standards in conjunction with a team of staff. He is doing this because a lot of the regional managers knew him and knew of his work and asked him to get involved.

## How can librarians improve visibility?

'Given the hierarchical nature of organisations, especially in the public sector, a lot of what the information specialist does is based on relationships with colleagues who you come to know, or whether someone comes to know you. The quality of your work, whether you are trusted, whether you deliver on time and how you are able to approach people all count. It is important to be able to listen to what people have to say and to be able to put other points of view to them in a non-threatening way. It's not easy to get this right every time, but if you aim to get it right 70–80% of the time, people do value that. At least then they know that they can come back and learn as well as being able to say things to you'.

**Table 27 Self-reported visibility rating of librarian at time of appointment versus today**

| Self-reported visibility rating at time of appointment: where 0 = invisible and 10 = highly visible | | | | | | | | | | |
|---|---|---|---|---|---|---|---|---|---|---|
| With key stakeholders | **0** | 1 | 2 | 3 | 4 | 5 | 6 | 7 | 8 | 9 | 10 |
| With staff (colleagues) | **0** | 1 | 2 | 3 | 4 | 5 | 6 | 7 | 8 | 9 | 10 |
| Self-reported visibility today (15 months after appointment): where 0 = invisible and 10 = highly visible | | | | | | | | | | |
| With key stakeholders | 0 | 1 | 2 | 3 | 4 | 5 | 6 | 7 | 8 | **9** | 10 |
| With staff (colleagues) | 0 | 1 | 2 | 3 | 4 | 5 | 6 | 7 | **8** | 9 | 10 |

## Do you think of yourself as a librarian, information specialist or research officer?

'Among other things, I do think of myself as a librarian. I tend not to advertise this because of other people's pre-conceived notions of a stereotypical librarian'. One of the regional managers recently exclaimed his surprise at the discovery that Bernard was a qualified librarian. However, a lot of the skills and professional knowledge that he gained came from studying librarianship. Through practice over the years, these skills have helped him in his job. For example, some of the principles of organisational management and information management he would use in systems administration in terms of database management. Managerial skills come into play in the way that he works with people, how he deals with finance and strategic planning. All of these practical skills are part and parcel of librarianship. 'You do not have to work in a library to be able to apply those skills and knowledge'.

## If you think back over your career, what has been your most successful method of increasing your visibility as an information specialist?

'Being able to listen and understand and relate to people on a one-to-one basis. To be able to deal with negativity, which isn't always easy, is important. It is essential to bring professionalism and equality to your role'.

## Do you use any formal method of reporting impact/value?

'Not at the moment, as it is not required'.

## Can you think of a challenging scenario in your role and how did you respond?

Bernard recalls a challenging time when his manager was putting job adverts on his desk as a hint. In the end, it was easiest to recognise what was happening – the superior was threatened by the skills and ability of the librarian – so he looked for other better opportunities to move on. Many of the managers in the public sector in his experience have no managerial qualifications or training. When their decisions or directions are questioned, they feel threatened by it and do not deal with feedback well. The insecurities around jobs occur because of this lack of experience and lack of training.

For example, in his previous job working in mental health – the department ceased to exist – so he was told one day 'Ok, you are moving'. He knew change was on the way, but it had not been widely communicated to him or other staff.

On one occasion, he was talking to a manager in child care who was younger than him, who was not keeping him in the loop about activities on a project he was involved in. He could not get any satisfaction from the situation, so he spoke to the area manager and explained that it was a waste of his time being involved in the project and something had to be done about it. He maintains it is important to be assertive and to stand up for yourself, no matter what your profession is. This in turn builds respect.

Redeployment to other departments in the public sector in Ireland can be a challenge. In the event of him being redeployed to a department that would have been completely unsuitable, then he would have 'kicked up a fuss' and gone to the trade union if need be.

### Do you think it is important for librarians to be able to demonstrate their value to their organisation through the means of, for example, a balanced scorecard/statistics/annual report?

'I'm not sure how important that is as most of it relates to service provision. I wouldn't rule it out, especially if there is a physical library. However, first and foremost, it is important to demonstrate the abilities and skills of the librarian. If you do this effectively, it becomes easier to argue for a place for the librarian, be it physical or virtual'.

'To demonstrate value effectively, the key thing is to build strong and even strategic relationships in the organisation. Demonstrating that you are trustworthy, that you are prepared to listen, also that you are prepared to admit that you do not know something or that you may have to seek advice on a query are all valuable traits'.

### What are your top tips for librarians working in health care to increase their visibility?

'Get out of the library, I think personally'.

'Learn to develop the intellectual component of being a librarian'.

By this, he means to be able to question things; for example, in health care, people talk about evidence-based practice. We need to ask what is evidence? We need to ask questions and find answers; otherwise, we will only be able to work within a certain niche. This is important because if one day someone comes along and questions what you do and your value, if you have not developed those critical thinking skills, then you will not be able to answer – instead, you will go into defensive mode – at which point you have lost the argument.

### Future of health sciences librarianship and thoughts on the 'embedded librarian'

When commenting on his thoughts of the future of health and medical librarianship as that of the embedded librarian, he felt that this was not a good future, from what he has read about the role. It is being seen as a survival strategy or an extension of an existing role rather than being something new or something that can be developed. 'If the model involves a librarian being part of a clinical team where they are sourcing literature, then it is not really anything new or original. We need to ask what does this really add to the team?'

## Advice to new entrants to the profession of librarianship in order to increase their visibility and impact

'To begin your career by taking a constructively critical approach to the profession and to take a critical approach to whatever they have been taught on the academic course as it may not always marry with what you find in practice'.

## What is your favourite thing about being a librarian?

'Always being open to the evaluation and learning of new knowledge and insights'.

# Case study 21: Research officer working as an embedded librarian at the Faculty of Medicine and Health Sciences

| Name: | Jane Burns |
|---|---|
| Organisation: | Royal College of Surgeons in Ireland (RCSI) |

**Mission of the organisation:** Founded in 1784 to train surgeons, today the college provides extensive education and training in the health care professions at the undergraduate and postgraduate level.

**The Faculty of Medicine and Health Sciences:** The Faculty of Medicine and Health Sciences is home to Ireland's largest medical school, one of the world's leading international medical schools, as well as the prestigious Schools of Pharmacy, Physiotherapy, Nursing and Midwifery, Postgraduate Studies and an Institute of Leadership. More information is available on the website (http://www.rcsi.ie/fmhs).

**The RCSI Health Professions Education Centre (HPEC)** was established in June 2013 in line with the college's strategic goal of achieving excellence in education. The RCSI strategy places an increasing emphasis on the professionalisation of teaching, learning and assessment within programmes and enshrines academic educational development and research across the institution. The RCSI HPEC will build on existing good practice and seek to generate opportunities for staff engaged in teaching and learning activities to create new, and strengthen existing, partnerships for the benefit of both students and staff. It will engage with the wider higher education community through dissemination of quality pedagogic developments and active research.

## Role of the research officer

Jane has worked here for 15 months. She is a professionally qualified librarian and has worked in many different libraries, including the National Meteorological Service, a children's hospital and many special libraries. She is also an occasional lecturer at the School of Library and Information Studies at University College Dublin. Jane works in the HPEC in the RCSI, which is a brand new department. The department is designed to support and interact with academic staff and develop the teaching curriculum. There are at least four strands to Jane's role. She manages Best Evidence in Medical Education (BEME) reviews. She is currently managing five systematic reviews and has to collaborate with researchers from all over the world, all in different specialities. In some of the reviews she acts as a reviewer; in others she manages the workflow involved in the review itself in terms of keeping people to timelines and using her project management skills.

In March 2014, they became the BICC (BEME International Collaborating Centres) along with 12 other universities around the world. The reviews are similar to Cochrane Systematic Reviews except they are qualitative. Anyone who would like to do a BEME review gets processed through the BICC. The protocols are read, subject experts are brought in and a decision is made on whether they go ahead or not. Another role that she has is direct involvement in research. She is the principal investigator on a piece of research being performed in conjunction with McGill University looking at the view of professionalism of general practitioners. The number of students interested in becoming general practitioners around the world is declining, with the exception of Ireland – this is the topic of her research. Another part of her role is providing research support. All academics come into her department when developing their academic curriculum. For example, their department has a learning and enhancement officer who would look at the technical approach to a course; Jane would look at the digital literacy element.

The other role she has is in teaching. She teaches academic writing. The aim of this is to improve the quality and quantity of research produced and to encourage people in the writing process. It is a combination of creative writing and academic writing. She brings in things such as understanding bibliometric, citation index and altmetrics. A spin off of this course is that they are introducing a short course on digital professionalism.

Jane rates herself as a 0 on the visibility scale when she first started the job. She states 'nobody knew who we were (in the department) and particularly nobody knew who I was'. It was a new role and a new department within the organisation, so the score is unsurprising in that context. The head of department is proactive and encourages staff to become members of committees within the organisation (Table 28).

She feels that now she scores highly among 'key stakeholders' who are academic departments within the RCSI. Among users or students, it is slightly more ambiguous. Her department teaches the teachers; therefore, there is a trickle-down effect to the students. If her department introduces a technology-enhanced learning solution, then this becomes part of what is happening in the classroom, but students may not necessarily know or understand her role or her department's role in this. The only direct involvement that Jane has with students is that she acts as the staff advisor for students setting up a creative journal. She does this in her own time in the evenings. She runs workshops, and this is her only direct interaction with students.

**Table 28 Self-reported visibility rating of librarian at time of appointment versus today**

| Self-reported visibility rating at time of appointment: where 0 = invisible and 10 = highly visible | | | | | | | | | | |
|---|---|---|---|---|---|---|---|---|---|---|
| With key stakeholders | **0** | 1 | 2 | 3 | 4 | 5 | 6 | 7 | 8 | 9 | 10 |
| With staff – academics (colleagues) | **0** | 1 | 2 | 3 | 4 | 5 | 6 | 7 | 8 | 9 | 10 |
| **Self-reported visibility today (15 months after appointment): where 0 = invisible and 10 = highly visible** | | | | | | | | | | |
| With key stakeholders | 0 | 1 | 2 | 3 | 4 | 5 | 6 | 7 | 8 | **9** | 10 |
| With staff – academics (colleagues) | 0 | 1 | 2 | 3 | 4 | 5 | 6 | 7 | **8** | 9 | 10 |

## What has been your most successful method of increasing visibility?

There are two things that have helped Jane to increase her visibility. One is joining committees. The other is having the opportunity to teach academics. They come to her from all different departments.

## What value have you brought to the organisation as a librarian?

Although Jane has the job title 'research officer', she considers herself as a librarian first and foremost. Her skills as a librarian such as being able to work with a multitude of end users, with a multiple range of resources and being practical and pragmatic have enabled her to add value to the organisation. In terms of research skills, she finds that she has added value to the organisation by managing reviews as a project. She organises the referencing and manages the information flow in a way that it was not being done before. She has set up several templates for grant proposals. She has brought information standards to the department and things that librarians do on a daily basis (e.g. managing references).

She works in conjunction with the library at the RCSI. The library and the HPEC are under the Faculty of Medicine. She has worked with librarians on several projects. There is a new course that they are running called 'The Peer Observation of Teaching', which is for academics. A guest lecturer was required to talk about subject searching and resources. This was a good opportunity to promote the library and librarians also within the organisation.

## Does your department have any formal way of measuring and reporting impact?

Because it is new, there is no formal reporting of impact in place so far. However, the department applies for research grants; therefore, their success in this process is a form of active measurement. Evaluation surveys are done for all classes that she teaches. For example, they ask people at the start of the creative writing course to hand in their list of publications to date. At the end of the course, they see if there is any increase in this. So far, 3 out of 15 people in the class have been accepted for publication. It is a slow burn because it can take a long time to get items published. They also measure the 'intent to write'. There are many younger members of staff who are very busy and working in a qualitative area. They have started to write and have been given the tools and workflows involved with research writing so this is also measured.

## Have you ever experienced a challenging scenario and how did you deal with it?

In most of her work experience, Jane has been as a solo librarian. Part of her challenge is that she always volunteers to do additional work. Managing people's expectations can sometimes be challenging. In one role, she was hired on a short-term contract to replace two librarians at a hospital library. She was working there for 20h a week to replace two full-time people. A lot of re-adjusting of service delivery had to be done. Because she was there only in a part-time capacity, she would assist people with searching or retrieval of information the first time that they asked. If they came back a second time, then she would direct them to an online tutorial. The deal was that she would help people get the papers they needed for a journal club or presentation, and she would sit with them and spend hours showing them how to do everything, but they had to do the tutorial the next time. There was some resistance to this – mainly down to a fear and apprehension about using the library. However, once people gained confidence and realised they could do the searching on their own, their usage increased. The staff had 24-h access to the library, so Jane could check Internet logs and could identify that they were active at 3:00 or 4:00 a.m. working on papers and downloading articles, etc.

The challenge was to get people to realise that they have the skills and empower them to do searching of medical literature and to get them to use the library as part of their work.

## Top tips for academic/embedded librarians to increase their visibility?

Jane recommends two approaches to increasing the visibility of the academic or embedded librarian. Managing your reputation within your organisation and within your profession via your professional library association. This is particularly relevant for solo librarians, and she feels that the best thing a solo librarian can do is to join a committee. This is an opportunity to develop skills.

'For example, if I am a solo librarian working in a hospital library, the chances of having an opportunity to understand the budgeting process are very small. If the librarian joins a committee and acts as a treasurer, they now have new skills that are transferable to the day job for budgeting and financial operations. Get involved with the events that happen with the library association and all of the different groups and sections.

Librarians do have expertise to offer. Understand that you do have expertise. You can speak at events; you can give workshops. Take a research approach to the work that you do. There are little things that you can do such as understanding evidence-based approach. For example, if I put a link to a database, will people use it more? So ask a research question and then think about how you are going to answer it'.

'Make yourself available. Step outside your role. A lot of people are resistant to that which is understandable for a number of reasons – if a salary has been cut for example and you say "I'm not doing this, it is not my job" – the problem with this approach is that it will ultimately limit you as well in your role as a professional librarian. Extending yourself and approaching people within an organisation with honesty e.g. "I really do not have a lot of time to do this, but I would like to sit on your Committee or could I come and do a presentation on X". This is an extra work, you may have to work outside the core hours, but for your own professional development and for your own visibility I think it is a better trade off'.

'Do a little bit more'.

## How important is it for the librarian to be visible to users in an online environment?

Jane feels it is absolutely essential for librarians to be visible to users in an online environment. In an online environment, there is no physical connection with a person. Going back to the late 1990s, when she worked in a meteorological library, she received some funding to purchase ScienceDirect™. They had an intranet and a library webpage. Jane put up a link from the intranet saying, 'ScienceDirect™'. She volunteered to be on the budget committee and she happened to be at a meeting that was reviewing funding for the coming year. One of the senior meteorologists asked, 'Why do we even need a budget for the library, sure we have ScienceDirect™ for free'. Jane had to explain that it was not free, it was coming out of the library budget and she was managing it. There was no appreciation at that time that she was even involved in it. Her role was invisible. After this experience, she made a point of branding everything. Right down to overdue notices; for example, 'This is sent to you from your librarian' together with her name and a link. You have to keep reminding people that resources are coming from the library and you have to brand everything. She put up a little photo of herself on ScienceDirect™ which she says, smiling 'tortured staff'.

Jane makes a comparison with publishers and database suppliers and librarians in an online environment. She says that librarians have become invisible to the user and publishers and suppliers are now also becoming invisible. In her experience, people are not too concerned with the journal or exact source that research is coming from. For example, she might ask someone, 'Where did you get that article?' The answer is often, 'On Google' or 'From PubMed'. They do not realise that PubMed is not a journal. If she probes and says, 'Where did Google get it from?', then they say 'I do not know, it's a Google document'….They are unaware of the actual journal it is from. Some are people with two PhDs, so they are 'double doctors' or 'doctor doctors' – medical doctors with a PhD too. These are not stupid people. This depends on the level of researcher, but people do not go directly to a journal website anymore (e.g. *BMJ*), they go to find the article regardless (within reason) of the source. They just want to find information.

## What is your most successful method of increasing visibility in an online environment?

'Be active in social media. I do not mean hanging out on Facebook all day, but at the same time Twitter is great'. She manages Twitter and Linkedin and is setting up a profile on ResearchGate. Use Twitter, ResearchGate and Linkedin. She is developing Orchid IDs for academics in the department. She explains it to researchers as having their 'own ISBN or unique number'. There are several foreign students and foreign academics with similar names and within the Irish staff there are approximately 20 staff members with the name 'O'Sullivan' or 'Murphy'. At a recent talk with post-graduate students, she encouraged them to start the Orchid ID now because this is when they start publishing. Engage in the online space and use Twitter – it is great for pre-publications and upcoming conferences and great for networking. A new technique is leveraging content from Twitter and pushing the information to the person she thinks would get value from the information. She gives an example of a pharmacy student; if she spots a paper coming up on Twitter, then she will email it to the student and say, 'I just saw this paper, I thought you might be interested in it'. They do not have to respond but they associate her with the online presence.

With regard to the use of email, Jane notes the following: 'I do not want people to dread seeing an email sent from me. I want them to see that the email is coming from me and think. Oh this is going to be good'.

Sometimes Jane will Tweet the student, or if it is an older member of staff she will email them; this is a generational thing, or it may depend on the individual. Sometimes she will call them to see if they got the email. She will always check the language of the end user and observe how they like to communicate and then use their chosen method of communication to communicate back to them.

'What you put in the subject line of an email is critical. You have to grab people's attention'. Jane explains that if she comes across a conference paper or an article, she would adapt her style of communication to match the language and style of the recipient. For example, she may observe the language people use when they send her an email or a tweet and match that when communicating back to them. She also would have casual conversations with people to find out what they are interested in. 'Research on email communications has shown that a pattern has emerged whereby subordinates email superiors (bosses and managers) using "I" a lot (Kacewicz, Pennebaker, Davis, Jeon and Graesser, 2013). They do this to try to impress. Managers who email subordinates never use the word "I". They say, "This is great", "Thanks very much", they do not personalise the method of communication'. This is useful to know for librarians as well as any working professional. For example, if you have a cantankerous customer or someone who may have been condescending toward you or your role, Jane is conscious to never use the word "I". She wants to ensure that she is on the same level as they are.

'If I really want to get somebody's attention, I call them. Because nobody calls anybody anymore. If the phone rings in our office, we all jump because we think someone is dead!'

Alternatively, she arrives at the person's door. The use of personal contact is usually well received.

## What advice would you give to new entrants to the profession?

Jane teaches Masters-level students in University College Dublin in the School of Information and Library Studies (SILS). She feels that she is in a fortunate position. She teaches management. She brings in guest lecturers as part of the course. She wants students to have a true picture of reality, of what library life is really like. She encourages students to network and to make networking a priority. For example, if a guest lecturer offers their email, then she encourages students to send them a simple one-liner email. Ireland is such a small country that the lecturer could be sitting opposite to them on an interview panel or they could become a future colleague.

In the SILS department, everyone else is an academic. Once students graduate, they typically would no longer have any contact with the faculty. For Jane, she views the students as potentially future colleagues. This makes her careful and conscientious about giving students advice. Find out who is in what area and what the specialities are. She also encourages them to volunteer. For example, things such as helping out at conferences. There is an Academic and Special Libraries Group, which is a division of the Library Association of Ireland, who accepted three volunteers to assist with a conference – in terms of planning and organising. This type of experience is invaluable and helps them to make contacts.

The other tip she has is 'be realistic'. 'The profession has changed dramatically. You are not going to be sitting down on a Friday afternoon having a story time with children. That is gone. You have to understand IT. You do not need to be a programmer, but if you are meeting with suppliers such as library management system suppliers or database providers, you need to have some knowledge to know what they are talking about. You need to understand XML code. Be flexible. Learn how to do research for other people, but learn how to do research for yourself. Make yourself visible through networking. Realise that you have a lot of good skills and students today have many opportunities to work in diverse areas, beyond the traditional library'.

## Embedded librarian/librarian in context – Is that the future?

'Yes. This is definitely the future. I always think of embedded war correspondent. They are on the frontline and can see what is happening. I am an embedded librarian and it is the envy of every other department'. The fact that she is a librarian in a research department has facilitated their work in ways that the department would not have even thought of beforehand. Colleagues in her department boast, 'We have our own librarian'. She feels she has eliminated a lot of wasted time by introducing smart information workflows. We assume that because people can book a holiday online and they can use a smartphone that people are technology savvy. However, they are not. From our training as librarians, we understand content in context. Not a lot of people get this. The way that content is organised, say in an online publication or a website, has relevance. A word in proximity to another word has a meaning. Many people do not understand that. The way that we process all kinds of information as librarians is valuable and unique to our profession.

One of the functions of the department is to write research grants. Every time one was done in the past, it was started from a scratch. Jane produced some templates. PhD students were fascinated by this. Jane also keeps a bank of bibliographic information. She has all references indexed using the Harvard system because this is popular in medicine. There is a fantastic repository at RCSI, but she has put together a small system just as a quick reference and record for her department. The record is kept as a spread sheet. People in the department writing the proposals refer to it for quickly looking up a reference. The organisation of this information is a library skill. Because librarians are used to functioning with small resources, they have to be organised. The other skill we have as librarians is that we very effectively re-purpose work. For example, if librarians present at a conference, much work usually goes into it. Jane would advise that librarians turn this into a short article for the organisation's newsletter or it may be the seed of an academic paper. She finds that this is a foreign concept to non-librarians.

If you work in a library with say 50 or more users, you develop a profile of them over time. Organising information in an appropriate way is part of our skills as librarians. Organising content in context is perhaps the unique selling point of librarianship today. For example, Bill comes into the library and you know what he is working on; you add value by recognising something you know he might be interested in that he may never have seen before – this is what librarians do best. This is a unique skill. She gives an example of work she did recently with an anatomist at the department who is looking at replacing the use of microscopes to look at tissue samples unless they are working in laboratories, where this skill is needed. What they found was that the margin of error for looking in microscopes and getting accurate results compared with the amount of training invested to get them to do this perfectly was not paying off.

Medical students are learning things such as histology. Now, they are using online visuals in a virtual learning environment instead of using microscopes. They have to click to say what disease is present, etc. The anatomist was trying to find research to see if this method of teaching was effective or not or whether it was more effective than using microscopes. So Jane sat with her and asked where she was looking and what she had found. The anatomist's reference was PubMed – all she had looked at were medical and scientific journals and sources. Jane suggested looking at Education Resources Information Center (ERIC) to find information from an educational perspective. The researcher was fascinated by this, and together they found many papers on this topic using ERIC. This changed the perspective of the researcher, and the librarian immediately brought value to the research process. This is a skill that librarians take for granted, but our information perspective allows us to take a research question and look at it through a 360° angle and holistic perspective.

## How do you see your specialist role evolving in 5 years?

The embedded librarian needs the e-library to back up her job. She could only do parts of her job if the RCSI e-library was no longer available to her. 'Ideally, there needs to be a bridge between the embedded librarian and the library and librarians working in the library. You have to have a library. You are only a bridge to content. Someone has to manage it and curate it and the embedded librarian provides the context for the content among other things. The library is very highly regarded in the institution'. If there was no library, then Jane feels that the organisation would be doing a big disservice to medical students, many of who will go on to become doctors, authors and teachers. 'Why would we deny them that experience of being a scholar? That is part of our role as librarians, whether we realise it or not, we are teaching people scholarship. Students need the library and the way that librarians contextualise content to experience scholarship. If they do not have that and everything is online, then it's the same as buying a pair of shoes – content becomes commercialised, not scholarly'. Jane says she would be very worried if people thought that the library was not needed.

## What is your favourite thing about being a librarian?

'It's not about books, although I do love books. My favourite thing about being a librarian is that it always changes and it always stays the same. I feel that I'm definitely part of the future but I definitely have a foot in the past'.

## Case study 22: corporate librarian working in a corporate setting

| Name: | Nicolas Carman |
|-------|----------------|
| Organisation: | Auckland Council, Auckland, New Zealand |

Nicholas Carman is the corporate librarian for Auckland Council in New Zealand. New Zealand performs well in many measures of well-being, as shown by its ranking among the top countries in many topics in the Organisation for Economic Co-operation and Development's 2013 Better Life Index. Auckland is a major part of New Zealand's economy. It is located on the North Island. With more than 1.4 million inhabitants, Auckland is the most populous city in New Zealand. According to the Census 2013, 33.4% of New Zealand's population live in Auckland. There are 94,554 people working in the city of Auckland. In the Mercer Quality of Living Survey, the city ranked 3 out of 50. Auckland Council is the governing body for the city. The Auckland Council organisation comprises council employees, who provide advice to 21 local boards, and a governing body, which is made up of an elected mayor and 20 elected members. Auckland Council also has seven key Council-Controlled Organisations (CCOs), which look after specific council assets, services or infrastructure.

### Vision of the council

The world's most liveable city.

*Source:* The Auckland Plan, Auckland:Auckland Council: 2014. Available from http://theplan. theaucklandplan.govt.nz/ Accessed 16.11.14.

### Online visibility of library and librarian

The corporate library is available online only via the intranet.

| Twitter: | http://twitter.com/nicholascarman |
|----------|-----------------------------------|
| Tumblr: | http://ncarman.tumblr.com/ |
| | https://klout.com/nicholascarman |
| Linkedin: | nz.linkedin.com/in/nicholascarman |

### Role in the organisation

Nicholas works for the Auckland Council corporate library. He looks after the information needs of Auckland Council's staff. They have a corporate library with magazines and research materials that are made available to staff. Research is also performed by librarians for the council staff. The corporate library is part of the Auckland public libraries group within the council. The corporate library is a 'funny offshoot' on the organisational structural tree, as Nicholas explains, 'nobody quite knows where to put us'. The council looks after Auckland's city's rate-payers. Until recently, there were four city councils which were amalgamated in 2009 to form the council. The librarian got his job on foot of this amalgamation.

The corporate library has regular customers who use the library a lot. There are people who occasionally use the library and have some awareness of who the librarians are but do not give the library much thought beyond the 'little things we do for them'. The research requestors are the ones who know the most about the library and understand it the best. There are large groups of people who are sent tables of contents of recent research who probably do not think about the library beyond that.

Nicholas explains that they have gone to some lengths to market themselves and spread awareness of what the librarians do, but it is always a bit of a struggle to get any recognition or traction. This can be a common experience of internal library services. The councillors are insulated a little from the corporate library. They are reached out to via local democracy services, and by the time they get the information back from the library via a secondary source, the councillors would probably not have any idea that it originated from the library. This is an interesting point: it appears that the corporate library as a source of information in certain instances is invisible to key stakeholders – the councillors.

Nicholas says that this is inconvenient because the corporate library is currently trying to convince councillors that they are worthy of rate-payers money. They are going through a restructure. A corporate library branch has already been lost, which was a type of symbolic cut. They had three library offices distributed around the city. The council has been trying to consolidate its buildings and locations and has been moving the bulk of its staff to a building in downtown Auckland. They had an office in Takapuna, but that office was lost and they have to re-locate the books that were there. No library staff members were lost, but Nicholas says, 'that could still happen'.

Nicholas rates his visibility as a zero at the time of his appointment (Table 29). There was no corporate library there before the amalgamation. They had to build up a library

## Table 29 Self-reported visibility rating of librarian at time of appointment versus today

| Self-reported visibility rating at time of appointment: where 0 = invisible and 10 = highly visible | | | | | | | | | | |
|---|---|---|---|---|---|---|---|---|---|---|
| With key stakeholders | **0** | 1 | 2 | 3 | 4 | 5 | 6 | 7 | 8 | 9 | 10 |
| With staff/users of the service | **0** | 1 | 2 | 3 | 4 | 5 | 6 | 7 | 8 | 9 | 10 |
| Self-reported visibility today (3.5 years after appointment): where 0 = invisible and 10 = highly visible | | | | | | | | | | |
| With key stakeholders | 0 | 1 | 2 | 3 | **4** | 5 | 6 | 7 | 8 | 9 | 10 |
| With key staff/librarians | 0 | 1 | 2 | 3 | 4 | 5 | 6 | **7** | 8 | 9 | 10 |

service from scratch, which Nicholas says, 'was fun'. Nicholas says he had a good boss who had a clear vision for what she wanted, and they have come a long way since they first started. However, now it is restructuring time, and everything is 'up for grabs'.

## What has been your most successful method of increasing visibility?

Nicholas says that this is hard to say. At present, they are trying to get hard data on this type of question. If he had to guess, then Nicholas would say that it was a combination of personal contacts at council and things such as running a monthly newsletter. Word of mouth and services, such as the table of contents (TOCs) service, branded as 'journal watch' in which they scan TOCs from magazines and journals and send it around to council staff, have worked well. They polished up the delivery of the journal watch service, and it has been a good marketing tool for the corporate library.

## What value do you think you have brought to the organisation as a librarian?

Nicholas feels he has brought an evidence-based approach to decision-making within the council. When people make decisions, they make them based on some information. Part of the function of the corporate librarian is to supply information and evidence to aid decision-making. Nicholas says that his value is shown every time somebody makes a decision based on the research service supplied by the librarian.

## Do you have any formal method of measuring and reporting your impact?

They have a customer satisfaction survey, which is run each year. Transactional statistics are counted and compiled. 'Impact is a tricky one'. They have a database of contacts who avail of the research service and the TOC alerts. Nicholas says the library plans to compare this with a complete list of council staff to see who is and who is not using the corporate library.

## Can you think of any challenging scenario in which you have had to prove the value or worth of the corporate library?

Restructuring is challenging; however, things have been stable for the past 3 years. The librarians have been left to their own devices to some extent during this time.

## What are your top tips for corporate librarians to increase their visibility and impact in their organisations?

'Meet people. Network. Go out on a team visit. Attend team meetings. Talk to people at gathering. Chatting with people is a very good way of promoting yourself. You also need more formal marketing methods such as newsletters, email, and mass broadcast emails'. The human resources department sends them new status lists of new people to the council. He joins them up to the library newsletter distribution list. He thinks that getting the library as part of staff induction would be invaluable, but they have not managed to get that slot yet. The powers that be do not deem them important enough to be part of induction.

There is a social media network, Yammer™, in use at Auckland Council. It has not been taken up with huge enthusiasm. However, Nicholas said that as soon as he saw it, he could see the potential it had for marketing library services and getting their message out.

## How important is it for librarians to be visible to users in an online environment?

Auckland Council intranet has a library presence, and this is very important. It is important for the library to be visible on whatever online portals are available to council staff. The library should have as prominent of a presence as the librarian can manage. Unfortunately, the corporate library is about three clicks away from the front page, and Nicholas does not hold much hope for them getting any more prominent of a presence on the intranet front page. Personally, Nicholas thinks it is very important to be visible on online services such as Yammer, Twitter and other social media outlets.

## What is your most successful method of increasing visibility in an online environment?

He finds Twitter very useful and a good way to professionally promote oneself. He goes on whatever is available. He finds Twitter™ very interesting and immediate. He does not particularly like Facebook™.

## What advice would you give to new librarians on increasing their visibility and impact?

'Be where your customers are. I think that is what we've always tried to do. We are temporarily based in the centre of town, if you want to engage key stakeholders – in our case councillors – then we need to be where they are, preferably in the flesh'. It is also important to be able to spread library services around so that people know where you are. The physical location of the library within a building is important. Nicholas says that in Takapuna the library was located next to the tea rooms, so it was a highly convenient location. The library could be seen on the way in and on the way out. Many people used to come in for this reason. The library was highly visible to people in the building.

'You cannot stay behind your comfy little desk and play with your computer all of the time; you've got to get out and get involved with people'.

One of the strategies that his library is currently looking at is getting librarians onto project teams. Rather than the corporate librarian being a 'bolt-on' or 'after thought', they will be there at the beginning of a project and will be part of the project team. This approach will make the librarian be more integral to teamwork within the council.

This is similar to the embedded librarian model that is popular in academic, special and health librarianship. Nicholas mentions Judy Peacock, an Australian librarian, who gave a keynote presentation at the Library and Information Association of New Zealand (LIANZA) 2014 conference that he found to be 'powerful'. Her presentation entitled 'Do. Discover. It's Time.' is available at http://lianzaconference.weebly.com/do-discover-its-time.html. It was about academic librarians re-inventing themselves, but Nicholas said her message resonated with him. He says it made him think, 'Don't get too comfy because your funding is about to get cut. So you better do something quick'.

## Where do you see the corporate librarian in 5 years?

'I wonder whether anyone will be called a librarian soon'. Nicholas holds a Masters of Library and Information Studies (MLIS) from the Victoria University of Wellington. However, a few years ago the 'Library' was dropped from this qualification. It is now called a Master of Information Studies. He thinks this was done because the term 'Library' can pigeonhole people. Likewise, because of the restructuring process that is currently on-going, he has visited five other libraries in Auckland. Of the five libraries, none of them use the word 'library' to describe themselves. They are called 'knowledge centres' or 'information services'; therefore, the word 'library' does not come into the picture anymore. These 'libraries' have hardly any hard-copy collections; the vast majority of resources are online. If customers need information, much of it may be sourced online and downloaded. He describes them as being 'very lean and mean'.

'It is just like public libraries: either you adapt your services and budget to what your customers want, or what you think they want, or you end up being cut back, like what is happening to some of the libraries in the UK'.

## What is your favourite thing about being a corporate librarian?

'It is probably the service mentality. I like being useful to people. I like making people happy and giving people information that they want. This is what keeps me going in this job. Giving people what they want and making them happy or occasionally exceeding their expectations is fulfilling, because a lot of people do not know what to expect from librarians. People do not really know what we can do. There is nothing particularly sophisticated about what we do for people, but we do things for people that they may not have time to do for themselves. Even Googling things or using the library databases to find information. I wish I could say that there was something wizardly about what I do, but there really isn't'.

## Case study 23: librarian employed as a legal information manager

| Name: | Sinéad Curtin |
|---|---|
| Organisation: | McCann FitzGerald, Dublin, Ireland |

McCann FitzGerald is one of the leading law firms in Ireland, with offices in Dublin, London and Brussels. The Dublin office is the headquarters of the organisation. Located in an up-and-coming area of Dublin City, known internationally as 'Silicon Docks', the newly built office enjoys striking views of Dublin City, overlooking the river Liffey and a new Samuel Beckett bridge crossing the river to a recently built national convention centre. Sinéad says smiling, 'There is nothing but lawyers and IT people here'. Google has its European headquarters around the corner from the building together with several other software giants and legal rivals. The building is nothing short of spectacular. Designed by Scott Tallon Walker Architects, it has an open central circular atrium that rises up to the skyline above, flooding the inside with natural light. The library occupies a prime location on the ground floor, with walls of glass making the space a transparent, open learning centre.

## Mission of McCann FitzGerald

A strong culture and a true partnership mean that our focus is on our clients, their business and commercial objectives.

*Source:* http://www.mccannfitzgerald.ie/firm.aspx Accessed 11.02.15.

## Mission of the McCann FitzGerald library

To provide good access to high-quality legal information resources and answer queries from our practitioners in a timely manner.

## Online visibility of library and librarian

Law firm website:          http://www.mccannfitzgerald.ie/

## Role in the organisation

Sinéad's official title is legal information manager, which she says, 'in short, librarian', and she has worked in McCann FitzGerald, a big law firm in Ireland, since 2006. She is an active member of the rather unfortunately named BIALL (British and Irish Association of Law Librarians) Irish group, and she previously worked at the law library of the Bar Council of Ireland. There are approximately 200 lawyers and 200 support staff at McCann FitzGerald. Sinéad has a team of three in the library. The team has a great deal of experience of working in the legal information sector. Sinéad's main role revolves around the organisation of information. She purchases electronic and print materials and arranges the materials as simply as she can. Her approach is to ensure that lawyers can access information quickly and easily so that they exploit the information resources available to them.

Sinéad says a big part of her role is as a teacher. She is surprised at just how much of her time is spent in a teaching role. She teaches trainee solicitors, and they are the heaviest users of the library service. She conducts formal instruction at the beginning of and during their 2-year traineeship. She encourages them to use the library and to contact library staff if they are unsure of anything or have information queries. She has good visibility with this group, and she sees them regularly. She finds that it is a gradual process to get to know them. This depends on where they have worked before, previous experience and what they are familiar with. After 2 years, she notices that their information search and retrieval skills have substantially improved.

The other main users of the library service in the firm are the fee earners including qualified lawyers, solicitors and partners. She also has a teaching role with them, and she handles queries. Queries are shared out among the three library staff members. Lawyers are encouraged to email the library with any information queries they may have. Whichever library staff member is available picks up the query. Sometimes the queries are quick and easy (e.g. to find a particular article or request for company documents). Other times the queries could be more involved and take longer to complete (e.g. researching a topic, perhaps offering guidance on how to research a topic and where to find information or which sources to try).

The library staff members are not legally qualified; therefore, there is a limit to the research that they perform. However, they are there to offer guidance and direction. There are some frequently asked questions, and queries on topical matters tend to be repeated. With experience, it becomes easier for the library team to answer these questions. Queries are logged by the library, which also helps to develop the team's knowhow. In general, Sinéad demonstrates good quality resources and lets the legal staff interpret the information themselves. 'This is what lawyers should be doing, especially trainee solicitors'.

Sinéad is responsible for the library budget, which includes negotiating prices for online resources and dealing with suppliers. The role is varied. Sinéad says, 'You never know quite what is going to happen. What I like about it is that things are constantly changing. I'm learning all the time. I'm learning about law and new legal queries come up all the time. New areas always emerge. The firm is always looking to the future. It's good to be involved in that'.

The training she delivers involves tips on how to search legal databases such as Westlaw™ and LexisNexis™ using protocols to cite case law as well as guidance on good hard-copy resources. Sinéad has found that despite some people thinking, 'Why do we need a library when everything is available online?', with the explosion of information available online, 'things have actually become more complicated. We mostly look at Irish, UK and EU resources. Irish legal resources are not as well developed as those in the UK, because it is a smaller market, so practitioners need to be made aware of the gaps in the online services that exist. The legal system in other jurisdictions such as the US are quite different to that in Ireland, so their case law is not as relevant'. She finds that it is important to remind trainees and solicitors not to rely on just one source; everything has to be cross checked.

The legal queries that you do in an academic setting and those in a practical setting can be different. To give an example, in legal practice, a lot can turn on the meaning of a phrase in legislation; therefore, the lawyer would need to research the background to that legislation and its interpretation by the courts and review commentary from secondary sources. At undergraduate level, this level of detail will not be required. It is usually sufficient to be familiar with the legislation that regulates an area of the law. That will usually be outlined in a good textbook on the topic. People sometimes need to be re-taught how to search. 'Google is fine, but people need to be aware that what they are finding there is not necessarily up to date or impartial and it is important to exploit the electronic resources that we pay for too'.

There is a great deal of free information out there now, and governments make a lot of information freely available. Sinéad feels that the online world is creating more jobs for librarians. There are different ways to search depending on which resource you use, and the resources are increasing all of the time.

## On a scale of 0–10, how visible do you feel to your key stakeholders?

Key stakeholders in the firm are the partners and managing partner. Sinéad feels that she is highly visible to them. They all know her. She finds that some rarely use the library, but that is because of the nature of their practice and they do not need to do much legal research. They might ask her to look something up and that would be sufficient. In other cases, she may see a lot of them or their trainees. Sinéad says, 'I find everyone needs you eventually'. People are directed to go to the library to find answers or to source information. She feels she scores an 8 because 'there is always room for improvement' (Table 30).

### Table 30 Self-reported visibility rating of librarian at time of appointment versus today

| Self-reported visibility rating at time of appointment: where 0 = invisible and 10 = highly visible | | | | | | | | | | |
|---|---|---|---|---|---|---|---|---|---|---|
| With key stakeholders | 0 | 1 | 2 | 3 | **4** | 5 | 6 | 7 | 8 | 9 | 10 |
| With staff/users of the service | 0 | 1 | 2 | 3 | **4** | 5 | 6 | 7 | 8 | 9 | 10 |
| Self-reported visibility today (8 years after appointment): where 0 = invisible and 10 = highly visible | | | | | | | | | | |
| With key stakeholders | 0 | 1 | 2 | 3 | 4 | 5 | 6 | 7 | **8** | 9 | 10 |
| With key staff/users of the service | 0 | 1 | 2 | 3 | 4 | 5 | 6 | 7 | 8 | **9** | 10 |

## On a scale of 0–10, how visible do you feel to readers and users of the library service?

Her visibility with readers and users of the library service (trainees, legal executives (paralegals), solicitors and partners) is very high. The main users are trainees. She says if she does not see them in the library, then she would wonder where they are because they do need to get assistance from the library staff and learn as they go along. On this scale, she feels that she rates 9 out of 10 (Table 30).

She has worked in this firm since 2006 – almost 9 years. When she first started, everyone in the firm knew that a legal information manager had been appointed but they would not have known her. It took a while for people to get to know her and vice versa. She is still making connections. She found it challenging at the start because of the size of the firm, which was a little overwhelming. Her previous position was at the law library, which was in fact much bigger with more than 1000 barristers, but the environment was very different. In the law library, the barristers would come into the library very frequently and be rushing into court. In the law firm, much more business is conducted virtually by email, and she would not see people in person as much as in the law library. However, she knows everyone in the firm now at least to see, even if she does not deal with them in person.

It took a little time to settle into the firm and get to know people. It was a gradual thing. She says, 'It took time'. The firm has had a library and qualified librarian for several decades. It is a role that is valued by the firm. Her visibility would have been a 4 for both groups.

## What has been your most successful method of increasing your visibility?

Sinéad says that the training, not just with the trainees but with the firm's practice groups, has been very successful. It can be difficult to get groups of lawyers together; however, some of the practice groups meet over lunch, and Sinéad can use this time, even if just 20 min, to introduce a new resource or generally just to keep people up to date. This works well. Particularly when she first started, she remembers one person coming up to her afterwards, saying that, 'I never knew we had access to that'. She said that focused training sessions even once a year for a practice group were very successful.

## What value have you brought to the organisation as a librarian?

Sinéad says candidly, 'I've saved the firm money. Having one person to deal with reps from companies to negotiate good prices has definitely saved money'. Sinéad now knows many of the reps and has good knowledge of quality legal resources. For example, some lawyers would express interest in a new subscription to a journal or online resource and Sinéad would look at this in conjunction with other resources that the library already has to avoid any duplication. 'I'm the person who oversees the budget and saves money along the way'. Another way that she brings value to the firm is by making material easier and faster to find. The library has a section on the firm's intranet, and she uses the library catalogue as a landing page. It has links out to legal databases and other in-house resources. It is a simple interface. She does not have a discovery layer or federated search option because, similar to many librarians, she does not think that it is needed. She describes such search facilities as, 'A bit rough and ready'.

She trains people in the resources that they do have and reminds them of what they have access to. This is a job in itself because she finds that people forget and it is difficult sometimes for non-librarians to keep up to date with the changing search interfaces and features of legal databases. Librarians are searching for information as a constant whereas a lawyer might not need to search a legal database for 12 months and when they come to search it, it may have substantially changed.

## What impact has the library service had on the organisation?

'We are making resources easier to find, which will in turn save lawyers time, making them more efficient. We make sure that we provide access to quality information that is reliable and up to date. I place a big emphasis on quality. We have good material to draw on, and it is organised properly. We keep people up to date by the detailed entries made in our catalogue and by providing current awareness services. We also work with professional support lawyers in producing the firm's weekly newsletter'.

## Does your department have any formal way of measuring and reporting impact?

'The reporting structure revolves around the financial budget'. She uses this opportunity to highlight achievements during the year. The financial information is extremely important. Sinéad's impact speaks for itself. She hears informally things such as 'The library really helped me out with that research' and generally gets good feedback. It is not a very formal environment in the sense that she is not required to provide a report with statistical information on the number of queries or training sessions she conducts, etc. Sinéad welcomes this and finds that it makes for a positive working environment. She goes to talk to one or to two people and decisions are made. Decisions are made quickly, and she appreciates this.

## Have you ever experienced a challenging scenario and how did you deal with it?

When the recession hit in 2008, things were tough in law firms and in all sectors. Everyone felt very insecure everywhere. The budget was affected, and some subscriptions were cancelled, but Sinéad found that overall it was a positive experience. She said that she improved her negotiation skills with suppliers and 'in hindsight, I learned a lot of new skills'. Lawyers appreciate that type of thoroughness, attention to detail and of course negotiation. 'Hard times are good for us occasionally; they force us to ask whether we really need things or if they are just "nice to have". It can give you an opportunity to rationalise your spending'. She cancelled some looseleafs, which Sinéad says, 'are a law library bugbear'. It is a loose unbound book of information in which a page can be taken in and replaced with more up-to-date information. However, it is very labour intensive. It is a dying 'technology', which online information has mainly replaced.

## What would your top tips be for law librarians to increase visibility?

'To meet your lawyers. Meet with them and ask them what they want. Ask them if the resources that they have are sufficient or if there are enough information resources available to them on their practice area. Do you feel you are being kept up to date? Do you know how to use material? Are you happy that the people in your team have sufficient search skills and knowledge? Small things such as fixing a person's login can make a big difference. It is the little things that can bother people. If you can fix those small things for people, this can be a quick but big win for you. These little irritants, if you can fix them, it makes life easier for people, especially lawyers, who can work long hours and are online a lot of the time'.

People will give you feedback on resources and give details about a resource that Sinéad feels she would not otherwise be aware of, because she is not a lawyer. Getting feedback like this is invaluable. Because the librarian is the central contact point, she can pass this knowledge on to lawyers or the next person to use that resource, whereas the lawyer may not necessarily share that feedback with everyone else in the firm. Again, as was seen in other case studies, the librarian can act as a knowledge broker within a company or organisation. They impart information to a multitude of people and have an invaluable role in sharing knowledge.

'Listen to your users. Ask people and talk to them'. Sinéad has not yet performed surveys. She gets a sense of what people like and do not like and feels she is in tune with her users' needs.

## How important do you think it is for the librarian to be visible in an online environment?

'I think that the physical library is still valuable space. It allows people to get away from their desks and to come in and perhaps read the paper'. Sinéad always invites people down to the library on the ground floor to give them guidance on a search. 'It is important that you are visible and open to people to come in. Having a friendly manner is very important for all of the library staff. Email conversations are at times efficient, but sometimes you are better off just picking up the phone'. There is no need for online chat in her environment. Having a library presence on the intranet is essential. It is also valuable for the librarian to have control over her intranet presence without having to run everything past the IT department.

### What advice would you give to new entrants to the profession of librarianship?

'To get known, go to any events that are on to hear about job opportunities. Try and get as much experience as you can. There are training courses available and try to go to these and get as much training as possible. The library world can be quite small, so if you meet people at events, your paths may cross again in the future'.

### Where do you see the law librarian/legal information manager in 5 years?

'There will be more and more information online. The print collection will dwindle. We have a role in business development aspect of work. Not just looking at legal research but looking at new areas of business. The online environment has given us more work to do, so I can see this continuing to grow. Librarianship is a growth area. The library here is getting busier and as soon as the recession hit, it got even busier. New areas of law will emerge. I can see more research going on and things have become more complicated. As you become better known to people, more people ask you things'. Visibility is self-perpetuating. Sinéad enjoys getting new, fresh queries and it makes the job more interesting.

### What is your favourite thing about being a librarian?

'For me it is the queries. It is the detective work – the digging for answers. I like when people are grateful for what they get. A thank you can go a long way. People are pretty good in here. Sometimes it can be a delayed thank you, but it is still nice to get it. There is good respect and appreciation here between different areas of the business'. Sinéad studied law and says that she 'loved it' but knew that she did not want to be a lawyer. She likes the subject, and it helps her to do her job well.

The following word cloud represents the combined tips of the three special librarians interviewed (Figure 10).

**Figure 10** Word cloud of tips for special librarians to increase their visibility.

# Summary

On the basis of the three interviews with librarians working in specialist roles, the following tips and strategies emerged for special librarians and research officers to improve visibility, impact and understanding of their value:

1. Get out of the library!
2. Get involved with leadership in your organisation.
3. Become part of project teams in the organisation.
4. Attend team meetings and contribute to them.
5. Gather impact data and make them visible.
6. Think about the word 'librarian' and whether this works as a job title in your organisation or if another job title would be more meaningful.
7. Similar to number 5, think about the word 'library' and whether 'knowledge centre' or 'information centre' would be more meaningful in your organisation to your key stakeholders.
8. The physical location of the library in the organisation is strategically important and ideally needs to be next to a busy area (e.g. canteen or reception area).
9. Have a prominent online profile within the organisation's online systems.
10. Network, network, network.
11. Make personal contact with people. Do not rely solely on email or social media to communicate with people in your organisation.
12. Manage your professional reputation and image – invest time in this.
13. Join strategic committees (those that align with your library's mission).
14. Do not be afraid to step outside of your comfort zone or role and take on challenging opportunities.
15. Question things and the way things are done. Look for answers that are based on evidence.
16. Use your critical-thinking skills.
17. Be a good listener.
18. Make effective use of social media.
19. Be proactive on Twitter and engage with patrons.
20. Use informal and formal marketing methods to communicate your messages to readers and stakeholders.
21. Take a research approach to your work.
22. Conduct informational interviewing.
23. Attend events and training for librarians.
24. Network within the profession and within your organisation.
25. Eliminate library jargon from physical and virtual library spaces.
26. Brand all e-resources with library branding.
27. Talk to your clients, ask them questions and act upon their feedback.

# Note

BEME International Collaborating Centres (BICCs) Centre, for more information see: http://bemecollaboration.org/BICCs/.

# State of play – measuring the current visibility of the librarian and library

## Introduction

It is impossible to move forward and plan ahead if you do not know how you are currently doing and what the current positioning and performance of the library is. It is useful to take a snapshot of current visibility to see whether this can be improved and identify any strengths and weaknesses. In order to determine how visible a librarian is, consider the visibility to both stakeholders and users or readers. Firstly take into account the visibility of the librarian to key stakeholders and secondly to readers or users of the library service. Equally important –if you have a library – is how visible the library is to the same two audiences. Finally online visibility must be measured and tracked. To determine the level of visibility, it is necessary to first describe what is meant by visibility.

## What is visibility?

In this hypothesis visibility encompasses three things. First, whether the librarian is recognised by name or by reputation. Second, whether what the librarian does is understood. Finally, and perhaps most importantly, whether the job and contribution of the librarian to the organisation is valued. Visibility is essentially a determinant of relevance. Librarians, like other professionals, strive for relevance in an increasingly competitive information space.

The same principle applies to the library. Do people recognise the library by name? Is it clear for visitors how to get to the library? Do readers know where the library is located within the building? Do people know or understand what the library has to offer? Finally, do people value the library as an institution? Consider the characteristics of low visibility and high visibility on the visibility scale (Figure 11).

| Low visibility | High visibility |
|---|---|
| • Library seen as a support service<br>• Nobody knows librarians name<br>• Library or librarian doesn't come to mind when strategic decisions are taken in organisation which would benefit from information<br>• Librarian carries out research without recognition<br>• Librarian develops online tutorials in isolation with low usage<br>• Librarian operates as a solo librarian in physical library | • Library seen as a strategic partner<br>• Key stakeholders know librarians by name or solid reputation<br>• Librarian is organisation's 'go-to' person for information to enable strategic decision making<br>• Librarian is a named author on research paper<br>• Librarian co-creates online learning material as part of a curriculum<br>• Embedded librarian programs in place |

**Figure 11** Visibility scale.

## Stakeholder analysis

Before determining the level of visibility, it is helpful to determine who the key stakeholders are by conducting a stakeholder analysis. Key stakeholders are going to be people in positions of power and influence in the organisation. There may be internal and external stakeholders. It is worth doing a short exercise to reflect upon and write down who the key stakeholders are.

There is an abundance of management and business literature that points to ways of finding out who the key stakeholders are. A popular and trademarked method is using six sigma. This looks at the balance between people with power and influence in organisations.

Value and impact are perceived differently by different people. In strategic management, the creation of a competitive advantage is a necessary condition for value (Fitzroy, Hulbert & Ghobadian, 2012). What librarians need to know is whether key stakeholders value them AND if working in a library is core to what a librarian does, do users value the library? What competitive advantage is the librarian and library offering its stakeholders over other information products and other information streams? To answer these questions, it is necessary to find out who the key stakeholders are.

A simple guide to finding out who key stakeholders are is mapped out by answering the questions below:

- Who allocates the library budget?
- Who has the power to shut the library down?
- Who will approve applications to hire new librarians/information professionals/library staff?
- Who is the CEO or Director General?
- Who is the Principal of the school?
- Who is a member of the Board of Directors/Management team/Hospital Board, etc.?
- Who writes the service plan/annual report for the organisation?
- Who is in charge of the corporate website and intranet?

- Who compiles the staff newsletter?
- Who are the major shareholders in the company?
- Who is the partner(s) in the firm?

# Determining value

Next it is necessary to find out what the key stakeholders consider or perceive to be valuable. Usually a librarian will already have an idea whether stakeholders value what they do or not. For example consider the following scenarios:

- Was there a budget increase recently?
- Has the librarian been able to hire new staff?
- Has the library expanded its service?
- Did management sign off on recent business cases submitted?
- Have staff got approval to attend that international conference?
- Has the librarian's salary increased in the last year?
- Has management been overheard singing the praises of the librarian?
- Has the librarian been asked to represent the company or organisation at a corporate event?
- Does the librarian regularly contribute to the curriculum of the school/university?
- Does the communications department contact the librarian to verify information?
- Are the researchers who have worked with the librarian crediting them on academic papers?
- Have any of the library staff ever received an 'employee of the month/year' award?
- Have the library staff or library received any award?

If a librarian can answer positively to all of the above then they are probably highly valued by their key stakeholders. If, however, there is uncertainty about some of these issues, then there is some work to be done. How can a librarian or information professional get a positive answer to all or most of the above? How can a librarian find out what their key stakeholders value from a librarian and/or library service?

The obvious answer here is to just ask them! If you meet them in a corridor, restaurant or lift just ask them if they can spare a minute or two of their time and simply ask 'What do you find valuable about the library (or name a core activity that you do (e.g. the role I have on the clinical effectiveness team?)' OR you could simply say 'I really need a budget increase. How can I prove to you that this is imperative?'

If your key stakeholders' response is to ask who you are then perhaps this is not the best method of getting their input. You can only try this if they know who you are and are likely to recognise you outside of your library or office.

Ideally this will lead on to further engagement with stakeholders, whereby a survey is circulated to them. A sample survey is listed in Appendix A. The survey could alternatively form the basis of a semi-structured interview with key people in the organization. This will yield relevant information and insight into their needs and what they perceive to be of value. This data will give a baseline from which to work and improve upon. Once an analysis of the data has been made, this will inform the visibility improvement plan (VIP), outlined in Chapter 8. Feedback and suggestions from stakeholders should be incorporated into the VIP. Lloyd (2004), an expert in the field of quality management, singled out listening to the 'voice of the customer' as a first step on the road to quality improvement.

See some examples of stakeholders for various types of librarians in Tables 31–35.

**Table 31  School librarian – example of stakeholders**

| Internal stakeholders | External stakeholders |
|---|---|
| School principal | Parents |
| Board of management | Professional school library association |
| Teachers | Local public library |
| School support staff (e.g. caretaker) | Local councillor(s) |
| Immediate boss | Fellow school librarians/peer group |

## School librarian – example of readers/users of school library service

Students, teachers, school principal, parents, visiting students, invited guests/speakers, etc.

**Table 32  Hospital librarian – example of stakeholders**

| Internal stakeholders | External stakeholders |
|---|---|
| Director of Finance (or equivalent) | Board of trustees |
| Immediate boss | Friends of the hospital |
| Consultants | Professional medical library association |
| Nurse managers | Fellow hospital librarians/peer group |
| HR manager | External funding agency (e.g. for research) |
| Hospital manager/Administrator | Affiliated academic institution (if a teaching hospital) |

## Hospital librarian – example of readers/users of hospital library service

Consultants, nurses, doctors, health and social care professionals, patients, the chaplain, the administrative staff, the managerial staff, and students.

Table 33 **Public librarian – example of stakeholders**

| Internal stakeholders | External stakeholders |
|---|---|
| Immediate boss/manager | Professional library association |
| Management team | Fellow public librarians/peer group |
| Local public councillors | School library |
| IT department | Local government |

## Public librarian – example of readers/users of public library service

The general public, minority groups, older people, toddlers, children, young adults, teenagers, single people, families, low, middle and high income earners, the unemployed, the homeless, and people with disabilities.

Table 34 **Academic librarian – example of stakeholders**

| Internal stakeholders | External stakeholders |
|---|---|
| Heads of faculty | Funding agencies for research |
| Provost | Academic library association |
| Head of research | Fellow academic librarians/peer group |
| Immediate boss/manager | Postgraduate training bodies |
| IT department | External accreditation boards |

## Academic librarian – example of readers/users of academic library service

Students, undergraduates and postgraduates, visiting students, lecturers, adjunct professors, alumni, and faculty.

Table 35 **Special/corporate librarian – example of stakeholders**

| Internal stakeholders | External stakeholders |
|---|---|
| CEO/partners | Special/corporate library association |
| Head of Finance | Fellow special librarians/peer group |
| Head of the department | Shareholders in company |
| IT department | Competitors (firms) – domestic and international |
| HR department | Professional association relevant to industry (e.g. Law association, research council) |

## What the librarian does

Librarians should think of this category from a strategic point of view. There is no need to list every operational task that is carried out. It is better to think like a key stakeholder might think. For example, the university provost may not be interested in how many books are borrowed from the library or how many people use the space but might be more interested in whether the reputation of the university is enhanced by the library and whether the library contributes to the attractiveness of the university to potential students.

So for example, if you are an **academic librarian**, a list of things could come under this category:

- Collaborate with faculty on strategic projects
- Make research output of the university openly accessible and discoverable via the institutional repository and research support system
- Make access to research literature easy for students and teaching staff alike
- Provide informed answers to information requests from students and teaching staff
- Ensure the library is a welcoming and student-friendly environment that encourages learning and the exchange of ideas and fosters knowledge creation and individual thought.
- Teach and deliver part of the academic curriculum
- Deliver a digital library, which enhances the reputation of the university and attracts students
- Provide makerspaces to facilitate experimental learning

If you are a **school librarian**, a list of things that would fall into the category might include the following:

- Collaborate with teachers to improve learning outcomes for all students
- Improve students' information, literacy and digital learning skills
- Provide an open learning environment with access to books and electronic media
- Run clubs for students to connect with each other and work collaboratively
- Select educational material aligned to the curriculum and to learning outcomes of the school
- Host events in the library based on the school calendar
- Organise stock buys and include students in the selection process
- Make the school library a welcoming space fostering creativity, innovation and learning for all students.

A list for a **hospital or health science librarian** might include the following:

- Enable immediate, seamless access to evidence-based resources for all hospital staff
- Manage the library space, making it fit its purpose
- Cocreate e-resources with clinicians that correspond to clinicians' learning and educational requirements
- Keep staff up to date with current and emerging literature through the supply of evidence updates
- Provide regular information updates to clinicians during Grand Rounds
- Co-author systematic reviews and research papers as part of the hospital's research output
- Provide expert information in a timely manner to inform patient care and evidence-based decision making
- Run a writing and journal club for hospital staff

For a **public librarian**, a list might include the following:

- Organise events in the library as informed by the needs of the local community
- Promote reading, learning and literacy to the general public
- Provide access to reading material in many formats to the community
- Manage the library as a physical place that is socially inclusive, welcomes the general public and caters for their learning, reading and leisure needs
- Providing training to the public on information literacy and digital literacy
- Support local businesses through the provision of information and space for them to use
- Offer a socially inclusive civic space free for everyone in the community
- Provide an outreach service for the community, including a mobile service for the housebound

The examples above are general in nature. Each individual librarian will know best what they do in their own job that is considered to be of value to their stakeholders.

## Prioritisation exercise: activities

Librarians are engaged in a variety of activities and offer diverse services. At this juncture, take the opportunity to decide what is a core activity and what is auxiliary. Reflect upon all current activities in conjunction with library staff. Then categorise them into core activities and those that are secondary, which have been used as add-ons. Auxiliary activities are those which perhaps are no longer offering a good return on investment (ROI) for the organisation or are of decreasing value. The value of an activity can be categorised into low, medium and high. A criteria for this categorization could include whether an activity or initiative is aligned to the overall mission of the organisation or not. If they are not aligned, they should be assigned with a low value. Activities and services provided by librarians inevitably change over time. A combination of waves of technological advances, heightened consumer expectations and a growing emphasis on accountability all converge to push new demands on librarians and libraries. New trends, such as the growth in digitization, repositories, open access, online learning and a focus on research data management, all necessitate a reprioritisation exercise of what is valuable today in the current information environment. See a sample of activities in Table 36.

The prioritisation exercise will be of even greater value if reader and stakeholder feedback on activities are included. It will generate a sense of ownership, buy-in and confidence around librarian-led initiatives. Traditional services may still be relevant but perhaps not all of them. To figure out which ones are worth continuing, measure their impact and assess their value according to a combination of data, the opinions of your own Library and Information Service (LIS) staff and those of your readers. Their opinions about what is core and what is auxiliary, together with those of the staff, make for a collaborative, multiperspective outcome. However watch out for what Google executives call the 'HiPPOs', or Highest-Paid-Person's Opinion (Schmidt & Rosenberg, 2014, p. 40), which is only relevant if it can be supported with accurate data and sound business sense. Librarians need to be wary of falling into what Frumento described as 'clerical traps' (Bardyn, Atcheson, Cuddy, & Perry, 2013), focussing on administrative tasks instead of value-added activities.

**Table 36  Prioritisation of activities and initiatives carried out by library staff**

| Activities/initiatives | Core or auxiliary? | Value (high, medium, low) (consider how the impact of activity aligns to the organisation's mission) |
|---|---|---|
| Participation in organizational committees | C | High |
| Staffed reference desk | A | Low |
| Cocreation of curriculum for information literacy | C | High |
| Individual training | A | Low |
| Librarian liaison to several departments | C | High |
| Reference management assistance | A | Low |
| Grant writing | C | Medium |
| Maintaining an active social media presence | C | High |
| Coffee station | A | Medium |
| Annual readathon | A | Medium |
| 3D printer | A | Low |
| Digitization project | C | Medium |
| Participation in campus visit for prospective students | C | High |
| Cocreation of data management plan | C | High |
| Service all branches | C | High |
| Library website upkeep | C | High |
| Print material collection | A | Low |
| Bibliometric report of institutional research output | C | High |

This is a useful exercise to help prepare staff for change. Traditional services might include current awareness, Selective Dissemination of Information (SDI), electronic table of contents (eTOC) alerts, document delivery and maintaining a staffed library reference desk. Reference queries and literature searches should be assessed for value. Information is a key resource for any learning organisation. However, libraries tend to be low on resources in terms of staff and budget so it is impossible for the library to be all things to all people. This is where another element of marketing comes into its own – segmentation. Segment your market to help determine what is worth continuing and what needs to either be revamped or discarded. Activities with a low value should be cut or transformed into an initiative with more value.

Categorisation of core and auxiliary services was investigated at the National Libraries of Wales and Scotland. Senior managers, librarians and library assistants were involved in the process. The categorisation proved somewhat difficult, due to the subjective nature of the interpretation of core and additional services (Broady-Preston & Swain, 2012). However, this approach to prioritisation is necessary to introduce change and to reflect upon current visibility. If activities are tied to positive impacts, resulting in better outcomes, then the job of prioritisation will be achievable. Use evidence as a guiding principle as it will not be possible to please all stakeholders all the time.

## Visibility of the librarian

### *Self-reported visibility*

Once you have determined who the key stakeholders in the organisation are and what they perceive to be valuable, as a librarian, you may begin to think of the following questions and rate yourself in your current job. On a scale of 0–10, where 0 = invisible and 10 = highly visible, how do you rate among the following individuals:

1. Key stakeholders
2. Readers/colleagues*/customers

*colleagues may be more appropriate than readers for librarians working in embedded roles.

To do this, fill out Tables 37 and 38.

This is a measure of self-reported visibility. If the librarian is unsure about answers to the self-reported visibility scale, feedback can be sought from peers or library colleagues. Ideally, librarians should aim high, at least 7 out of 10 in at least two of the four categories.

Next, consider your visibility to readers of the library, colleagues (if you are in an embedded role) or customers (if you are in a corporate role).

## Measuring your visibility according to your stakeholders

Aside from self-reported visibility, it is also important to measure visibility from the point of view of (1) key stakeholders and (2) readers/users of the service. To gain feedback from stakeholders about the visibility of the librarian, simply ask a small number

**Table 37  Visibility to key stakeholders (sample)**

| Visibility of librarian to key stakeholders | 0 | 1 | 2 | 3 | 4 | 5 | 6 | 7 | 8 | 9 | 10 |
|---|---|---|---|---|---|---|---|---|---|---|---|
| Recognise librarian upon sight? | | | | | | | | | x | | |
| Recognise librarian by name or reputation? | | | | | | | x | | | | |
| Understand what the librarian does? | | | | x | | | | | | | |
| Value what the librarian does? | | | | | | | x | | | | |
| Average visibility score of librarian: | 6 | | | | | | | | | | |

**Table 38  Visibility to readers/colleagues/customers**

| Visibility of librarian to readers/colleagues/customers | 0 | 1 | 2 | 3 | 4 | 5 | 6 | 7 | 8 | 9 | 10 |
|---|---|---|---|---|---|---|---|---|---|---|---|
| Recognise librarian upon sight? | | | | | | | | | | | |
| Recognise librarian by name or reputation? | | | | | | | | | | | |
| Understand what the librarian does? | | | | | | | | | | | |
| Value what the librarian does? | | | | | | | | | | | |
| Average visibility score of librarian: | | | | | | | | | | | |

of key stakeholders in the organisation the questions in the table above. Carry out the survey listed in Appendix A to gain feedback from readers or colleagues about the visibility of the librarian. As mentioned previously, combine the survey approach with a focus group or semi-structured interviews with key users and stakeholders.

Self-reported scores and those obtained from users of the service and key stakeholders should be compared to obtain an average visibility score. There may be a variation depending on the audience: view this as a big opportunity. In John Kotter's recent work "Accelerate", he talks about a dual operating system consisting of a traditional hierarchy and a new network to bring about active, sustainable change in organisations. The dual system centres around what Kotter describes as 'The Big Opportunity' (Kotter, 2014). Kotter offers eight accelerators to drive the big opportunity. Librarians are faced with a dilemma in a fast paced world where information has become a prime commodity. This should be turned into the big opportunity. The work of librarians and the social, economic and cultural values they contribute to society must be seen. Librarians have to increase their visibility to thrive in the new economy.

# How did you score?

## 0–3 You're invisible! ☹

If you scored an average visibility score of between zero and three, you have some serious work to do. But do not fear, there are plenty of ways to increase your visibility, which will get you back on track. Chapter 8 details a visibility improvement plan with 10 steps that should get you started.

## 4–5 You're visible, but only just. You have some work to do. ☺

Concentrate on areas where you scored the least. If people do not recognise you, consider whether that is in fact necessary in your job. Are you working as a cataloguer or in a back office in perhaps a systems role? Is this where you are having the biggest impact? If it is, there may not be a need for people to recognise you, at least in person. However, if people should recognise you but do not, then you have some work to do. Cataloguers and people working in systems roles will do their work better by engaging with users and finding out first-hand what users are looking for from a library catalogue or a library website. Three of the librarians interviewed in the case studies emphasised the importance of interaction with patrons to improve their experience and to provide a reader-centric library and information service. This idea of cocreation of library services between patrons and librarians is found in the literature to be successful (Marquez & Downey, 2015). Start by introducing yourself to key people in the organisation, attend meetings and get involved with committees. If you are in a systems role, set up a user group and gain feedback from patrons on their user experience. Get your presence known and contribute to the organisation in other ways beyond your daily routine.

Increasing visibility at the organisational level will require the librarian or LIS team to step outside the comfort zone of the physical library. This has been repeatedly emphasised by librarians interviewed in the preceding case studies. Developing leadership skills and emotional intelligence will aid you on this journey. You will need to be prepared to network in order to be accepted as a key member of staff. To do this, join some active committees and encourage members of your staff to join them.

If people do not recognise your name or reputation, this is an area that can be improved. For example, if a senior person in the organisation receives an email from you and they do not know you or worse still, delete it, you need to work on your reputation and get your name out there. Some ways to do this are by publishing or by adding your name to library products such as an 'Evidence Update', an e-zine, or any products that are sent out to readers and managers. All products should be branded. If you are the library manager, you need to have your library brand (logo, slogan and library name) and your personal name on the delivered products. Your reputation and library brand must align. Everything the librarian says and does and everything that stakeholders say about the librarian and the library combine to define your reputation.

Talk to managers and find out what their information needs are, then make sure you deliver a targeted product that meets their needs. Keep up to date with current and emerging literature in key strategic areas that the organisation works in. More than one of the library managers interviewed in the case studies emphasised the importance of delivering upon promises made and responding to needs identified in a proactive way. The response given will enhance the reputation and value of the librarian. Recruit brand champions who will become library ambassadors. Have your lift speech or elevator pitch ready. See more on this speech in Chapter 8.

There is an art to communicating effectively, and it can take some practice to get it right with management. For example, if emailing the management with an update or news item, it needs to be worded carefully. The subject line needs to speak to them. Ideally the body of the email should be short, to the point and it should include a call to action. A common approach in sales and marketing is to place fear, uncertainty and doubt (FUD) in the user's mind to make them think that they are in need of a product or service. This type of technique is common in commercial sales pitches. Usually this is accomplished by pointing out negative features of competitive products. In the case of librarianship, it is pretty easy to market our expertise over the Internet or search engines. People get frustrated with hundreds of thousands of meaningless search results and while they value the speed of response, the time taken to filter information is not appreciated. When it comes to information, managers are looking for clarity, certainty and fact-based information to keep them informed. Try sending them a link with a synopsis of fact-based information and offer them an opportunity to discuss the item further with the librarian.

Do people understand what you do? First of all, do they need to? Perhaps not every detail needs to be known, but it is very important that key stakeholders understand your role. This in turn leads them to have a perception about your value and impact in the organisation. Have you told them what your role is? How have you told them? Has your message been clear and free of jargon? Prepare a performance report or annual achievements document that is sent to management on at least an annual basis. The message must be a key performance message and one that aligns to the overall vision of the organisation. There is more about this topic in Chapter 8 (Figure 11).

### 6–8 You're getting there, but there is still a little room for improvement ☺

If you scored between six and eight you are quite visible to key stakeholders and readers in the organisation. Examine areas where you scored less. What is it that is impeding visibility in these areas? Is there anything you can do in the short or medium term to improve visibility? Think about quality improvement processes such as the Deming PDSA cycle plan-do-study-act. This is also known as the Shewhart cycle. Quality improvement is an iterative process and needs buy-in from the outset. Do not be afraid to make mistakes, but try to learn from them and keep improving. To keep motivated, start with 'quick-wins', plan areas where you know that success can be achieved. This might be something as simple as sending interesting and relevant tweets from your library Twitter account on a regular basis. Plan to do this daily. Predict how many new followers you will achieve in a six-month period. Decide who is going to do this and when. Implement the plan (i.e. start tweeting). Study the metrics associated with this (e.g. number of retweets, favourites, new followers, direct tweets or contacts made). Begin analysing the data. Compare predictions of the number of followers with the reality. Reflect upon what worked and what did not work. Act upon areas where improvements are needed. Introduce changes to make improvements happen. Then start the cycle again. See Figure 12.

A self-appraisal may help to identify what works and areas for improvement. An example is the STAR method, used by the Office of Human Capital Management of the US Department of Agriculture. The STAR method may be a useful way of determining areas where visibility could be improved. It is a type of reflective piece that looks at describing a situation (S) and task (T), the action (A) taken and the results (R) achieved.

### 9–10 Good job! Well done! Keep up the good work. You are on the path to enlightened librarianship. ☺ 👍

Your tactics are working. You are a strategic thinker and have built up a good reputation for your work. Why not spread your ideas and your successes? Contribute to the

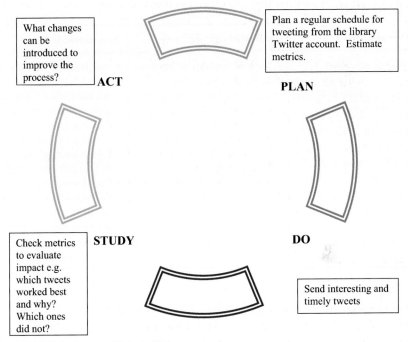

**Figure 12** PDSA cycle applied to a library scenario.

LIS community by giving presentations at conferences or writing for the academic LIS journals and journals in other disciplines. You could even share your ideas on the **theinvisiblelibrarian.com Blog.**, which has been set up as a follow up to this book.

## Root cause analysis

In terms of self-reported visibility, if any areas are low or high scoring, it is useful to write down the reasons that the librarian feels that he or she is not doing well in some areas and is doing better in other areas. Getting to the root cause of any successes or failures is the first step in planning to fix them. Root cause analysis (RCA) is a process designed for use in investigating and categorizing the root causes of events with safety, health, environmental, quality, reliability and production impacts (Rooney & Heuvel, 2004). It generally consists of a four step process:

1. Gather data
2. Chart causes
3. Identify root cause
4. Make and implement recommendations

Consider this fictional scenario as an example. Mary is a hospital librarian who asks the Head of Education if she can give a 10-minute presentation during Grand Rounds coming up next month. This is the first time the Head of Education has met Mary, and he refuses her request, stating that it is already a packed programme and

**Table 39  Paths to root cause analysis**

| Causal factor 1 | Paths through root map | Recommendations |
|---|---|---|
| Head of education refuses librarian participation in Grand Rounds | • Lack of visibility of librarian to Head of Education<br>• Head of Education does not understand value that librarian adds<br>• No standard bill of librarian inclusion in Grand Rounds<br>• Notice of one month not sufficient in a busy hospital | • Ask Head of Education what his information needs are and deliver a response to at least one identified need.<br>• Communicate value of librarian to Head of Education (e.g. invite them to a 10 min sample talk)<br>• Collaborate with Head of Education or nominee from department to schedule policy of dedicated schedule for librarian to attend Grand Rounds |

he does not see the relevance of the librarian slot to Grand Rounds. The causal factor, paths and recommendations are outlined in Table 39.

RCA was used to determine stakeholders' perceptions of the value of the library at one academic research institution (Nitecki & Abels, 2013). The researchers adopted the 'Five whys' approach to carry out the RCA. The stakeholders included faculty, students, university administrators, librarians, donors and library employees. Through a mixed-method approach using interviews, a focus group and literature review, several root causes of perceived value were outlined. A value wheel represents the diverging perceptions of stakeholders. This research is an evidence-based approach to identifying value and tailoring a library response based on root causes.

# Visibility of the library

Next decide how visible the library is. Complete Table 40 as a self-reported exercise on the visibility of the library. Carry out this task in conjunction with all library staff. This is an attempt to capture the library staff's perception of the visibility of the library to its readers. This is an opportunity to enhance teamwork through communication and working towards a common goal – the increased visibility of the library.

# Library visibility to readers according to readers

To gain feedback on the visibility of the library from readers or potential readers, the easiest thing to do is to ask them. Use the survey from Appendix A as a template and

**Table 40** **Self-reported visibility of the library to readers**

| Visibility of library to readers | 0 | 1 | 2 | 3 | 4 | 5 | 6 | 7 | 8 | 9 | 10 |
|---|---|---|---|---|---|---|---|---|---|---|---|
| Do readers know where the library is? | | | | | | | | | | | |
| Do readers recognise the library by name or reputation? | | | | | | | | | | | |
| Do readers know what services the library has to offer? | | | | | | | | | | | |
| Do readers appreciate the value of the library? | | | | | | | | | | | |
| Average visibility score of library: | | | | | | | | | | | |

make it available online, in paper format or both. The survey should be adapted for different library types, in particular with regard to the question about library services awareness, as this will vary depending on the library.

To determine the visibility score of the library, take an average score of the visibility of the library according to both library staff and readers.

# How did the library score?

## *0–3* ⊗

If the self-reported consensus from library staff is that the library scores an average of between zero and three, then the library is invisible. There is some serious work to be done to improve its visibility. First off, look at the signage in the local area and building. Can visitors find the library? It should be obvious to anyone visiting the organisation or town/city where the library is. Secondly, embark upon a marketing plan. If people are unaware of library services, begin a library awareness campaign. Use social media and host events in the library and outside the library to raise awareness. The library ideally should have a logo and identifiable brand, including a tagline or slogan. Running a competition to come up with a logo and slogan may be an option if one is not already in place. This, in turn, will raise awareness and buy-in from readers. It needs to be a slogan that is believed and valued by staff. According to Google's executive managers, 'If you do not believe your own slogans you will not get very far' (Schmidt & Rosenberg, 2014, p. 23). See more information on branding later in this chapter.

Adopting a retail approach to marketing is something that offers unique opportunities to libraries. Learning from the best and most successful retail industries will make marketing a successful strategy for libraries. First let's start with the customer. Customers and users or readers of an LIS have expectations, which generally will not differ radically from their use of any other service industry. Put yourself in the customer's shoes for a moment. Think of what you might expect from a service. It might include:

- Easy access
- Speedy delivery
- Wide choice
- Range of delivery platforms
- Expertise
- Premium services
- Options
- Membership
- Discounts

Consider each of these elements in relation to your library. Is the library offering these benefits to readers? If these benefits are available, perhaps readers are unaware of them. Create a promotional leaflet highlighting benefits using an infographic. For example:

**Library membership benefits**

#1 We save you time.

We know that you are busy juggling multiple tasks and deadlines. That's why we have made Library and information resources easy to access and use for our Members.

You can get what you need – fast. For example, most of our online tutorials are 30 minutes in length. You can find the solution to a niggling problem in just half an hour!

#2 Membership is free!

#3 We bring you carefully selected, quality resources in subjects you are interested in.

#4 We adopt a partnership approach and are open to working with your department and new teams to get the best results, based on the most up-to-date, data-driven information.

#5 We help corporate teams make better decisions based on the latest data.

## 4–5 ☺

The library is barely visible to readers. There is some work to be done. Identify areas of strengths, weaknesses, threats and opportunities using a Strengths, Weaknesses, Opportunities and Threats (SWOT) analysis. Concentrate on achievable improvements, again using the PDSA cycle described earlier. Carry out a needs assessment with readers and start making small incremental changes that will improve visibility. Perhaps there is a lack of awareness about some or all of the services the library offers. Highlight the benefits of services to readers using a targeted marketing campaign. This can be done using social media and traditional marketing methods, such as email or a poster campaign. Carry out a review of any promotional materials that the library has. Are they working? Is awareness increasing? Perhaps the materials need to be revamped or reimaged in a new format.

Set up a blog for the library. Post interesting current items that will appeal to your audience on the blog. Include a 'Spotlight of the week', such as an e-book collection or special collection item that might need promotion. Collections can be promoted throughout the blog and social media. Try to engage library champions in cocreation of content for the blog. Invite reviews from readers on books and other media items. Blogs can be set up around specific subject areas. Pick subjects of interest to readers and stakeholders (e.g. health and well-being or corporate management). Public and school libraries have transformed some spaces in their libraries to become makerspaces. Consider whether this may raise the profile of the library to the community.

Does the library need a fresh look or a new and improved layout? The only way to find out is to ask people who use it what they think. Try to look at the library through fresh eyes, as if you are seeing it for the first time. Invite a nonuser to act as a 'secret-shopper' and ask them to provide a narrative based on their impression and experience. It would be useful to invite new members to give you immediate feedback on the layout and environment of the library. A survey could be carried out with library members and interviews could be held with people in the building who do and do not use the library. It is equally important to hear from people who do not use the library to find out why that is the case. Take steps to respond to user feedback and make the space a welcoming and inviting place to be. It should align with the overall ethos and objectives of the organization.

## 6–8 ☺

The library is quite visible to readers. There may be small areas where improvements can be made. Check on the progress of marketing campaigns in use and check the online visibility of the library. If readers are under appreciative of the value of the library, launch a value statement and reader charter. Read more about engaging with readers in Chapter 8. Do not forget to look after your fan base. Are readers coming back for repeat business? How do they perceive your value? Do they feel satisfied; do they envisage areas where your value could be enhanced? New opportunities may exist, but it is vital to keep the lines of communication open, to gather regular feedback and to empower customers to 'have their say'. Listen to their 'pleas and causes' like one of the most successful football managers of our times:

> *I have always tried to be the bridge between the club and the fans and I have tried to support the fans in a lot of their pleas and causes.*
> *Sir Alex Ferguson former manager of the football club Manchester United*

Do you have a 'Comments' or 'Suggestions' box in the library? Is it located in an area of privacy? Does your website allow online comments or a feedback mechanism? Ideally you should have both options always available for customers to use, both in person and online. Feedback should be gathered on a routine basis for all services offered, including literature searches, training, document supply, physical spaces and facilities, etc. A library must be user-centric. Why else does it exist if not for people to use it?

Keeping services as close to user needs as possible is essential. This means that regular engagement with users or customers is an absolute must. Otherwise, the library's function is likely to drift. Planning, implementing a marketing strategy and getting feedback should be a regular occurrence for any librarian who wishes to improve their visibility and impact. The marketing strategy should feed directly into the strategic plan of one to three years. Feedback on regular services should be embedded within them.

### 9–10 ☺ 👍

The library is ubiquitous. The marketing, promotion and awareness activities that the library has embarked upon are a resounding success. Other librarians have library envy due to the success of the library. Why not share the success story of the library? Add your story to the theinvisiblelibrarian.com blog. Other libraries may learn from this. Enter for a recognised award to try to get recognition for efforts made.

## Management techniques for determining visibility – how are you going to get more visible?

Some management techniques have been discussed, such as quality improvement using the PDSA system and getting to the root of the problem using root cause analysis. Further techniques frequently used in business environments, including positioning, auditing, SWOT and Political, Economic, Social, Technological, Legal and Environmental (PESTLE), are now explored in relation to library environments. In parallel to the visibility check, a number of these techniques will assist librarians in their journey to improved visibility.

## Positioning

The positioning of the library or librarian in the organization chart of the institution is important. Positioning determines how resources are allocated, how stakeholders perceive the library/librarian and their business fit within the organisation. If librarians wish to evolve beyond being perceived to be a 'support service', then their positioning needs to be core to the organisation and aligned to similar departments with key roles such as research, business intelligence or knowledge management. If the library is bundled in with divisions such as student services, employee services, information and communications technology or human resources it will always be stuck in support mode. Supporting roles always have to fight for resources and prove their worth to the organisation, as they are seen as 'nice to have' but not absolutely essential. This is where librarians must step up and embrace change; the profession must evolve beyond playing a supporting role. Librarians must start to be seen as the main act.

A small change that librarians can make to increase their visibility is simply this: librarians need to stop using the word support. Change it to partner or collaborator. This is particularly relevant in academic and special librarianship. For example, if someone asks for assistance on a literature review, offer to meet with them and discuss the topic and offer to help as long as you receive acknowledgement as a co-author.

## Information audit and skills audit

Conducting an information audit and a skills audit is a useful way to take stock and identify any gaps or areas where additional training is required. Human and financial resources may be factors that could be hampering visibility. The audits contribute to an environment of continuous quality improvement.

## Information audit

To start any audit, a rigorous approach is required. Information must be identified that meets the strategic objectives of the organisation. Any gaps in information provision should be identified. For an information audit to be successful, input from readers is required. Take into account the information needs of readers and whether the library/librarian is meeting those needs. Consider how information is being made available, what platforms are used, what information types are provided and when a reader can expect to have a request for information answered. The information audit should take into account the collection development policy that is in place and input from the acquisitions librarian, special collections manager, systems librarian and digital library/repository manager (where present) should be sought. The information audit will look at content and usage. Usage statistics using international standards such as Counting Online Usage of NeTworked Electronic Resources (COUNTER) compliant statistics should give an indication of the usage of electronic resources. Some libraries also compile statistics on ultimate use, which shows what the user does with the digital object they have acquired from the library. An example of this is the Digital Cart Service in use at the University of Houston Library, Texas (Reilly & Thompson, 2014). All of these statistics inform collection development and digital library management and give an indication of the visibility of content and collections to readers.

A detailed example of a quality improvement process using an evidence-based approach is provided by Griffin, Lewis and Greenberg at the University of South Florida (USF) (Griffin, Lewis, & Greenberg, 2013). The Special and Digital Collections (SDC) department at USF began to take assessment seriously following budget cuts and loss of library staff. They used qualitative and quantitative methods to assess the needs of their department and patrons. The tools used included Google Analytics, Desk Tracker, LibGuides, SQL queries via Fedora Commons Repository software and Aeon. This holistic, data-driven approach to measuring current impact empowered the department to make informed decisions to improve quality. For example, patron needs in relation to a reading room were identified by analysing data from a one-minute, one-page survey. Feedback was captured from readers using the room over a two-year period. This was analysed in combination with the traffic patterns of readers. Notably the department acted upon the feedback and matched opening hours to readers' usage patterns and through successful application for a grant, funded a new overhead scanner for the reading room.

It is striking that in just two years, the SDC successfully introduced a significant change management initiative of continuous assessment. The authors report that this strategy has become part of their culture. The outcomes have been transformative. They have successfully aligned outcomes of the SDC to priorities set by the university and are able to extract data on a routine basis or for formal reviews, which support the positive impact of SDC.

In addition to usage statistics, feedback should be compiled from readers, especially where special and unique collections are in place. Often, specialised content can present a unique selling point for a library. This needs to be nurtured and promoted far and wide. Entry points to specialised content should be made as straightforward as possible. Conduct regular usability testing to quality assure this. The outcome of the audit should identify information gaps, inform a revised collection development policy and highlight opportunities for the improved visibility of collections and information products for the organisation.

## Skills audit

Find out what skills your staff have by conducting one-to-one consultations with staff or by developing an online skills directory. Generally, library staff will have profiles on social media platforms such as LinkedIn, which effectively acts as an electronic résumé. Other popular sources are ResearchGate or Academia.edu. Ideally library staff will have personal development plans in place, which should be reviewed annually. These plans will inform the skills audit. Assess the current skill set of the library staff to help determine strengths and weaknesses. Relevant library associations should be consulted to obtain guidance policies on education and competencies for librarians. Conducting a training needs analysis. This should correspond to gaps in visibility, which need to be addressed. For example, perhaps there is a skills deficit around using social media platforms or compiling e-resource statistics. Perhaps training in critical appraisal or research methods such as crowdsourcing is required. These gaps will come to the fore when a baseline of skills are identified and areas for improvement indicate a skills deficit.

Creating training opportunities for staff will offer an incentive and have a motivating influence on library staff. Growth and personal development are part of Maslow's hierarchy of needs under self-actualization. While financial rewards are not always possible in libraries, opportunities for continuing professional development and learning are. This will pave the way to gradually introduce a change management programme to heightened visibility.

## SWOT and PESTLE

Strategic management techniques will enhance the key steps in identifying current visibility and identifying any underlying causes. Use tried and tested management techniques to find out underlying reasons for visibility level and areas that affect visibility. For example, carry out a SWOT and PESTLE analysis. The SWOT will identify strengths, weaknesses, opportunities and threats to visibility.

**PESTLE**: PESTLE has been used frequently as a management technique to help to understand the external environmental conditions under which we work. It outlines Political, Economic, Social, Technological, Legislative and Environmental factors that affect something in an organisation or a business. This can be applied to factors effecting the visibility of a librarian or library.

**Political factors**: the stability of the country that the librarian works in. The stability of the organisation and its governance should be taken into account.

**Economic factors**: Consider the budget that the library has or should aspire to have. The budget required to run as a value for money operation should be examined vis-à-vis costs, pay and non-pay related, staffing, overhead and demand.

**Social factors**: Trends in consumer interaction with information particularly on the internet will affect visibility of the librarian and library. Social inclusion is an important factor to count.

**Technological factors**: Consumer use of technology, the prevalence of mobile and tablet use ( as well as other devices), generational consumer approaches to IT (generation X and Y), the proliferation of digital information on the internet and competitors in the information industry all impact librarian visibility. Consider awareness levels of emerging technologies and the use of them within the organisation and/or discipline/industry.

**Environmental factors**: Design of the exterior library building and effect of the building on the environment. Does the library have sustainable energy programmes, recycling facilities and implementation of a green approach? Libraries have shared their approach to sustainable buildings, for example, the green design of Zhengzhou library in China (Xuan & Hongyan, 2011). There is a green library Facebook Group and blog dedicated to sharing environmentally friendly tips for librarians.

**Legislative factors**: Copyright, data protection and intellectual property rights and laws. Monitor legislative changes and emerging laws that are relevant to data protection, intellectual property, copyright, etc.

If you are unsure how to capture a PESTLE analysis for your library, why not try a crowdsourcing technique and collate the collective thinking of like-minded librarians and other professionals. This was successfully captured by Matt Holland, a UK librarian with the North West NHS Ambulance Service, on a clinical librarian blog in 2015 (Holland, 2015).

This is a starting point to measure current visibility and set objectives for improving visibility. Objectives for improving visibility need to be SMART – specific, measured, achievable, realistic and time-bound. Some quick-wins for increasing visibility are identified in the examples below. Longer-term change is outlined in the VIP in the next chapter.

For example, if you are a school librarian and only some of the teachers in the school recognise you, a smart objective might be to ensure you are recognised and known by name by every teacher in the school before the next school break. To achieve this, the librarian could ask if she could give a short presentation in the staff room at the next staff meeting or invite teachers who do not know her to bring their classes to the library at a designated time.

For a public librarian who is not recognised or known to readers or users of the service, it is important to be physically available for the public and to be seen in the public eye at events. For example, the librarian could begin a regular 'meet and greet' to people visiting the library and give library tours the first Tuesday of every month for three months. Her recognition after three months could be measured by a simple survey or by the observation of an increase in people greeting her by name.

For a hospital librarian who feels that she is not recognised by users of the service, he could have a smart aim to give a presentation during Grand Rounds once a month or every quarter to increase visibility.

For a corporate librarian, giving a presentation at a board meeting or hosting a special event, such as a seminar on a topic of interest to the firm (e.g. during national library week), would be a smart way to increase visibility.

Academic librarians may offer to meet with any new faculty members or attend faculty meetings. Teaching and giving lectures as part of the under/postgraduate curriculum is key to ensuring heightened visibility. Hosting special events, such as a writing for publication workshop during international open access week, could also heighten visibility.

Embedded librarians could offer to get a speaking slot at departmental meetings to talk about their role or they could use hot-desking to sit with different teams in the organisation and get to know people.

## Measuring visibility, impact and value

Chapter 9 will detail examples from the LIS literature of libraries that have successfully measured and evaluated the impact that they have on their readers and users. The definitions of visibility, impact and value are explored here to give an introduction to these concepts. Why is visibility important? Visibility matters for librarians who want to have an impact, who want to demonstrate value and who want to make a positive difference to people's lives. Visibility is defined as 'the degree to which something has attracted general attention; prominence' (Oxford ED 2nd ed. 2010). Undoubtedly visibility of librarians and libraries is essential for both professional growth and for the growth of the profession.

A definition of impact is 'a marked effect or influence' (Oxford English Dictionary). To find out what the impact of a library service is having, it is useful to explore what is understood by impact. Impact, according to Brophy, may be any of the following:

- Negative or positive
- What was intended or something different
- Result in changed behaviours, attitudes, outputs (e.g. research outputs), be short- or long-term and be critical or trivial.

Value is defined as 'the regard that something is held to deserve; the importance, worth or usefulness of something' (Oxford ED). Value is seen as an indication of the beneficial effects of the library (Orr, 1973). Value for key stakeholders in an academic library setting is defined by Oakleaf in terms of saving time or saving money. She defines impact as what LIS services allow the reader to do (Oakleaf, 2013). We have looked at measuring visibility, but now we will turn to the various methodologies in use for measuring the impact and value of libraries.

# Measuring impact and value in academic libraries

In academic libraries, evaluation methods include LibQUAL, participation in national student surveys and external accreditation standards. The Association of College and Research Libraries (ACRL) has made a toolkit available to measure the value of academic libraries since 2010. ACRL Standards for libraries in Higher Education include Key Performance Indicators (KPIs) for institutional effectiveness 'Libraries define, develop, and measure outcomes that contribute to institutional effectiveness and apply findings for purposes of continuous improvement' (ACRL Standards, 2011). The Rubric Assessment of Information Literacy Skills (RAILS) initiative in the USA is assisting academic librarians to produce campus-wide rubrics for assessment, with a focus on information literacy outcomes. Some countries have established national groups, such as The Society of College, National and University Libraries (SCNOUL) in the UK and Ireland, covering national and academic libraries. The Performance and Quality Strategy Group of SCONUL uses benchmarking, assessment techniques and performance data for its participating libraries. The Joint Information Systems Committee (JISC)-funded Library Analytics and Metrics project (LAMP) is developing a basic student attainment and retention dashboard for all universities and colleges. In the UK, the Customer Service Excellence Standard can be used for accreditation. The implementation of standards fosters active engagement and partnership with customers, which is 'imperative if academic library services are to become not only valued, but vital to their parent organisations' (Broady-Preston & Lobo, 2011). In Australia, the Council of Australian University Librarians (CAUL) provides members with resources for measurement of impact, including performance indicators and case studies of best practice. Kaplan and Norton's Balanced Scorecard is a popular model for many libraries. It is supported by librarians at the University of Washington, McMaster University, University of Virginia and Johns Hopkins University as 'an excellent organizational performance model' (Hiller, Lewis, Mengel, & Tolson, 2010).

# Measuring impact and value in public libraries

For public libraries, the impact they have on their communities is what is needed to demonstrate value. Researchers have called for more qualitative methods, such as the social audit of Newcastle and Somerset library services (McMenemy, 2007). The use of quantitative statistics, such as book issues and the number of readers, do not give an adequate picture of value, in fact, they can weaken the position of the library. The real value of a public library is the positive experience that a person has when they use a library, online or in person. This is why it is difficult to measure the value of the public library, as it is difficult to measure experience. The critical incident technique is a useful qualitative method that has been used in public libraries to evaluate the quality of service (Wong, 2013). The societal impact of a public library on its community is where the social value of a public library lies. Whether the public library lends itself to a more informed citizenry needs to be measured. Qualitative methodologies, such as profiling, have been successful at making the societal benefits of public library use tangible. Profiling has enabled UK Online Centres (UKOC) to translate faceless data into outcomes that are 'tangible, practicable and workable' (UKOC, quoted in Rooney-Browne, 2011). Profiles of how public libraries are helping people in UK communities are available on ukonlinecentres.com. Rooney-Browne provides a comprehensive overview of methods for measuring public library value (Rooney-Browne, 2011).

It has been observed that the best way to measure impact is to do so over a long period of time (Brophy, 2006). In libraries where readers are fairly static (e.g. academic and school libraries), this may be easier to achieve. With school libraries, reading scores of students can be measured over a two- or three-year period, for example. For academic libraries, ranking of universities and student grades can be measured over time, particularly if librarians are delivering courses that form part of the curriculum.

Brophy introduced a LoI (Level of Impact) scale from −2 to 6 when evaluating the level of impact The People's Network (PN) had in public libraries in the UK. PN involved the installation of computers in public libraries. In the US, the Washington iSchool is measuring the impact of internet accessibility in US public libraries. Over 800 US public libraries have registered for the impact survey. Another way for librarians to measure value/impact is to align services to (1) the mission of the organisation and (2) standards for libraries in their specialist area. A Public Library Improvement Model for Scotland was launched in 2014 with five quality indicators. In Wales, a framework for public libraries was published in 2014 (Welsh Government, 2014), which includes impact measurement for the first time. Alarmingly, in England there are no national standards or national impact measures for public libraries. This is devolved to local authorities on a voluntary basis (Anstice, 2014). The Sieghart report does not include a recommendation for standards for public libraries in England. This is out of step with best practice internationally. The USA, Australia and Canada all have standards for public libraries. The Australian Public Library Alliance offers benchmarking calculators and the US Public Library Association (PLA) offers public library service data including outcome measures to its members. The PLA is putting a strategic emphasis on impact measurement and is due to launch its 'Project Outcome' with a three-year strategic plan in June 2015. Project Outcome includes a set of survey instruments, data entry and analysis tools, online training and support for libraries' implementation and advocacy efforts.

An innovative ranking system has been developed for public libraries in Europe by two Scandinavian librarians, Berndtson and Öström. The Library Ranking Europe (LRE) will certainly improve the visibility of participating public libraries. The aim of the project is to stimulate benchmarking and the development of quality among some 65,000 European public libraries. Interestingly, the visibility of libraries is part of the criteria for ranking libraries from a scale of one to six using stars. More criteria may be accessed from the libraryranking.com website.

## Measuring impact and value in health science libraries

In health science librarianship, the National Library of Medicine has shown leadership by publishing research on impact known as the 'Value Study' (Marshall et al., 2013). This used a mixed-methods approach using qualitative and quantitative research. In hospital libraries where patient outcomes are measured, outcomes have immediate impact. It may be difficult to relate patient outcomes directly to any librarian involvement, but in some cases, it can be proven (e.g. the supply of information at the point of care just in time for decision making that effects a patient). The main body of research about the impact of library and information services to patient care has shown that the involvement of a librarian has a positive impact on clinical decision making and saves time (Marshall, 1992, 2013; Perrier et al., 2014). Lack of time is a major obstacle to information-seeking in hospitals where the immediate availability of information is a major asset (Kostagiolas, Ziavrou, Alexias, & Niakas, 2012). Other methods for measuring impact include the critical incident technique (Marshall, 2014), systematic reviews of the literature (Weightman & Williamson, 2005; Wagner & Byrd, 2004; Brettle et al., 2011) and a hospital survey linked to performance indicators based on institutional mission (Dalton, 2012). Eldredge (2004) compiled a useful inventory of research methods used in librarianship with particular reference to the health sciences.

## Measuring impact and value in special libraries

The Financial Times, in conjunction with the Special Library Association, commissioned a report into 'The Evolving Value of Information Management', published in 2013. One of the striking findings of this report, which surveyed 882 people, was the differences in perceptions of the value of the knowledge provider. According to the report, knowledge providers overestimated their value to executives, with 55% stating that they added 'a lot of value'. However only 34% of executives reported the same to be true. This would suggest that special library and information professionals need to work on demonstrating their impact and value. The LibQUAL™ and SERVQUAL™ instruments are widely used in academic and research libraries as a method of measuring service quality and library performance. In the national library of Iran, LibQUAL™ was used as a gap analysis model reviewing clients' views of service quality (Neshat & Dehghani, 2013). In special libraries, Total Quality Management (TQM) and European Foundation for Quality Management (EFQM) are proving useful methods for measuring excellence in quality (Moghaddam & Moballeghi, 2011).

Unless librarians begin to measure impact, there can be no credible way of justifying having a librarian employed in an organisation or having a library as an information service. People may take comfort in knowing that the organisation has a library or librarian, but that is not enough if the organisation falls on hard times and everything is fair game for cuts. Many hospital librarians, particularly in the USA and public libraries in the UK, have felt the effects of recessionary times with closures and cuts to library services and job losses for librarians. Measuring impact is a critical tool in effective strategic planning. It will assist in determining which services have the greatest and least impact. It will aid decisions about which services to cut or reduce and inform decisions about which services should be boosted with more resources. One of the formidable qualities of librarianship is the exchange of information and collaboration between librarians. Impact stories and research on impact have been generously offered by many researchers, who offer research instruments for local use by other librarians. Examples of such research will be outlined in the next chapter.

# Measuring online visibility

In tandem with the visibility of the library and librarian in person, another area that is key to the professional growth of librarianship is the visibility of the library and librarian on the internet. How visible is the library and librarian on the web? In order to take stock of current visibility, adopt a three step approach:

- Step 1: determine the visibility of the library brand against two predefined checklists (see below).
- Step 2: identify visibility gaps from the list and check feasibility and the need to fill those gaps
- Step 3: measure usage and impact metrics in relation to all internet access points from both checklists.

## Step 1: Determine visibility of library brand against two predefined checklists

Visibility of the library and librarian in the online environment is heavily reliant on the library having a strong, consistent brand. The brand should consist of a logo with the name of the library and a motto or slogan if possible. All potential pathways to information and services that the library provides should be linked to highly branded library resources that the reader is likely to instantly recognise and immediately associate with the library. The identification of the library brand will provide a certain level of reassurance to the reader that they are uncovering quality resources and reliable information during their online search activity. Not only this, but online library users may then realise that electronic resources are made available to them thanks to the library, if the branding is visible. Otherwise they may not make the connection between the resource and the library at all. One of the case studies highlighted a lack of visibility of the library in relation to the product ScienceDirect™. Customers did not realise that it was being provided via the library due to the absence of library branding.

# Branding

The first thing to do is check whether the library has a brand and logo and whether it is instantly recognisable by library users. If no brand exists, many library associations have sections on their websites that relate to library marketing, promotion and branding where more information can be gathered. For example, the International Federation of Library Associations and Institutions (IFLA) have a section on their website devoted to library branding, which has further guidance and tools that librarians may use. The American Library Association has a selection of slogans for school libraries to use. Once the library branding has been decided upon, stick to this as the house style. Unless your organisation undergoes rebranding, do not be tempted to change or 'update' your logo or tagline every few years. Companies who have done this lose brand recognition and consumer loyalty. When Kellogg attempted to change its Coco Pops brand to Choco Krispies, there was an outcry, and Kellogg resorted to a public vote, which asked for it to be changed back (Crawford, 1999).

Having a brand that is easily recognisable is crucial to help increase awareness of your existence and makes you and your library instantly visible. Branding is important to get right. If working as a school, academic or hospital librarian, the organisation may have its own logo. Ideally use the colours of that logo to create one for the library and information services. If you can avail of in-house skills to do this, it is a good opportunity to work with other departments in your organisation, or you could run a competition to generate some interest in the library. The name of the LIS should be part of the logo. It may be worth creating a tagline or motto depending on the LIS. Have a look at library websites that are in the same category as yours for some examples. Generate new ideas by looking at the logos and old and new taglines of major brands (e.g. NIKE 'Just do it'; McDonalds 'I'm lovin' it', Google 'Standing on the shoulders of giants'; 'Apple. Think different'; 'BMW. The ultimate driving machine'; 'Fly with Ryanair and save money'; AUDI 'Vorsprung durch Tecnik'; Microsoft 'Where do you want to go today?' etc.). According to Forbes (2014), the top 25 most valuable brands in 2014 were dominated by the technology sector, with Apple, Microsoft and Google coming out on top. Inspiration may be gained by reading some examples of library slogans listed in Table 41.

The library brand must be prominently displayed at every online access point. Create an inventory of all possible sites where the LIS and librarian has a presence. This will be used to make up two checklists. These should be audited at least annually. As sites change, it would be wise to also carry out a spot check at least once during the year. Initially there is quite a lot of work involved, but once done, the LIS should find that people will begin to recognise the LIS brand and usage should increase. In terms of online visibility, ensure that wherever your LIS is represented that your logo is prominently displayed, particularly in social media spaces (e.g. LinkedIn, Twitter, Facebook, Google Groups, ResearchGate, Virtual Learning Environments (VLEs), etc.).

Consider the social media presence of the library and librarian. Is the library and librarian social media friendly? Social media toolbars should be available on all online library access points, including the library website, discovery tool, library catalogue, repository and library blog. The library brand should be on the library website, LIS pages on the corporate or the organisation's website and intranet, all email signatures of all library staff, all interactive online tutorials, Libguides™, online chat, blog(s), subject guides, all subscription-based databases (Ovid, Ebsco, Proquest, Westlaw, etc.), A to Z journal listings, individual journal publisher websites, online catalogues, discovery tool, e-book platform, legal databases, etc. Branch out and include the LIS logo on professional association websites and partner organisations where the LIS may have reciprocal arrangements. The Institutional Repository (IR) and other relevant IRs in your region and country should have the library brand. The key thing is to keep a consistent look and feel that readers will familiarise themselves with.

**Table 41  Sample library slogans**

| Library type | Library name | Slogan |
|---|---|---|
| Research library | British Library | Explore the world's knowledge. |
| Public library | New York Public Library | But above all things, truth beareth away the victory |
| Public library | Queens Library, New York | Enrich your life |
| Public library | Calgary Public Library, Canada | Everything you're into |
| Public library | Plainfield Public Library, Illinois, USA | Educate – captivate – connect. |
| Public library | Boston Public Library, USA | Books are just the beginning |
| Public library | Chicago Public Library | It's free. It's easy. |
| Public library | Bibliotheque Montreal | Pour aller plus loin. |
| University library | Cofrin Library, University of Wisconsin, Green Bay, USA | Your guide to answers. |
| University library | Borland Library, University of Florida, USA | Opening the door to knowledge. |
| University library | Kings Western University, Canada | Experience the heart of king's |
| University library | Z. Smith Reynolds Library, Wake Forest University | Get better answers. Discover new ideas. Do great things. |
| University library | University of the Philippines Diliman libraries | Discovering Connections, Connecting Discoveries |
| School library | Queenstown Primary School, New Zealand | To help create motivated and engaged young readers |
| School library | Knoxville Christian School, USA | Read to succeed |
| School library | Scoil Mhuire Community School, Ireland | The Truth will set you free |
| School library | King James School, UK | Inform – inspire – achieve |
| Special/Health science library | National Institutes of Health USA | Turning discovery into health |
| Consumer health library | VCU's Community Health Education Center, VA, USA | Where knowledge empowers people |
| Special library | National Geographic Library, Washington DC, USA | "The 10 minute rule." That means, if you haven't found what you are looking for in 10 minutes, call us. |
| Special library | New Zealand National library | Collect, connect, co-Create |
| Special library | British Library | Inspiring future knowledge |

Consider the visibility of the librarian on all of these sites. A photo of the librarian adds a human touch for the reader who is searching for information online, and it gives the reader a more personalised user experience. It means that if the reader has an opportunity to meet the librarian in person, that they will be recognised, heightening the visibility of the librarian. If the librarian is not visible on premium online access points, the old adage of 'out of sight, out of mind' will be the unfortunate outcome for the library.

Two sample checklists are supplied below:

## Checklist for online access points where library brand/logo should be visible

- Dedicated library website
- Library microsite or pages on parent organisation website
- Library microsite on organisation intranet
- Institutional repository
- Discovery tool
- Library catalogue
- Library portals
- In search engines (e.g. Google Scholar Library Links)
- In third-party bibliographic databases (e.g. PubMed Linkout tool, ERIC, Web of Science, Scopus, CINAHL, Lexis-Nexis, etc.)
- On publisher websites (e.g. 'access provided by X library')
- On point-of-care tools
- Branded library 'Link Resolver' icon
- On e-book platform, digitised collections and e-publishing sites
- Links to library website from professional associations websites (e.g. health professionals, teachers, lecturers, etc.)
- In virtual learning environments used by learners of the organisation
- Social media platforms (e.g. Facebook page, Twitter account, LinkedIn)
- Apps provided by third-party vendors
- In web exhibitions, such as those using OMEKA open source software
- Email signatures
- PowerPoint presentations given by library staff
- Online tutorials prepared by library staff

## Checklist for online access points where the librarian should be visible

- LibGuides or alternative library subject guides, including a profile for librarians with a photo and contact details
- Chat or 'ask a librarian' feature
- Photo of librarian in Library blog
- Photo of librarian in Library ezine or organizational ezine

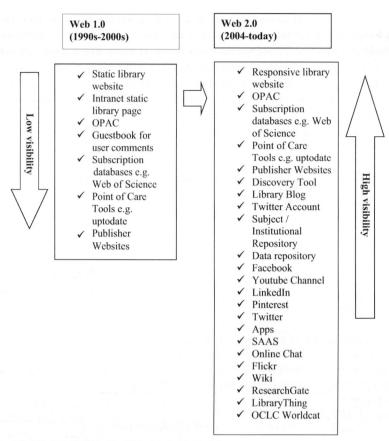

**Figure 13** Library visibility in Web 1.0 and Web 2.0.

- Research platforms (e.g. ResearchGate and Academia.edu)
- Photo of librarian in LinkedIn profile
- Photo of librarian on professional Twitter account

In the Web 2.0 world, libraries have ample opportunities to increase visibility by engaging with social media and developing digital libraries and repositories, which make use of search engine optimization and protocols for metadata harvesting such as OAI-PMH. The transition from Web 1.0 to Web 2.0, also known as the social web, has been profound with increased platforms for librarians to become visible on.

See diagram in Figure 13.

## Step 2: Identify visibility gaps from the list and check feasibility and need to fill those gaps

Some online access points from the checklists may not be suitable for all libraries and librarians. For example, a repository may not be a requirement of the organisation. Facebook and Pinterest may also not be relevant for some libraries. This is context-dependent and is dependent on the needs of the client base. It depends on the resources used versus the return. Each access point should be measured for its ROI. The promotion of library collections is essential in helping to create an increased awareness and in turn, visibility of library services and collections. This translates into the increased use of collections augmenting the value of the library. Raising awareness helps people find connections through the library, building up a reputation for the library as a useful and relevant asset to the reader, organisation and user. Promotion aids people's understanding of the role of the library and creates knowledge about what librarians do and what they have to offer. If the library has unique or special collections, these can be promoted by hosting a lecture series or by developing dedicated webspaces for the collections using, for example, Lib-Guides™ or web exhibition software, such as OMEKA, and contextualising the content by providing extra research material on the exhibit topics. Promotion of these types of collections offers opportunities to collaborate with internal and external partners (e.g. faculty, administration or local public/school libraries, etc.). Barriers to the visibility of content is a data quality issue. Online Computer Library Center (OCLC) found that incomplete data, lack of synchronization of metadata with library holdings data and multiple formats of data were all potential barriers to discovery and access to content (Kemperman et al., 2014). These are three areas of data quality which librarians must address to increase visibility of content.

## Step 3: Measuring usage and impact metrics

Measuring usage is relatively straightforward with widely available free analytical tools such as Google Analytics for websites. A step-by-step guide for developing a web analytics report for a library website using Google Analytics has been created by Yang and Perrin (2014). Google offers free courses and online resources for beginners and experts using their analytics products via their Google Academy website. Visual.ly's Google Analytics Report is an app that creates a custom infographic of your website's activity and performance. Third-party vendors offer usage statistics as a normal part of their service offering for databases, e-books, OPAC, discovery tools, etc. Service level agreements with external vendors and partners should include a qualitative element. Social media tools, such as Facebook, Twitter, LinkedIn, etc., come with their own set of analytics for measuring their impact. Social engagement and user experience as metrics are emerging areas.

Once the performance of the website and social media tools are being tracked, eventually a benchmark can be established around normal performance. Incremental improvements can then be put in place to improve ranking, activity and engagement. Tracking performance after changes have been installed will prove whether the changes worked and led to better performance or not. Continue this pattern of quality improvement until visibility improves. Breeding (2008) outlined three rules for a successful library web presence that remains valid today: content, community and visibility. Any barriers that are present that block or delay access to content has the potential to lower visibility to the information navigator. Having clear pathways to content and simple navigation is key. The growth of community features on the social web has created ample opportunities for customer engagement. Finally visibility and finding library resources is about putting them in the user's space, making LIS visible along the natural pathways that your users take.

MEDLIS (Model for Evaluation of Digital Libraries and Information Services) is a generic model for the evaluation of digital libraries (outlined in Chowdhury et al., 2008). Tools for social media management include but are not limited to the following: Hootsuite, Keyhole, Quintly, Buffer, IFTTT, SocialOmph, Crowdbooster, SproutSocial and TweetDeck. Social media management is a growing market with multiple options. The best strategy is to try some tools out and decide on which works best for the library's profile. An example of some of the common metrics available with future references are listed in Table 42. It is important that metrics are aligned to the key strategic objective, which is to increase visibility.

**Table 42** **Common metrics of digital and social media tools**

| Digital tool | Metrics |
|---|---|
| Library website | No. of visits, Pages requested, Pages not used, device used to access, demographic data, browser and OS used to access, referring URL (see Welch, 2005; Fagan, 2014) |
| Discovery tool | No. of sessions, visits, no. of full-text downloads, no. of e-books used, resources with low usage |
| Blog | Page views over time, no. of subscribers, content analysis of comments, no. of tweets |
| Twitter | Number and growth of followers, likes, tweets, retweets, favourites engagement rate, link clicks, analysis of hashtags, lists, questions answered, queries through direct messages |
| Repository | Position in ranking web of repositories; downloads, unique visitors, returning visitors, no. of researchers registered, citations, reuse of data/publications, integration of altmetrics |
| YouTube | Top referring websites to each video; user comments, favourites, subscribers, views, likes, dislikes, comments, sharing, estimated minutes watched (see Colburn & Haines, 2012) |
| WIKI | No. of recent visits, updated pages and how usage translates into standardisation of internal work and high performance teams. Application of Bradford's and Lotka's laws (see Lin & Hong, 2011) |
| Facebook | No. of fans, followers, likes, |
| | Questions answered, comments acted upon (quality improvement) |
| | Page likes, wall posts/reposts, total reach, engaged users (page, post level), edgerank |
| | Engagement rate (people talking about this divided by total page likes), traffic (see Gonzalo, 2012) |
| LinkedIn | Pagereach, engagement rate, follower demographics, viewing activity, user profile views, updates views, likes, comments, network growth, long-form posts |
| Library catalogue | Information retrieval patterns, referring URLs, transaction logs, search terms (see Fang & Crawford, 2008) |
| Digital collections | Relative visibility index (divide new users to the site by returning visitors) proposed by Pérez and Montesi (2013) |
| Social media ROI | Number of visits to the website per post created, number of interactions per post created (Lee-King, 2014) |

## Summary

The aim of any library is, in part, to connect people to knowledge. In health care, it could be to inform health care practitioners about the latest evidence in their field and have a positive impact on a patient's journey; in education at the primary and secondary level, it is to educate the young and provide access to reading and learning material; in third level, it is to generate new knowledge. In special libraries, it is to respond to needs identified by its working environment and stakeholders. In public libraries, it is to provide happiness and learning and respond to the needs of its community. Librarians must not lose sight of the reader or of their mission. If they do, their customers and stakeholders will, in turn, lose sight of them.

## Notes

See http://impact.ischool.washington.edu/.

For sustainable energy tips for libraries see http://thegreenlibraryblog.blogspot.ie/ and http://www.facebook.com/group.php?gid=32308457042.

ACRL value of academic libraries toolkit see http://www.ala.org/acrl/issues/value/valueofacademiclibrariestoolkit.

RAILS initiative see http://railsontrack.info/.

SCONUL http://www.sconul.ac.uk/.

CAUL – http://www.caul.edu.au/

PLA Project Outcome: http://www.ala.org/pla/performancemeasurement.

Library Ranking Europe: http://www.libraryranking.com/.

IFLA Branding. http://www.ifla.org/at-your-library/ways-to-use.

ALA slogans for school libraries http://www.ala.org/advocacy/advleg/publicawareness/campaign@yourlibrary/prtools/schoollibrary/schoolslogan.

# Visibility improvement plan (VIP)

*All we have to decide is what to do with the time that is given us.*
**The Fellowship of the Ring by J.R.R. Tolkien**

## Introduction

The previous chapter challenged librarians to reflect upon their current level of visibility to help identify gaps in visibility or potential areas for improvement. Improvement processes work best when implemented as part of a quality improvement framework. Librarians who take time out to reflect upon how they can improve their visibility and impact will inevitably find that certain activities they undertake or services that they provide are not offering them an adequate return on their investment. Resources – both human and financial – are often strained in librarianship. This means that measuring outcomes based on the value and impact that services have is crucial to good quality management practice. Such forms of outcome measurement will quickly reveal any potential areas that are counterproductive to the visibility of librarians. In some cases the results may show that some radical choices may have to be made. For example, a library might have to be closed. Or certain services will perhaps have to be limited or suspended, for example document supply. Other changes, such as ceasing one-to-one training and replacing it with group training or migrating learners to virtual learning environments with tailor made library tutorials, may be perhaps the best way forward.

We are living in an era of 'big data'. Librarians have always meticulously gathered statistics and data to inform their decision-making processes. The current era suits librarianship. The problem is whether the correct data is being measured. What does the number of visits to the physical library tell us? How about the number of people who visited the library and found what they were looking for or had a positive experience? The latter tells us more about *value* than the former. It is the difference between quantitative and qualitative information. However, much research continues to focus on the quantitative, for example analysis of open libraries is still talking about the number of visits and number of issues. Such research is not adding to the evidence base of librarianship, which needs to expand.

Borrowing from the process of strategic planning, the visibility improvement plan is a form of a strategic plan with a focus on visibility. The same process of strategic planning applies. The plan should ideally be a three-year plan. Each year the plan should be reviewed to evaluate its success, and adjustments or contingencies should be made in response. Six sigma has a phased improvement process which involves five steps (DMAIC): define, measure, analyse, improve and control.

# Let's get visible! v-i-s-i-b-i-l-i-t-y

## Step 1: V is for visualise

The first step to take on your path to increased visibility is to visualise where you will be in one, two and three years' time. Organise a team day and invite a library champion and key stakeholders to come along and join you for the duration of the vision-finding exercise. The team day must include library staff and a representative sample of stakeholders in the organisation. It is imperative to get them on board and include them in imagining a shared vision for the library from day one. Try to reach a shared vision through a participative, iterative process. It is important for librarians to factor in reflective time, which is helpful for practising critical thinking. Close your eyes and imagine what your work place will look like. Will the library have changed in any way? Take in the colours, objects, people and the environment you see around you. What does it look like? What would you like it to look like, ideally? What do you think you will need to make that dream a reality? What staff do you envisage needing – will you need less or more staff? What skills and attributes will they need to be successful? What hardware and equipment will you need? What potential barriers will you face? What challenges might be put in your way? What disrupters and opportunities will there be? Who is going to help you to achieve your vision?

Vision statements need to be aspirational and inspiring. Vision statements are dreams: dreams of a better place, a better environment and a better world. To have a vision is to have a desired image of the future.

It is absolutely essential that the following statements are derived and agreed upon collectively from the start: vision, mission and value statements. Each statement must align with that of the parent organisation. In other words, if the CEO of the organisation reads the vision statement for the library, she will instantly recognise that it ties in with that of the organisation.

Start by revising an existing or devising a new vision and mission statement. The key point here is that the statement must align with that of the organisation. This notion of alignment is essential. Alignment is enabled, for example, by using the business language that is contained in a service plan or annual report for your organisation. Use language that your CEO or Director General will understand. Use terms that will have meaning from a management perspective. Avoid library or technical jargon. If your organisation does not have a vision or a mission statement, then search for examples of statements of similar organisations to yours for inspiration and direction. It is advisable to involve all library staff in this exercise. Buy-in from staff is crucial. All library staff should agree on their raison d'etre, which is essentially what a mission statement is all about. The vision statement is usually a broad view of where the library should be striving towards, and the mission is the broad aim. If all staff understand what they are striving towards and what their mission is, it is more likely that they will work collectively towards it. Having a shared vision has been shown to increase collaboration, improve staff morale and enhance team performance and group learning capacity. It is also a sign of an effective organisation. The effectiveness of shared vision has been demonstrated in several working environments, including healthcare (MacFalda,

1997; Smith, 1991); higher education (Lord, 2015; Leong, 2014); schools (Price, 2012); non-profits (Chen & Graddy, 2010) and industry (Schippers, Den Hartog, Koopman, & van Knippenberg, 2008). Lord demonstrated that 'open-mindedness', or what others call 'reflection' (Dewey, 1933), combined with shared vision positively effects group learning capacity.

If we look to the literature we can take the example of the Taubman Health Sciences library in Michigan, which started the transformational journey of a reimagined library with a redefinition of its mission statement. Its emphasis on partnership and collaboration to replace *support service* was deliberate (Allee et al., 2014). The mission of the library changed from having an internal focus to an external focus. The mission is 'to be a valued partner, fully integrated into the work of the university, providing leadership in knowledge management for education, research, patient care and community outreach'. The successful transformation of the library and redefined role of librarians started with this statement of intent. This type of leadership in transformative librarianship is badly needed in the health arena, where change is constant.

## Step 2: I is for improvise

Once you and your staff and relevant stakeholders have established a shared vision, it is time to improvise. When is all of this going to happen? Define realistic timelines and prioritise which activities will be pursued first. Ask why you are introducing changes? What will the impact be? What will the advantages, value and outcomes be? How are you going to measure and keep track of your achievements? It's important to build upon the momentum achieved by realising the vision. A certain level of preparedness is necessary as you are about to embark upon a change process. Any change requires careful planning, where possible, and preparing staff for change. Incorporate the feedback gained from stakeholders and readers gathered when current visibility was measured here.

Michie, van Stralen, and West (2011) introduced a behaviour change wheel (BCW) to characterise and inform behaviour change interventions. Behaviour change is essential in translating what we know into practice or, as it is known in healthcare, evidence-based practice. At the heart of the BCW is a COM-B system. The COM-B system encapsulates capability, opportunity and motivation, which all influence behaviour change, as seen in Figure 14. An understanding of this system may assist library administrators and managers when introducing a change management approach. Capability is an individual's psychological and physical ability to engage in activity; opportunity is influenced by external factors that make actions happen and motivations are drivers that direct action, such as habits. These three components make up behaviour. Some organisations may find that two of the components are present, but perhaps motivation is lacking. Areas to consider when trying to influence behaviour change in the area of opportunity is sufficient human and financial resources. To ensure staff are capable and act as enablers to achieve the vision, continuing professional development must be prioritised. Finally motivation is driven by strong leadership, setting realistic goals, recognising achievements and self-motivation.

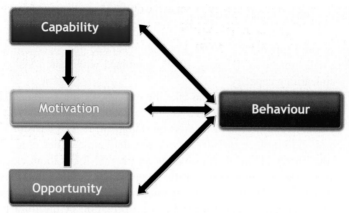

**Figure 14** The COM-B system – a framework for understanding behaviour.
© 2011 Michie et al.; licensee BioMed Central Ltd. CC BY 2.0.

## Capability – training and continuing professional development

Training may be an area that is identified as a requirement for existing library staff. Fortunately there are many open-access options available in the form of Massive Open Online Courses (MOOCs). The growth of MOOCs offers opportunities for librarians to freely upskill themselves, as long as they can build sufficient time into their working lives. Some recent MOOCs of interest to librarians include the University of Toronto's MOOC on library advocacy; UNESCO has introduced a free curriculum on Open Access online; Vanderbilt University has a MOOC on Data Management for Clinical Research, John Hopkins University offers a Data Scientist Toolbox course and IMARK has Digital Libraries, Repositories and Documents MOOCs. Four Irish academic libraries have produced a MyRI open access online toolkit to support bibliometrics training and awareness available at ndlr.ie/myri. Librarians may subscribe to updates from MOOC directories for free, such as mooc-list.com. Aside from online learning, there are librarian exchange schemes available through professional library associations. Mentoring and pairing staff together also works well, particularly in the area of teaching. Team teaching has been shown to increase the confidence of the librarian and helps validate the librarian's identity as a teacher (Matlin & Carr, 2014). It may also be possible to learn from others in your organisation. For example, if there is a communications department, an approach could be made to ask if their team could impart skills to the library team about the effective use of social media, issuing press releases, etc. An Information Communications and Technology (ICT) department could be contacted to give basic or advanced database skills; people working in the Human Resources department may be able to assist with business case or report writing. This is also a good way of networking and collaborating with other people within your organisation.

It is vital that all staff have a personal training or continuing professional development (CPD) plan in place. Ideally this should be carried out annually and done in consultation with the library manager or director. CPD plans are informed by the strategic plan and standards of service set at the outset. As outlined in Chapter 7, a staff skills audit will ensure that any areas for improvement have been identified. The skills audit, in combination with feedback obtained from library users, will identify areas where there may be a skills deficit. At a minimum, all library staff should be trained in customer service, using the library management system, dealing with complaints and feedback and escalating queries to senior staff. Librarians need to continually review their performance and skills. An area for continuous improvement is research methodologies and technical skills. While budgets may restrict access to formal training, Twitter remains a powerful tool for professional development. Collaboration with fellow librarians from other sectors is always worth considering.

## Opportunity

Creating opportunities to realise the vision involves looking at resources, both human and financial.

## Resources – human

You may find that you need more staff, but there may not be any funding available for recruitment. Think of alternatives to recruiting new staff, such as taking on volunteers or graduate placements. Some library associations offer staff exchange programmes, which will enable you to introduce staff with complementary skillsets to your library.

## Resources – financial

You may need to find more funding to realise the vision. Make a business case based on data and projections of future outcomes and impact from the changes you intend to introduce. Include testimonials. Alternatively it may be necessary to introduce some cutbacks. For example, some resources may have to be temporarily dropped, such as electronic database subscriptions, unless funding can be sourced directly from other departments, third parties or faculty.

## Motivation

A correlation was found to exist between perceived motivation, job satisfaction and commitment in library staff in research and academic libraries in Nigeria (Tella, Ayeni, & Popoola, 2007). John Adair's seminal work on leadership and motivation includes a framework for motivation. Adair's framework includes eight key points. It starts with self-motivation, building a team of motivated individuals, treating each as an individual, setting realistic and challenging aims, demonstrating progress, creating a motivating environment, providing just rewards and recognising achievements (Adair, 2006). Aim to implement these eight key points for motivating the library team.

### Step 3: S is for strategic planning

*Setting goals is the first step in turning the invisible into the visible.*

Tony Robbins, Life Coach

One of the oldest management traits and one that has stood the test of time and scrutiny is strategic planning. Strategic planning is a process of deliberating over the path that the organisation or department is going to take and setting its course for a number of years into the future. Regardless of what stage you are at in the academic or school year, you can start increasing your visibility by having a strategic plan in place. It is never too early or too late to start strategic planning. Strategic planning is an essential component of any visibility improvement plan. A starting point for measurement is strategy. Libraries are often focused on output measurement and recording, such as the number of books loaned each month, instead of outcomes, such as whether a new immigrant population to a community had registered and used the library. Outputs are important, particularly for operations management, but they must inform an overall strategic approach. Elements that make up an effective strategic plan include the following: a vision statement, a mission statement, a value statement and a list of goals and objectives. These components are outlined with an example for a school library in Table 43. At this point, a shared vision and mission statement should be agreed upon. The remaining components: goals and objectives are outlined next. Guiding documents, such as a value statement, standards of service and a reader charter enhance the overall connectedness of the library with its readers and should be considered as supporting documents to the strategic plan.

A number of components will inform the strategic plan, including a literature review identifying best practices and emerging trends; visiting other libraries with a similar remit to the existing library; usage data and feedback gained from engagement with stakeholders and readers as outlined in the previous chapter. A further process that enhances the strategic plan is to set up focus groups inviting stakeholders, library staff and patrons. Ideally, employ an independent facilitator to guide the focus group process. An authoritative source for running focus groups is the Focus Group Kit (Morgan, Krueger, & King, 1998). Inviting patrons and stakeholders to participate in long-term planning for the library demonstrates to them that library staff are customer focused, acts as a good public relations exercise and shows stakeholders that the library is strategically aligned to the mission of the organisation. It also energises library staff and gives them practice at active research with a valid data output, which can be used in the strategic planning process. The number and composition of the focus groups will have to be determined locally. The planning process can take some time. This will depend on the resources available. A library who has successfully used focus groups as part of a strategic planning process found that it 'raised the library's profile on campus and reinforced the perception of the library as a customer-orientated department' (Higa-Moore, Bunnett, Mayo, & Olney, 2002).

## Goals

The goal is an overarching aim with several objectives acting as subaims of the overall goal. The goal should be informed by needs of the organisation and needs of readers, which were identified in Chapter 7. Typically a strategic plan will have between four and five strategic goals. Each goal will have several subobjectives that relate to it. Every goal in the plan will compete with other goals for resources, therefore less goals

**Table 43  Key components of a strategic plan – sample school library strategic plan**

| Component | Description | Alignment | Measurement/assessment | Example for a school library |
|---|---|---|---|---|
| Vision statement | The vision statement describes the overall aspiration of the department/library. It should encompass values and an overall ethos | Align to similar statements of organisation | | The vision of X school library is to be a source of enlightenment for all pupils |
| Mission statement | The mission statement sets out in broad, clear terms the overall aim of the department/library | | | The mission of X school library is to facilitate (education and) learning for all pupils |
| Goal | A goal is an overarching aim that the department/library aspires to achieve. Each goal will ideally require a number of SMART objectives aligned to the goal to make them a reality | Align to areas of improvement identified in Chapter 7 through engagement with key stakeholders and users | At least one KPI should be set against the overall goal | The library will provide innovative, flexible learning spaces for all students |
| Objective | Objectives should be aligned to one goal and they should be set out in a SMART format:<br>• Specific<br>• Measurable<br>• Achievable<br>• Realistic<br>• Time bound<br>Each goal will typically have 3 or more objectives. | Each objective should align to one goal | Each objective should have a KPI<br>(e.g. the observation of social interaction of students)<br>(e.g. Students use the space to collaborate on group work activity and projects)<br>(e.g. all IT equipment in working order) | 1. Space will be allocated for 15 computers/tablets and 15 open desks for use by pupils for reading and computer use by April XXXX.<br>2. Movable seating, tables and desks with built-in access to power and data will be purchased.<br>3. Computer/tablet requirements in line with space and pupil intake will be reviewed and updated every school term.<br>4. Use of open desks and computers/tablets/ICT equipment will be monitored monthly |

*Continued*

**Table 43**  **Continued**

| Component | Description | Alignment | Measurement/assessment | Example for a school library |
|---|---|---|---|---|
| Value statement | A statement that encompasses the ethos of the library/information unit | Align to preferred behaviours | | Our actions are guided by the following values: inclusiveness, innovation, responsibility, active engagement and respect |
| Standards of service | Based on ISO standards for library and information units | | | |
| Reader charter | A document outlining the rights of the reader and the librarian, similar to a contract | | | |

will give a greater return. Goals need to be clearly understood by those who will be implementing them. Set achievable goals that will gain credibility and backing for the library.

## Objectives

Objectives should be SMART (Specific, Measurable, Achievable, Realistic and Time bound) and aligned to a specific goal. A key performance indicator (KPI) should be assigned to each objective. Another way of looking at this is to set objectives that are feasible in a reasonably short timeframe that will make a significant difference. These are what Prof. R. Rummelt calls 'proximate objectives' (Rumelt, 2011). Objectives need to guarantee a win for political and financial reasons and to build momentum.

## Key performance indicators

KPIs need to be meaningful. Bernard Marr suggests that Key Performance Questions (KPQ) can help form KPIs. He describes a KPQ as 'a management question that captures exactly what managers want to know when it comes to reviewing each of their strategic objectives' (Marr & Creelman, 2014, p. 120). For example, a strategic objective of a library might be to create a community-centred library. A supporting KPQ is 'Do we know what the needs of the community are?' and 'How well do we know the demographics of our community?' A resulting KPI is 'Community needs analysis'.

## Value statement

Once the strategic plan is agreed upon, start working on a value statement. Again, this must align with organisational values. The value statement can be a very powerful message to your users and key stakeholders in the organisation. It can be a useful reference both in good times and in bad. A value statement is what you believe in: it expresses ethos and a sense of commitment.

A sample value statement:

> We are committed to professional conduct, accountability, integrity, respect and community enhancement.

## Standards of service

It is useful to develop a 'standards of service' statement to accompany the value statement. When creating the statement, you can look to ISO standards for libraries, or you can be informed by customer feedback. Many libraries have standards in place. Usually published by library associations, specialised standards exist for different library types: health libraries, school libraries, academic and public libraries. The standards of service will set out what the user may expect to receive in return for being a member or user of the library services. Standards of service are a way of managing user expectations and demonstrate a commitment to quality. The standards need to take into account staff timetables, availability and resources. For example, a standard of service might be that all requests for journal articles will be supplied within the user-specified timeframe when possible. This could mean that a user requests a journal article urgently, but you may not have a subscription for it or a means to supply it via other library agreements. This maybe an exception, but it is important to set standards that can realistically be met. There is room for improvisation and innovation here. A 'DEAL' should be made with your customers and with library staff. The deal is that if a reader or stakeholder walks into the library or approaches a member of staff they should 'Drop Everything And Listen'. Talk to staff about this and try to build a culture among library staff of engagement with readers and listening to what they have to say. If readers are listened to and asked for opinions, they will provide feedback. Once the staff really listen to readers, they will be better positioned to respond accordingly. Lloyd (2004) talks about listening to the voice of the customer three times. Preservice, at the point of service and postservice. Methods vary for this, such as surveys, focus groups, interviews, 'mystery shoppers' or touchpads for real-time feedback. Whatever the method, it is a key standard of quality that the voice of the customer is listened to at all stages of the service cycle, which is highly applicable to libraries. Standards of service inform operational plans for libraries and are a useful management tool. If done in consultation with library staff, they can have an empowering and cohesive effect of bringing a team together and motivating staff to set and keep standards in place.

## Reader charter

A reader or customer charter is a useful reference to make visibly available in the library both in print and online. It outlines expectations of the library for readers and vice versa. It is also an opportunity to highlight any specialised library services.

Table 44 may be used as an example.

Start communicating your key messages to key stakeholders. The vision mission and value statements of the library should be accessible on the library's website at a minimum (Figure 15). The vision statement could be over the library entrance or prominently displayed in the library.

Aim to get sign off for the strategic plan with key stakeholders in your organisation. This could be a leadership team or direct line manager. It needs to be someone in a position of power and influence in the organisation. It is a good opportunity to set up a meeting with them and to discuss the plan and get the library on the agenda and radar of the organisation.

### Step 4: I is for 'implement your plan'

Aim to get all staff on board and start working on the goals in the strategic plan. Get 'doing' and implementing. Implementation science is a method that is suited to

**Table 44** **Sample library reader charter**

| Reader charter | |
| --- | --- |
| **As a member of or visitor to the library, you are entitled to:** | **Our library staff have rights too and we ask that you:** |
| • A quiet space to read, reflect and think<br>• Uninterrupted time to browse library collections during opening hours<br>• Use of WIFI free of charge<br>• Use of computer equipment onsite<br>• Lending rights: borrow 6 items (including any combination of books, DVDs, paintings) for 4 weeks; or 2 items (including laptop, tablet, MP3 player) for 3 weeks<br>• Access to self-service kiosks for loans and returns<br>• Courteous and responsive service from library staff<br>• A clean and environmentally friendly library space<br>• Accessibility for the disabled<br>• A response to all online queries within 48 h | Respect library staff, other library users, library equipment and resources. |

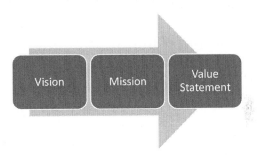

**Figure 15** Vision, mission and value statements.

healthcare organisations and others for getting evidence into practice. It works as a four-stage process: exploration, installation, initial implementation and full implementation. The visualization exercise corresponds to the exploration phase described in step one above. The installation process is similar to the improvisation process described in step two above, which is about preparing staff for change and putting resources in place to make change happen in practice. The next phase involves actual implementation. This is about putting your plan into action incrementally. It may be necessary to pilot certain changes first, which corresponds to phase three of the implementation science approach: initial implementation, to see how best they might work for you and the organisation. The initial implementation phase corresponds to the Balanced Scorecard approach, which has been tried and tested at many libraries (Sayed, 2013; Poll, 2001). According to Marr and Creelman (2014), a combination of a strategy map and a balanced scorecard describe the strategy and its implementation.

**Table 45  Strategy map: sample for a school library**

| Vision: be a source of enlightenment for all pupils | |
|---|---|
| Mission: to facilitate education and learning for all pupils | |
| **Stakeholder perspective**<br>• Attractive, welcoming place for students and parents<br>• Enhance the reputation of the school<br>• Improve learning outcomes for students | **Reader perspective**<br>• Excellent library and technology services<br>• A student's sanctuary, different from the classroom<br>• A fun place to learn, read and work with others |
| **Internal perspective**<br>• Library as a source of pride for the school<br>• Excellent use of timetabled library classes<br>• Good return on investment of library reading material, technical equipment and furniture outfit | |
| **Learning and growth perspective**<br>• Highly motivated librarian<br>• Culture of innovation, including experimentation with emerging technologies<br>• Professional approach to quality improvement based on data and research | |
| Value statement: inclusiveness, innovation, responsibility, active engagement and respect | |
| **Standards of service** | |
| **Reader charter** | |

They can act as a common point of reference for everyone on the team. It may be useful to set up library committees or a Library Advisory Group depending on the corporate language used by the organisation. They will assist in the implementation of the plan. Such a group or committee will need strong leadership from a library director (Fitsimmons, 2013). A committee or advisory group will help to keep the plan on track while simultaneously raising the visibility of the librarian and library staff within the organisation.

The work of the strategic plan is already complete, so all that has to be done is to translate this into a strategy map.

A template for a strategy map based on the balanced scorecard is given in Table 45. The example used is for a school library.

## Step 5: B is for 'be proactive'

Do not wait for your readers or customers to come to you: go to them. The importance of getting outside the library is evident in the LIS literature and has been echoed by many of the librarians interviewed in the case studies outlined in this book. Being proactive is a two-fold process. On the one hand, physical contact and in-person communication with people who are readers or customers must be constant and on the other hand, engagement with your audience through social media should also be constant. Librarians should aim to get an even balance between the physical and virtual worlds of readers through effective communication. In the business sense, marketing is essential to generate revenue and turn over a profit. Libraries generally are social organisations and operate as not-for-profit entities. However, this does not mean that they can afford to ignore marketing. Any library that offers a service needs to have a marketing plan to stay open and stay in business. Marketing is key to creating and improving the visibility of the librarian and the library. Achieving increased awareness of your LIS and visibility comes down to two key factors:

- Having a plan
- Getting staff on board and motivated to carry it out

## Promotional materials

Despite futurist claims of an office 'without hardcopy' in a Business Week article by George E. Pake, former head of Xerox Corporation's Palo Alto Research Center in 1975, libraries without a photocopier or paper available for use are in the minority. It is worth developing a suite of promotional material every one to two years. Bookmarks, post-its, pens, pencils, badges, A5 flyers detailing LIS services, USB keys, recyclable bags and posters (whatever the budget allows) are all worth investing in. Printing costs have decreased in recent years. Mousemats in the library at computer terminals can be branded, as well as branded screensavers for computers/tablets/laptops not in use. There is little point in producing a 10-page bulky brochure with information that is likely to go out of date in a few months. People do not read that much promotional literature anymore. Think of all the households that explicitly state 'No junk mail' on their post boxes; there is a need to be more environmentally conscious (also junk mail as a type of promotional literature is a potential source of annoyance). People are now used to bite-sized pieces of information, making 'less is more' a good rule of thumb for written promotional literature. Infographics are an increasingly popular method for producing promotional messages. According to Karr (2013), over 87% of website visitors tend to read text placed on infographics, and on average, traffic to a website increases by 12% after uploading an infographic. Infographics can enhance a business by 82% by creating brand awareness. Infographics are not only a sure way of successfully promoting the library, but software is also available to create them for free. They are a win–win promotional tool.

Some publishers will offer to promote their product using the LIS in-house branding. This is particularly useful when seeking to promote a new online product and is usually done for free. General rules to guide a writing style of any promotional material include the following:

- Keep it simple
- Get to the point (ideally in the first line)
- Do not use jargon
- Be consistent with the use of font and colour – keep to the house style
- Avoid long paragraphs of text – use bullets instead
- Do not repeat or try to pad anything out
- Sell benefits, not features
- Read it out loud
- Get a colleague or critical friend to proofread and check grammar, punctuation and spelling – the designers will not do this for you

- If possible, ask a reader for feedback before it goes to print
- If you have a press office or communications department, contact them for advice
- Make use of people within your organisation – not only does this help you with your tasks, it also helps build up relationships and visibility at the local level.

## Advertising

Consider advertising your LIS in a journal read by professionals you are trying to attract to your service. This could be a linked logo on a publisher's website or a professional association's website. Advertising the library and information service is best achieved through promotional messages sent using social media platforms.

Social media tools are valuable for getting a library's message across, for promoting events and for creating awareness about what libraries offer and what librarians do. They facilitate dialogue and the exchange of information between library and patron and are an open platform to hear the voice of the customer. Essentially social media is a high-end visibility platform. Some countries prefer some tools over others: in the USA and Germany, Facebook is the most popular tool. Turkey has one of the highest country ratings in Facebook (Sendir, 2014). In China, video formats are preferred. In Hong Kong, Facebook and Twitter are the most accepted tools (Jain, 2014).

## Twitter

If you are not already using Twitter, set up an account for your library. Start tweeting on a regular basis. There are many online tools that facilitate management of social media accounts, such as Twitter, Facebook and LinkedIn. The advantage of these tools is that ultimately they will save the librarian time. Prescheduled tweets, for example, and multiple Twitter accounts can be managed using tools such as HootSuite, Buffer App and Reachpop. Rotate this among library staff and you will see an instant return. A library without a Twitter account today is completely invisible to a potential audience of 284 million users per month (twitter.com). With that seismic opportunity, there is no excuse in the world for not having a Twitter account. It is completely free – as long as the library has Internet access – which, for the most part, is a given. It is easy to use, it forces brevity and it is a ready-made online marketing and promotional tool just willing people to take advantage of its potential. Twitter + librarians = perfect match. Even the mission of Twitter echoes what most librarians wish to do:

> To give everyone the power to create and share ideas and information instantly, without barriers.

> *twitter.com*

Some librarians have resisted Twitter as they are worried about perhaps saying the wrong thing or making a mistake. Others worry about 'Who is going to manage the library's Twitter account?' Nobody likes taking on extra work, particularly if the library is short-staffed and morale is low. However, as mentioned previously, there is no excuse left for not using Twitter: the only reason may be that readers of the library may not use Twitter. If that is the case, encourage them to start using it. Another exception may be that tools such as Twitter and Facebook are restricted, which is the case in China. Alternatives are available, such as Sina Weibo. Social media is a key tool for increasing the visibility of librarians. One researcher summed it up succinctly when she said, 'Avoiding them is like refusing to have a telephone or a meeting room' (Lloret Romero, 2011).

It is important to find your own voice and identity on Twitter. The Twitter accounts of many national and public libraries offer good examples of distinct voices. See, for example, @NLIreland, @britishLibrary, @ActuBnf, @librarycongress, @DNB_ Aktuelles and public libraries @nypl, @BPLBoston, @SPLBuzz, @parisbiblio and @obamsterdam. In 2011, Tay carried out a Klout score on library Twitter accounts, which are listed on his blog Musings about Librarianship. Many of the accounts analysed in 2011 have doubled or quadrupled their followers in just four years since Tay's analysis. Not surprisingly, Barack Obama has the highest Klout score of 99, followed by other celebrities, including Justin Bieber at 92. Public and national libraries have the highest library Klout scores. The Klout score uses 400 signals from eight different networks to measure the impact of social media and is a number between 1 and 100 (Klout.com). It is not just a quantitative measure about the number of followers or retweets, but it aims to capture the level of engagement with followers. A more recent study of public libraries on social media found that the accounts of Sao Paulo, Seoul and Stockholm were the most active public libraries on average, with over two posts per day. Of the 31 public libraries examined, 22 had active social media accounts (Mainka, 2013).

Twitter is also an incredibly useful way to connect with other librarians and to swap ideas and collaborate with others in an online environment. This has been commented upon in the professional LIS literature as a useful tool for building professional knowledge and for interprofessional communications (Kraft, 2013). This has also been backed up by the case studies with one of the interviewees, Hugh Rundle, also declaring that Twitter is '*the best professional development tool I have ever used*'.

## *Facebook*

Facebook has three main social functions: for friends, fun and family. Despite this social dimension, libraries have embraced Facebook, and there are many who have been successful. Facebook is not for everyone, and it is not for all librarians or libraries. It can be particularly useful for public and national libraries or those that are public facing. Special libraries, such as corporate, law and health libraries, may not find Facebook a useful social media tool. Their readers may use Facebook for social purposes only and not for work. However, public, academic and national libraries are using Facebook to develop their social media presence and engagement with readers. Everything comes back to what the needs of the readers are. If a need is identified for a librarian or library to have a Facebook page, then it should be set up. In a study of public libraries in informational world cities, Sao Paulo, Seoul and Stockholm were found to have the most active public library Facebook activity on average, with over two posts per day. Four types of posts on Facebook made up their activity: status posts, photo posts, video posts and URL posts to events organised by the library (Mainka et al., 2013).

## LinkedIn

All library staff should build a professional profile on LinkedIn. A profile should also be built for the library. This is like a 'shop window' for the library and a profile photo of the inside of the library should accompany it. It is an opportunity to highlight any awards that the library has received and what the vision and mission of the library is. LinkedIn identifies other people in the organisation who the library can connect with. It is an instant way of heightening the online visibility of both the librarian and the library and a proactive way of managing a professional online reputation. There are interesting features including groups, discussion lists and long-form publication. A library with a LinkedIn profile shows readers and stakeholders that the library adopts an open culture and is open about what it does, what its achievements are and what its purpose is. It also says that the library is open to receive comments and suggestions and to respond to them.

## Blog

Set up a blog for the library. Blogging software is mainly free and easy to use. The key thing is to keep it up to date and to keep it interesting. A blog allows room for creativity and a certain amount of freedom of expression. The blog should have a personality and reflect that of the library and librarian. It is a difficult balance to achieve, particularly if a blog has multiple authors among the library staff. Engage with your audience and invite them to write guest posts. Blogs need to be kept up to date and topical.

## Events

Plan to attend conferences that your customers attend and be one of the exhibitors (e.g. an ICT/health/nursing/medical/school/law/academic/education conference). Invest in a penguin stand and flyers, bookmarks, gadgets and free giveaways. Usually the organisers will waive fees for exhibitors if they are a not-for-profit organisation. If the conference is for education purposes, a library with a stand is usually welcomed. This is a great way to make connections and network with potential and existing users. It guarantees immediate exposure and opportunities to meet with people whom you wish to reach out to. Tweet about the conference and engage with social media via blogs and the conference website, professional association website, etc.

Tips for manning a stand at a conference:

- Bring sweets/chocolate/coffee to give away and attract people to your stand
- Have a tablet/laptop with a demo prepared
- Bring promotional material

- Have a competition with prizes
- Gather people's contact details with a 'business card drop off', a notebook to take details or a scanner to scan attendee information from their conference badge.

## *Canteen/cafeteria*

Increased visibility can start in-house. Most organisations have a restaurant or cafeteria, which is an ideal place to promote the work of the librarians. This has been used by academic, special and health librarians, with some examples highlighted in Chapter 9. Librarians interviewed in the case studies also found that this approach works well. Two librarians found that the use of colour effected their marketing prospects. They provided tabletop demos over 20 weeks at two different university hospital cafeterias. When they wore red or blue shirts, black pants and a colour matched tablecloth, they found that these colours attracted more attention, they received more questions and had more conversations with patrons. They found that this method was an 'inexpensive and effective way of increasing our library's visibility' (Patridge & Shack, 2010). Colour psychology has a place in marketing. Librarians could use the colours of their library brand or organisation's logo when engaging in marketing activities. One of the librarians interviewed in the case studies, Niamh Headon-Walker, integrated the colours of the university's logo into the library's Website. The library furniture also reflects the logo. The chairs and couches are red, the tables are white and the carpet is blue, which reflects the colours of the Institute's logo.

## *Online tutorials*

Develop e-tutorials and embed them within the online places that your readers occupy, such as the virtual learning environment, professional association websites and your parent organisation's website and intranet. It should also be available on the library website but, first and foremost, these tutorials should be available in the online spaces that your users occupy.

## Videos

There are many visual social tools that are freely available and offer great potential for libraries and librarians to increase their visibility. Among the most popular are You-Tube, VINE, Instagram and Snapchat. Practical tips for using social media tools are freely available on David Lee King's blog, and tips for using video have been shared by Ned Potter (Potter, 2012). The popularity of watching and sharing videos on the internet is growing, with 78% of American adult internet users reported to watch or download videos (Purcell, 2013).

## YouTube

Libraries are investing time and resources into creating their own YouTube Library channel and playlists. This is an instant promotional opportunity, as it educates readers about the services and benefits of using the library. Many excellent examples exist from literally thousands of libraries. University and public libraries are particularly prominent on YouTube. The number of likes and views is an instant indication of the popularity of the video and the dissemination of the message. This service is free for libraries. All that is needed is time, equipment, a bit of imagination and someone to write the script, be comfortable in front of the camera and get rolling. Some examples worth looking at are the Toronto Public Library, Essex Libraries, the Kansas City Public Library, the Arizona State University Library Minute playlist, the Ponderosa High School Library and the New Zealand National Library. Videos are a good medium for explaining library facilities, for example a simple explanation of the use of self-service machines in Harper Adams University is given by the librarian on YouTube. A service of particular value to any organisation with a research department or that has research as part of its mission statement is bibliometrics. This is an area where academic libraries in particular may excel. Producing a research impact report for the university and breaking it down into the faculty/department level is a really practical and useful way to show the immediate value of the skills of the librarian to the university. It also aligns the library to the mission of the organisation. Producing a YouTube video demonstrating research impact using bibliometrics is an instant way to capture the value of the library. See, for example videos produced by University College Dublin library from Ireland using YouTube.

## Chat reference

Similar to the tutorials above, make online chat available to users in the online spaces that they use for their continuing professional development (Zhang & Mayer, 2014).

## Step 6: I is for 'inform'

Inform everyone about your plans and new initiatives. Do not let the strategic plan gather dust on the virtual or physical stacks. Communicate the plan and outcomes frequently. Take specific steps that communicate to management that the library is evolving and moving towards a new future. Hold a launch day or special event to mark any milestones identified in your strategic plan. Get outside of the library. Bring food. Go to your staff canteen during busy times, like lunchtime, and set up a stand. Hand out flyers, such as an infographic demonstrating achievements and feedback. A good way to profile success and engagement with readers is to have a 'You said, we did' infographic highlighting actions taken by the library based on reader feedback. Have promotional giveaways to act as a talking point. This is one of the best ways to talk to people in your organisation and to increase your visibility to them.

Inform management at your institution about KPIs and outcome measures. Communicate your value to the organisation. Use KPIs from the strategic plan to draw up a one page document. Call this document a KPI sheet or 'Library Achievements' or a 'Values Scorecard'. This document should be named according to the business or educational language in use at your institution. A values scorecard can be used to create a picture of the benefits and strengths of the library contribution to the organisation (Town & Kyrillidou, 2013). It should align with any annual reports or departmental report mechanisms for reporting impact. The language used in the reporting of the KPIs should equally match that of the institution. The CEO must be able to read and understand the page quickly and easily. He must also be impressed by the data therein.

Draw up an infographic based on data from your KPIs. Make this available on your website and Tweet about it. Print this out as a large poster or e-poster and display it outside the library, on a TV screen or whiteboard or in a suitable place in your organisation.

### Step 7: L is for lift speech or elevator pitch

Have a lift speech ready and practised for any encounters with senior people in the organisation. All library staff should be briefed on the speech or at least the techniques to deliver a good lift speech. In 2014, the Harvard Business Review has made a free article available from a corporate communications consultant, Tim David. His four tips for a lift speech: start with a verbal slap, then ask a problem question, go to the noddable and finally finish with a curiosity statement (David, 2014). If this is translated to a scenario where the librarian meets the CEO, for example in the elevator, and is asked: 'So what do you do in the library?' the verbal slap needs to be an individual response that the librarian comes up with herself. Ideally humour would work well here, as it needs to be something that the CEO is not expecting to hear to keep him or her interested. Secondly, ask a problem question such as 'Don't you find that with so much information available on the Internet that it is sometimes difficult to filter out the noise?' He then suggests that you use a quote that you think will return an agreeable nod. So, for example 'It is quality of information and not quantity that really counts', which should produce a nod of agreement. Finally proceed with a curiosity statement. David's formula for this is 'I help/teach _____ (ideal client) to _____ (feature) so they can _____ (benefit).' In the case of the librarian, it might be something like 'I help managers to filter out erroneous information so that they can make data-driven decisions'.

This usually can get a conversation started and may initiate a follow-up meeting. The key thing is that it will generate an interest and get the librarian remembered by a key person in the organisation. David stresses that it needs to be authentic and must be thought up by each individual to suit each person's personality.

## Step 8: I is for 'improve'

Improve quality using quality improvement techniques. Review the strategic plan on an annual basis by evaluating and reflecting upon the KPIs and successes of the plan. These include things like developing and implementing solutions. For example, using bibliometrics to position the librarian as an expert and key stakeholder in research management in an organisation is a solution for research departments. Adopt a quality improvement cycle to look at core activities, which was discussed in the previous chapter. An example is highlighted in Chapter 9 of the University of South Florida, who looked at their core services and used data-driven techniques to evaluate their effectiveness. Look at each core activity, which was an exercise outlined in the previous chapter. Deal with each core activity using a quality improvement cycle outlined in Figure 16.

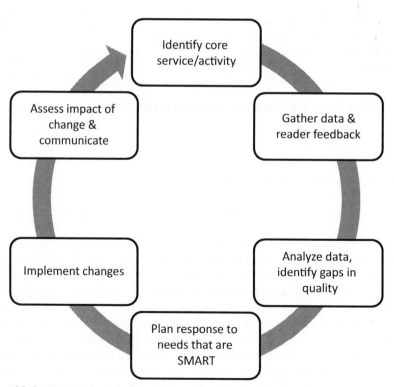

**Figure 16** Quality improvement cycle of core library activities and initiatives.

## Step 9: T is for 'tailor'

Tailor your services and your outlook to suit your readers. This is essential. It has to do first and foremost with alignment. The librarian has to deliver services that align to the overall mission of the organisation. The embedded librarian must act as a team member contributing to projects that align to the organisation's projected outcomes. Whether this is being part of a multidisciplinary quality team in a hospital, a faculty team in a university or part of a library association special interest group, all of these activities count and allow you to make a visible contribution to your organisation either from the outside or from within.

Find out what makes your users tick and provide information products and services that respond to their needs. Products need to be based on strong technical insights (this is a core principle of Google, which is also in the information business). Librarians' underlying expertise is in information. For example, the data deluge is causing information overload. Managers need up-to-date data and research to inform their decision making. Deliver a product that responds to this need. The format, frequency and content will depend entirely on the audience, so this will need to be figured out locally and ideally in consultation with key managers. Do not make the mistake of 'build it and they will come'; gather feedback from managers from the outset to inform the design and look of the content you deliver. As Tim O'Reilly, an open source advocate, said, 'Users must be treated as co-developers.' (Perpetual beta, 2015). There is much research emerging on the 'user experience', and this is a growth area in librarianship. A new open access journal 'Weave', set up in 2014, is dedicated to user experience in librarianship. One example is from Montana State University, where they used an A/B testing process involving students to improve their experience of the library website (Young, 2014). Jakob Nielsen, a user advocate and principal of the Nielsen Norman Group, has a free weekly newsletter that is relevant for any librarian involved in web design.

## Step 10: Y is for 'you can do it!'

*Don't aim for success if you want it; just do what you love and believe in, and it will come naturally.*

*David Frost*

Librarians need to have self-belief. The profession is one of the oldest professions in the world. Librarians are credible, trusted, qualified individuals with so much to offer any organisation. They are needed now more than ever as the proliferation of information continues to dominate our society. If you experience any level of self-doubt, think about catching up on some reading. Three of the many motivational books worth mentioning include 'How to Win Friends and Influence People' by Dale Carnegie, Stephen R. Covey's 'The Seven Habits of Highly Effective People' and 'Drive: The Surprising Truth About What Motivates Us' by Daniel H. Pink. Alternatively there are some inspirational Ted talks available, including Daniel H. Pink's 'The Puzzle of Motivation', Amy Cuddy's 'Your Body Language Shapes who You Are' and Alain de Botton's 'A Kinder,

Gentler Philosophy of Success'. Some Tedx talks by librarians are motivational and moving, such as Pam Sandlian Smith at TEDxMileHigh and Helen Shenton at TEDx-Dublin. Practising mindfulness has been shown to reduce stress and enhance wellbeing (Grossman, Niemann, Schmidt, & Walach, 2004). Mindful leaders have the ability to influence others, which is essential for good leadership (Sutton & Booth, 2014).

# Visibility checklist

This visibility improvement plan is summarised in Table 46 as the visibility checklist.

**Table 46  Visibility checklist**

| | | |
|---|---|---|
| 1. | Visualise the future | Put a half day aside for this event. Involve all library staff, invite library champions and between one and three stakeholders |
| | | Use brainstorming techniques to visualise the future |
| | | Invite an independent facilitator for the event |
| | | Agree upon a vision statement |
| 2. | Improvise | Put in place resources using a creative approach to realise the vision |
| 3. | Strategic plan<br>    Vision statement<br>    Mission statement<br>    Value statement<br>    Reader charter<br>    Standards of service | Engage all library staff in the strategic planning process<br>The vision informs the strategic plan. Build upon this by deciding upon:<br>• A mission statement and<br>• A value statement through consensus<br>Agree on goals and objectives<br>• Develop a reader charter<br>• Create a standards of service document |
| 4. | Implementation plan | Start with some 'quick wins' to keep staff on board and motivated (e.g. set up a library twitter account and blog) |
| 5. | Be proactive<br>    Attend events<br>    Develop online tutorials<br>      and place them in your<br>      users' online space | • Use social media effectively and proactively<br>• Invest in a display stand and promotional material and start attending professional conferences in areas outside of librarianship<br>• Make information tutorials available in your users' space<br>• Advertise your LIS<br>• Embed chat reference in your users' space |
| 6. | Inform everyone about the changes you are making | • Host a significant event to launch or market key milestones in your strategic plan<br>• Have an information-related event in your canteen/ staff restaurant at least quarterly<br>• Create a visually appealing display of your key achievements and send this to management annually |

**Table 46**  **Continued**

| 7. | Lift speech/Elevator pitch | Practise your lift speech and revise regularly; take opportunities where they arise (not necessarily always in a lift). Corridors, restaurants and meetings are all equally good places to make your speech heard |
|----|----------------------------|--------------------------------------------------------------------------------------------------------------------------------------------------------------------------------------------------------------------------|
| 8. | Improve – quality improvement methods | |
| 9. | Tailor | Conduct a needs analysis. Get feedback from your users and nonusers. Run a survey, focus group and interview some readers and nonreaders. Tailor your services according to the needs of the people most likely to benefit from LIS services or from the librarian being included on their team |
| 10. | You can do it! Have self-belief | Try to make time for continuing professional development. Include time for reading, listening to Tedtalks and practising mindfulness, whatever approach is your preferred learning style. Librarians are professional, credible, trusted and reliable information experts. We need to build our self-confidence to go forth and improve information processes and management in our organisations for the betterment of all |

# Notes

UCD Library YouTube Channel: https://www.youtube.com/watch?v=fepRJaccUqI.
Harper University YouTube Channel: https://www.youtube.com/watch?v=eaLE6C-Gv0s.

# Strategies that work to improve the visibility, value and impact of the librarian and library

**9**

*Progress is impossible without change, and those who cannot change their minds cannot change anything.*

**George Bernard Shaw**

No profession in the business of information can survive without adapting to the rapidly changing pace of information technology and consumer expectation levels. Librarians are no exception. They cannot afford to stand still or rely on the 'goodwill factor' for their library to remain open or their role as librarian to stay viable. They cannot continue to do what they have always done and think that they will survive. In the information age, people expect instant results and instant information. Librarians in the main have not stood still, and there are many examples from the library and information science (LIS) literature and indeed popular media that show this. Some examples are selected here and highlighted as strategies that work. There are ideas used in practice that other librarians can ponder in their own situation and perhaps use or adopt as appropriate.

Librarians need to be prepared during 'peace time', including times of economic prosperity. Similar to the strategy that centres for disease surveillance adopt to prepare for emerging infectious diseases and threats, librarians need to have a system in place for prevention, preparedness, detection and response. To prevent the threat of invisibility, librarians need to have an elevator pitch ready – they need to be able to pull out a one-page document that outlines in management terminology what their key performance indicators are and how they are adding value to the organisation. To be prepared, librarians need to horizon scan, be aware of upcoming trends and changes and detect any potential threats to the profession through keeping up to date with current literature and media. If librarians are not prepared at all times, then if knocks do come and cuts strike, they will be left floundering. There is no use finding oneself knee deep in an economic crisis and wondering why executives or governments want to force cuts that impact readers, librarians and information workers. It is also too late at this point to start coming up with a knee-jerk reaction such as pulling out business plans compiled in the eleventh hour for improving the situation or worse again plans to 'save' the library when it is already too late. This defensive stance that librarians sometimes adopt does not work. The ship will have sailed and as a worse-case scenario the librarian will be left unemployed. The response must be evidence-based librarianship, and all librarians must get in on this act. It is not about saving jobs or saving libraries; it is about growing the profession and taking it to the next level.

Regardless of the approach used in the literature that follows, for the librarian to increase visibility, value and impact, all activities pursued and resources provided, basically everything that the librarian does, must align to the needs of the organisation. The focus must be on value-added interactions. There is no point in continuing auxiliary services just because 'this is what we have always done' or because of tradition. Therefore, the starting point is to determine those needs through research and by talking to key people, readers and potential readers in the organisation. This is covered in Chapter 7. The examples shown in this chapter work in certain environments and should be adopted and used if deemed a good fit by librarians in similar situations. These examples scratch the surface of good practice in librarianship; this is a rapidly evolving landscape and more research is continually evolving.

# Leadership and advocacy

## *Library associations*

Professional associations representing librarians and information professionals worldwide have an important advocacy and leadership role to play in advancing the profession of librarianship and improving the visibility of librarians to the world. Part of improving the visibility of the profession is through explaining to the general public what it is that librarians do and what value libraries offer to them. The American Library Association (ALA) has done a good job of expanding the role of libraries and librarians to society via the 'ilovelibraries' initiative. The ALA has a campaign for U.S. libraries in place with support from the ALA's Library Champions campaign. Previous ALA campaigns such as '@your library' were successfully adopted by other associations, such as the Brazilian Federation Librarians Association (FEBAB). The Chartered Institute of Library and Information Professionals (CILIP), the U.K.-equivalent of ALA, is a member of the Speak Up for Libraries movement and has an entire section of its website devoted to advocacy, awards and projects. It supports advocacy for all types of library and information professionals in many diverse settings. Similar to other library associations, CILIP is particularly active in election years, and 2015 is set to be a busy year for their 'Electionwatch' campaign.

The International Federation of Library Associations and Institutions (IFLA) has made an online learning programme available to members that includes a module on advocacy entitled 'Libraries on the Agenda' and a module comprising statistical data in support of advocacy. IFLA also has a school library advocacy kit available online. In 2013, IFLA conducted a survey with responses from 300 librarians around the world. The results were summarized, and nine best-practice strategies were found to be effective for successful advocacy through partnerships. These are available on their website.

In the United States, the Medical Library Association (MLA) has recognised the challenges that are facing librarians working in health care and has put in place several programmes to tackle these challenges. Hospital librarians in the US have been faced with significant challenges for the past decade. The MLA captures the changing status and trends in U.S. hospital libraries as per a recommendation from the Vital Pathways Task Force. The results are worrisome. In 2013, the data reported that 25% of the changes reported were positive or neutral whereas 75% were negative (Medical Library Association, 2013). The MLA has responded by putting advocacy campaigns in place to assist hospital librarians (e.g. return on investment (ROI) calculators) and other resources available from their website. The MLA has a benchmarking network that is helpful for comparative analysis, management decision-making and research. The MLA has 'Standards for Hospital Librarians', which are invaluable for hospital librarians when stating their case. The MLA has an option for international membership that is highly recommended to any health care librarian regardless of what country they work in.

In Europe as well as specialized associations such as the European Association for Health Information and Libraries (EAHIL), who advocate for health science librarianship, the European Bureau of Library, Information and Documentation Associations (EBLIDA) lists lobbying for European libraries as its core activity. EBLIDA plans to create an online knowledge and information centre to assist librarians in advocating for access for all to the information society. It lobbies for libraries and other information sectors to European and international institutions. It also supports national member organisations.

The Australian Library and Information Association (ALIA) representing librarians and information workers in Australia makes details of advocacy campaigns in place since 2012 available on its website. In 2015, the FAIR campaign focuses on freedom of access to information and resources. Likewise, in New Zealand, the Library and Information Association of New Zealand (LIANZA) proactively engages with parliament on any issues likely to affect the value communities receive from libraries in all sectors.

The Pakistan Library Association has an explicit action related to the aims and objectives of its constitution: 'the development and improvement of the library services, the library professionals and the librarianship itself to enhance their social image and to ensure respectful survival in society' (Pakistan Library Association, 2013).

In Africa, the African Library and Information Associations and Institutions (AfLIA) was launched in 2013 with one of its aims to put the library and information profession on the national and continental agendas.

Despite codes of ethics and constitutional documents that govern library associations, they have not been immune to criticism for not advocating for librarians and for falling short when it came to taking active measures to support the profession. The Canadian Library Association has been criticised for its lack of support for librarians (Lockhart, 2012).

Many library associations have developed whole sections of their websites to advocacy; there are times of the year that are devoted to librarianship, events to mark librarianship and awards to promote and recognise the profession. Library associations have developed standards to drive professionalism in librarianship and to enhance growth. For a short list of library associations, please refer to Table 47.

## The power of the voice of the customer

Library patrons such as readers and writers have actively shown their appreciation for libraries, and their impact has had a positive effect. For example, in Liverpool,

**Table 47  Professional associations representing libraries and librarians**

| Name | Year founded | Mission | Advocacy pages/links | Country/continent |
|---|---|---|---|---|
| International Federation of Library Associations and Institutions (IFLA) | 1927 | IFLA is the international organisation for library and information associations, institutions and librarians in the user communities they serve throughout the world. | http://www.ifla.org/publications/school-library-advocacy-kit http://www.ifla.org/ES/book/export/html/8688 | ALL |
| American Library Association (ALA) | 1876 | To provide leadership for the development, promotion and improvement of library and information services and the profession of librarianship to enhance learning and ensure access to information for all. | http://www.ala.org/united/powerguide http://www.ala.org/aasl/advocacy http://www.ala.org/advocacy/advocacy-university | USA |
| Medical Library Association (MLA) | 1898 | The MLA is organized exclusively for scientific and educational purposes and is dedicated to the support of health sciences research, education and patient care. MLA fosters excellence in the professional achievement and leadership of health sciences library and information professionals to enhance the quality of health care, education and research. | https://www.mlanet.org/advocacy/librarian-advocacy | USA |
| Special Libraries Association | 1909 | The Special Libraries Association promotes and strengthens its members through learning, advocacy and networking initiatives. | http://www.sla.org/about-sla/vision-mission-core-value/#sthash.dLDzGL7u.dpuf | USA |

| | | | | |
|---|---|---|---|---|
| Chartered Institute of Library and Professionals (CILIP) | 2002 (Formerly library association 1977 merged with Institute of information Scientists 1958) | CILIP exists to<br>Promote and support the people who work to deliver this vision.<br>Be the leading voice for information, library and knowledge practitioners, working to advocate strongly; provide unity through shared values and develop skills and excellence.<br>• See more at http://www.cilip.org.uk/cilip/about/vision-and-mission#sthash.TrW6OoOL.dpuf | http://www.cilip.org.uk/cilip/advocacy-awards-and-projects/advocacy-and-awards | UK |
| School Library Association (SLA) | 1937 | We believe that every pupil is entitled to effective school library provision. The SLA is committed to supporting everyone involved with school libraries, promoting high-quality reading and learning opportunities for all. | http://www.sla.org.uk/advocacy.php | UK & Ireland |
| African Library and Information Associations and Institutions (AfLIA) | 2013 | It is the trusted African voice for the library and information community and drives equitable access to information and knowledge for all. | http://aflia.net/index.php/about-aflia | Africa |
| European Bureau of Library, Information and Documentation Associations (EBLIDA) | 1992 | EBLIDA lobbies to defend and promote the interests of the library, archive and information sectors and professionals in Europe, mainly following the policy agenda of the European Commission. | http://www.eblida.org/activities/position-papers.html<br>http://www.eblida.org/activities/advocacy-and-lobbying-for-libraries-in-europe.html | Europe |
| Australian Library and Information Association (ALIA) | 1937 | ALIA is the national professional association for the Australian library and information sector. | https://fair.alia.org.au/ | Australia |

Continued

**Table 47  Continued**

| Name | Year founded | Mission | Advocacy pages/links | Country/continent |
|------|-------------|---------|---------------------|-------------------|
| Library and Information Association of New Zealand (LIANZA) | 1910 | Powered by our members, LIANZA provides strong leadership, growth opportunities and a community of practice to support the provision of quality library and information services to communities throughout New Zealand. | http://www.lianza.org.nz/our-work/campaigns | New Zealand |
| Pakistan Library Association | 1957 | To provide leadership and to serve as a collective voice and advocate for advancement of libraries in the country. | http://www.pla.org.pk/ObjectivenFuturePlan.html | Pakistan |
| Brazilian Federation Librarians Association (FEBAB) | | | | South America Brazil |
| Canadian Library Association (CLA) | 1946 | CLA is the national voice for Canada's library communities. | http://www.cla.ca/AM/Template.cfm?Section=Advocacy&Template=/CM/HTMLDisplay.cfm&ContentID=16552 | Canada |

the Love Letters campaign saved the closure of 11 libraries (Flood, 2014). The campaign involved over 500 writers, musicians, actors, artists, illustrators and educators who wrote letters to the mayor about why their library mattered to them. They protested and held rallies and consultations. In the end, the voice of the customer was heard and the council reversed its decision to close the public libraries. This campaign was picked up by Book Week Scotland, and *The Guardian* newspaper is collecting stories from readers all over the world using the Love Letters campaign. In a similar vein, volunteers have come together to support public libraries via a national charity in the United Kingdom simply called 'The Library Campaign'. The campaign converses with the media and among other things hosts a national Speak Up for Libraries conference.

# Librarians as leaders

Individual librarians have an advocacy role to play and some have shown a strong commitment to the plight of libraries. For example, in the United Kingdom, Ian Anstice is chronicling public library closures and makes many resources available on the Public Libraries News website. In the United States, Jennifer LaGarde runs an award-winning blog, 'Adventures of Library Girl', and acts as a librarian ambassador, particularly in the area of school librarianship. Andy Woodworth, public librarian and advocate, moderates the Save NJ Libraries Facebook group with more than 15,000 members. Nancy Kranich, special projects librarian and lecturer at Rutgers University, has been selected to receive the 2015 ALA Ken Haycock Award for Promoting Librarianship. Advocacy can be achieved through publication and research. Aaron Tay, academic librarian in Singapore, regularly tweets and runs a blog, 'Musings about librarianship', with great technical tips that advance librarianship. Notable leaders in the field of health science librarianship such as J.C. Marshall, A. Brettle, A.L. Weightman and others have significantly contributed to the evidence base of health librarianship. Publishing evidence-based research to test library services and librarianship is increasingly important as an advocacy tool. Individual librarians can and do make a difference. *Library Journal*'s annual 'Movers and Shakers' award has been shining a light on emerging leaders since 2002. Leaders are needed now more than ever because the profession of librarianship continues to evolve with increasing speed. There is no magic list of an ideal leadership profile because the emphasis is on flexibility and continuous innovation (Sutton & Booth, 2014).

## Schools of library and information studies/iSchools

The University of Toronto offers a massive open online course (MOOC) in library advocacy called 'Library Advocacy Unshushed: Values, Evidence, Action', available in 2014 and 2015.

## Advocacy groups

There are independent groups in addition to library associations that have aims in common with librarians such as the right to literacy and free access to information. One such group is the Reading & Writing Foundation, which has broadened its scope from look-ing at literacy in the Netherlands to improving literacy internationally through the Public Libraries 2020 programme. One of the highlights is the Public Libraries 2020 tour that features YouTube videos from librarians and readers in the European Union (EU) with a unifying theme: libraries change lives. The website sends a positive and real message about the positive impact of public libraries in the lives of everyday citizens of the EU.

# Examples from academic librarianship of increasing visibility, value and impact

## *Proactive reference*

The first set of examples is from academic libraries. Academic libraries have seen the decline of reference queries over the last decade or so, with the progression of the Inter-net and the explosion of information readily available online. There has been much dis-cussion and debate in the literature over the decline of reference and in particular the reference desk. VanScoy (2010) identified six areas of interaction with users and refer-ence librarians: information provision, instruction, interpersonal dimensions, guidance, counselling and partnership. Of these six, Solorzano (2013) argues that only information provision has declined because of vast reference sources available on the Internet. Free resources such as Wikipedia and a growing number of Google products make freely available information resources instantly to users. The other five areas continue to be of value to users and organisations. Librarians still offer a credible role through counsel-ling users to filter results and use advanced search techniques to source more relevant research results. The Internet offers highly interactive tools to enhance the delivery of the traditional reference interview, which 'librarians should be taking advantage of…instead of trying to compete with it' (Solorzano, 2013). Skype, instant messaging, FaceTime and chat software all offer an enhanced user experience of interacting with a librarian online.

In the area of instruction, Oakleaf and VanScoy (2010) identified eight instructional strategies based on educational theories to maximize the impact of digital reference on student learning. If student learning is core to the mission of the academic library, then these strategies are worth considering for reference librarians working with students. The strategies include catch them being good; show, do not tell; chunk it up; let users drive; be the welcome wagon; make introductions and share secret knowledge. The authors argue that inclusion of these strategies in digital reference will have a positive impact on student learning with improved outcomes.

The interpersonal dimension of reference interactions is illustrated by Maksin's (2014) description of research conversations. They maintain that these conversations between librarians and students 'reinforce students' experiences with constructivist learning and personalized attention outside the library, and can situate the academic library as a partner in broader institutional goals related to student learning' (Maksin, 2014, p. 175). This approach is also referred to as 'research consultations' by others in the literature. The sea change that has occurred in reference librarianship is captured by the word 'partnership'. Instead of readers being seen as 'service users' and librarians as 'delivering a service', both are now treated as equal partners in the research process. This strengthens librarianship beyond the 'service and support' mode and strengthens the readers' role beyond a passive information consumer.

The library of the University of New Mexico (UNM) introduced three new initiatives that they show are successful strategies: (1) engagement and community building, (2) reverse reference and research immersion and (3) meeting users where they are. It took some 10 years to gradually make the move to a more proactive, integrated model of their services. The 'reverse reference' model that UNM developed moves reference librarians from the desk to a more proactive role in the university's instruction services. This is reported to have given them the freedom to engage directly with their communities and build up relationships, partnerships and collaborations. The latter point aligns the services of the library directly with the mission of the university, which is crucial.

UNM introduced a virtual reference desk (VRD) with one phone number, one email address and one chat for the entire university. The authors report that the Association of Research Libraries (ARL) statistics increased on all levels in just 3 years. Chat reference increased by 56%, phone enquiries increased by 69% in the first-year and email queries were up from 854 in 2008 to over 1400 in 2009. This evidence shows that making simple things such as contact details easier for the user of the library results in increased use. Meeting users where they are works. Importantly, these activities increased the online visibility of the library services, bringing them to where the users are located and removing the barrier that the traditional physical reference desk creates. The authors state that the VRD in particular 'increased the accessibility and visibility of the library…in an electronic environment' (Aguilar, Keating, Schadl, & Van Reenen, 2011).

Likewise, proactive chat was introduced by Grasselli Library at John Carroll University (United States). The library had offered virtual reference services since 2002. Various types of software and models of participation were used. Some 10 years later in 2012, they switched the online reference and chat service to a more proactive approach. The software in use featured a trigger-initiated chat. This type of chat is commonly found in commercial websites, where after a set period of time a user spends browsing a website, a chat box opens up (or is triggered) with an offer of assistance. The university library reported that switching to a proactive chat reference model increased the visibility of their chat service that, in turn, increased patrons' use. Over a 6-month period, 70% of all chat reference queries were initiated by trigger, with only 30% initiated by patrons (Zhang & Mayer, 2014).

## Roving librarians

Another type of proactive reference seen in academic libraries is roving librarians. This is where librarians are available for reference queries to students on campus and they usually have a mobile device such as a tablet, iPad or laptop to demonstrate how to find information. However, the experience of this has been mixed. Some report that this presents a barrier to users (Caperon, 2014) whereas others found that it was well received and gave librarians an insight into how users were working in the building (Cason Barratt, Acheson, & Luken, 2010). The University of Huddersfield (United Kingdom) reported success with their roving librarian initiative that concentrated on subject librarians roving outside of the library. They went to places such as campus cafés, busy thoroughfares, resource centres and social areas. Sharman (2012) found that it created closer working relationships with staff outside of the library and led to informed conversations with students that would not have taken place at the subject inquiry desk. Strong branding of roving librarians helped students to identify them out of context and having free giveaways such as sweets made the librarians more approachable to students. More information can be found on this on-going project at https://sharmana.wordpress.com/.

Other universities have followed the roving librarian model with success. The University of East Anglia branded their project 'Librarians Let Loose!' complete with a logo and dedicated webpage. This was modelled on the Huddersfield approach and faculty librarians roved outside of the library. The roving experience was adopted as a student and staff engagement exercise. Use of tweets and promotion through the library blog proved successful. A 30-min time slot was found to be perfect for maximum effect. Librarians had to be proactive and directly approach students. They kept a record of comments or questions asked by students. Of the 286 comments made, 140 were positive. Sharples (2014) found that this type of outreach to students helped to raise the profile of the library. The 'Librarians Let Loose!' project proved very successful with nursing students in particular, who are located in a more remote area of the campus. The University of Edinburgh library had a library pop-up series with a blog devoted to the pop-up library. They reported meeting with 2200 people in just 9 weeks (Edinburgh University Library Blog, 2014).

## Trend spotting

The Horizon report identifies short-, medium-, and long-term trends in education that are likely to affect teaching and learning. In the 2014 report, one of the medium-term trends, likely to drive changes in 3–5 years, was students becoming creators, as opposed to consumers, of content. Libraries have responded to this trend by creating makerspaces – places where students can experiment with various physical and digital tools such as wood, metal and three-dimensional printers to create new products. Some libraries loan equipment such as video recorders, digitizing equipment and publication services that support content creation and production. The DeLaMare Science and Engineering library at University of Nevada Reno was listed as one of the best makerspaces in the United States by *Make* magazine in 2015. Libraries also provide gaming rooms where students can play videogames and experiment with learning through gaming. Libraries can play a central role in supporting experimental learning where it is valued by their parent organisation. A solvable trend outlined in the same report is the low level of digital fluency among faculty. This is solvable by librarians embedding digital literacy instruction into curriculum and providing faculty with digital literacy resources. University libraries adopting a proactive approach to assisting faculty and students with digital literacy included in the report are Texas University library, Plymouth, and Fresno State University library.

The 2015 Horizon report found that a medium-term trend was the use of new sources of data as a way to measure performance. Libraries such as Nottingham Trent University have linked aggregated data to measure library use, attendance and grades (Johnson, Becker, Estrada, & Freeman, 2015, p. 12). Another medium-term trend was the proliferation of open educational resources. Librarians are adding value to universities by selecting open educational resources and embedding them within the context of student learning spaces. Northshore Community College has included the promotion of open education resources with faculty as one of the points in their 2014–2015 library action plan. Interestingly, the same college has a dedicated goal for increasing visibility in the action plan containing eight goals. 'Promote the Library to Increase its Visibility and Presence on Campus and in the Community' (Danvers, 2014).

Where learners are using physical spaces on campus, librarians in universities can create such spaces in their libraries to heighten their visibility as educators. This strategy was used successfully at Purdue libraries, where a renovated learning space, the LearnLab, in the Management and Economics library led faculty, students and administrators to 'understand the reality of the changing paradigm of librarians as teachers' (Maybee, Doan, & Riehle, 2013).

## Role of the library and librarian in research

The importance of librarians as research partners in higher education must be plain and clear in the mind of the academic research community. If it is not, then libraries may face a hard battle in convincing their administrators to grant them renewed and increased budgets. Librarians at Wayne State University (WSU) in the United States identified opportunities for increasing the visibility of the library and its role in research. They shared their strategies for other librarians to use and adopt as necessary. WSU engaged in several collaborative initiatives with the Division of Research at their university. The participation of librarians in continuing professional development seminars organised by the Division of Research proved fruitful. Librarians gave overviews of funding opportunities, grant writing resources, mentoring and tools for keeping up to date. The advantage of this participation was that it enabled the librarians to promote and market their resources and their expertise directly to researchers who formed part of a large, targeted and interested audience. Other collaborative initiatives included the joint hosting of a training session promoting the use of research profile databases, which the author described 'increased visibility of WSU libraries and their resources' (Healy, 2010). Faculty orientation sessions included librarians' input, and the handbook included a library section. The librarians also contributed to the online newsletter. The WSU collaboration with the Division of Research proved that joint working toward a common goal – to enhance the research mission of the university – proved successful. WSU librarians also responded to the needs of the organisation. For example, the Office of Technology Transfer contacted the library for assistance in providing staff with training on searching databases, locating information and articles. The office identified a need, and the library responded by creating a liaison librarian role for them.

Other areas where librarians at WSU increased their visibility included working with post-doctoral researchers and graduate students. Librarians gave 2-h workshops in scholarly communication on topics such as writing, presentation skills, doing a literature review and avoiding plagiarism. The librarians took a proactive approach by initiating contact with the graduate school, offering their participation in workshops.

An analysis of 24 research universities in the United Kingdom found that university libraries offering dedicated spaces for researchers improve service visibility (Corral, 2014). Examples of universities offering researcher spaces such as 'research commons' include the University of Warwick library, Queen Mary, Birmingham, Durham and York.

## *Virtual visibility*

Measuring online visibility of the library must match the objectives of having a digital presence for the library in the first place. For example, if the objective of the online library is to increase usage of library collections (online public access catalogue (OPAC), databases, repository, e-books, etc.) and library services (online tutorials, document supply, chat and email queries), then these should all be measured. Ahmad and Abawajy (2014) have detailed a quality assessment model for measuring the impact of third-party sourced services on digital library service quality. It encompasses three elements: environment quality, delivery quality and outcome quality. Seven points to consider for digital library evaluation include aligning local usage data to national norms; use of census data over samples; web usability testing; content is still king; usage data analysis can direct service improvements and finally digital libraries are operating in an increasingly competitive information space, making outcomes for users ever more important (Franklin, Kyrillidou, & Plum, 2009).

A second objective of having a digital library presence is to measure the quality of service that the library offers from a user's point of view. This incorporates user expectations and user satisfaction and it can help predict repeat business and future trends. To measure quality of service, user surveys should be performed as well as focus groups or interviews with key stakeholders. An emerging area is the analysis of ultimate use data. Digital libraries may collect use data, which captures the usage behaviours of people who use content retrieved from digital libraries. A recent study has shown that a Digital Cart Service was an effective tool for informing digital library management, specifically in the areas of metadata creation, marketing and promotion, content selection and system design (Reilly & Thompson, 2014). Measuring quality enables continuous improvement of services in line with what users expect and are happy with. It may identify gaps, areas that need work and importantly services that perhaps should be stopped altogether. It can help librarians to focus on what is working and strengthen the personalisation of services to user needs and increase interaction with users and potential users of the library.

Xia (2009) successfully demonstrated that Facebook groups at two research university libraries enhanced the visibility of the library to students and faculty. As he has noted, visibility is a primary concern for librarians and technology can be used to address this: 'increasing the visibility of their library through high technologies has become the top priority of librarians' (p. 470).

## Repositories and open access

Librarians who successfully manage subject or institutional repositories are directly involved in fulfilling university-wide missions (i.e. to increase the visibility of the institution by showcasing its scholarly output). However, librarians must work to ensure that key stakeholders in the organisation are aware of the important role that librarians play in achieving this. For example, the skills involved in making a repository interoperable, visible, current and useful are due to the librarian's information management skills, expertise in metadata, attention to providing long-term preservation of research and by raising awareness of repositories within the academic community. Librarians are the ones making research output of individual researchers in a university more discoverable and more visible. Are they losing out on their own visibility while hoisting up that of others?

The value of repositories becomes evident to researchers when they are integrated into a researcher's routine workflow and become almost 'invisible' to them. As Aschenbrenner, Blanke, Flanders, Hedges, and O'Steen (2008) have pointed out, researchers are the most important users of repositories. Integration of repositories with a current research information system (CRIS), with the SWORD (Simple Web Service Offering Repository Deposit) protocol and features such as dynamic researcher pages all enhance their value to researchers. Expanding integration and connectivity of repositories with multiple platforms is being performed at several institutions, including VIVO (a research-focused discovery tool) at Cornell University, Building the Research Informaiton Infrastructure (BRII) at the University of Oxford and researcher pages at the University of Rochester (Russell & Day, 2010).

The utilization of repository metrics to support research grant applications is a key added value of repositories. Repository managers are reporting impact of repositories in different ways. There is no standard as yet for repository metrics. In the interim, repositories are listed in online repository directories such as OpenDOAR an Open Directory of Open Access Repositories and Registry of Open Access Repositories (ROAR), which give a breakdown of the quantity of research per repository. In the EU, funded research is mandated to be made available via open access. European repository managers are responding to this by liaising with researchers at their institutions to ensure any funded research output is made available via university and subject repositories. This includes research data under the EUs biggest research and innovation programme Horizon 2020, with nearly €80 billion of funding available over 7 years (2014–2020). The Consejo Superior de Investigaciones Científicas (CSIC), a public research organisation in Spain, maintains an online 'Ranking Web of World Repositories' via its Cybermetrics Lab, and this is an advocacy tool that repository managers can use to promote open access and the visibility of their repository worldwide.

## Engaging with stakeholders

In Briggs library at South Dakota State University (SDSU), librarians embarked upon an innovative project to engage with one of their key stakeholder groups – university administrators. Five librarians were assigned to 10 research projects. It was found that through this engagement, librarians actively contributed to the university's mission in specific areas. The authors report that positive feedback was received and librarians increased their visibility on campus in an innovative way (Kott, Mix, & Marshall, 2015). Another important group of stakeholders are prospective students. The role of the campus visit is key in attracting new students to universities. Librarians have been proactive in getting involved in the campus visit. Librarians at Miami University contacted the director of admissions to set up a meeting to involve librarians in the university-wide mission of attracting more students. This simple step led to increased visibility of the library and worked together toward a shared goal – increasing student enrolment. The outreach librarian provided a voice for libraries during the campus visit and acted in an ambassadorial role. Librarians can actively add value by joining campus-wide efforts to attract students (Miller, 2012).

## Communicating value

Once librarians have found that they are contributing to a university's mission, it is important to effectively communicate that value. Higher grade point average (GPA) was linked to library electronic resource usage at Samford University. Rollins and Cherry make sure that key stakeholders are informed of this value by submitting their findings via a report that is presented to every college dean at the start of the school term. The deans immediately see the link between library contribution and academic success (Davidson, Rollins, & Cherry, 2013).

## Assessment

In the United States, there is a growing emphasis on assessment and measuring outcomes in academic libraries since the Association of College and Research

Laboratories (ARCL) report in 2010. The University of Colorado Denver developed a research protocol to measure the value of the library that they invite other librarians to test in their institutions. Their approach is based on recommendations outlined in the ARCL report – namely the integration of collaboration, purposefulness and longevity. It is a good example of translating existing evidence into practice. What is interesting about this research is that it demonstrates again that a proactive approach works and collaboration with stakeholders outside of the library works. It began with the librarian sending an email to the chemistry instructor and led to a 3-year interdisciplinary study with positive outcomes. As the authors state, 'exciting opportunities can be possible when librarians leave the library, meet and engage with faculty and capitalize on serendipity' (Pan, Ferrer-Vinent, & Bruehl, 2014).

# Examples from health librarianship of increasing visibility, value and impact

Examples of successful strategies that lead to improved visibility for librarians and libraries in the health sciences have been sourced from the LIS literature. In the U.K. National Health Service (NHS), there are annual Sally Hernando awards for Innovation in NHS Library and Knowledge Services under a Library Quality Assurance Framework. Some of the award winners are excellent examples of increasing the visibility and value of health science librarians to their trusts and the wider health care community. The NHS Library and Knowledge Services' Wiki lists past winners. Some of the winning initiatives included the following:

- Aligning research publication metrics review with an organisational appraisal and validation process.
- Self-guided murder mystery trail in the library.
- Storage, classification and dissemination of patient stories.
- Mapping literature search topics to strategic priorities of the organisation.
- Social network analysis map (measures relationships and information flows between staff in the organisation) can show how people share information.
- Monthly science cafe in a hospital where the public can come in and access experts and information on current health issues.
- Mental health film club.
- Staff art exhibition.
- Clinical librarians' use of evidence summaries to underpin trust procurement decisions.

## Getting outside of the library

Getting physically out of the library is a must for all librarians wishing to make an impact in their organisation. If people do not see the librarian, then they will not necessarily realise who she or he is or that a library even exists in house. An example from nursing literature is a mobile medical library initiative, which took the librarian out of the library and into 17 nursing units at a community teaching hospital. The librarian brought a mobile cart colourfully decorated with a Computer on Wheels (COW) and a selection of books, journals and bookmarks for nursing staff. The librarian educated nursing staff about medical databases available in the units and how to access them. The authors reported that this initiative helped nurses to become acquainted with the medical librarian so that if they needed assistance with a literature search or assignment as part of a degree programme, then they would know who the librarian was (Ryan & Joseph, 2012). It also helped increase awareness of the hospital's nursing research team and encouraged participation in it. It was viewed as an initiative to strengthen nurses' evidence-based practice, and the librarian was contacted by a nurse manager of another nursing service requesting a visit. Initiatives such as these help increase awareness of librarians and their skill set in hospital settings.

Getting out of the library has never been more pertinent. Setting up clubs in a hospital such as a journal club or a writing club is an effective way of increasing visibility of the librarian's work outside of the library. A clinical librarian at North Wales NHS Trust found that the structured support offered through a journal club she set up was valued by clinical staff (Urquhart, Turner, Durbin, & Ryan, 2007). Two health science librarians reported their success at presenting and participating at non-library-related conferences. The conferences included NHS procurement and two international conferences in Delhi, India. One was co-presented with a clinical colleague. The benefits included personal development, increase in contacts, local learning and a deeper understanding of evidence-based practice in a global context (Blagden, Pratchett, & Treadway, 2014).

## Going mobile

The ubiquitous nature of mobile technology and mobile devices offers unique opportunities for libraries and librarians to increase their visibility. Caperon (2014) spoke of the 'wake-up call' that a medical student, Harding, gave to academic librarians when he challenged them to facilitate the 'paperless student' of the future. Support for wireless devices in universities and other organisations is now commonplace, and libraries must avail of this opportunity to become highly visible in the mobile world that students, clinicians and the general public increasingly occupy.

The University of Leeds in the United Kingdom has looked closely at how mobile library services could be effectively delivered to their students and staff. Through qualitative and quantitative research methods, including an online survey and focus group, the need for potential delivery of specialized library services through mobile technology was assessed. Services included text messaging, Quick Response (QR) codes, library guides and tutorials. The university already had an app in place that included the ability of readers to check their library account, renew and reserve items, search the catalogue and perform other library-related functions. The results of their research informed strategic decisions relating to which library services to pursue and which to cease. This kind of research and data-driven approach to library services is a successful way to offer a reader-centred library and information service that responds to their needs in a meaningful way. On the basis of feedback from the focus group, it was decided that two library services should cease: staff roving with iPads and instant chat with a librarian.

Boone (2009) warned of the danger of librarians becoming invisible on smartphones. Librarians need to be visible in the research workflow of their readers, and if this workflow includes mobile technology, then the librarians need to be bumped into along the researchers' way. Boone argued that 'a rise in the number of mobile apps will result in a decrease in the visibility of librarians'. He was concerned that any library branding would be removed from publisher's databases when accessible as an app from a mobile device and not necessarily through the library website. However, as mobile technology and apps have rapidly advanced and continue to do so, librarians must work with vendors to ensure that library branding appears on vendors apps. Contact details for some apps can include customised library contact information, although more work needs to be done. The visibility of the library in mobile apps and websites optimised for mobile viewing is essential.

At the University of Loughborough, website traffic displayed an increase in access via mobile devices. The library systems team produced a prototype mobile app for the library. They report that the time to develop the app and the cost involved was minimal. This was because of the skill of the in-house team and the use of jQuery Mobile frameworks. Local branding was incorporated into the app and use of the app was high. Work continues on the app and further functionality is due to be incorporated into the app on the basis of user feedback (Cooper & Brewerton, 2013).

## Collaboration with clinicians

Librarians are often tasked with creating online tutorials and videos promoting the best use of electronic resources to readers. This can be a time-consuming task and not without an element of risk to its usefulness to the reader. One way of improving online tutorials is through collaborating from the outset with the viewing audience in a co-creative endeavour. Hery and Weill (2015) describe a unique collaboration between doctors and librarians in France that led to a 'DocToBib' YouTube channel packed with videos on how to get the most out of the popular biomedical database PubMed using the free citation manager tool Zotero. The videos were jointly produced and created by librarians and doctors. The outcome was a resounding success, with the videos being watched in several countries beyond their origin, including North Africa, Canada and Sweden. This type of collaboration between librarians and clinicians is an excellent example of increasing the impact and visibility of health science librarians to clinicians and raising their profile in clinical settings.

## Expanding staff to include a therapy dog

Many academic, special and health libraries are having fun with new part-time staff members such as registered therapy dogs. Pet therapy is an intervention that helps the 'physical, social, emotional and/or cognitive functioning of a client' (Anger & Akins, 2014). A study has found that any risk associated with having a therapy dog in a controlled health care environment in urban Europe or North America and with responsible human behaviour is far outweighed by the benefits (Brodie, Biley, & Shewring, 2002).

Benefits include reduced stress and anxiety for various population cohorts, including students preparing for exams (Young, 2012), hospitalized women with high-risk pregnancies (Lynch et al., 2014) and patients with dementia (Tribet, Boucharlat, & Myslinski, 2008). Certified library therapy dogs such as Monty at Yale Law School and Cooper at Harvard Medical School's Countyway library can be checked out in the same way as a book or laptop by library patrons. Other libraries including school and public libraries are following suit. Weibling, a librarian at Savannah Elementary School in Aubrey, Texas, introduced a reading therapy dog programme to third-grade students that was reported to have increased their interest in reading and improved their comprehension (Inklebarger, 2014). Glencoe Public Library in Illinois offers a K9 Reading Buddies programme for children. Therapy dogs are certified by trusted pet therapy organisations. Some libraries have quarterly dog visits around exam times, such as the University of California Santa Cruz library. Emory University's Robert W. Woodruff law library and others offer pet hugs once a month such as the University of California Berkeley library. Stress levels of workers in global economies are increasing, resulting in substantial economic overheads. Between 50% and 60% of all lost working days are attributed to work-related stress (European Agency for Health and Safety at Work, 2014). Therapy dogs as part of a library service are one way to tackle work-related stress and are particularly relevant in health care work settings where stress affects nursing, medical and administrative staff (Schmid, Drexler, Fischmann, Uter, & Kiesel, 2011). Apart from the health benefits of having a therapy dog available in a library, it is a novel and cost-effective way for libraries to increase their visibility in their organisation and improve outcomes for their communities and parent organisation.

## Embedded librarianship

If managing a team of library staff, then it is worth examining the opportunities for 'loaning' a librarian to a team in an embedded role for a set duration and measuring the impact of this venture. In health care settings, this model is an attractive option from a management point of view because staff members are usually under severe pressure in terms of time and resources. The LIS literature has concrete examples of successful embedded librarianship models in various settings. It is worth exploring this as part of a strategic planning process. Consultation with faculty and management should be sought from the outset to identify the demand. It may even lead to a business case for seeking an extra librarian post. Examples of successful embedded librarian roles are outlined in Table 48.

Wu and Mi (2013) outline practical steps for embedded librarians in health science settings that will increase their value and impact in their organisations. They can be summarized as having a cultural and physical presence, build close relationships with key stakeholders, collaborate, contribute to curriculum development, act as a faculty team member, serve on committees and engage in outreach to connect the institution to the community. It is a brave new world for health science librarians, and embedded librarianship offers an opportunity to stay relevant and revitalise the profession.

## Research

Evidence-based librarianship (EBL) is a natural fit for health science librarians because it goes hand in hand with evidence-based medicine or practice (EBM/EBP). EBP is a movement that has its origins in the late 1990s. Its most common definition is from Dr D. Sackett, who defined it as 'the conscientious, explicit and judicious use of current best evidence in making decisions about the care of the individual patient. It means integrating individual clinical expertise with the best available external clinical evidence from systematic research' (Sackett, Rosenberg, Gray, Haynes, & Richardson, 1996). EBL evolved shortly after with a seven-part conceptual framework proposed by Eldredge (2000). The purpose of EBL is to help librarians to take a rigorous approach to decision-making and to base those decisions on the best available evidence. In health science librarianship, many systematic reviews have been published to build an evidence base of the profession. EBL can play a strong role for advocacy for all libraries and assists librarians in increasing visibility of their impact and value.

The evidence-based approach used by Abels, Cogdill, and Zach (2002) to develop a taxonomy of the value of library and information services to hospitals and academic health science centres is one that hospital librarians could use in their organisation to increase visibility and display their value to their hospitals. It is based on the balanced scorecard approach to quality improvement, which is also outlined in Chapter 7.

In Ireland, health science librarians have become involved in the support of research and clinical guideline development at the national level. This has increased the visibility of librarians in the health system by enabling them to work more closely with clinical teams and promoting library services and resources at the national level (Smith & White, 2014).

Table 48 **Examples of reported impact of embedded librarians**

| Type of embedded role | Institution | Reported impact |
|---|---|---|
| Information literacy programmes | University of Rhode Island, Community of Vermont | Stronger connections with students |
| Embedded liaison programmes | Welch Medical Library, John Hopkins University | Increased frequency and depth of librarian–faculty interactions |
| Facilitator model liaison programme | University of Texas Southwestern Medical Center Dallas | Heightened awareness of liaison programme (82.5%), Demand for further liaisons from departments (Crossno, DeShay, Huslig, Mayo, & Patridge, 2012) |
| Research project and programme-based embedded librarian | Purdue University Library, National Solar Observatory | Strengthen relationships with faculty and develop active partnerships Flexible organisation, asset management. |
| Law firm embedded librarian 'senior information officer' | Finance and capital markets, Clifford Chance, LLP | Operates in consultancy – expert capacity aligns with organisation's goals (Andrews, 2014) |
| Embedded librarian in residence halls | University of Illinois | Librarian is 'extremely visible in the students' lives' (Long, 2011) |
| Embedded librarian with at-risk populations | University of Wyoming | Increase view of librarians as 'teachers' and 'consultants' (Fisher & Heaney, 2011) |
| Embedded librarian working as a media manager | BBC Archives | Greater visibility and more engagement (Williams, 2014) |

# Critical success factors for increasing visibility

- Partnership working – list existing partnerships, set a key objective for the next 1–3 years (i.e. how many partnerships/collaborations is envisaged and with whom? How will the impact be measured?)
- Build relationships with key stakeholders (identify them, name actions to make relationships and connections happen, create an action plan)
- Grow networks within the LIS community – learn from experts in the field and share experiences
- Embrace and use social media, track and measure its impact (number of likes, retweets (RTs), followers, comments, shares, posts, reach, etc.)
- Start small, think big

Jane Blumenthal, librarian and past president of the MLA, shared some pertinent tips for health science librarians that are key to the success of the profession into the future: stop selling services and resources, look at areas where librarians add value to the institution, present the library as an equal partner, be part of the curriculum, be an author not just an acknowledgement and do not be afraid of failure (Blumenthal, 2014).

## Online visibility – strategies that work

Embedded librarianship lends itself well to increasing the online visibility of the librarians, and there are many examples of this. In particular, in online instruction, there are great opportunities for librarians to increase their visibility. Ann Schroeder describes her programme at the Community College of Vermont, where she offered an embedded librarian programme to all courses. This is an example of where an innovative approach to a library service can really pay off. The embedded information literacy (IL) programme replaced face-to-face instruction. Despite reported reservations by faculty staff of this switch, a year later a survey revealed an increase in faculty and students' confidence in using the library. The value of the embedded librarian programme was proven (Schroeder, 2011).

An Australian university also has an example of an embedded IL programme. This is reported to have been a successful way to involve librarians directly in better outcomes for the faculty of Buit Environment and Engineering. Milne and Thomas describe how the IL evolved over a 3-year period from 2007 to 2009 at the Queensland University of Technology. On the basis of pre- and post-test evaluation, they were able to demonstrate using data the improved learning outcomes of students in the course because of the IL programme. Resources included an openly accessible custom written text, which was made visible via their institutional repository; a library quiz; a library lecture; library tutorials and a final exam (Milne & Thomas, 2011).

Duke University embedded library subject guides within the learning management system of the university. Using an automated system, guides were mapped to each of the 1700 courses offered to students. Outcome was assessed using surveys and web usage statistics. Survey results proved that students found the guides useful or very useful, and the web traffic showed an increase over two semesters (Daly, 2011).

The concept of embedded librarianship is not exclusive to academic or health science librarians. Special and corporate librarians have explored this as a viable option for increasing impact and value. Reynolds investigated the impact of a three-team information unit in a commercial property firm. Using surveys and interviews of staff and partners of the company, she found that overall interviewees felt that the unit did have an impact although it was not always easy to define. The researcher concluded that to improve the impact of the information unit, they would create a marketing strategy, introduce an impact monitoring policy and notably work to embed the unit in the work of the teams of the organisation (Reynolds, 2013).

## Examples from school librarianship of increasing visibility, value and impact

Gildersleeves reports on a pilot research project asking the question, 'Do school libraries make a difference?', which looked at secondary schools in England, Scotland, Wales and Northern Ireland. Outcomes were defined as 'results generated from particular service activities and the effects of activities'. Impacts were defined as 'differences experienced by the consumers of the services' (Gildersleeves, 2012, p. 406). Impact of the school library was measured in relation to its value to pupils and the wider school community. The project looked at mapping school library presence with schools' ranking in the national league table and at perceptions of stakeholders – teachers and pupils – of the contribution made by school libraries and librarians to student learning and development. There was a focus on non-librarian consultation (i.e. parents, students, head teachers and staff) during the research, which was adopted to offer a neutral standpoint on school library and school librarian advocacy. Findings from the pilot phase of the study reveal that pupils value the school library for different reasons. Help given to find relevant information for school work; improving writing through reading; and having a place to study, play games, use computers and socialize were all reasons given by pupils about why they value school libraries.

A relevant finding was that librarians furnishing annual reports to school management teams were not always presenting them within the context of the school's learning goals. Gildersleeves found that when reports were framed in context to include items such as pupils' comments, they were then easily communicated to the wider school community (p. 411). There was variation in online visibility of the school library: some had websites and others had only internal pages. Most case material found by the School Library Commission had never publicly been shared. The full research was due to take place during 2011–2012; however, no publication of the findings has been made available at the time of writing. The findings of the pilot suggested that school libraries do have a positive impact on pupil learning and development. A case bank of good practice examples is due to be made available by the University College London Department of Information Studies.

School libraries are a statutory requirement in Scotland, but despite lobbying for this to be the case in both England and Wales, the issue has not progressed.

Extensive research has been performed in the United States about the impact of school library media programmes and library media specialists on academic achievement of public school students. The results have been positive, with correlations between student achievement and best practices found. Best practices include good staffing, good funding and active information literacy programmes in schools with libraries (Tepe & Geitgey, 2005). Small and Snyder describe two phases of a study of the impact of school libraries in New York State, where certified school library professionals are mandated only at the secondary level. They look at the impact of the school library on achievement, motivation for learning and technology use. Two online surveys were used and validated. The first was a general survey sent to 1612 school librarians and 832 principals. The second was more focused and was sent to 47 school librarians, 134 classroom teachers and 1153 students from 47 schools. The instruments used are made openly available and the authors appeal to school library professionals to use them to assess the impact of their libraries on students and teachers in their areas (Small & Snyder, 2010). In addition, resources for continuing professional development are available to school librarians through project ENABLE to deliver effective services to students with disabilities. Jennifer LaGarde has made a marketing template available on her award-winning school library Blog (librarygirl. net) for school librarians to share and use in their own school libraries.

One of the champions of school librarianship in the United States was Mary E. Hall, who was the second professionally qualified school librarian in the States (Alto, 2012). She set up an exemplary school library at Girls High School in Brooklyn in 1903. She convinced education leaders a century ago that the school librarian was needed to cultivate 'a love of reading, academic achievement and independent learning skills' (p. 11). These principles of school librarianship remain true today, but it appears that intense lobbying is required and the profession needs new champions such as Hall to explain the importance of school librarianship to students today. One such champion is Keith Curry Lance, who has performed multiple impact studies across many states that demonstrate the positive effect of school libraries and library media programmes. Lance identified the importance of collaboration between the library media specialist (LMS) and teachers and collaboration between the LMS and principals. Where this is absent, the LMS must assume a leadership role to advance this. Technology is seen as an essential part of any successful library media programme in schools. Support staff plays an important role in freeing up time for the LMS to participate in meetings such as those to win and keep the support of the school principal. Three areas are important for the success of school libraries:

1. The employment of a professionally qualified librarian and the presence of support staff
2. Collaboration
3. Technology.

His research has wide-reaching appeal with the United States with First Lady Laura Bush featuring his research at a White House conference on school libraries in 2002. The Ontario Library Association also featured his research at a summit on school libraries the same year. By identifying two key stakeholders who took on the role of champions – a person in a position of significant power and an organisation with an advocacy and leadership role for librarians – the research was made highly visible to a large heterogeneous audience. According to Lance, having tangible research, demonstrating the value of school libraries to both educators and the general public at these two events 'helped to move research-based school library advocacy beyond "preaching to the choir"' (Lance, 2002, p. 6).

Advocacy for school librarianship and all librarianship needs a dual approach. On the one hand, a grass roots approach through lobbying by individual librarians, library associations and most importantly school children, teachers and parents is needed. On the other hand, this needs to be coupled with a strategic government approach via departments and organisations with statutory responsibility for education. In South Africa, this approach has worked toward the beginnings of an improved school library system. Hart (2014) describes how two initiatives converged to improve school libraries. The first initiative was taken by the National Council for Library and Information Services (NCLIS) who commissioned an LIS Transformation Charter. The second initiative was a campaign entitled 'One School, One Library One Librarian', launched by the civic action group Equal Education. What is striking about this battle for school librarianship is the effectiveness of the participation of school children in lobbying. This has shown to be successful in Ireland through case studies in Chapter 3 and again in the literature by Hart describing the situation in South Africa where 'a series of marches by thousands of school children... put pressure on government to address the dire school library situation' (p. 6).

Despite a growing body of evidence to support the link between a school library and librarian and better learning outcomes, there is still more to do. Cuts to school librarian posts and reduction in funding for school libraries prevail. There is a clear lack of visibility of school librarians in all continents from Asia to Africa to the United States.

School libraries in Asia are the first to get a budget cut from school administrators because of a lack of understanding of the value of school libraries and school librarians (Lo, Chen, Dukic, & Youn, 2014). Calls for school librarians to make their contributions clearly known to stakeholders continue. A recommended way to achieve this is via the EBP model (Richey & Cahill, 2014, 2015). This must be strengthened with activism, a grass roots line of attack with a savvy approach to media and public relations. It is not enough to produce glossy reports highlighting evidence to support school libraries; it must be acted upon and lobbied for.

School libraries are innovative spaces, and some are offering makerspaces for students to experiment with their creativity, such as the Grand Center Arts Academy public charter school in St. Louis and an elementary school in Pennsylvania (Collette, 2015).

### Tips to improve visibility for school librarians

- Develop a page on the school's website for the school library.
- Document testimonials about the school library from students, parents, teachers and the broader community. Publicise the testimonials on the website and in promotional literature.
- Align annual reports or reports about school library achievements with the school's mission and objectives.
- Perform a survey using validated instruments to gather feedback and research on the impact of the school library and school librarian.
- Widely publish the results of the research.

# Examples from special librarianship of increasing visibility, value and impact

Perhaps in special libraries, more so than any other type of librarianship, librarians are under pressure to demonstrate impact and value to their organisations. Professional library associations have taken the initiative to lead the way by informing the discussion about the value of librarians in society. The Special Libraries Association performed a 2-year alignment study with a key objective to 'Highlight the value of information professionals in today's information economy' (Special Library Association, 2008). Publishers are also working in this space. For example, Elsevier produces a LibraryConnect online space for librarians with webinars on a series of topics. Springer has a Corporate and Government Library Advisory Board made up of 30 information professionals. The board developed an ROI study together with Outsell (Outsell Inc., 2007). The study found that users of information products value three areas most: currency of information, saving time and saving money. These are important areas in which librarians need to demonstrate relevance and ROI. Springer has put together an ROI dashboard, which was presented to librarians at the Special Libraries Conference in 2009 by its director of channel marketing (Scotti, 2009). On the basis of their research on corporate and government libraries, Scotti recommended three areas to demonstrate ROI: value (penetration and use), utilisation (citations, authors, decisions supported) and time saved. The ROI dashboard consisted of a five-step approach to demonstrating impact and ROI: (1) review organisational strategies and identify key knowledge workers; (2) determine what is to be measured; (3) conduct internal research using qualitative and quantitative methods; (4) create a dashboard aligned to organisational goals; and (5) communicate with management, present the dashboard and review as required.

Botha, Rene, and Van Deventer (2009) report on the impact of a special library and information service on researchers using the library at the South African Council for Scientific and Industrial Research. Using qualitative and quantitative research methods, the results show that researchers save time and are more successful in research by using LIS. The authors developed a measurement instrument, which is available for use by academic, special and research libraries, to adapt in their own environments.

An example of the impact of a corporate library is described by Reynolds (2013) in her research about an information unit based in Drivers Jonas Deloitte, a commercial property consultancy. Interviews were conducted with 10 partners and associates and 75 responses were received to a questionnaire. The results showed that the service was visible to those interviewed, although they were unclear about what other teams in the organisation might use it for. The interviewees were in agreement that the information unit did have an impact, although they were hesitant to describe the nature of the impact in detail. A future direction for building impact of the information unit was to embed it into the work of teams at the firm, develop a marketing strategy and impact monitoring policy.

Presidents of the SLA always deliver powerful themes to their members that are centred around empowerment. Being proactive, taking risks, expanding skills and investing in ourselves were all part of the advice to overcome stereotypes about librarians by the SLA President, Deb Hunt, in 2013. Adding and demonstrating value, becoming part of the leadership team in organisations and 'being part of the solution, not the overhead' was a key message (Hunt, 2013). The SLA President, Jill Strand, had a message for members for 2015 to 'lean into the curve' (Strand, 2015). The profession is seeing unprecedented change, and she challenges librarians to go with the changes because it will position them to come out faster and gather speed as they turn the corner. In particular, she implores librarians working in specialist roles to communicate their value and impact to their organisations and their employers.

Nolin (2013) suggests that special librarians focus on added value services to researchers via personalized meta-services. Such services would mean that the librarian needs a degree in the subject area of the research as well as a Master's degree in LIS and knowledge of research processes. It presents a challenging scenario for special and academic librarians, but one that may elevate the profession to an equal member of the research team that Neway envisaged (Neway, 1985). The danger is that the librarian becomes invisible in this process, as Nolin states 'the better the librarian becomes in working and supplying online services at a distance, the more invisible this profession becomes for researchers' (Nolin, p. 516). The best way to counteract this is through regular communication and contact in person with researchers. Special librarians in this scenario will need to increase awareness about their skills and contribution to increased quality of research output. They will arguably be better equipped to do this, given the advanced research skills they will be using in practice; therefore, this approach will mean that librarians will be adept at using research methods to measure their value.

## Co-creation

Co-creation of information products by consumers of information in conjunction with information professionals is a growth area. This is an area in which the librarian becomes highly visible in the value chain. Examples noted above of doctor–librarian co-creation of PubMed tutorials and of chemistry instructor–librarian co-creation of a research protocol are successful strategies for demonstrating value and increasing visibility. This approach is particularly useful for readers and consumers to gain first hand an understanding of what it is that librarians do. For special librarians, there is a clear opportunity in co-creation, particularly in a corporate environment where competition is key to organisational intelligence. Allbon (2005), a law librarian, had success with Lawbore, a website she set up in conjunction with a first-year law student at the City University London. She describes how it put the library at the centre of the university by linking staff, students and alumni and how it altered students' perception of the library, where they now see the library as a dynamic useful resource.

Working outside of the library with customers helps to build loyalty and improves retention. The social web is the perfect sandbox for co-creative experimentation. Crowdsourcing is one way to appeal for participation or highlighting a joint need with a key stakeholder in the organisation. The challenge is to build relationships with key people and to identify champions or a 'lead user' (Schachter, 2013). It is important to anticipate new trends. This is possible by monitoring literature in a customer's subject area, attending conferences in their discipline and blending information skills with the information needs presented by a customer's field of expertise.

## Collaboration

Examples exist in the literature of how librarians and libraries have increased visibility, impact and value, and this chapter has highlighted just a few examples from different sectors of librarianship. Networking and collaborating with other librarians and other disciplines is a sure way to increase visibility and impact. One of the foundations of the discipline of librarianship is sharing. Librarians are resourceful people. Sharing best practice and learning from our successes and failures is what makes the practice of librarianship stronger. All librarians can learn from reading outside of their immediate discipline or speciality. Therefore, a medical librarian may learn from best practice in academic librarianship and vice versa. A school librarian may learn from reading about best practice in public librarianship and vice versa. A strategy from school librarianship 'DEAR' (Drop Everything and Read) was successfully adopted to suit a corporate health service environment, with positive results (Ni Bhrian, 2015). As Cmor (2010), an academic librarian, highlighted, we can all get by with a little help from our (special, public, school, law and medical librarian) friends.

Reading the literature and acting upon it is one way of learning from others and improving visibility of individual librarians and libraries. However, setting up a collaborative group of librarians from different sectors perhaps in a local area is another way of building partnerships and forming collaborative groups. It pushes the boundaries of special librarianship, it builds confidence and it improves the visibility of all librarians and libraries to the wider community.

# Examples from public librarianship of increasing visibility, value and impact

## *Greater opportunities*

The Access to Research project in the United Kingdom has opened up a world of research to public library users. For the first time, access to a wealth of academic journal articles and papers may be accessed through public libraries throughout the United Kingdom for free. More than 4 million articles are included with more than 20 participating publishers. This initiative was born out of one of the recommendations of the Finch Group, convened by the U.K. government, to make access to publicly funded research more widely available. This is a successful example of collaboration between publishers and public libraries. The project is set to run for 2 years and started in February 2014. Data are being gathered to analyse the impact of the project. The intention is that access to research will enhance the work of independent researchers, small businesses, students and give greater opportunities to the general public.

## *Lifelong learning and bridging digital divide*

In an increasingly connected society, public libraries offer community spaces to bridge the digital divide between the digital literate and the digital illiterate. Participation in modern democracies is increasingly dependent on having a digitally literate citizenship. In public libraries, impact is captured by demonstrating levels of civic engagement and community improvements such as increased confidence in using the Internet and understanding information that is digitally retrieved. Nygren (2014) highlights several projects taking place in public libraries in the United States, the Netherlands and Sweden that embrace the connected learning movement. The value of libraries acting as community hubs for lifelong learning has been illustrated.

## Maker movement

The maker movement is a potential growth area for libraries. Makerspaces are transforming the idea of libraries with great potential for public libraries. Makerspaces are places where people gather together to use technology to create. The first library in the United States to create a makerspace was the Fayetteville Free Library in 2011. The public library of Knivsta launched Sweden's first public library makerspace in 2013. This trend is set to continue and is a type of library re-imagined. The same principle of a library as a place of learning applies. A packed audience of librarians listened intently to Mark Frauenfelder, a key advocate for libraries embracing makerspaces, at the annual conference of the American Library Association in 2013. Librarians know that public libraries are about so much more than books. However, the general public may not know this. Makerspaces offer public libraries an opportunity to engage with their communities and collapse the boundaries of the traditional public perception of the 'library equals books' brand. The impact of makerspaces is still to be determined, but it is an exciting new wave of innovation that libraries of varying types are embracing with gusto.

## Engagement with readers inside and outside of the library

Lloyd describes an innovative idea of a participatory display in which anyone who visits the Eden Prairie Public Library writes on a board the reason for their visit (Lloyd, 2014). This is a participative and original way to engage with everyone who visits the library in a visual way. It is a quick win and one that would be successful at many types of libraries, including public, school, academic and perhaps special. There is an increasing emphasis on health and well-being in Western societies where the latest epidemic is obesity. Obesity has more than doubled worldwide since 1980. In 2014, 39% of adults aged 18 years and older were overweight and 13% were obese (World Health Organization, 2015). Health and public libraries have a duty to engage with their readers about healthy eating and healthy cooking. Woodworth describes a series of cooking events held at a public library in New Jersey. The most successful cooking demonstration was one that was held outside of the library, in the parking lot, showing the local community how to grill pizza (Woodworth, 2014). This is a novel idea for raising the visibility of the library in the community and engaging with readers. It demonstrates again that getting outside of the physical library increases the visibility of the librarian and library. In Scotland, the East Dunbartonshire Leisure & Culture (EDCL) trust launched a pop-up health library complete with books and health information. This is in line with the EDLC commitment to promoting health and well-being (New Pop-Up Library, 2015). This innovative approach to providing services outside of the library promotes the visibility of public libraries to the community in a key strategic area for the trust and for society.

Aligning public library impact to societal big issues such as health and well-being, obesity and ageing is a strategic way for librarians to demonstrate value to their communities. Every country in the world is reported to have an increasingly ageing population.

People aged 60 or older are estimated to make up 21.1% of the world's population by 2050 (United Nations, 2013, p. xii). Dublin City's Central Public Library collaborated with an advocacy group called Age Action during Positive Ageing week on a human book event. The aim of the event was to get people talking and thinking about stereotypes that can affect both young and old people. Age Action reported that 'the simplicity of the event had a meaningful impact' (Age Action Ireland, 2013). The World Health Organisation has set up a website, www.agefriendlyworld.org, to promote age-friendly cities and communities. This represents an opportunity for librarians working in those cities and communities to engage in a global societal initiative to promote healthy ageing and increase awareness of their contribution in the process. Customer service has on occasion been found to be lacking, particularly as was found by the research that led to the creation of the Idea Stores in London. This is an area that is important to readers and influences their experience. The service attitude of library staff and the ambience of the library are also valued (Nagat, Sakai, & Kawai, 2007). The use of facilities for community groups and cultural activities such as author visits, readings, poetry sessions and so forth also adds value. Extending services to local businesses also adds economic value to communities. In developing countries, public libraries add social and economic value (Nasir Uddin, Quaddus, & Islam, 2006).

## Social media

Use of social media at two diverse Canadian public libraries was found to be valuable for the generation and dissemination of community-generated knowledge. Twitter was found to engage users in deep interaction and a successful strategy was to approach local influencers – people with large social followings in a community – to re-tweet library announcements or participate in online conversations (Forcier, Rathi, & Given, 2013). Many public libraries are beginning to use products such as Zinio and Overdrive to make information products such as e-books and e-zines more accessible to the public. The strength of social media lies in the way that readers create and share content to market such products independently of libraries. For example, this YouTube video created by a reader (and author) gives an overview of how to use these products with his choice of public libraries: https://www.youtube.com/watch?v=tH4XqZhSl3c. Products such as LibraryThing, Bibliocommons and Acquabrowser have opened up public library OPACs to enable a social discovery experience to readers. Reviews on the Bibliocommons website from multiple public libraries and readers are positive. Research shows that user-generated lists (e.g. I own this) and ratings are used, but other features are underused (Spiteri & Tarulli, 2012). Public libraries that adopt knowledge management strategies 'ensure their survival, provide excellent services to society, gain competitive advantage…innovate and adopt best practices' (Teng & Hawamdeh, 2002). With regard to social media, Forcier et al. (2013) developed a knowledge management framework for social media use that may be of interest to public librarians.

## Co-location and open libraries

Benstead, Spacey, and Goulding (2004) found that rural communities benefited from an evolved approach to the traditional mobile and public library service to rural communities in England. The new improved service is co-located library services. Research gathered from 40 local authorities demonstrated that 26 of them worked with partners to deliver library services to rural areas. Twenty-two of them were delivered through shared use of community facilities – most through local village halls or community centres. A minority were delivered through the few remaining village shops and post offices. In Asfordby, an Information and Study Centre provides Internet access, study facilities and library services coupled with a traditional mobile library service operating in the evenings and on weekends. A survey showed that social inclusion, lifelong learning and heightened awareness of the mobile library service were successful outcomes of the centre.

Of the 500 public library service points in Denmark, 81 operate open libraries (Johannsen, 2012). Open libraries offer communities a third place. Oldenburg describes the home as the first place, work as the second and areas where communities congregate for creative endeavour as the third place. The third place is important for civil society, democracy and connectedness. Public libraries arguably already fulfil the role of third place, but open libraries do so in a more coherent way because they are by default more open; therefore, they are more accessible to all. Open libraries are essentially staffless libraries, where members of the community in possession of a smart or swipe library card gain access to the public library space and materials. It would seem that the librarian is completely invisible in open libraries because they are physically absent. The impact of open libraries on the visibility of the librarian has not been researched in the LIS literature and represents a significant gap in evidence. It could be argued that in the case of public libraries their raison d'etre is to provide reading and learning material and a space to readers so that the involvement of a librarian in open libraries is secondary. However, that represents a lack of understanding of what a public librarian does. Open libraries do not pop up out of nowhere. The librarian is in the background using her acquisition skills to choose a collection of materials for the library; her organisation skills to plan events in the library that attract authors, musicians and artists; her management skills to ensure that the library operates smoothly and is a safe place for the community; her creative skills to make the library a welcoming and social space for readers; and her technical skills to facilitate self-service, ease of browsability and access to all formats of materials.

In an era of self-service and heightened Internet connectivity, the importance of social interaction with a librarian or library staff that a public library visitor of any age might expect to gain is absent in staffless and even in some staffed libraries. The low cost and convenience of self-service has been well documented and is here to stay (Zhong, 2007), but readers and librarians may well lose out if the social gap is not addressed. Furthermore, some people with mental health issues find solace in staffed public libraries. One study showed that their experience of visiting public libraries where library staff knew them and their interests enhanced the value of the experience to them (Brewster, 2014). The users' experience of a public library is not something that is taken into account when closures are decided upon; more research is needed in this area. Self-service frees up librarians and library staff from routine tasks and offers an opportunity to bridge the social gap by engagement with readers in a more visible way. Self-service challenges librarians to step outside of their comfort zone and 'requires more of librarians' (Zhong, 2007, p. 105). For example, librarians can raise their profile by providing Internet training sessions held in the library or by developing online tutorials for finding quality information. Public librarians must review provision to local communities, including rurally isolated and deprived urban areas, according to the needs of those individual communities.

In some ways, digital libraries and portals are similar to open libraries in which the librarian is unseen and completely invisible. The Digital Public Library of America (DPLA) 'opened its doors' in April 2013 after more than 2 years of development. Development involved librarians, archivists, museum workers and digital system designers. It is an excellent example of collaborative work that showcases the best of the nation's public domain content. Complete with apps and personalized features, it has been described as 'an amazing frontier for information' (O'Leary, 2013). The European equivalent is Europeana, a similar digital cultural heritage portal launched in 2008 with strong political endorsement at the highest European levels (Purday, 2009). Purday stresses that a critical success factor for Europeana is the application of standard metadata practices across the participating institutions. Metadata represent an area of expertise for librarians. The success of Europeana and the DPLA is down to several interdependent factors and players, but without librarians, neither project would have gotten off of the ground.

The role of the librarian in the provision and management of public library services regardless of format (open or staffed or digital) is one that must be incessantly highlighted to decision-makers in councils. The public librarian must not lose sight of the three core values that have stood the test of time: books, free access and the library as a place in the current disruptive technological climate (Sheppard, 2006). In 2006, Sheppard argued that a unifying vision for the future public library was lacking and causing ambiguity for public librarians. However, almost a decade later, librarians have responded to disruptive technology by embracing it, as seen previously with the advent of makerspaces and open libraries. Public libraries are still a community stronghold. They respond to Maslow's highest level of need – 'self-actualisation'. It is simply not possible to have public libraries without librarians. This message must be driven home to stakeholders making decisions about closures. When Sheffield public library closed for 8 weeks in 1995, a study showed that readers 'missed the library for a reason related to their social value or because it had become an indispensable part of their lives' (Proctor, Usherwood, & Sobczyk, 1997). Future research will show what the effect of current public library closures in the United Kingdom in the future will be.

In London, a complete re-branding of the public library took place with the launch of Idea Stores over 10 years ago. It is essentially a brand overhaul because much of the activities and events that happen in Idea Stores are similar to public libraries today. However, it is open 7 days a week, and there is a deep emphasis on education, with up to 900 courses run a year. The staff members of the Idea Store are all highly visible to their visitors, with staff employed as 'floor walkers' and no longer hidden behind desks. It is a highly inclusive brand with community members working in front-facing, customer service roles. However, very few qualified librarians are employed, making up just 10% of the staff. In Tower Hamlets, the Idea Store was set up in response to a large public consultation project with its community. Over 600 people were interviewed. The consultation was undertaken by an external market research company. The secret of the success of Idea Stores consists of significant investment, re-branding and a response to an identified need. The deputy head of the Idea Store, Sergio Dogliani, says its success is about keeping values: 'It is the attention we have always put on people (customers, staff), not just on things (buildings, books)' (Godowski & Dogliani, 2014). The three values of Ideas Stores are 'engage, empower and enrich'. A full interview is available on the This Week in Libraries Vimeo channel. The Idea Store has inspired other libraries in Europe, including a public library in Piacenza, Italy (Maltoni, 2013).

## Publishing research

Publishing research in LIS journals is a useful way to actively contribute to the LIS profession. However, for librarians to increase visibility to potential customers, then it is worth picking a topic of interest to this audience, researching it and publishing it in an academic journal outside of the LIS sector. For health sciences, try a medical/ nursing/multidisciplinary journal. For academic libraries, try a journal for higher education. For school libraries, try an educational journal or newsletter. Topics of interest to all professions include 'how to find accurate information online', 'how to do a literature review in X topic/discipline', 'using social media to keep up to date in X topic/discipline', getting the most out of X search engine or getting references right first time...the possibilities are many. As a librarian, *you are the expert* in these areas and you may be surprised to find that many professionals engaged in research are interested in the experts view on this. In large organisations including universities and national health organisations, the value and importance of the role of the librarian is seldom understood or ill perceived. Walton and Grant state that 'Publishing in LIS literature and other disciplines will put you on an equal footing with other academics and will go some way to boosting the reputation of the LIS profession' (Writing up Your Project Findings, 2013, p. 192).

The examples that have been drawn from the literature in this chapter highlight commonalities in the following ways:

- Change and improvement take time. In more than one example, increasing the impact of a service took more than 10 years.
- Change requires that people have a shared vision and are able to work together as a team.
- Collaboration is a successful way of demonstrating impact and brings value to the work that librarians do in the eyes of faculty or other departments within an organisation and collaboration with external organisations.
- Students, researchers and general readers appreciate help, and when they can make this positive association of assistance with a librarian, this in turn increases the value of the librarian to them.
- The model of embedded librarian works well in some settings. Librarians need to be cautious about defining roles and responsibilities in an embedded scenario; that is, they should not be taking on the work of academics, nor should they lose contact with other librarians within their organisation.

- If introducing a change, then it is crucial to measure the impact that this has by comparing data (qualitative, quantitative) before and after the change intervention takes place.
- Librarians will be successful if they actively respond to their community's needs.

It was mentioned at the outset that librarians need to be ready in times of economic crisis and economic prosperity. Being ready means being visible. Heightened visibility is the key to successful librarianship. It is proposed that a visibility emergency kit should be assembled and revised every 6 months. Contents of the kit are outlined in the next section.

## Visibility emergency kit

In times of emergency, when a librarian is fearful for their position or library, the following elements are recommended to make up a visibility emergency kit:

- Critical scientific papers showing evidence of the value and impact of librarians and libraries.
- Vision, mission and value statement of library.
- One page of key performance indicators aligned to strategic organisational outcomes in two formats – one page and an infographic.
- One recent month's supply of positive feedback from readers and key stakeholders.
- Spare budget for visibility campaign.
- Pop-up portable library display ready to take to the next available event to promote the work of the library staff and usefulness of their work to the organisation.
- One month's advance supply of scheduled social media posts (blog, Twitter, Facebook).

Know where to get reliable information during an emergency.

- Contact details for library association and union.

## Notes

Access to Research Project: http://accesstoresearch.pls.org.uk/.
Book Week Scotland: http://www.scottishbooktrust.com/reading/book-week-scotland/love-letters-to-libraries.
School library survey instruments: http://digital-literacy.syr.edu/RESOURCES/Surveys.
Project Enable: http://projectenable.syr.edu/.
Public Libraries News: http://www.publiclibrariesnews.com/.
The Library Campaign: http://www.librarycampaign.com/.
EBLIDA: http://www.eblida.org/activities/advocacy-and-lobbying-for-libraries-in-europe.html.
FAIR Campaign: https://fair.alia.org.au/.
LIANZA: http://www.lianza.org.nz/our-work/campaigns.
AFLIA: http://aflia.net/index.php/about-aflia.
Interview with Sergio Dogliani: https://vimeo.com/101355018.

# Into the future: the future is now

*There is nothing like a dream to create the future.*

**Victor Hugo**

## Libraries

Behind every good library is a good librarian. However, not every good librarian needs a library. A librarian's unique personality often filters through to the reader's experience of a library and information service. Librarians are flexible and may effectively work in a variety of environments including outside a physical library. As has been shown through the interviews with librarians in this book, increasingly they engage in outreach activities and heighten their visibility by working outside the confines of a library.

Good librarians are the people who make everyone feel welcome. They go out of their way to meet the information need of the reader. They make a 'deal (drop everything and listen)' with visitors to the library. It does not matter what task a librarian is working on. If they receive a phone call, an email or someone walks into the library or office with a query, librarians must make a DEAL with them. They may be just looking for directions to another part of the building, they may want to know the time, they may be interested in the latest stem cell research available and whether the library can provide them with a literature search; regardless of how big or small their query is, they have come looking for assistance. If the librarian considers herself to be part of the service industry, then it is essential that they stop and listen. This type of personal interaction and outreach to people is part of the essence of librarianship. All librarians interviewed alluded to the importance of making connections with people in a professional and courteous way.

Librarians are committed professionals. Two of the librarians from the case studies took demotions to follow their dreams and take positions in librarianship where they felt they could really make a difference. Librarians select material and content based on readers' needs and preferences. Libraries are special places. However, they simply would not be as successful if there was no librarian to manage it, to make sure the space responds to the whole community, to meet the needs of as many citizens as possible and to make the space an inviting and inclusive one.

## Neutral generalists

Two librarians interviewed talked about the 360° perspective that librarians hold within any organisation. Because librarians are neutral, they do not take sides.

They may be seen as a trusted asset in an organisation. They often know more about what is going on in an organisation than other people, including management. Librarians offer a unique perspective to a problem. They can bring an alternative way of looking at a situation, which may help to turn it around. Librarians make connections and have an ability to approach a problem from a 360° angle, not just a right angle. This makes librarians key to emerging trends such as team science. Librarians can join any team and offer an alternative way of looking at a topic.

## Democracy

Libraries uphold the principles of democracy, promoting free access to ideas, through literature and digital media. The value of books and libraries must never be underestimated. The willful destruction of literature, books and libraries is an attack on democracy. Events like the burning of books in Berlin in 1933 under the Nazi regime and the ransacking of the Central Library of Mosul and other libraries in Iraq in 2015 by Islamic extremists, demonstrate this all too well. Even through tumultuous times such as those in South Africa where 20 public libraries were burnt down and the destruction of Sarajevo's National Library, libraries represent a cultural identity of a people. This must be protected. Visibility in these instances is fraught with danger, but it is a battle that must be won. As Lor (2014) has stated, 'The risks of invisibility outweigh those of visibility'. The reaction to risk must be to draw upon expertise in our profession and work together to build a more robust library outlook. Librarians have to walk the talk as leaders and share the remarkable positive impact that they have on people's lives with the world.

## A societal good

There are some things that are not easy to qualify or report back as evidence of the inherent societal good that libraries and librarians add to the communities they work in and people who engage with them. A snapshot of this is captured by two librarians interviewed, one a school librarian, who stated:

> Some things that are not measured are things like the boy with special needs who finds it hard to make friends or a student who is lonely who uses the school library like a type of haven and place for him to go during breaks.

The other, a public librarian who recalled:

> I know that I may be the only person that this old lady gets to speak to the whole day, or even the whole week.

## Openness

Finland is a type of democratic library utopia, where the principle that underpins libraries and democracy – openness – is not just an ideal, but a citizen's reality. Everyone has access to every library, regardless of their status or position in society or what memberships they hold. For example, all citizens can access academic libraries or the parliamentary library. Library access is a citizen's right. The rest of the world can learn from the Finnish example and can model it as best practice. The outcomes of this openness and the value placed on information, which extends to a right written in the Finnish constitution, have been a highly literate, happy populace. Finland consistently scores among the highest literacy rates in the world. According to the Organisation of Economic Co-operation and Development (OECD), roughly every fifth Finn reads at high levels. These levels mean that that they can perform multiple-step operations to integrate, interpret or synthesise information from complex or lengthy texts that involve conditional and/or competing information. In addition, they can make complex inferences and appropriately apply background knowledge as well as interpret or evaluate subtle truth claims or arguments (OECD, 2013). Finland ranked sixth in the world as the happiest country in 2015 according to the *World Happiness Report* (Helliwell, Layard, & Sachs, 2015). They too have fallen on hard economic times, resulting in re-structuring and downsizing, but the Finnish answer has been a human one, with a focus on helping each other through collaboration and networking (Tuominen & Saarti, 2012).

## Change

There has been a fundamental shift in what librarians do in the past 10–20 years. So much change has happened and often with such a swift pace that the librarian has barely had time to notice. For example, in health libraries, transactions are primarily made in a virtual environment; librarians spend less time on administrative tasks and more time on value added initiatives. Fewer people are using hospital libraries in the traditional sense. Health care professionals still use library spaces, but in new and exciting ways. It is no longer to browse their favourite journal, as they can do this in the palm of their hand thanks to the access that librarians set up with publishers. They come to the library to meet with colleagues, to give lectures, to get a cup of coffee, to pet the therapy dog or to liaise with the librarian on a joint research project. Health science librarians are becoming strategic partners and collaborators in health teams; they are evolving beyond a support service.

In school libraries, there has been a shift in emphasis away from the printed book and towards multiple formats of information. The focus is on learning outcomes and making creative learning environments where students can thrive. Makerspaces are gaining popularity, and librarians are experimenting with these in their school libraries.

What public libraries offer to their communities is changing, but the principles of public libraries are staying the same. The physical space that library buildings offer is being used but in new and innovative ways. For example, in the United Kingdom, libraries have been welcoming musicians since 2005 via the 'Get It Loud in Libraries' initiative, which has attracted crowds of over 28,000 people. This sees up-and-coming bands perform live in libraries and gives young people opportunities to engage with cultural and artistic events. In the United States, some public libraries such as Connecticut's Westport Library and Chicago Public Library are making robots available to visitors. Librarians see this as a way to teach children and young people programming skills. Initiatives such as these are making the headlines in major publications, including the *Wall Street Journal* (When Robots Join the Library, 2014). As we know from Oscar Wilde, 'There is only one thing worse than being talked about, and that is not being talked about'. These are examples of public libraries responding to their communities and reclaiming libraries as true community spaces in the new Internet century.

## Trends

There is a lot going on in libraries today that is innovative. Libraries are turning areas into makerspaces and lending out robots for young people to learn programming skills. The information world is a rapidly evolving landscape. The International Federation of Library Associations and Institutions (IFLA, 2013) has noted five key trends likely to change our environment. Each trend has its own implications for libraries and librarians. The trends are around the areas of access to information, online education, privacy, global empowerment of connected societies and the transformation of the economy through technology. Each trend represents big opportunities for librarians in traditional areas such as digital preservation, copyright and data protection, privacy and managing information. Opportunities are also emerging for librarians in new areas such as managing data, open access, open learning, consumer technology, gaming, cloud computing and transparency of government.

## The world is online

A global digital snapshot taken in January 2015 of over 240 countries in the world shows that over half of the world's population (i.e. 3.649 billion people) are mobile phone users. This penetration is forecast to continue. Over 3 billion people are using the Internet, and 2 billion have active social media accounts. The world is online and ever more inter-connected (We Are Social, 2015). According to the IFLA trends report (2013), by 2016, the Middle East and Africa will see a 104% increase in mobile data traffic. Sixty-four percent of U.S. adults own a smartphone (Pew Research Center, 2014c). What do mobile users need? They need websites that are designed and optimised for mobiles. Librarians need to focus on this need as a priority. Seventy-four percent of U.S. adults use social media (Pew Research Center, 2014b). What do social media users need? They need reminders about the value of librarians and libraries to society.

Librarians need to proactively use social media to engage with users in their online space by responding to their information needs.

Anyone commuting on a train, subway, metro, underground, tram or city/suburban bus will notice the sheer number of workers with their vision firmly focused on a mobile screen of various size. Take a look across the train platform on a rush hour working day and just observe how everyone's head is buried in a phone, tablet or mobile device. Information anytime, anyplace, on any device is the new norm, particularly for people on the move. The ubiquitous nature of information today makes it absolutely essential for the librarian to be embedded into mobile technology.

## Collective intelligence and collaboration

Raising awareness and visibility through collaboration with other librarians from different sectors in the community is a safe and proven strategy that works (e.g. school libraries working with public libraries, public libraries working with academic libraries and health libraries with public or academic libraries, etc.). We now have the tools to collaborate in a virtual world where there is the potential to reach out and engage with other librarians to further our collective intelligence for the good of the profession. Tools such as Wikis, Flickr, Linkedin, open source technologies, blogs and specialised open-access journals give a collective voice to librarians. For example, the potential for librarians to collectively find better information solutions beyond the current array of discovery tools and library management systems is vast. Virtual collaborative spaces for librarians to reach out and connect with each other will enable librarians to combine larger data sets and analyse them for better evidence and better solutions.

## Professional reputation

With the outside world, the professional reputation of librarians in general is partly managed mainly through professional library associations. However, there is an onus on individual librarians to manage their professional reputation in a coherent way themselves. There is a need to cultivate a collegial approach to managing librarians' reputations. This extends to social media profiles as well as interaction with readers and others online and in person.

## Rise of smarts

Google senior executives talk about how they employ 'smart creatives', employees who are encouraged to run with their own ideas, take risks and combine technical depth with management expertise and creativity. They differ from 'knowledge workers', a term coined by Peter Drucker in 1959, who develop expertise in specific areas, but rarely in more than one set of distinct skills. Google executives maintain that 'Smart creatives are key to achieving success in the Internet Century' (Schmidt & Rosenberg, 2014, p.17). Government rhetoric talks of 'smart cities', which are 'Enabling and encouraging the citizen to become a more active and participative member of the community' (Department for Business Innovation & Skills, 2013). Smart cities are seen to be attractive locations to live, work and visit. Urban dwellers are invited to participate in open source participative programs such as SmartCitizen (smartcitizen.me) to connect people with their environment and city. The purpose of this initiative is to create more effective and optimised relationships between resources, technology, communities, services and events. Librarians have opportunities to become involved in projects such as these, which are perhaps slightly outside of their immediate zone of vision. By 2030, 70% of the world's population is projected to live in cities (IFLA, 2013). However, smart cities and smart economies are going to need smart librarians.

## Evidence-based librarianship

Two areas of research need attention to increase the value of librarianship to other disciplines. The areas are visibility and quality. The visibility of research undertaken by librarians needs to increase. The quality of research needs to be enhanced across all sectors of librarianship. This requires a culture shift, including adopting an evidence-based approach to measuring impact and value and publishing findings as research. New graduates must be encouraged to come to the workplace wearing an evidence-based hat. A grounding in evidence-based librarianship must be given to students in Masters of Library Science (MLS) programmes. Repositories are one way to increase visibility and access to library and information science (LIS) research. However, library associations, national libraries, iSchools and publishers have a role to play here. Some publishers publish virtual open access issues of LIS journal titles to coincide with library conferences (e.g. *Health Information and Libraries Journal*) and the European Association of Health

Information and Libraries (EAHIL). Publishers also give discounts to librarians on LIS periodicals. EBSCO makes library and information research abstracts available as a free library research database called Library, Information Science & Technology Abstracts (LISTA). Emerald makes a library resources section available on their website. Elsevier makes Library Connect available to librarians for free, which includes white papers, multimedia resources and an extensive archive of webinars.

Progress is evident. For example, some specialised LIS open-access journals are appearing, such as *Collaborative Librarianship* http://www.collaborativelibrarianship.org/, http://weaveux.org/, http://journal.radicallibrarianship.org/, *Weave* and the *Journal of Radical Librarianship*. The University of Alberta libraries in Canada have played a strong leadership role in managing the Evidence-Based Library and Information Practice (EBLIP) open-access journal. Open access journals and Blogs such as *In the Library with the Lead Pipe* http://www.inthelibrarywiththeleadpipe.org/, http://www.libfocus.com/, http://blogs.lse.ac.uk/impactofsocialsciences/, Libfocus, Informed, Impact of Social Sciences blog and academicwritinglibrarian.blogspot.ie are all adding to the evidence base of librarianship. Library associations that produce library journals should aim to make these openly accessible. Notwithstanding the argument about a journal being a membership benefit, there is an option of making a current volume available after a 6- or 12-month embargo. Some library associations such as CILIP make access to LIS bibliographic and full-text databases available as a member benefit, which enhances the value of personal membership to librarians.

Leadership has been shown by IFLA, which launched an open-access repository (library.ifla.org) in 2013, making all IFLA papers, policies and research freely and openly available. This preserves this important body of research for future generations and makes access to research for librarians seamless.

The quality of research in LIS needs attention. There has been a recent call for LIS researchers to move beyond the survey as a research method (Halpern, Eaker, Jackson, & Bouquin, 2015). They found that the contents of 1880 articles in LIS journals were analysed with results that showed only 16% 'qualified as research'. Elevating the quality of research methods taught and used is a job for university heads of departments with responsibility for curriculum for library and information studies at the graduate and undergraduate level. At a minimum, the LIS curriculum should include an introduction to evidence-based librarianship.

# Fishing

Wah and Choh (2008) proposed a content delivery model for libraries using the analogy of fishing. Readers go on the Internet and fish for information. Libraries can sprinkle content bytes into the sea, rivers and pools where they fish (i.e. search engines, social networks, research portals). What libraries have in abundance is content. What users rate above anything else is good content. The ways and means by which content is obtained by surfers needs to be absolutely free of hassle. Thus far, no library website has claimed to have mastered ultimate reader engagement. In the absence of this, meeting surfers and fishermen where they are is the answer. It is also about seeing the quest for information from the fisherman's point of view and stepping into their shoes.

# Power through collaboration

Greater collaboration is required among national, academic, public and special libraries with regard to electronic resources, database subscriptions, e-journals and e-books. This is an on-going problem. The temptation and attractiveness of big deals continues to prevail. As a consequence, smaller libraries and readers with little or no affiliation continue to make up the 'information poor'. Leadership is required, especially from large, powerful libraries and librarians to bring subscriptions into a level playing field. Publishers' grip on library budgets must loosen. Finlib offers a utopian model in which all citizens access any library. Can other librarians follow this lead? As has been observed, in an online world 'the user does not care which library serves him the document – he is just interested in getting the information' (Mainka et al., 2013). This concept was taken on board by the National Library Board of Singapore. Its online catalogue service was made available via the application program interface (API) to the developer of a book club portal called Bookjetty. This increased access to their catalogue by 1000 visits per week (Wah & Choh, 2008).

# Synthetic biology

Synthetic biology holds massive potential for the future of information storage, a natural domain of librarians. Scientists have discovered that DNA is a robust and energy-free way to store data and information. Everything from Shakespeare's sonnets to the complete collections of all TV, film and videos ever made can be coded to synthetic strings of DNA (Moore, 2013). This is a growing area that librarians can observe with interest.

# Space

Library as a place is an evolving area of debate. The needs of communities need libraries to fit into a smart culture. Self-service has evolved, but the role of the librarian in all of this needs to be highly visible. People will always need a place to stop and think, reflect and just be. Libraries in whatever forms will be needed as places for people to gather. The use of physical libraries has changed and will continue to change and evolve.

# Recognition

Serious lobbying is required to elevate the status of librarianship, in particular school librarianship. As has been noted, a grass roots approach through library associations and librarians has been attempted, but more needs to be done. A more co-ordinated approach through state departments and governments with evidence to back up the value of the school librarian is needed on a grand scale to effect real change.

# Robots

In July 2014, *Wired* magazine included an article on what jobs robots were likely to take from humans in the future. Of the seven jobs highlighted, librarians were one. The argument was that as technology advances and self-service becomes commonplace, the need for librarians or library technicians to check out books will be obsolete. This demonstrates a fundamental lack of understanding about what librarians do or at least the breadth of their jobs. The problem is one of context. 'The library does not have a product problem. The library does not have a book problem. The library has a context problem' (OCLC, 2014, p. 91). Librarians need to make their roles known to society more openly and proactively.

# Consumer choice

No time in history has had a greater impact on consumerism that the age in which we now live, the information age. People have immediate access to information 24/7 and to people from all over the globe via the Internet. This fuels growth and innovation, enhances collaboration and brings people together in a virtual world for all kinds of initiatives. One is to make products for consumption. This is when Darwin's theory of survival of the fittest has high applicability to information products. Three-dimensional printers are now available on desktop computers. Public and academic libraries are dabbling in their use.

# The future

Eric Schmidt, Executive Chairman of Google, has a practical approach to planning a future strategy. His advice is 'Start by asking what will be true in 5 years and work backward' (Schmidt & Rosenberg, 2014, p. 92). In 5 years, we know that people will use mobile technology, the World Wide Web and social media to connect, discover and learn. In 5 years, we know that people will need help with finding, filtering, managing and trusting information. In 5 years we know that reading and writing will still be important. These are starting points for librarians.

When it comes to the future, there are at least four potential realities: one that is plausible, possible, predictable or probable (Table 49). It is almost impossible to predict what the librarian or library will be doing or look like in 5 or 10 or even 50 years. The challenge is the fast pace of change. Librarianship has evolved tremendously in the last 20 years, which was caused primarily by technology, the rise of the Internet and the

Table 49  **The four futures**

| Plausible | Possible |
|-----------|----------|
| Predictable | Probable |

consumer-driven society in which we live. For example, in some areas of librarianship, the health sciences the future is now. The pace of change in health care is on a par with the pace of change in technology. As health care is driven by technological developments and scientific discoveries, the pace of change for health librarianship is doubled.

The possibilities of the future are limitless. If we pause to look at how far the human race has come in the last few centuries, we see that some incredible advances have been made, particularly in technology and communications. The invention of the telephone in 1876 led to interconnected communications across the world. In the early 1990s, the Internet and World Wide Web globally revolutionised telecommunications and contact between humans. Just 20 years ago in the developed world, people walked to a telephone booth to make a phone call. Today, a call can be made from any place with a mobile phone. The mainframe computers of the 1960s led to developments in terminals to interface with them in the form of personal computers in the 1980s. Today, the personal computer is found in the average adult's pocket in the form of a smartphone. Technology has advanced at incredible speed in the past 50 years. The next 50 will plausibly show more radical changes that we cannot yet imagine. The tablets of today will be replaced by a new, yet to be imagined technology. Keyboards and the mouse may be things of the past. The written word may no longer be written by a human. Verbal communication will increase with voice recognition software. Interactions and communications in real time are already possible. Facebook has only been around since 2007 and has 1.44 billion monthly active users in 2015 (Statisca.com).

## Planning for the future

Daniel Goleman (1995) refers to emotional intelligence as the way that we manage ourselves and our relationships. Being emotionally intelligent is a measure of how self-aware we are, how motivated we are and how well we can tune into other people. There are five strands to being emotionally intelligent as defined by Goleman. They are worth reiterating here because they will assist librarians to progress and make a difference in their working lives. The five areas are self-awareness, managing ones emotions, staying motivated, being empathetic to others and finally social skills. These qualities arguably can be developed and learned. They will assist you as a librarian and assist your team to thrive and do well. They are fundamentally leadership traits. Leadership takes strength, dedication, durability and sensibility. Leadership will empower you to follow through on your visibility improvement plan.

Librarians are now equipped with a visibility emergency kit, a VIP 10-step plan to embrace the Big Opportunity. Librarians everywhere must be ready for change under all circumstances. Scenario planning is a good way to embrace change. Librarians need to be ready with a response for the day when the chief executive officer walks into the library and says, 'I may have €50,000 left in the budget, would you be able to come up with a viable plan for its effective use?' That day may not be so far in the future. The librarian needs to have an eye on the future and be ready with a business plan to make the best of the resources available, whether they are presented with an additional €50,000 or a €50,000 cut.

# Universal access to knowledge

Recalling the words of Brewster Kahle (computer scientist, digital librarian and founder of the Internet Archive), who said in 2008, 'It's a great time to be a librarian. Universal access to all knowledge is within our grasp'. This is the Enlightenment ideal. The conviction of the Enlightenment that scientific investigation of nature and society leads to improvements and progress extends to the values of many libraries.

# Values stay the same

The values and principles of librarianship have not changed. Ranganathan's wisdom presented in 1928 remains true today:

Books are for use
Every reader his book
Every book its reader
Save the time of the reader
A library is a growing organism

For librarians, five similar principles may guide them:

Society needs librarians
Every librarian its organisation
Every organisation its librarian
Save the time of the organisation
A librarian never stops learning

The past centuries have been the centuries of the library. This is the century of the librarian. The focus needs to shift from the library to the librarian. It needs to be embraced wholeheartedly by all librarians, who need to use all of the tools at their disposal, such as technology and ideas, while remaining true to the values and ethics of librarianship. Be proactive, be responsive and be brave and then you will be on the road to career fulfilment and total visibility.

# Notes

**Get it Loud in Libraries**: For more information see http://www.getitloudinlibraries.com/.
**Team Science**: This is defined by the National Cancer Institute as a collaborative effort to address a scientific challenge that leverages the strengths and expertise of professionals trained in different fields. See https://www.teamsciencetoolkit.cancer.gov/public/WhatIsTS.aspx.

# Appendix 1

## Public library visibility survey

Q1  When was the last time you visited your local public library?

In the last week ☐
In the last month ☐
In the last year ☐
Between 1–5 years ago ☐
Never ☐

Q2  Do you know where your local public library is?

Yes                         No

Q3  Have you ever visited your local public library's website?

Yes                         No

Q4  Did you know about the following services available at your local public library's website?

| | | |
|---|---|---|
| Download e-books | Yes | No |
| Download audiobooks | Yes | No |
| Read newspapers and magazines online | Yes | No |
| Learn languages online | Yes | No |

Q5  Please circle your age group:

1–18            19–35            36–55            56–65            66+

Q6  Please select your current status:

| | | |
|---|---|---|
| Employed (full time) | Employed (part time) | Self-employed |
| Unemployed | Homemaker | Retired |
| Schoolchild (primary and secondary education) | | Student (third level) |

Thank you!

# References

Aabø, S. (2005). Are public libraries worth their price?: a contingent valuation study of Norwegian public libraries. *New Library World, 106*(11/12), 487–495.

Aabø, S. (2009). Libraries and return on investment (ROI): a meta–analysis. *New Library World, 110*(7/8), 311–324.

Abels, E. G., Cogdill, K. W., & Zach, L. (2002). The contributions of library and information services to hospitals and academic health sciences centers: a preliminary taxonomy. *Journal of the Medical Library Association, 90*(3), 276.

Adair, J. E. (2006). *Leadership and motivation: The fifty-fifty rule and the eight key principles of motivating others.* London: Kogan Page Publishers.

Age Action Ireland. (October 2013). *Finding out what's under the cover.* Ageing Matters. p. 14.

Aguilar, P., Keating, K., Schadl, S., & Van Reenen, J. (2011). Reference as outreach: meeting users where they are. *Journal of Library Administration, 51*(4), 343–358.

Ahmad, M., & Abawajy, J. H. (2014). Digital library service quality assessment model. *Procedia-Social and Behavioral Sciences, 129,* 571–580.

Aitken, E. M., Powelson, S. E., Reaume, R. D., & Ghali, W. A. (2011). Involving clinical librarians at the point of care: results of a controlled intervention. *Academic Medicine, 86*(12), 1508–1512.

Allbon, E. (2005). IT'S ALIVE! The birth of LawBore and the indispensability of the law librarian. *Legal Information Management, 5*(4), 211–215.

Allee, N. J., Blumenthal, J., Jordan, K., Lalla, N., Lauseng, D., Rana, G., et al. (2014). One institution's experience in transforming the health sciences library of the future. *Medical Reference Services Quarterly, 33*(1), 1–16.

Allsopp, J. (July 30, 2014). *We bean counters need to speak out about NHS cuts.* The Guardian. Retrieved from http://www.theguardian.com/healthcare-network/2014/jul/30/finance-managers-speak-out-cuts-nhs. Accessed 15.10.14.

Alto, T. (2012). Mary E. Hall: dawn of the professional school librarian. *School Library Monthly, 29*(1).

American Library Association. (2014). *School library legislation: Elementary and Secondary Education Act (ESEA) Talking Points.* [Web log]. Retrieved from http://www.ala.org/advocacy/esea-tp.

Andrews, R. (March 2014). *The thick of it – Being an embedded librarian in a law firm* CILIP Update, 28.

Anger, W. H., Jr., & Akins, S. (2014). Pet therapy. *Journal of Consumer Health on the Internet, 18*(4), 396–400.

Anstice, I. (2014). *Public library standards in England.* Retrieved from http://www.publiclibrariesnews.com/useful/documents/public-library-standards-in-england.

Aschenbrenner, A., Blanke, T., Flanders, D., Hedges, M., & O'Steen, B. (2008). The future of repositores. *D-Lib Magazine, 14*(11/12).

Association of College and Research Libraries. (2011). *Standards for libraries in higher education.* Retrieved from http://www.ala.org/acrl/standards/standardslibraries.

Australia, Boroondara City Council. (2014). *City of Boroondara annual report 2013–14.* Retrieved from http://www.boroondara.vic.gov.au/. Accessed 07.02.15.

Australian Library and Information Association. (April 2014). *Putting a value on 'priceless':* *An independent assessment of the return on investment of special libraries in Australia.* Canberra, ACT: Australian Library and Information Association. Retrieved from www.alia.org.au/roispecials.

Bardyn, T. P., Atcheson, E., Cuddy, C., & Perry, G. J. (2013). Managing and revitalizing your career as a medical librarian: a symposium report. *Journal of Hospital Librarianship,* *13*(3), 220–230.

Baxter, S. J., & Smalley, A. W. (2003). *Check it out! The results of the school library media* *program census, final report.* St Paul, MN: Metronet. Retrieved from http://www. metrolibraries.net/res/pdfs/2002final_report.pdf.

Benstead, K., Spacey, R., & Goulding, A. (2004). Changing public library service delivery to rural communities in England. *New Library World, 105*(11/12), 400–409.

Blagden, P., Pratchett, T., & Treadway, V. (March 2014). *Supporting advocacy outside the* *profession.* CILIP Update pp. 42–43.

Blumenthal, J. (2014). The library of the future is present. *Journal of the European Association* *for Health Information and Libraries, 10*(4), 4.

Boone, T. (2011). Ensuring the visibility of librarians. *Information Outlook, 15*(1), 10–12.

Botha, E., Rene, E., & Van Deventer, M. (2009). Evaluating the impact of a special library and information Service. *Journal of Librarianship and Information Science, 41*(2), 108–123.

Bowles-Terry, M. (2012). Library instruction and academic success: a mixed-methods assess-ment of a library instruction program. *Evidence Based Library and Information Practice,* *7*(1), 82–95.

Breeding, M. (2008). Content, community, and visibility: a winning combination. *Computers* *in Libraries, 28*(4), 26–28.

Brettle, A., Maden-Jenkins, M., Anderson, L., McNally, R., Pratchett, T., Tancock, J., et al. (2011). Evaluating clinical librarian services: a systematic review. *Health Information &* *Libraries Journal, 28*(1), 3–22. http://dx.doi.org/10.1111/j.1471-1842.2010.00925.x.

Brewster, L. (2014). The public library as therapeutic landscape: a qualitative case study. *Health* *& Place, 26*, 94–99. http://dx.doi.org/10.1016/j.healthplace.2013.12.015.

Broady-Preston, J., & Lobo, A. (2011). Measuring the quality, value and impact of academic libraries: the role of external standards. *Performance Measurement and Metrics, 12*(2), 122–135. http://dx.doi.org/10.1108/14678041111149327.

Broady-Preston, J., & Swain, W. (2012). What business are we in? Value added services, core business and national library performance. *Performance Measurement and Metrics, 13*(2), 107–120.

Brodie, S. J., Biley, F. C., & Shewring, M. (2002). An exploration of the potential risks associated with using pet therapy in healthcare settings. *Journal of Clinical Nursing,* *11*(4), 444–456.

Burgin, R., Bracy, P. B., & Brown, K. (2003). *An essential connection: How quality school library* *media programs improve student achievement in North Carolina.* RB software & Consulting.

Callinan, J. (2011). Attitudes and experiences towards setting up a bibliotherapy service for the bereavement support service. In *European Association of Health Information & Libraries* *Workshop.*

Callison, D., & Baker, K. (2014). *Elements of information inquiry, evolution of models &* *measured reflection.* Knowledge Quest.

Callison, D. (November 2004). *Survey of Indiana school library media programs: A collabora-tive project between the Association for Indiana Media Educators & Indiana University –* *Indianapolis, School of Library and Information Science.* Paper presented at the 2004 AIME Conference, Indianapolis, IN. Retrieved from http://www.ilfonline.org.

Canada needs a Health Care Accord. (April 2014). *The council of Canadians*. Retrieved from http://www.canadians.org/2014accord. Accessed 15.10.14.

Caperon, L. (2014). Developing adaptable, efficient mobile library services: librarians as enablers. *Ariadne, 73*.

Cason Barratt, C., Acheson, P., & Luken, E. (2010). Reference models in the electronic library: the Miller Learning Center at the University of Georgia. *Reference Services Review, 38*(1), 44–56.

Chen, B., & Graddy, E. A. (2010). The effectiveness of nonprofit lead–organization networks for social service delivery. *Nonprofit Management and Leadership, 20*(4), 405–422.

Chowdhury, G., McMenemy, D., & Poulter, A. (2008). MEDLIS: model for evaluation of digital libraries and information services. *World Digital Libraries, 1*(1), 35–46.

Chung, H. -K. (2007). Measuring the economic value of special libraries. *The Bottom Line, 20*(1), 30–44.

Cmor, D. (2010). Academic reference librarians: getting by with a little help from our (special, public, school, law and medical librarian) friends. *Library Management, 31*(8/9), 610–620.

Colburn, S., & Haines, L. (2012). Measuring libraries' use of YouTube as a promotional tool: an exploratory study and proposed best practices. *Journal of Web Librarianship, 6*(1), 5–31. http://dx.doi.org/10.1080/19322909.2012.641789.

Collette, J. (2015). *Littlebits education community case study: Elementary school library makerspace*. Retrieved from http://littlebits.cc/case-study-elementary-school-library-makerspace.

Cooper, J., & Brewerton, G. (2013). Developing a prototype library WebApp for mobile devices. *Ariadne, 71*.

Cordray, R. (July 2014). *What jobs will robots take from humans in the future*. Wired. Retrieved from http://www.wired.com/2014/07/jobs-will-robots-take-humans-future/.

Corrall, S. (2014). Designing libraries for research collaboration in the network world: an exploratory study. *Liber Quarterly, 24*(1), 17–48.

Cox, B. L., & Jantti, M. (2012). Capturing business intelligence required for targeted marketing, demonstrating value, and driving process improvement. *Library & Information Science Research, 34*(4), 308–316.

Crawford, A. M. (May 13, 1999). *Coco pops back after vote*. [Web log post]. Retrieved from http://www.marketingmagazine.co.uk/article/57359/coco-pops-back-vote.

Creaser, C., & Spezi, V. (2012). *Working together: Evolving value for academic libraries*. Loughborough: Loughborough University.

Crossno, J. E., DeShay, C. H., Huslig, M. A., Mayo, H. G., & Patridge, E. F. (2012). A case study: the evolution of a "facilitator model" liaison program in an academic medical library. *Journal of the Medical Library Association, 100*(3), 171.

Dalton, M. (2012). Key performance indicators in Irish hospital libraries: developing outcome-based metrics to support advocacy and service delivery. *Evidence Based Library and Information Practice, 7*(4). From http://ejournals.library.ualberta.ca/index.php/EBLIP/article/view/17442.

Daly, E. (2011). Instruction where and when students need it: embedding library resources into learning management systems. In C. Kvenild, & K. Calkins (Eds.), *Embedded librarians: Moving beyond one-shot instruction* (pp. 79–91). Chicago: ACRL.

Danvers. (2014). *Northshore Community College Library action plan 2014–2015*. Massachusetts: Northshore Community College. Retrieved from library.northshore.edu/about/pdf/action-plan.pdf.

David, T. (December 30, 2014). *Your elevator pitch needs an elevator pitch*. [Web log post] Harvard Business Review. Retrieved from https://hbr.org/2014/12/your-elevator-pitch-needs-an-elevator-pitch.

Davidson, K. S., Rollins, S. H., & Cherry, E. (2013). Demonstrating our value: tying use of electronic resources to academic success. *The Serials Librarian, 65*(1), 74–79.

Dempsey, M. (2011). Blending the trends: a holistic approach to reference services. *Public Services Quarterly*, 7(1–2), 3–17.

Department of Agriculture. Office of Human Capital Management. (2009). *Tracking performance accomplishments and writing self-assessments*. Washington, DC: Department of Agriculture. Retrieved from http://www.dm.usda.gov/employ/employeerelations/docs/PerfAccomplishmentsSelfAssessment.pdf.

Department for Business Innovation & Skills. (2013). *Smart cities: Background paper*. London: UK Government. Retrieved from https://www.gov.uk/government/uploads/system/uploads/attachment_data/file/246019/bis-13-1209-smart-cities-background-paper-digital.pdf.

Department for Culture, Media & Sport, Department for communities and Local Government. In B. Lewis, & E. Vaizey (Eds.), (2014). *Independent library report for England*. London: UK Government. Retrieved from https://www.gov.uk/government/publications/independent-library-report-for-england.

Dewey, J. (1933). *How we think: A restatement of the relation of reflective thinking to the educative process*. Lexington, MA: D.C. Heath and Company.

Dublin City Council. (2009). *Dublin City Council 2010–2014 corporate plan*. Dublin: City Council.

Dublin City Council. (May 2011). *Dublin City Council workforce plan 2010–2014*. Dublin: Dublin City Council. Retrieved from http://www.environ.ie/en/LocalGovernment/PublicationsDocuments/FileDownLoad, 27321,en.pdf.

Edinburgh University Library. (February 24, 2015). *Tag it, find it!: pop up library on tour*. [Web log Post] Retrieved from http://libraryblogs.is.ed.ac.uk/popuplibrary/.

Eldredge, J. D. (2000). Evidence-based librarianship: an overview. *Bulletin of the Medical Library Association*, 88(4), 289.

Eldredge, J. D. (2004). Inventory of research methods for librarianship and informatics. *Journal of the Medical Library Association*, 92(1), 83. Retreived from http://www.ncbi.nlm.nih.gov/pmc/articles/PMC314107/.

European Agency for Safety and Health at work. (2014). Retrieved from https://www.healthy-workplaces.eu/en/stress-and-psychosocial-risks/facts-and-figures.

European Commission. (2009). *Strategic framework – Education & training 2020*. Retrieved from http://ec.europa.eu/education/policy/strategic-framework/index_en.htm.

Exeter Health Library user charter. (February 2014). Retrieved from http://services.exeter.ac.uk/eml/EHLusercharter.pdf.

Fagan, J. C. (2014). The suitability of web analytics key performance indicators in the academic library environment. *The Journal of Academic Librarianship*, 40(1), 25–34. http://dx.doi.org/10.1016/j.acalib.2013.06.005.

Fang, W., & Crawford, M. E. (2008). Measuring law library catalog web site usability: a web analytic approach. *Journal of Web Librarianship*, 2(2–3), 287–306.

Feld, K. (2013). *Launching the new library of Birmingham: A case study*. Retreived from Culturehive.co.uk.

Financial Times Corporate. (2013). *The evolving value of information management*. Virginia: Special Library Association. Retrieved from http://www.ft.com/sla.

Finch, J. (2012). Accessibility, sustainability, excellence: how to expand access to research publications. In *Report of the Working Group on Expanding Access to Published Research Findings*.

Fisher, R., & Heaney, A. (2011). A faculty perspective: strengthening at-risk students' transition to academic research through embedded librarianship. In C. Kvenild, & K. Calkins (Eds.), *Embedded librarians: Moving beyond one-shot instruction* (pp. 35–45). Chicago: ACRL.

Fister, B. (June 23, 2014). *Shocking secrets revealed! What big libraries pay for big deals.* [Web log post] Retrieved from https://www.insidehighered.com/blogs/library-babel-fish/shocking-secrets-revealed-what-big-libraries-pay-big-deals.

Fitsimmons, G. (2013). The institutional library committee, part I: a tool for garnering support. *The Bottom Line, 26*(1), 18–20.

FitzRoy, P., Hulbert, J., & Ghobadian, A. (2012). *Strategic management: The challenge of creating value.* London: Routledge.

Flood, A. (November 2014). *Authors claim victory after Liverpool drops library closure plans.* The Guardian. Retreived from http://www.theguardian.com/books/2014/nov/11/liverpool-library-closure-plans-carol-ann-duffy-caitlin-moran.

Forbes. (2014). *The world's most valuable brands.* Retrieved from http://www.forbes.com/powerful-brands/list/. Accessed 30.12.14.

Forcier, E., Rathi, D., & Given, L. M. (2013). Knowledge management and social media: a case study of two public libraries in Canada. *Journal of Information and Knowledge Management, 12*(04).

Francis, B. H., Lance, K. C., & Lietzau, Z. (2010). *School librarians continue to help students achieve standards: The third Colorado study* (Closer Look Report). Denver, CO: Colorado State Library, Library Research Service.

Franklin, B., Kyrillidou, M., & Plum, T. (2009). From usage to user: library metrics and expectations for the evaluation of digital libraries. In *Evaluation of digital libraries. An insight into useful applications and methods* (pp. 17–40).

Furness, R., & Casselden, B. (2012). An evaluation of a Books on Prescription scheme in a UK public library authority. *Health Information & Libraries Journal, 29*(4), 333–337.

Germano, M. (2011). The library value deficit. *The Bottom Line, 24*(2), 100–106.

Gildersleeves, L. (2012). Do school libraries make a difference? Some considerations on investigating school library impact in the United Kingdom. *Library Management, 33*(6/7), 403–413.

Gilson, T. V. (2011). Reference services today and tomorrow. *Searcher, 19*(7), 32–35.

Godowski, S., & Dogliani, S. (2014). *Idea stores: The next generation.* Retrieved from http://www.designinglibraries.org.uk/?PageID=242.

Goleman, D. (1995). *Emotional intelligence.* New York: Bantam Books.

Gomez, R., Ambikar, R., & Coward, C. (2009). Libraries, telecentres and cybercafés: an international study of public access information venues. *Performance Measurement and Metrics, 10*(1), 33–48.

Gonzalo, F. (November 12, 2012). *How to get Facebook engagement… without paying for it?.* [Web log post] Retrieved from http://fredericgonzalo.com/en/2012/11/12/how-to-get-facebook-engagement-without-paying-for-it/.

Google Academy, https://analyticsacademy.withgoogle.com/explorer.

Gratz, A., & Gilbert, J. (2011). Meeting student needs at the reference desk. *Reference Services Review, 39*(3), 423–438. http://dx.doi.org/10.1108/00907321111161412.

Griffin, M., Lewis, B., & Greenberg, M. I. (2013). Data-driven decision making: an holistic approach to assessment in special collections repositories. *Evidence Based Library and Information Practice, 8*(2).

Griffiths, J. M., King, D. W., & Lynch, T. (2004). *Taxpayer return on investment.* [Report] Prepared for State Library and Archives of Florida (pp. 5–6) [Online]. Retrieved from http://dlis.dos.state.fl.us/bld/roi/pdfs/ROISummaryReport.pdf/. Last accessed 25.01.15.

Grossman, P., Niemann, L., Schmidt, S., & Walach, H. (2004). Mindfulness-based stress reduction and health benefits: a meta-analysis. *Journal of Psychosomatic Research, 57*(1), 35–43.

Halpern, R., Eaker, C., Jackson, J., & Bouquin, D. (March 2015). *#DitchTheSurvey: Expanding methodological diversity in LIS research.* In the Library with the Lead Pipe. Retrieved from http://www.inthelibrarywiththeleadpipe.org/2015/ditchthesurvey-expanding-methodological-diversity-in-lis-research/.

Hart, G. (August 16–22, 2014). *Converging paths in the drive for school libraries in democratic South Africa.* Lyon, France: IFLA World Library and Information Congress. Retrieved from http://library.ifla.org/991/1/213-hart-en.pdf.

Haslett, D. (2005). *Room for reading: The junior certificate school programme demonstration library project.* Dublin: JCSP Support Service.

Hay, L. (2006). Student learning through Australian school libraries part 2: what students define and value as school library support. *Synergy, 4*(2), 27–38.

He, L., Ellinghaus, S., & Chaudhuri, B. (2012). An outcome study on the learning programs at the Novartis Knowledge Center (NKC). In *Proceedings of the 9th Northumbria international conference on performance measurement in libraries and information services: Proving value in challenging times, University of York* (pp. 141–148).

He, L., & Juterbock, D. (2012). Quantitative evaluation of the impact of Novartis Knowledge Center information services in drug discovery and development. *QQML, 3*, 357–366. Retrieved from http://www.qqml.net/December_2012_issue.html.

Health Education England. (2014). *The Health Education England Strategic Framework 2014-29.* Framework 15. Retrieved from http://hee.nhs.uk/2014/06/03/framework-15-health-education-england-strategic-framework-2014-29/.

Healy, A. M. (2010). Increasing the visibility of the library within the academic research enterprise. *Issues in Science and Technology Librarianship, 63*, 2.

Helliwell, J. F., Layard, R., & Sachs, J. (2015). *World happiness report 2015.* Sustainable Development Solutions Network. Retrieved from http://worldhappiness.report.

Hendriks, B., & Wooler, I. (2006). Establishing the return on investment for information and knowledge services: a practical approach to show added value for information and knowledge centres, corporate libraries and documentation centres. *Business Information Review, 23*(1), 13–25.

Henefer, J. (2007). *More than a room for reading: JCSP Demonstration Library Project.* Dublin: Junior Certificate School Programme Support Service. Retrieved from http://www.pdst.ie/sites/default/files/390_More_Than_a_Room_for_Reading_-_Final.pdf. Accessed 19.10.14.

Hery, L., & Weill, C. (2015). DocToBib: PubMed, the physician and the librarian…or the fantastic story of doctors and librarians producing videos together. *Journal of the European Association for Health Information and Libraries, 11*(1), 20–22.

Hicken, M. (2004). 'To each according to his needs': public libraries and socially excluded people. *Health Information & Libraries Journal, 21*(s2), 45–53.

Higa-Moore, M. L., Bunnett, B., Mayo, H. G., & Olney, C. A. (2002). Use of focus groups in a library's strategic planning process. *Journal of the Medical Library Association, 90*(1), 86.

Hiller, S., Lewis, V., Mengel, L., & Tolson, D. (October 25–27, 2010). *Building scorecards in academic research libraries.* Baltimore, MA: Library Assessment Conference. Retrieved from http://libraryassessment.org/archive/2010.shtml. Accessed 10.04.15.

Hunt, D. (2013). Creating strategic value: forging a brand. *Information Outlook, 17*(5).

IFLA. (2013). *Riding the waves or caught in the tide? Navigating the evolving information environment: Insights from the trend report.* Retrieved from http://trends.ifla.org/insights-document.

IFLA/UNESCO School library manifesto. (Revised 2006). Retrieved from http://archive.ifla.org/VII/s11/pubs/manifest.htm.

Indecon International Economic Consultants. (2013). *Evaluation of JobBridge final evaluation report.* Retrieved from http://www.welfare.ie.

Ingham, A. (2014). Can your public library improve your health and well–being? An investigation of East Sussex Library and Information Service. *Health Information & Libraries Journal, 31*(2), 156–160.

Inklebarger, T. (2014). *Dog therapy 101.* American Libraries Magazine. Retrieved from http://americanlibrariesmagazine.org/2014/12/22/dog-therapy-101/.

International Association of School Librarianship IASL. http://www.iasl-online.org/advocacy/make-a-difference.html.

International Federation of Libraries Associations and Institutions (IFLA). (2006). IFLA/UNESCO School Library Manifesto. Retrieved from http://archive.ifla.org/VII/s11/pubs/manifest.htm.

International Federation of Libraries Associations and Institutions (IFLA). (2012). *IFLA code of ethics for librarians and other information workers.* Retrieved from http://www.ifla.org/news/ifla-code-of-ethics-for-librarians-and-other-information-workers-full-version.

Ireland. (2001a). *Local Government Act.* IRL.

Ireland. (2001b). *Department of health. Report of the National Advisory Committee on Palliative Care.* Dublin: National Advisory Committee on Palliative Care. Retrieved from http://lenus.ie/hse/handle/10147/42522.

Ireland. Local Government Management Agency. (2012). *Public Library Authority Statistics Actuals 2011.* Retrieved from http://www.askaboutireland.ie/aai-files/assets/libraries/an-chomhairle-leabharlanna/libraries/public-libraries/publications/2011-library-statistics-actuals.pdf.

Irish Blood Transfusion Service. (2003). *Irish blood transfusion service annual report 2002.* Dublin: IBTS.

Ismail, L. (2010). What net generation students really want: determining library help-seeking preferences of undergraduates. *Reference Services Review, 38*(1), 10–27.

Jain, P. (2014). Application of social media in marketing library & information services: a global perspective. *International Journal of Academic Research and Reflection, 2*(2), 62–75.

Janke, R., & Rush, K. L. (2014). The academic librarian as co–investigator on an interprofessional primary research team: a case study. *Health Information & Libraries Journal, 31*(2), 116–122.

Jantti, M., & Cox, B. (2013). Measuring the value of library resources and student academic performance through relational datasets. *Evidence Based Library and Information Practice, 8*(2), 163–171.

Johannsen, C. G. (2012). Staffless libraries-recent Danish public library experiences. *New Library World, 113*(7/8), 333–342. http://dx.doi.org/10.1108/03074801211244959.

Johnson, L., Becker, S., Estrada, V., & Freeman, A. (2014). *Horizon report: 2014 higher education.* Retrieved from http://www.editlib.org/p/130341/report_130341.pdf.

Kacewicz, E., Pennebaker, J. W., Davis, M., Jeon, M., & Graesser, A. C. (2013). Pronoun use reflects standings in social hierarchies. *Journal of Language and Social Psychology.* http://dx.doi.org/10.1177/0261927X13502654.

Karr, D. (August 24, 2013). *Why infographics are so popular.* [Web log post]. Retrieved from https://www.marketingtechblog.com/infographics-popular/.

Kemp, S. (2015). *Digital, social & mobile worldwide in 2015.* We are social. Retrieved from http://wearesocial.net/blog/2015/01/digital-social-mobile-worldwide-2015/.

Kemperman, S. S., Brembeck, B., Brown, E. W., de Lange-van Oosten, A., Fons, T., Giffi, C., et al. (2014). *Success strategies for electronic content discovery and access: A cross industry white paper.* Dublin, OH: OCLC. Retrieved from http://www.oclc.org/content/dam/oclc/reports/data-quality/215233-SuccessStrategies.pdf.

Kostagiolas, P. A., Ziavrou, K., Alexias, G., & Niakas, D. (2012). Studying the information-seeking behavior of hospital professionals: the case of METAXA Cancer Hospital in Greece. *Journal of Hospital Librarianship, 12*(1), 33–45.

Kott, L., Mix, V., & Marshall, N. (2015). Administrative research support service. *The Reference Librarian, 56*(1), 22–33.

Kotter, J. P. (2014). *Accelerate: Building strategic agility for a faster-moving world.* Harvard Business Review Press.

Kraft, M. (2013). Using Twitter for professional knowledge. *Journal of the European Association for Health Information and Libraries, 9*(4), 10–12.

Kuon, T., Flores, J., & Pickett, J. (2014). The biggest classroom in the building: libraries staffed with certified librarians in many schools hold unexploited potential to raise achievement and meet the more rigorous demands of the common core. *Phi Delta Kappan, 95*(7), 65.

LaGarde, J. (2013). *School library marketing 101: It's about students not stuff.* [Web log post]. Retrieved from http://www.librarygirl.net/2013/04/school-library-marketing-101-its-about.html.

Lance, K. C. (1992). *The impact of school library media centers on academic achievement.* Prepared for the U.S. Department of Education Office of Educational Research & Improvement Library Programs.

Lance, K. C. (2001). Proof of the power: quality library media programs affect academic achievement. *Multimedia Schools, 8*(4), 14–20.

Lance, K. C. (2002). How school librarians leave no child behind: the impact of school library media programs on academic achievement of U.S. public school students. Student achievement. *School Libraries in Canada, 22*(2), 3–6.

Lance, K., & Hofschire, L. (2012). *Change in school librarian staffing linked with change in CSAP reading performance, 2005 to 2011.* Denver, CO: Colorado State Library, Library Research Service.

Lee King, D. (August 27, 2013). *12 tips on making better vine videos.* [Web log post]. Retrieved from http://www.davidleeking.com/.

Lee-King, D. (August 21, 2014). *Analytics for social media – ROI.* [Web log post]. Retrieved from http://www.davidleeking.com/2014/08/21/analytics-for-social-media-roi/.

Leong, J. (2014). Purpose-driven learning for library staff. *The Australian Library Journal, 63*(2), 108–117.

Leong, J., & Vaughan, M. (2010). Preparing new librarians for career and organisational impact. *Library Management, 31*(8/9), 635–644.

Lewis, S. D., & Stowe, Z. N. (2014). Pet therapy program for antepartum high-risk pregnancies: a pilot study. *Journal of Perinatology, 34*(11), 816–818.

*Library of Birmingham cuts weekend opening to six hours.* (April 2015). BBC News UK. Retrieved from http://www.bbc.com/news/uk-england-birmingham-32146016.

Lin, S. C., & Hong, M. C. (2011). Application of Bradford's law and Lotka's law to web metrics study on the wiki website. *Journal of Educational Media and Library Sciences, 48*(3).

Lloret Romero, M. N. (2011). ROI. Measuring the social media return on investment in a library. *The Bottom Line: Managing Library Finances, 24*(2), 145–151. http://dx.doi.org/10.1108/08880451111169223.

Lloyd, R. (2004). *Quality health care: A guide to developing and using indicators.*

Lloyd, E. (February 13, 2014). *Why did you come to the library today? Participatory display.* [Web log post]. Retrieved from http://shelfcheck.blogspot.ie/2014/02/why-did-you-come-to-library-today.html.

Lo, P., Chen, C. C., Dukic, D., & Youn, Y. R. (2014). Attitudes and self-perceptions of school librarians in relations to their professional practices: a comparative study between Hong Kong, Shanghai, South Korea, Taipei, and Japan. *School Libraries Worldwide, 20*(1). London: Jones and Bartlett Publishers.

Lockhart, A. (2012). *The Canadian library association's failure to advocate for librarians and libraries*. [Web log post]. Retrieved from https://plglondon.wordpress.com/2012/01/27/the-canadian-library-associations-failure-to-advocate-for-librarians-and-libraries/.

Lockyer–Benzie, M. (2004). Social inclusion and the City of Swan public libraries in Western Australia. *Health Information & Libraries Journal, 21*(s2), 36–44.

Long, D. (2011). Embedded right where the students live: a librarian in the university residence halls. In C. Kvenild, & K. Calkins (Eds.), *Embedded librarians: Moving beyond one-shot instruction* (pp. 199–209). Chicago: ACRL.

Lor, P. (2014). Risks and benefits of visibility: librarians navigating social and political turbulence. Paper presented at: IFLA WLIC 2014-Lyon – libraries, citizens, societies: confluence for knowledge in session 200-library theory and research In *IFLA WLIC 2014, 16–22 August 2014, Lyon, France* Retrieved from: http://library.ifla.org/view/conferences/2014/.

Lord, M. (2015). Group learning capacity: the roles of open-mindedness and shared vision. *Frontiers in Psychology, 6*, 150. http://dx.doi.org/10.3389/fpsyg.2015.00150.

Luther, J. (2008). *University investment in the library: What's the return? A case study at the University of Illinois at Urbana.*

Lynch, C. E., Magann, E. F., Barringer, S. N., Ounpraseuth, S. T., Eastham, D. G., Lewis, S. D., et al. (2014). Pet therapy program for antepartum high-risk pregnancies: a pilot study. *Journal of Perinatology, 34*(11), 816–818.

MacFalda, P. A. (1997). Performance improvement: how to get employee buy-in. *Radiology Management, 20*(1), 35–44.

Mainka, A., Hartmann, S., Orszullok, L., Peters, I., Stallmann, A., & Stock, W. G. (2013). Public libraries in the knowledge society: core services of libraries in informational world cities. *Libri, 63*(4), 295–319.

Maksin, M. (2014). From ready reference to research conversations. In C. Forbes, & J. Bowers (Eds.), *Rethinking reference for academic libraries: Innovative developments and future trends*. London: Rowman & Littlefield, 2015.

Maltoni, I. (2013). Un Idea Store a Piacenza?: Dalla collaborazione virtuosa tra architetti del futuro, bibliotecari e AIB prende forma un'interessante ricerca di tesi. *Biblioteche oggi, 31*(10), 35–42.

Marquardt, L. (2008). The Leopard's spots on the move: school libraries in Europe. In *Report submitted to international federation of library associations and institutions*. Retrieved from http://eprints.rclis.org/14272/1/marquardt_final4IFLA_20080818.pdf. Accessed 19.10.14.

Marquez, J., & Downey, A. (2015). Service design: an introduction to a holistic assessment methodology of library services. *Weave: Journal of Library User Experience, 1*. (2). http://dx.doi.org/10.3998/weave.12535642.0001.201.

Marr, B., & Creelman, J. (2014). *Doing more with less: measuring, analyzing and improving performance in the not for profit and government sectors* (2nd ed.). Basingstoke, Hampshire: Palgrave Macmillan.

Marshall, J. G. (1992). The impact of the hospital library on clinical decision making: the Rochester study. *Bulletin of the Medical Library Association, 80*(2), 169.

Marshall, J. G., Morgan, J., Klem, M., Thompson, C., & Wells, A. (2014). The value of library and information services in nursing and patient care. *The Online Journal of Issues in Nursing, 19*(3).

Marshall, J. G., Sollenberger, J., Easterby-Gannett, S., Morgan, L. K., Klem, M. L., Cavanaugh, S. K., et al. (2013). The value of library and information services in patient care: results of a multisite study. *Journal of the Medical Library Association, 101*(1), 38. http://dx.doi.org/10.3163/1536-5050.101.1.007.

Matlin, T. R., & Carr, A. (2014). Just the two of us: Those who co-teach, co-learn. *Collaborative Librarianship, 6*(2), 61–72.

Matthews, J. (2006). The Library Balanced Scorecard. *Public Libraries, 45*(6), 64–71.

Maybee, C., Doan, T., & Riehle, C. F. (2013). Making an IMPACT campus-wide collaboration for course and learning space transformation. *College & Research Libraries News, 74*(1), 32–35.

McGarry, A. (June 13, 2008). *China's pain fires Olympic dream.* [Web log post]. Retrieved from http://blogs.abc.net.au/olympics/.

McGowan, J., Hogg, W., Campbell, C., & Rowan, M. (2008). Just-in-time information improved decision-making in primary care: a randomized controlled trial. *PLoS One, 3*(11), e3785.

McMenemy, D. (2007). What is the true value of a public library? *Library Review, 56*(4), 273–277.

Medical Library Association. (2013). *Summary of hospital library status forms as of September 2013.* Retrieved from https://www.mlanet.org/resources/vital/index.html#stats. Accessed 01.04.15.

Michie, S., van Stralen, M. M., & West, R. (2011). The behaviour change wheel: a new method for characterising and designing behaviour change interventions. *Implementation Science, 6*(1), 42.

Miller, L. (2012). The library and the campus visit communicating value to prospective students and parents. *College & Research Libraries News, 73*(10), 586–589.

Milne, C., & Thomas, J. (2011). Embedding a library program in the first-year curriculum: experiences and strategies of an Australian case study. In C. Kvenild, & K. Calkins (Eds.), *Embedded librarians: Moving beyond one-shot instruction* (pp. 47–60). Chicago: ACRL.

Moghaddam, G. G., & Moballeghi, M. (2011). Quality management in special libraries. Proving value in challenging times. In *Proceedings of the 9th Northumbria international conference on performance measurement in libraries and information services: Proving value in challenging times, University of York* (pp. 119–124).

Moore, T. (January 23, 2013). *Huge amounts of data can be stored in DNA.* Sky News. Retrieved from http://news.sky.com/story/1041917/huge-amounts-of-data-can-be-stored-in-dna.

Morgan, D. L., Krueger, R. A., & King, J. A. (1998). *The focus group kit* (Vols. 1–6). Thousand Oaks, CA: Sage Publications.

Nagata, H., Sakai, K., & Kawai, T. (2007). Public library and users' lifestyle in a changing context. *Performance Measurement and Metrics, 8*(3), 197–210.

Nasir Uddin, M., Quaddus, M., & Islam, S. (2006). Socio-economic-cultural aspects and mass information need: the case of public library uses in Bangladesh. *Library Management, 27*(9), 636–652.

National Network of Libraries of Medicine. Middle Atlantic Region and the University of North Carolina at Chapel Hill. Value of Library and Information Services in Patient Care. Retrieved from http://nnlm.gov/mar/about/value.html.

Neshat, N., & Dehghani, M. (2013). Review of the current gap between clients' expectations and perceptions of received service in national library by using gap analysis model. *Performance Measurement and Metrics, 14*(1), 45–60.

*New pop-up library aims to help you stay fit and healthy.* (March 2015). UK: Kirkintilloch Herald. Retrieved from http://www.kirkintilloch-herald.co.uk/news/local-headlines/new-pop-up-library-aims-to-help-you-stay-fit-and-healthy-1-3733182.

Neway, J. M. (1985). *Information specialist as team player in the research process.* London: Greenwood Press.

Ni Bhrian, D. (April 25, 2015). *Time to drop everything and just read.* Irish Times. Retreived from http://www.irishtimes.com/culture/books/time-to-drop-everything-and-just-read-1.2187674.

Nitecki, D. A., & Abels, E. G. (2013). Exploring the cause and effect of library value. *Performance Measurement and Metrics, 14*(1), 17–24.

Nolin, J. M. (2013). The special librarian and personalized meta-services: strategies for reconnecting librarians and researchers. *Library Review, 62*(8/9), 508–524. http://dx.doi.org/10.1108/LR-02-2013-0015.

Nygren, Å. (2014). *The public library as a community hub for connected learning.* Lyon, France: IFLA World Library and Information Congress. Retrieved from http://library.ifla.org/1014/1/167-nygren-en.pdf.

Oakleaf, M. (2010). *The value of academic libraries.* Chicago: Association of College & Research Libraries.

Oakleaf, M., & VanScoy, A. (2010). Instructional strategies for digital reference. *Reference & User Services Quarterly, 49*(4), 380–390.

OCLC. (2014). *At a tipping point: Education, learning and libraries: A report to the OCLC membership.* Dublin, OH: OCLC.

OECD. (2013). *OECD skills outlook 2013. First results from the survey of adult skills.* OECD Publishing. http://dx.doi.org/10.1787/9789264204256-en.

OECD. PISA 2012 results. Retrieved from http://www.oecd.org/pisa/keyfindings/pisa-2012-results.htm.

O'Leary, M. (July/August 2013). *The digital library of America opens its doors.* Information Today.

Osorio, N. L. (2012). *Consortia and the big deals: A new way of doing business or the end of the technical library?.* Retrieved from http://docs.lib.purdue.edu/cgi/viewcontent.cgi?article=1586&context=iatul.

Outsell, Inc. (November 2007). *Information management under fire: Measuring ROI for enterprise libraries.* Retreived from http://www.outsellinc.com.

Pake, G. E. (1975). *The office of the future.* Business Week. Retrieved from http://www.businessweek.com/stories/1975-06-30/the-office-of-the-futurebusinessweek-business-news-stock-market-and-financial-advice.

Pakistan Library Association. (2013). Retrieved from http://pla.org.pk/ObjectivenFuturePlan.html.

Pan, D., Ferrer-Vinent, I. J., & Bruehl, M. (2014). Library value in the classroom: assessing student learning outcomes from instruction and collections. *The Journal of Academic Librarianship, 40*(3), 332–338.

Pan, D., & Fong, Y. (2010). Return on investment for collaborative collection development: a cost-benefit evaluation of consortia purchasing. *Collaborative Librarianship, 2*(4), 183–192.

Patridge, E., & Shack, C. (October 2010). What color is your library? How color impacts library promotion in a hospital setting. In *Poster session presented at the meeting of the South Central Chapter of the Medical Library Association, Austin, TX.* Retrieved from http://hdl.handle.net/2152.5/1162.

Pérez, Y. E. R., & Montesi, M. (2013). Visibilidad y uso de colecciones digitalizadas: propuesta de un indicador de visibilidad relativa. *Ibersid: revista de sistemas de información y documentación, 7*, 123–129.

Perrier, L., Farrell, A., Ayala, A. P., Lightfoot, D., Kenny, T., Aaronson, E., et al. (2014). Effects of librarian-provided services in healthcare settings: a systematic review. *Journal of the American Medical Informatics Association, 21*(6), 1118–1124.

Pew Research Center. (2014a). *Health fact sheet.* Retrieved from http://www.pewinternet.org/fact-sheets/health-fact-sheet/. Accessed 14.12.14.

Pew Research Center. (2014b). *Social networking fact sheet.* Retrieved from http://www.pewinternet.org/fact-sheets/social-networking-fact-sheet/. Accessed 27.04.15.

Pew Research Center. (2014c). *Mobile technology fact sheet*. Retrieved from http://www. pewinternet.org/fact-sheets/mobile-technology-fact-sheet/. Accessed 27.04.15.

*Perpetual beta*. (2015). *Wikipedia, the free encyclopedia*. Retrieved from http://en.wikipedia. org/wiki/Perpetual_beta. Accessed 21.05.15.

Poll, R. (2001). Performance, process, and costs: managing service quality with the balanced scorecard. *Library Trends, 49*(4), 709–717.

Poll, R. (2014). *Bibliography impact and outcome of libraries*. IFLA Statistics and Evaluation Group The Hague: IFLA. Retrieved from http://www.ifla.org/files/assets/statistics-and-evaluation/publications/bibliography_impact_and_outcome_2014.pdf. Accessed 08.03.15.

Potter, N. (December 17, 2012). Marketing with video: it's now essential, and easier than you might think. *Library Journal*. http://lj.libraryjournal.com/2012/12/marketing/marketing-with-video-its-now-essential-and-easier-than-you-might-think/#_.

Poulter, A., Mcmenemy, D., & Chowdhury, G. (2008). MEDLIS: model for evaluation of digital libraries and information services. *World Digital Libraries, 1*(1), 35–46.

Price, H. E. (2012). Principal–teacher interactions how affective relationships shape principal and teacher attitudes. *Educational Administration Quarterly, 48*(1), 39–85.

Proctor, B., Usherwood, R., & Sobczyk, G. (1997). What happens when a public library service closes down? *Library Management, 18*(1), 59–64.

Public Library Association a Division of the American Library Association. (2014). *The 2014 public library data service: Characteristics and trends*. Counting Opinions (SQUIRE) Ltd. Retrieved from http://www.plametrics.org/PLDS2014.pdf.

Purcell, K. (October 2013). *Online video 2013*. Pew Internet Project. Available from http://pewinternet. org/Reports/2013/Online-video.

Purday, J. (2009). Think culture: Europeana. eu from concept to construction. *The Electronic Library, 27*(6), 919–937.

Reilly, M., & Thompson, S. (2014). Understanding ultimate use data and its implication for digital library management: a case study. *Journal of Web Librarianship, 8*(2), 196–213.

Renn, O., Archer, M., Burkhardt, C., Ginestet, J., Nielsen, H. P., Woodward, J., & PDR Library Affairs & Copyright Group. (2012). A blueprint for an ideal corporate information centre. *Nature Reviews Drug Discovery, 11*(6), 497.

Reynolds, T. (2013). To what extent does a corporate information unit impact upon the company in which it is based? *Performance Measurement and Metrics, 14*(1), 61–70.

Richey, J., & Cahill, M. (2014a). School librarians' experiences with evidence-based library and information practice. *School Library Research, 17*. Retrieved from http://www. ala.org/aasl/sites/ala.org.aasl/files/content/aaslpubsandjournals/slr/vol17/SLR_Evidence-BasedLibrary_V17.pdf.

Richey, J., & Cahill, M. (2014b). What's a school librarian's evidence in, of and for practice? *Evidence Based Practice, 43*(3), 69–73. Retrieved from http://files.eric.ed.gov/fulltext/ EJ1049068.pdf.

RIN and RLUK. (2011). *The value of libraries for research and researchers*. London: Research Information Network.

Rooney, J. J., & Heuvel, L. N. V. (2004). Root cause analysis for beginners. *Quality Progress, 37*(7), 45–56.

Rooney-Browne, C. (2009). Rising to the challenge: a look at the role of public libraries in times of recession. *Library Review, 58*(5), 341–352.

Rooney-Browne, C. (2011). Methods for demonstrating the value of public libraries in the UK: a literature review. *Library and Information Research, 35*(109), 3–39.

Roswitha, P. (2001). Performance, processes and cost: managing service quality with the balanced scorecard. *Library Trends, 49*(4), 709–717.

Rumelt, R. (2011). *Good strategy bad strategy: The difference and why it matters*. London: Profile.

Russell, R., & Day, M. (2010). Institutional repository interaction with research users: a review of current practice. *New Review of Academic Librarianship, 16*(S1), 116–131.

Ryan, M., & Joseph, C. B. (2012). A mobile medical library initiative: promoting nurses' professional development and information-searching skills for evidence-based practice. *MED-SURG Nursing: Official Journal of the Academy of Medical-Surgical Nurses, 22*(1), 57–59.

Sackett, D. L., Rosenberg, W., Gray, J. A., Haynes, R. B., & Richardson, W. S. (1996). Evidence based medicine: what it is and what it isn't. *BMJ, 312*(7023), 71–72.

Satell, G. (April 16, 2013). *4 Principles of marketing strategy in the digital age*. [Web log post]. Retrieved from http://www.forbes.com/sites/gregsatell/2013/04/16/4-principles-of-marketing-strategy-in-the-digital-age/.

Sayed, E. N. (2013). Aligning planning with outcomes. *Performance Measurement and Metrics, 14*(2), 100–117.

Schachter, D. (2013). Creating value by building relationships: information professionals may find it more valuable to build relationships with their customers rather than simply engage them in developing new products and services. *Information Outlook, 17*(5).

Schippers, M. C., Den Hartog, D. N., Koopman, P. L., & van Knippenberg, D. (2008). The role of transformational leadership in enhancing team reflexivity. *Human Relations, 61*(11), 1593–1616.

Schmid, K., Drexler, H., Fischmann, W., Uter, W., & Kiesel, J. (2011). Which occupational groups in a hospital are particularly stressed? *Deutsche Medizinische Wochenschrift (1946), 136*(30), 1517–1522.

Schmidt, E., & Rosenberg, J. (2014). *How Google works*. London: John Murray Publishers.

Schroeder, A. (2011). Replacing face-to-face information literacy instruction: offering the embedded librarian program to all courses. In C. Kvenild, & K. Calkins (Eds.), *Embedded librarians: Moving beyond one-shot instruction* (pp. 63–78). Chicago: ACRL.

Scotti, G. (June 14–17, 2009). *ROI 2.0. Presentation at special library association conference*. Washington, DC. Retrieved from http://www.springer.com/cda/content/document/cda_downloaddocument/SLA.ROI.Presentation.6-09.ppt.

Sendir, M. (2014). Health sciences libraries and public health education awareness in social media platforms. *Journal of the European Association for Health Information and Libraries, 10*(4), 13–14.

Shaffer, C., & Casey, O. (2013). Behind the glasses and beneath the bun: portrayals of librarians in popular cinema and a guide for developing a collection. *Collection Building, 32*(2), 39–45.

Sharman, A. (2012). The roving librarian. *ALISS Quarterly, 7*(4), 6–8. ISSN:1747-9258. Available at http://eprints.hud.ac.uk/14523/.

Sharples, C. (2014). *Librarians let loose! An experience of roving at the University of East Anglia*. *Sconul Focus*, 62, 31–34.

Shenton, H. (2004). The future shape of collection storage. In *Where shall we put it?: Spotlight on collection storage issues: Papers given at the national preservation office annual conference, held 4 October 2004 at the British Library*. Retrieved from http://www.bl.uk/aboutus/stratpolprog/collectioncare/publications/articles/2004/HShentonNPO%20Conf2004.pdf.

Sheppard, T. (2006). Intellectual gambling: betting on the future public library. *New Library World, 107*(11/12), 512–522.

Sievert, M., Burhans, D., Ward, D., Jones, B. B., Bandy, M., Carlson, J., et al. (2011). Value of health sciences library resources and services to health care providers in medium and large communities across two mid-continental states. *Journal of Hospital Librarianship, 11*(2), 140–157.

Slee, T. (September 2014). *Breathing new life into the school library*. CILIP Update p. 30.

Small, R. V., & Snyder, J. (2010). Research instruments for measuring the impact of school libraries on student achievement and motivation. *School Libraries Worldwide, 16*(1), 61.

Smith, R. (1991). First steps towards a strategy for health. *British Medical Journal*, *303*(6797), 297.

Smith, B., & White, G. (2014). Irish health science librarians supporting national clinical guideline development. *Journal of the European Association for Health Information and Libraries*, *10*(3), 9–11.

Solorzano, R. M. (2013). Adding value at the desk: how technology and user expectations are changing reference work. *The Reference Librarian*, *54*(2), 89–102. http://dx.doi.org/10.1080/02763877.2013.755398.

Special Library Association. (January 21–25, 2008). In *Positioning SLA for the future: Principles & process for the alignment initiative SLA leadership summit* Louisville, KY. Available at http://hq.sla.org/content/SLA/alignment/portal/explore.html. Accessed 29.09.14.

Spiteri, L. F., & Tarulli, L. (2012). Social discovery systems in public libraries: if we build them, will they come? *Library Trends*, *61*(1), 132–147.

Stone, G., & Ramsden, B. (2012). Library Impact Data Project: looking for the link between library usage and student attainment. *College & Research Libraries*, crl12–406.

Strand, J. (February 19, 2015). *Communicating the value of the information professional*. [Web log post] SLA Blog. Retrieved from https://www.sla.org/communicating-value-information-professional/.

Suber, P. (November 4, 2006). *CERN builds support for ambitious OA project*. [Web log post]. Retrieved from http://legacy.earlham.edu/~peters/fos/2006/11/cern-builds-support-for-ambitious-oa.html.

Sutton, A., & Booth, A. (2014). The librarian as a leader: development of leadership in the library and information profession. *Journal of the European Association for Health Information and Libraries*, *10*(4), 16.

Tella, A., Ayeni, C. O., & Popoola, S. O. (2007). Work motivation, job satisfaction, and organisational commitment of library personnel in academic and research libraries in Oyo State, Nigeria. *Library Philosophy and Practice*, *9*(2), 13.

Teng, S., & Hawamdeh, S. (June 2002). Knowledge management in public libraries. *Aslib Proceedings*, *54*(3), 188–197. MCB UP Ltd.

Tenopir, C., Volentine, R., & King, D. W. (2012). Scholarly reading and the value of academic library collections: results of a study in six UK universities. *Insights: The UKSG Journal*, *25*(2), 130–149.

Tepe, A. E., & Geitgey, G. A. (2005). Student learning through Ohio school libraries, introduction: partner-leaders in action. *School Libraries Worldwide*, *11*(1), 55–62. Retrieved from http://www.iasl-online.org/pubs/slw/jan05-tepe.htm.

Thomas, S., Burke, S., & Barry, S. (2014). The Irish health-care system and austerity: sharing the pain. *The Lancet*, *383*(9928), 1545–1546.

Todd, R. J., & Kuhlthau, C. (2005). Student learning through Ohio school libraries, part 1: how effective school libraries help students. *School Libraries Worldwide*, *11*(1), 63–88.

Town, J. S., & Kyrillidou, M. (2013). Developing a values scorecard. *Performance Measurement and Metrics*, *14*(1), 7–16.

Tribet, J., Boucharlat, M., & Myslinski, M. (2008). Animal-assisted therapy for people suffering from severe dementia. *L'Encéphale*, *34*, 183–186.

Tuominen, K., & Saarti, J. (2012). The Finnish library system open collaboration for an open society. *IFLA Journal*, *38*(2), 115–136.

Twomey, A. (May 3, 2010). *New school library under threat*. Northside People. Retrieved from http://issuu.com/dublinpeople/docs/northside_people_west_may19_2010.

United Nations, Department of Economic and Social Affairs, Population Division. (2013). *World population ageing 2013*. ST/ESA/SER.A/348.

Upton, M. (June 3, 2010). *Adjournment debate – Demonstration library programme*. Ireland Dail Debates, 711.3. Retrieved from http://debates.oireachtas.ie/dail/2010/06/03/00028.asp.

Urquhart, C., Turner, J., Durbin, J., & Ryan, J. (2007). Changes in information behavior in clinical teams after introduction of a clinical librarian service. *Journal of the Medical Library Association, 95*(1), 14.

VanScoy, A. (2010). The meaning of reference work for the academic reference librarian: A phenomenological investigation. Unpublished doctoral dissertation, University of North Carolina at Chapel Hill, Chapel Hill, NC.

Wagner, K. C., & Byrd, G. D. (2004). Evaluating the effectiveness of clinical medical librarian programs: a systematic review of the literature. *Journal of the Medical Library Association, 92*(1), 14.

Wah, C. P., & Choh, N. L. (2008). Libraries without borders. Content delivery, Singapore Style. Paper presented at "Libraries without borders: navigating towards global understanding" – world library and information Congress In *74th IFLA general conference and council. Québec, Canada*. http://archive.ifla.org/IV/ifla74/papers/074-Wah_Choh-en.pdf. Accessed 06.04.15.

Walton, G., & Grant, M. J. (2013). Writing up your project findings. In M. J. Grant, B. Sen, & H. Spring (Eds.), *Research, evaluation and audit: Key steps in demonstrating your value*. London: Facet Publishing.

Weightman, A. L., & Williamson, J. (2005). The value and impact of information provided through library services for patient care: a systematic review. *Health Information & Libraries Journal, 22*(1), 4–25.

Welch, J. M. (2005). Who says we're not busy? Library web page usage as a measure of public service activity. *Reference Services Review, 33*(4), 371–379.

Welsh Government. (2014). CyMAL: museums archives and libraries wales. In *Libraries making a difference: The fifth quality framework of Welsh Public Library Standards 2014–2017*. Aberystwyth: Welsh Government. Retrieved from http://gov.wales/docs/drah/publications/140425wpls5en.pdf.

Wexford County Council. (2004). *Council's corporate plan 2004–2009*. Retrieved from http://www.wexford.ie/wex/YourCouncil/Publications/CorporatePlans/Thefile,515,en.pdf. Accessed 28.09.14.

Wexford County Libraries. (October 2014). *Library mission statement*. Retrieved from http://www.wexford.ie/wex/Departments/Library/. Accessed 26.10.14.

Wheaton, K., & Murray, A. (2011). The future of the The future: the continuing saga of the knowledge librarian. *KM World, 20*(10). Retrieved from http://www.kmworld.com/Articles/Column/The-Future-of-the-Future/The-Future-of-the-The-Future-The-continuing-saga-of-the-knowledge-librarian-78464.aspx.

When robots join the library. (September 29, 2014). *Wall Street Journal*. Retrieved from http://www.wsj.com/video/when-robots-join-the-library/632795B5-2C6E-4C22-B673-21AA55CEB4F0.html.

Williams, L. (November 23, 2014). *Embedded information professionals – Making the leap from library to workplace*. CILIP Update.

Wong, A. C. Y. (2013). Using the critical incident technique to evaluate the service quality perceptions of public library users: an exploratory study. In *Proceedings of the eighth international conference on conceptions of library and information science, Copenhagen, Denmark, 19–22 August, 2013. Information Research 18*(3), September, 2013. http://www.informationr.net/ir/18-3/colis/paperS10.html#.VSu4eqNPOmR.

Woodworth, A. (May 6, 2014). Programs that boil, bake, and sizzle! Programs that pop. *Library Journal*. Retrieved from http://lj.libraryjournal.com/2014/05/opinion/programs-that-pop/programs-that-boil-bake-and-sizzle-programs-that-pop/#_.

World Health Organisation. (2015). *Obesity and overweight*. Factsheet No. 311. Retreived from http://www.who.int/mediacentre/factsheets/fs311/en/.

Wu, L., & Mi, M. (2013). Sustaining librarian vitality: embedded librarianship model for health sciences libraries. *Medical Reference Services Quarterly, 32*(3), 257–265.

Xia, Z. D. (2009). Marketing library services through Facebook groups. *Library Management, 30*(6/7), 469–478.

Xuan, W., & Hongyan, L. (2011). *Energy saving and green building design of libraries: a case study of Zhengzhou Library*. San Juan, Puerto Rico: IFLA World Library and Information Congress. 13-18 August, 2011. Retrieved from http://conference.ifla.org/past-wlic/2011/library-buildings-and-equipment-section.htm.

Yang, L., & Perrin, J. M. (2014). Tutorials on Google analytics: how to craft a web analytics report for a library web site. *Journal of Web Librarianship, 8*(4), 404–417.

Young, J. S. (2012). Pet therapy: dogs de-stress students. *Journal of Christian Nursing, 29*(4), 217–221.

Young, S. W. H. (2014). Improving library user experience with A/B testing: principles and process. *Weave, 1*(1). http://dx.doi.org/10.3998/weave.12535642.0001.101.

Zhang, J., & Mayer, N. (2014). Proactive chat reference getting in the users' space. *College & Research Libraries News, 75*(4), 202–205.

Zhong, H. (2007). Research on reader self-service in a public library. *Library Management, 28*(1/2), 101–106.

# Index

CPI Antony Rowe
Eastbourne, UK
November 19, 2015